D1214181

THE SLAVS
THEIR EARLY HISTORY AND
CIVILIZATION

The Slavs
Their Early History and
Civilization

BY

FRANCIS DVORNIK

Professor of Byzantine History at Dumbarton Oaks
and Member of the Faculty of Arts and Sciences, Harvard University

BOSTON

AMERICAN ACADEMY OF ARTS AND SCIENCES

1956

936.7
D98s

SURVEY OF SLAVIC CIVILIZATION

VOLUME II

Published with the assistance of and under the sponsorship of Curt Reisinger and the Committee for the Promotion of Advanced Slavic Cultural Studies in cooperation with the Department of Slavic Languages and Literatures at Harvard University. Volume I, Dmitry Cizevsky, *Outline of Comparative Slavic Literature,* 143 pp., paper cover, $2.00, was published in December 1952.

© COPYRIGHT 1956 BY THE

AMERICAN ACADEMY OF ARTS AND SCIENCES

To the Memory of
my Mother

CARNEGIE INSTITUTE
OF TECHNOLOGY LIBRARY

CONTENTS

MAPS

PREFACE

The idea of publishing a book on early Slavic history and civilization originated in 1951 when I was giving a course on this subject in the Slavic Department of Harvard University. Professor Michael Karpovich, then Chairman of the Department, and his colleagues, especially Professor Roman Jakobson, asked me to make the lectures available in book form to a larger public. My original intention was to publish the course as it was given, with only slight additions, for the use of English speaking students. Professor Jakobson, however, urged me to develop the lectures quite extensively in order to make the book useful also to scholars not familiar with early Slavic history. I followed his advice the more willingly because there does not exist any study dealing with the mediaeval history of all Slavic nations and their relations with Byzantium, the Franks, and the Germans. By thus enlarging the scope of the original course of lectures I was able to make use of some of the material I had collected on this subject in recent years, and to realize, at least in small part, my idea, conceived in London during the war years, to write a mediaeval history of the whole of Central and Eastern Europe, a project which, for various reasons, I had to give up. My book, *The Making of Central and Eastern Europe*, published in 1949, was also a part of this original plan.

With the above brief outline of its background, the double character and purpose of this book becomes clear. It is intended to be a handbook on early Slavic history and civilization for students in history, as well as for a larger public, and, at the same time, to give to specialists in Slavic studies a succinct account of the present state of research on the many problems connected with the historical and cultural development of the Slavic nations, from their origins to the middle of the thirteenth century, when an important phase in their history came to a close.

In order to avoid unwieldy bibliographical data, I have limited myself to works written in non-Slavic languages, on the assumption that it will be easy for any student desiring to consult works in Slavic to complete his bibliography from the works indicated, and I have thought it useful also to add a collection of the main sources for each chapter. The reader can thus, in each chapter, easily control the statements based on sources.

I am greatly indebted to the members of the Slavic Department of Harvard University for their encouragement and help. Professor Roman Jakobson kindly read the whole manuscript and gave me most valuable advice, especially in the field of Old Slavonic literature. Without his advice and help, for which I am very grateful, this book would not have been published in its present form. I am also grateful to the Chairman of the Department, A. B. Lord, for the interest he took in seeing this book through the press.

I wish to thank George Soulis who helped with the first draft of the maps and undertook the compilation of the Index. D. Obolenski, Reader in Mediaeval Russian and Balkan History at Oxford University, was kind enough to read a part of my manuscript.

I am obliged to The American Academy of Art and Sciences which agreed to publish my work, and to its editors, Professor Taylor Starck and Dr. Walter Muir Whitehill. The publication could not have been achieved without the subsidy provided by the Slavic Department of Harvard University, which decided to include it in the series, *Studies in Slavic Civilization*, financed by the Reisinger Fund and The American Academy. Although it should have appeared in 1954, as announced in the second volume of the *Harvard Slavic Studies*, unforeseen difficulties caused its delay.

I dedicate this book to the pious memory of my mother, who died in Moravia in June, 1951, while I was finishing my course at Harvard.

Dumbarton Oaks   December 8, 1954
Washington, District of Columbia

1

Origins and Migrations of the Slavs

Original home of the primitive Slavs — New theories — Greek and Roman writers on the Slavs — Abortive attempts by the Romans to reach Slavic territory — Commercial intercourse between the Baltic and the Black Sea and migrations of Scythians, Slavs, Germans and Sarmatians — Eastern Slavs, Goths and Iranians — Hunnish invasion, the Antês, Croats and Serbs — Slav penetration through Hungary towards the borders of the Roman Empire — Spread of the Western Slavs, Southern Slavs and Byzantium — Avar invasion — Destruction of Christianity in Illyricum and its consequences for the history of mankind.

It may seem strange that one of the first essential steps towards an evaluation of medieval Slav civilization should be to determine the whereabouts of the original habitat of the primitive Slavs. It is a problem which has preoccupied scholars for a considerable time and has received a great deal of their attention, particularly since the nineteenth century. The naive explanation that the Slavs came from the Danubian region was abandoned long ago, and though many other answers to this question were put forward, none was satisfactory. Archaeologists and philologists are still combining their efforts in the hope of arriving at the correct solution.

On philological grounds it was commonly agreed among modern scholars that the cradle of the Slavs was located in the marshes of the Pripet basin, a region known as Polesie. It was observed that the primitive Slavs had no term for the trees, beech, larch, and yew, whereas they did have a word for hornbeam. From this evidence it was argued that the original habitat of the Slavic race must have been located beyond the limit of the above-mentioned trees, that is to say, east of a line running from Königsberg in modern Prussia (now Kaliningrad) to Odessa. The marshy ter-

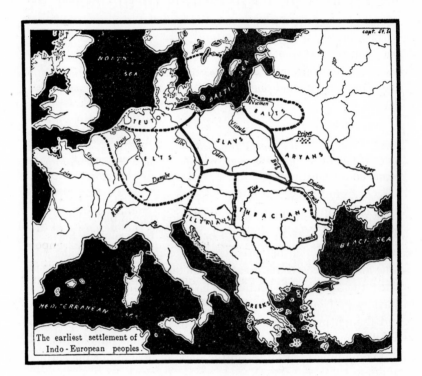

The earliest settlement of
Indo-European peoples.

rain of Polesie, which was especially suited to the hornbeam, was thus regarded as the primitive home of the Slavs. This surmise met with ready acceptance, particularly in circles where the Slavs were regarded as an inferior race, because it was considered that the civilization developed by a people living for centuries in an unhealthful tract of marshes would have been of a poor and squalid kind. Such a theory was somewhat rashly developed by F. Peisker, who pictured the primitive Slavs as a people harassed for centuries by Mongolian nomads, enslaved by them from time to time and constantly endeavoring to hide from their terrible tormentors by skulking in the trackless marshes and impenetrable forests.[1]

Some scholars, Germans and Czechs among them, at first accepted this theory; but it soon became evident to others that a people confined for centuries to a territory of such small dimensions could not possibly have developed into the mighty nation which, from the sixth century A.D., astonished all contemporary Byzantine and Latin writers by its vast numbers and by the robust vitality manifested as it breached the defenses of the Roman Empire in southeastern Europe. Because of this important consideration, some archaeologists extended the primitive habitat of the Slavs from the Pripet basin southwards towards the Carpathian Mountains and westwards towards the Vistula.

It is agreed that the primitive Slavs must have lived for a long period as neighbors of the Germans, the Balts, and the Thracians, who together with the Slavs, the Celts, the Proto-Italians, Illyrians and Greeks, formed the European branch of the great Indo-European group of nations. No one harbors any doubts about the primitive habitat of the Germans in southern Scandinavia, Denmark and the islands and part of the coast be-

---

[1] A summary of F. Peisker's argument can be read in Vol. II of the *Cambridge Medieval History* (Ch. XIV: "The Expansion of the Slavs"). His ideas on the enslavement of the Slavs by the Mongolians are absolutely false and his philological arguments in support of his strange theory were long ago refuted by specialists in Slavic archaeology and philology. It is strange that such a fantastic story could have been printed in an English standard work on medieval history.

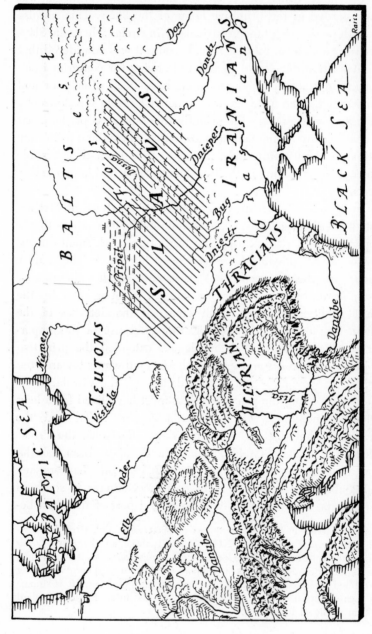

The Original Habitat of the Slavs according to M. Vasmer
(Die ältesten Bevölkerungsverhältnisse Russlands im Lichte der Sprachforschung)

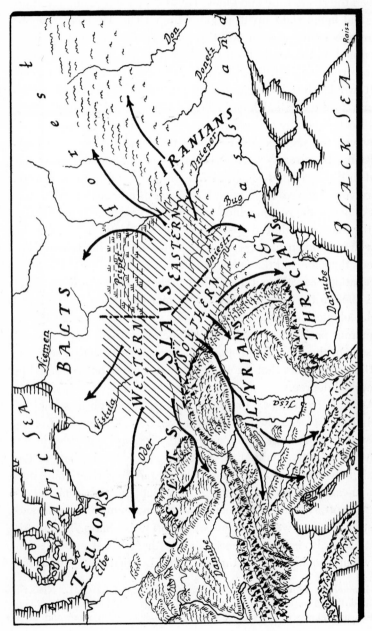

The Original Habitat of the Slavs according to L. Niederle (*Slovanski starožitnosti*)

tween the rivers Elbe and Oder. The Balts have remained in their original home right up to modern times. The Thracians, whose primitive home was in what is now Hungary, seem to have occupied, in the north, both slopes of the Carpathian Mountains, whose very name still recalls their presence.

It would thus be logical to locate the primitive Slavs much nearer to the original home of the Germans and the Balts than has been generally accepted. Against this supposition there was, however, the philological argument mentioned above. This difficulty has been resolved only recently, when it was demonstrated that in the early prehistoric period climatic conditions in Europe were very different from what they were at a later date, and that not only was the region which was regarded as the original habitat of the Slavs outside the area where the beech, the larch and the yew were known to grow, but so also were the lands lying between the Elbe and the Oder, the Vistula and the Bug. Moreover, excavations carried out by Polish archaeologists between 1920 and 1938 in the region of the Pripet marshes failed to yield any archaeological evidence which would support the theory that a numerous people had made a prolonged stay there in prehistoric times. On the other hand, the evidence suggests that it was not until Roman times that the Pripet region came to be populated in a marked degree.

Arguing from these premises, the modern Polish school of archaeologists, led by John Szekanowski, L. Kozłowski, J. Kostrzewski and T. Sulimirski, came boldly forward with the theory that the primitive habitat of the Slavs should be located in the lands between the Elbe, Oder, Vistula and Bug rivers and that the so-called "Lusatian culture," of which the rich remnants — mostly pottery — are to be seen in all the museums of Central and Eastern Europe, was a product of the primitive Slavs. This possibility was also seriously considered by the greatest authority on Slavic archaeology of our time, the late L. Niederle.[1] The prob-

---

[1] *Manuel de l'Antiquité Slave* (Paris, 1923), pp. 20 seq. L. Niederle situated the primitive home of the Slavs, in general, between the rivers Vistula and Dnieper. He seemed, however, to have been more and more

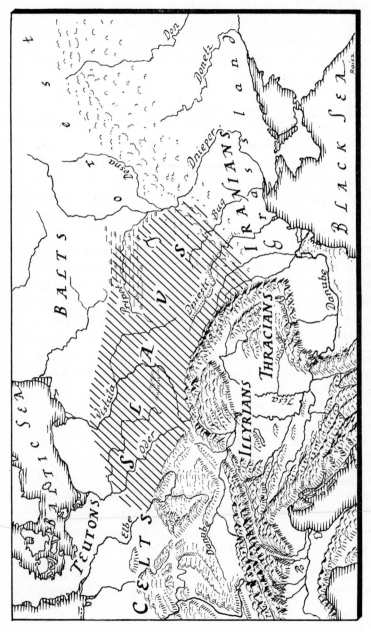

The Original Habitat of the Slavs according to K. Yazdzewski
(*Atlas to the Prehistory of the Slavs*)

lems associated with the "Lusatian culture" were, however, far too complex at the time he was writing his works and he did not dare to go as far as the Polish school does today. Polish scholars seem to have clarified some of these problems so that today their theory appears to be a not unreasonable hypothesis. The matter cannot be finally solved until the results of further archaeological research are made known. One of the greatest puzzles which continue to baffle archaeologists is the origin and evolution of the Lusatian culture, remnants of which are also to be found in eastern Bohemia and Moravia. It has not yet been possible to determine which people created the Lusatian culture, although many theories have been advanced. Some have attributed it to the Illyrians or to the Thracians; others to an unknown people, or to several ethnical components, whose place was later taken by the Slavs. Most of the prehistoric maps show a vacuum in the lands where the Lusatian culture flourished. On several grounds it would seem reasonable to fill this vacuum with the Slavs. Such a hypothesis would render more understandable the rapid expansion of the Slavs in historical times.[1]

Recent discoveries help to resolve another difficulty associ-

---

inclined to extend the prehistoric habitat of the Slavs towards the west, beyond the Vistula. In his Czech "Handbook of Slavic Antiquities" (*Rukovět Slovanské archeologie* [Prague, 1931], p. 15) he reviewed the results of recent archaeological findings in the field of Lusatian culture and came to the following conclusion: "If we deny the Slavic character of the archaeological material of Lusatia, Silesia and Przeworsk (in Poland) there would then be, from the archaeological point of view, no room in the Roman period for a great Slavic people west and east of the Vistula. This would be absurd because Tacitus and Ptolemy locate the Slavs east of the Vistula and speak of them as a numerous people."

[1] Soviet experts in Slavic prehistory (cf. P. I. Tretjakov's book *Vostočno slavjanskie plemena* [East Slavic tribes] published by the USSR Academy, 1948, reviewed by M. Artaminov in *Voprosy istorii* IX (1948) pp. 97–108) look for the origin of the Slavic race in the vast agricultural territory between the Elbe and the Dnieper. The Slavic race, they argue, is the result of a long evolution from different ethnical and biological elements. Thus Soviet authorities differ from the Polish school in one main respect. They regard the Lusatian culture as one of the elements which contributed most notably to the origin of the primitive Slavs and their culture. Czech experts, especially J. Filip and J. Poulík, side with Russian archaeologists.

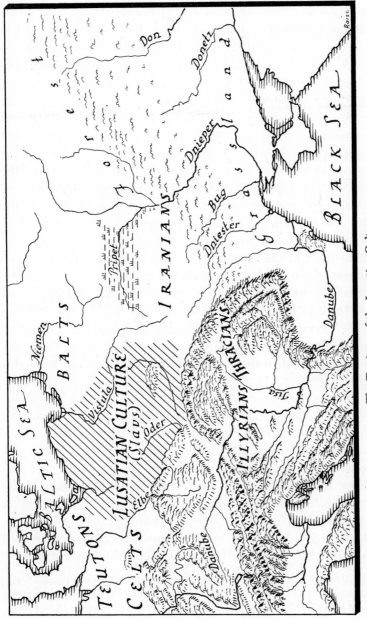

The Territory of the Lusatian Culture

ated with the Lusatian culture. It is known from archaeological
evidence that the centers of this civilization — especially in its
western part — were destroyed about the year 500 B.C. From
that time onwards, this culture shows quite different features,
which are evidenced also in the eastern part of the territory. The
cause of the destruction of these Lusatian centers appears to
have been a hostile incursion by the Scythians. These were an
Iranian people closely related to the Ossetians, who still live in
the northern Caucasus. They came to eastern Europe in the
eighth or seventh century B.C., if not earlier,[1] and founded an
empire in southern Russia. This extended westwards to the
Danube, eastwards to the Don and northwards to the sources of
the Dnieper and the Bug. The famous Greek historian of the
fifth century, Herodotus, who visited the Black Sea region, gives
us some detailed information concerning them.

The track of the Scythian invasion of Central Europe can be
followed through Silesia, Moravia and Bohemia. It is marked by
a series of destroyed "Lusatian" strongholds and also by numerous Scythian tombs which lie on the route of the invasion and
in the territory of the Lusatian culture. As the eastern part of
this territory seems to have suffered less destruction, it may be
that the population there surrendered to the invaders without a
fight.

This invasion must have considerably weakened the native
population, thus permitting envious neighbors to raid and pillage.
This weakening enabled the Germans to press towards the Oder,
and the Celts, who until then were settled in modern France and
western and southern Germany, to move towards the east and
occupy Bohemia, Moravia, parts of Silesia and the lands of the
upper Vistula. This was the beginning of the great migration
and expansion of the Celts; it caused a violent upheaval in Italy,
where, in 390 B.C., they sacked Rome and threatened to conquer the whole country. It also shook Asia Minor where some of

[1] See T. Sulimirski's study: "Scythian Antiquities in Central Europe," *The
Antiquaries' Journal* XXV (1945), pp. 1–20. On the Ossetians see the
recent study by V. I. Abaev, *Osetinskij jazyk i folklor* (Moscow, 1949), vol. I.

the Celtic tribes found a definite home and became the Galatians to whom St. Paul addressed one of his epistles.

If we suppose that the people who created the Lusatian culture were Slavs, we can readily understand the great setback which their civilization suffered as a result of this Scythian blow. On the other hand, if we cannot accept that the Slavs were responsible for the Lusatian culture, it is natural to surmise that after the Scythian invasion the native population of the Lusatian territory was gradually replaced by Slavs advancing towards the Elbe and the Baltic. On the ruins of the Lusatian culture there arose another civilization, this time undeniably Slav, which archaeologists call "Venedian" and which attained its zenith in the first century of our era.

2

Our task of determining more precisely the origins of the Slavs and of following more accurately their prehistoric evolution would become very much easier if we could find more information concerning them in the works of the classical Greek and Roman writers. However, the fact that the Slavs were originally settled so far from the lands of the Mediterranean civilizations explains why they remained for so long unknown to the Greeks and the Romans. Of the early Greek historians, only Herodotus may have been aware of their presence beyond the sources of the Dniester and the Bug and on the middle Dnieper. The Neuroi and the Budini, whom he locates there, were probably Slavic. It might also be that the "Scythian Plowmen," whom he distinguishes from other Scythians, were also partly Slavs.

After Herodotus we find no mention of the Slavs in Greek literature until the second century of our era, when they are mentioned on the map of Claudius Ptolemy. As early as this, Ptolemy calls the Carpathian Mountains the Mountains of the Slavs (Οὐενεδικὰ ὄρη), and some of the tribes located by him in that region should be regarded as Slavs. The Baltic he also calls

CARNEGIE INSTITUTE
OF TECHNOLOGY LIBRARY

Sea of the Slavs (Οὐενεδικὸς κόλπος) and refers to Slavs on the Vistula.

Before him Pliny the Elder (A.D. 23–79) knew that there were Slavs (Venedi) living on the Vistula, and Tacitus (about A.D. 55–120), in his description of Germania, places the Venedi east of the Germans.[1] After that we have to wait until the sixth century for more precise reports on the migrations of the Slavs and their culture.

The scarcity of information about the Slavs in the works of the old classical writers helps to explain why the civilized peoples of the West were so little interested in the historical and cultural evolution of the Slavs. It is necessary to bear in mind that all historical and geographical knowledge in the Middle Ages was based upon the writings of the classical authors, above all, on those of Caesar, Pliny, Tacitus and Ptolemy. The works of the Byzantine writers, who have provided us with so much information on the history of the Balkans and southern Russia, and even of Central Europe, were mostly unknown to the peoples of the West before the Renaissance. Even later, modern historical research, which has remained deeply indebted to the same sources, has been slow and laborious; and so it is no wonder that even in recent times the historical evolution of the Slavs and of Central and Eastern Europe in general has been much neglected and at best perhaps looked upon as a curiosity.

3

Matters would have been quite different if the Romans had come into direct contact with the Slavs, as they did with the Celts and the Germans. This would not have been impossible; for twice the Romans came very near to the territory inhabited by the Slavs.

[1] Among the many etymologies of the word Venedi the most probable is that which recognizes in the word a proto-Indo-European root, "ven'd." Names derived from this root are common also among other Indo-European nations.

The first of these opportunities occurred when the Romans tried to subdue the Germans, who had been moving gradually since 1000 B.C. into northern and central Germany. By about the year 100 B.C. the Germans had compelled the Celts to abandon parts of southern Germany and had occupied it completely themselves. Gaul — the habitat proper of the Celts — came firmly into Roman hands between 58 and 51 B.C. and was in process of being latinized. The attacks of the Germanic tribes on Gaul forced the Romans to attempt their subjugation and subsequent latinization. We learn from Caesar himself, the conqueror of Gaul, how keenly he was aware of the Germanic danger. His genius saved Gaul for Rome, and his victory was followed by a new Roman offensive against the Germans. Already Agrippa had started to latinize some Germanic tribes which victorious Roman arms had forced to settle on the left bank of the Rhine.

Before launching the new offensive against the Germans, Rome first of all secured possession between 35 and 8 B.C. of Raetia and Pannonia, which were inhabited by populations of old Illyrian stock. It was then that Augustus gave the order to attack and his son-in-law, Nero Claudius Drusus, penetrated from the North Sea to the rivers Ems and Weser. The Germanic tribes which were settled in the regions he had overrun — the Batavians and the Frisians — had to accept Roman domination (12 B.C.) and this conquest was followed by the occupation of the territory between the Rhine and the Weser. The Chatti (Hessians) were in the same position as the Batavians and the Frisians, and Roman legions were garrisoned at Alisso on the river Lippe to exercise control over the new subjects of the Empire and ensure their loyalty.

The Romans continued their advance, and in the year 9 B.C. Drusus camped on the Elbe. A little later he set up his headquarters at Mainz. Frightened by these quick successes, the Marcomanni and Quadi, Germanic tribes of the Swabian family who then dwelled on the Main, began to move eastwards in search of a new home. This they eventually found in modern

Bohemia, Moravia and Slovakia, after they had expelled the Celtic Boii.

The victories of Drusus were completed by his brother Tiberius. The territory between the Rhine and the Elbe became a Roman province. In spite of frequent revolts, the country could hardly have escaped the fate which overtook the Celts in Gaul, if the Romans had continued steadily to pursue their offensive policy in these regions. Germanicus, the son of Drusus, avenged the massacre of Varus and his three legions in the Forest of Teutoburg (A.D. 9) and smashed the insurgent Germanic bands in the years A.D. 14 to 16. This aggressive policy was, however, abandoned by Tiberius, who reigned from A.D. 14 to 37. The country seemed too poor to excite the interest of the conquerors, while the new subjects were too wild and undisciplined, so that the pacification and administration of Germania appeared to be too costly a project. Hence, Tiberius ordered the evacuation of the territory lying between the Ems and the Elbe, and at a later date Claudius (A.D. 41–54) ordered the legions to re-cross the Rhine.

From the point of view of Roman interests, it was a great mistake to leave Germania to its fate. The ferocity of the Germanic tribes, which the Roman legions had experienced more than once, should have been a warning to the Roman government. Roman generals little thought when they led their troops back to the Rhine that the short-sighted policy of their leaders would one day bring the savage hordes they had conquered back with re-doubled fury. They could not foresee that the northern barbarians would, in their turn, cross the Rhine and smash the Roman Empire. It is not difficult to imagine how different the fate of Europe would have been if Germania had been civilized and latinized as Gaul had been. It is, indeed, a solemn thought to realize how momentous and far-reaching for the evolution of the whole of mankind the mistakes of rulers may become.

4

The victories of Drusus and Germanicus brought ancient Rome to the point where it most closely approached Central Europe and the Slavs from the northwest. It seems, however, that the Emperor Trajan (A.D. 98–117) came to the conclusion that this defensive policy of containment had been a great mistake. He endeavored to rectify it by conquering the peoples beyond the Danube in order to protect the Empire from any danger which might threaten it from this direction.

The Dacians, a nation of Thracian origin who had already proved a source of considerable trouble to both Augustus and Domitian, were attacked and defeated by Trajan. Their king preferred suicide to Roman captivity. Trajan's famous column and the *Tropaeum Traiani*, the triumphal monument discovered in the village of Adam-Klissi in the Dobrudja, commemorate this victorious Roman campaign.

A new province, Dacia, was formed comprising Transylvania, Wallachia and Moldavia, the Rumania of 1918–1940. It was designed to be an important bulwark of Roman civilization, protecting the Empire against any attack from Germanic tribes established in what are now Slovakia, Moravia and Bohemia, and from the Sarmatians, the successors of the Scythians, who occupied the region between the Carpathian Mountains and the Black Sea; but it is here that the Romans made their greatest mistake. They would have been wise to have occupied the whole of the Danubian basin and to have established the frontier of the Empire on the Carpathian Mountains, because this would have involved the subjugation of the Sarmatian Iazyges, who dwelt between the Tisza (Theiss) and the Danube and threatened both Dacia and Pannonia.

Trajan's successor, Hadrian (A.D. 117–138), failed to pursue this new political course. His defensive policy is still recalled today in Britain by the long wall which bears his name and which was designed to protect Roman Britain from the savage Picts, Scots and other tribes of the north. It was left to the future to show that this policy was wholly ineffectual and that no man-made barrier could save Roman Britain from the fury of barbaric invaders.

Marcus Aurelius (A.D. 161–180) tasted the bitter fruits of this misguided policy in the years which he had to spend battling with the Germans, who had been left too long in peace. In A.D. 162, the Chatti (Hessians) launched an attack against the provinces of Raetia and *Germania Superior*, and the Marcomanni and Quadi, established, as indicated, in modern Czechoslovakia, followed their lead in attacking the Romans. The Sarmatian tribe of the Iazyges, from the Tisza (Theiss) and the Danube, joined forces with the Germans, and Rome had many anxious moments. For fourteen years Marcus Aurelius had to wage an almost constant struggle against these allied attackers, but his legions emerged victorious. They penetrated further than the middle Danube and their garrisons were dotted over the whole of southern Slovakia and southern Moravia. The Emperor wrote one book of his "Meditations" in the country of the Quadi — "on the river Hron" — in modern Slovakia. It is said that when he pondered there on the distant prospect of the high peaks of the Carpathian Mountains, his main preoccupation was to contemplate the extension of the Roman Empire as far as this great natural boundary. Two new Roman provinces had now to be created: Sarmatia, comprising the territory between the Theiss and the Danube, and Marcomannia — the Bohemia, Moravia and Slovakia of today.

If it is true that Marcus Aurelius contemplated such far-reaching projects, it is a further proof of the genius of this great Emperor; but he was denied the experience of seeing the realization of such plans, for he died on the 17th of March, A.D. 180, at Vindobona, the modern Vienna.

The entire future of Central Europe and of the Slavs would have taken quite different shape if the Romans had been able to maintain their position beyond the Danube and to continue the work of the imperial philosopher. It seems, however, that Rome did not then possess sufficient strength to pursue a prolonged offensive policy in those regions. All that recalls the ancient *limes Romanus* in southern Slovakia and southern Moravia are a few remains of Roman camps and forts, and a Roman inscription beneath the Castle of Trenčín, at the foot of the Tatras in northern Slovakia, which informs the world that sometime about the year A.D. 179, Roman legions camped there, thus reaching the most northerly point in their push towards the Carpathian Mountains.

5

So it happened that the Romans failed to establish direct contact with the Slavs. In the meantime, while the Romans were trying to reach the Carpathians, the Slavs had been moving in the direction of the middle Dniester and Dnieper long before the Scythian invasion in 500 B.C. It was a slow-moving penetration from the upper Vistula and upper Bug, motivated by the increase in the population, which was now growing too large for the original home. But other tribes were now appearing in the region, which at the present day is southern Russia, preceding the Slavs in their movement towards the Black Sea. The Bastarnae, a Germanic tribe — although some scholars regard them as Celts — left their primitive home between the fifth and third centuries B.C. and, accompanied or followed by other Germanic tribes, traversed the territory inhabited by the Slavs, appearing about 230 B.C. on the lower Danube and the Black Sea. The Goths, whose original habitats were in southeastern Sweden, moved from there to the shores of the Baltic and the region of the lower Vistula in the first century of our era. After a prolonged stay, they followed in the footsteps of the Slavs and the Bastarnae and reached the borders of the Roman Empire at the beginning of the third century. The division of this mighty tribe into Visigoths (*Tervingi, Wise,* called also *West Goths*) and Ostrogoths (*Greutingi, Brilliant,* called also *East Goths*) was probably effected after they had reached the Black Sea.

This steady migration of primitive tribes towards the lower Danube and the Black Sea may seem a strange one, but it can easily be explained. Historians were formerly accustomed to look upon the evolution of Europe from the point of view of the Romans, to whom the Carpathians appeared to form an impenetrable barrier for primitive peoples, but they forgot to take into account other geographical features which were favorable to half-nomadic and half-agricultural mass movements. These features were the waterways of the Russian plains, which not only made commercial exchanges possible, but considerably developed them between the peoples of the interior of what is now Russia and those on the shores of the Baltic.[1] Greek colonists were the intermediaries in this trading intercourse.

Colonization of the shores of the Black Sea by the Greeks had begun as early as 700 B.C. The trading posts set up by Greek merchants developed into busy townships. From the mouth of the Dniester to the Sea of Azov, a series of flourishing Greek city-states came into being, one of them, Panticapaeum (the modern Kerč), providing the nucleus around which the so-called Bosporanian kingdom sprang up. So mighty did this kingdom become that, under Mithridates II, King of Pontus (124–88 B.C.), it became a center of fierce resistance against Roman penetration into this part of Europe and Asia Minor.

The Greek colonists developed a brisk commerce with the interior of what is now Russia, and their traders, following the easy Russian waterways, penetrated as far as the Baltic. They also built up and maintained lively commercial relations with Asia Minor and the Middle East. The people who benefited most by this intercourse were the Scythians who, up to about 200 B.C., dominated the whole of what is now southern Russia, and it is more than probable that they were in touch with the Slavs. If the tribes mentioned by Ptolemy, settled in the modern Ukraine, were Slavs, they were the first Slavic tribes to come into contact with Greek civilization as it spread from the Greek city-states

[1] For details see M. Rostovtseff, *Iranians and Greeks in South Russia* (Oxford, 1922).

on the shores of the Black Sea. As a result of this Greek cultural influence, the upper class of the Scythians became partly hellenized and the whole nation abandoned its nomadic existence and settled down.[1]

About the year 200 B.C., a new nation, the Sarmatians, who were akin to the Scythians, made an appearance in southern Russia and defeated the Scythians, whom they then proceeded to absorb. The Sarmatians founded their own empire, which extended over the whole southern Ukrainian territory, from the river Don to the Danube. The relations of the Greek colonists with the Sarmatians, at least in the early days, were not as happy as those maintained with the Scythians; but under the Roman protectorate, or that of the Bosporanian kingdom, the Greek merchants survived the difficult period and continued their trade with the interior of Russia.

This commercial intercourse between the Baltic and the Black Sea brought to the notice of the nations in the north the many advantages of living in the warmer and richer lands lying on the confines of the Roman Empire and Greek civilization. There must have been an important trading post — a forerunner of Kiev — on the middle Dnieper, which held out particular attractions for them, and it is no wonder that the Slavs first began to move slowly but steadily towards it. This center and the Don and Donets region, into which the Slavs were moving, were controlled, after the defeat of the Scythians, by the Sarmatians, and the Slavic tribes which entered this territory naturally came under their political and cultural influence.

6

The eastward movement of the Slavs was hastened by the activities of the Goths. As we have seen, this great tribe had occupied part of the Baltic coast for about two centuries, and

[1] Many interesting details concerning the evolution of the Scythians under the influence of Greek culture can be obtained from M. Rostovtseff, *Skythien und der Bosporus* (Berlin, 1931) and E. H. Minns, *Scythians and Greeks* (Cambridge, 1913).

they subjugated the greater part of the Slavs, whose presence in this area was attested by Pliny the Elder, Tacitus and Ptolemy. The steady flow of the Slavs towards the east was not slowed down when the Goths abandoned their home on the Baltic and started moving towards the Black Sea, following the Dnieper waterway. The presence of the Goths in southern Russia, however, caused a considerable upheaval in that region. The Ostrogoths pushed on in the direction of the Black Sea and about A.D. 200 the Greek cities on the coast became a glittering prize for the new barbarian invaders, and only the cities in the Crimea were able to resist successfully. The Visigoths spread towards the lower Danube, and in the middle of the third century they conquered Dacia from the Romans. Thus, the Goths had established an empire which comprised the whole of southern Russia as far as the shores of the Sea of Azov, and the Slavic tribes which had peacefully penetrated these regions, now under Gothic rule, came under the political and cultural influence of the new masters of the area.

It should, however, be emphasized that Sarmatian influence was exerted on the Slavs before that of the Goths. The fact that the Slavs who had penetrated towards the Don and Donets region had come under the domination of the Sarmatians before the arrival of the Goths is confirmed by the testimony of two sixth-century writers — Jordanes and Procopius. Jordanes, the historian of the Goths, records that a part of that nation, having crossed the Dnieper, probably in the region of Kiev, attacked the Spali, a tribe which lived in the region of the Donets river. After defeating them, the Goths turned towards the Sea of Azov and penetrated into the Crimea, this encounter taking place in the second century of our era. The Spali supposedly belonged to the Alanic group of Sarmatians and must be identified with the Speroi or Speri mentioned by Procopius. Since Procopius says that in the old days all Slavs — meaning, of course, only the Slavs known to him — were called Sporoi or Spori, we are entitled to conclude from this statement that the Slavs in this region were, before the arrival of the Goths, controlled by the Alanic Spali.

We find additional evidence for this in the fact that in the language of the ancient Slavs, the word for "giant" is *spolin* (Russian *ispolin*, Polish *stolin* or *stolim*), a word obviously derived from "Spali" — the giant, master nation.

The power of the Spali was broken by the Goths; but it seems that the Sarmatians did not entirely relinquish their hold on the Slavs. The place of the Spali appears to have been taken by the Antês, whose origin is not yet quite clear. Pliny the Elder in his *Natural History* (Book VI, chap. 35) mentioned the "Anti" among peoples living between the Sea of Azov and the Caspian. Ptolemy was also aware of their existence in this area and Greek inscriptions placed them in the region of the Crimea. At that time, this area was inhabited by Sarmatian tribes. If Pliny's Anti could be identified with the Antês, their Slavic origin should be excluded. It is possible that the Sarmatian "Anti" were settled in the basin of the Don and Donets as early as the second century of our era and that they then took over the leadership of the Slavs in that region.

Some scholars, however, regard the Antês as a Slavic tribe. Their name — although regarded by some as Iranian — could, in reality, be Slavic, and derived from the same common Indo-European root as the name of the Veneti, Venedi. It is quite admissible that an Iranian tribe and a Slavic tribe bore similar names formed from a common root.

Jordanes and Procopius, sixth-century writers to whom we owe most of our information about the Antês, are not very helpful in solving this problem. Jordanes distinguishes three groups of the Slavs — the Venedi, the Sclavini and the Antês. In another passage he stresses that the Antês spoke the same language as the Slavs. This statement is confirmed by Procopius who, however, strictly distinguishes them from other Slavs. Does this mean that both writers were aware of a non-Slavic origin of the Antês? It is possible, but their statements furnish no conclusive evidence for either opinion.

In any case, a strong Sarmatian political and cultural influence on the organization of the Antic state can hardly be ex-

cluded. The Slavs governed by the Antês and the Sarmatian
tribes were immediate neighbors, and it is possible that some
of them helped the Antês to establish their political supremacy
over other Slavic tribes. At least, some of the names of prominent
Antês mentioned by the Byzantine writers Procopius, Menander
and Agathias seem to be Iranian. In any case we can conclude
from the statements of Jordanes and Procopius that, by the sixth
century, the Byzantines regarded the Antês as Slavs. If there
was any admixture of Iranian elements among the Antês, they
were, at that period, already completely slavicized.

The fact that the Goths were occupied elsewhere must have
greatly helped the Antês to consolidate their position in the area
of the Don, Donets and middle Dnieper. As the Antês are said
to have established a dynasty, supported by numerous tribal
chiefs, we may suppose that their domination of this part of a
region which is now Russia must have been of quite ancient
date. If all this is true, and there are no serious reasons for rejecting these statements and suppositions, then the first attempt
at organizing the Slavs in the present day Ukraine into a kind of
State was made by a tribe which, even if Slavic, was under
strong Sarmatian influence.

The Antês also assumed the leadership of the opposition to
the Goths. It was because of this that Ermanarich, King of the
Goths from A.D. 350 to 370, before starting upon his march to the
north to win his short-lived Gothic empire, first attacked and
defeated the Antês and forced them to submit to his rule. The
Slavs who did not belong to the Antês group and who were called
Sclavini by Jordanes submitted only in part to the Goths. Some
of them preferred to migrate towards the north, settling in the
region of the future Novgorod. This suggests that the Slavs were
rather averse to the idea of being ruled by the Goths. Ermanarich also forced the Slavs of modern Poland — the Venedi of
Jordanes — to accept him as their overlord. He founded an empire which embraced all the Slavic and German tribes and some
of the Finnish tribes living between the Baltic and the Black
Sea. Had this empire survived, the Goths and not the Scandina-

vians would have amalgamated the Eastern Slavs into a single political body, which would have been called *Gothia* instead of *Russia*.

7

But the Gothic empire did not last. Ermanarich's hopes were dashed to the ground by the first Asiatic invasion of Europe — that of the Huns. The Huns were masters of North China when they were attacked and defeated by the Avars, a kindred tribe established between the Targum and the Korean peninsula. The Huns fled in panic towards the west and, after cutting through the Indo-European tribes, established themselves in southern Russia, whence they launched their attack upon the Goths. In a single battle in A.D. 370, this first Germanic empire was completely destroyed. This fact alone shows that the Gothic rule over subjugated nations must have been loose in the extreme, and the Goths did all the fighting. Ermanarich committed suicide — or was murdered by his own subjects, who were appalled at the disaster which had overtaken them. The new king, Vinitharius (Withimer), after gathering together the remnants of the Ostrogoths and of the Germanic tribes which had followed them, tried to retreat by way of the Dnieper to the old home of the Goths, but he found the way barred by the insurgent Antês. The Goths were desperate, but they won the ensuing battle and, to terrorize his opponents, Vinitharius killed Boz, the King of the Antês, together with all his sons and seventy chieftains. This massacre took place in the year 375. Acts of terrorization, however, could not save Vinitharius or his empire. In the following year he was attacked and thoroughly beaten by the Huns, or more precisely by the Sarmatian Alans, who had joined forces with them and formed an important contingent of the Hunnish hordes. Thus the Antês had their revenge and breathed again. When the Huns moved into modern Hungary, which became the center of their empire under Attila (445–453), the Antês were presented with a new opportunity of affirming their hold over the territory of the middle Dnieper and the Slavs inhabiting it, and when the Hunnish empire disintegrated after the death of Attila, the Antês moved the frontier of their own possessions nearer to the lower Dniester and the lower Danube.

The invasion of the Huns was one of the most important events at the end of ancient history. They overthrew the whole existing order in Central Europe and set the Goths in motion who, after being allowed to settle in the eastern parts of the Roman Empire, initiated the process which contributed so greatly to its ruin. But the Hunnish invasion had other consequences which were bound, directly and indirectly, to affect the Slavs and to influence their history. We have seen that the Sarmatian Alans largely threw in their lot with the Huns. It seems, however, that the upheaval caused by this invasion had forced two other Sarmatian tribes — the Croats and the Serbs — to look for new places in which to settle. Greek inscriptions from the second and third centuries of our era, found at the mouth of the Don, mention the name Choroathos or Chorouathos. This region was settled by Sarmatians and was considered by contemporary Greek sources to belong to Asiatic Sarmatia. This provides the strongest argument for maintaining that the Croats, or at least their ethnic name, were of Sarmatian origin.[1] The evidence for

---

[1] P. S. Sakač thinks that he discovered the name "Croats" in Darius' inscriptions from the sixth century B.C. There an old Persian province and people are mentioned, called Harahvaiti, Harahvatis, Horohoati ("Iranische Herkunft des kroatischen Volksnamens" in *Orientalia Christiana Periodica* XV [1949], pp. 313–340). The province was situated in southern Persia near the frontiers of what is now Afghanistan. Sakač's theory is that the Harahvatis were driven away from their country by the Indians and migrated towards the Caucasus. This theory presents some difficulties; for how is their migration across the whole Iranian plateau to be explained when they could probably have found other chances of settling down nearer their own country? It is, however, possible to imagine that a part of this Iranian tribe did not follow the rest during the Iranian immigration into modern Persia, but stayed in the steppes between the Caspian and the Aral Seas, whence it moved later towards the Sea of Azov and the Caucasus. All this shows that the problem of the origin of the Croats and the Serbs is complicated and that many questions have to be answered before it can be definitely solved.

the Sarmatian origin of the Serbs is not so strong, but seems to be reasonably well founded.[1]

Trying to escape from the onslaught of the Huns, the Croats and the Serbs fled towards the northeast, beyond the middle Dnieper, where the Antês were settled. Here the Croats may have been joined by a Gothic tribe, and together they established themselves beyond the Carpathian Mountains and gathered the Slavic tribes of Galicia, Silesia and the eastern part of Bohemia — already abandoned by the Quadi and occupied by Slavs — into a kind of state. We have sufficient evidence from the Byzantine imperial writer Constantine Porphyrogennetus, from Arabic sources and also from the Anglo-Saxon King Alfred of the existence of a Croatian State beyond the Carpathians called White Croatia. The Serbs were in some regions mixed with the Croats, especially on the upper Vistula. The bulk of them, however, pushing more towards the northwest and following in the footsteps of the Scythian invaders of about 500 B.C., imposed their rule on the Slavic tribes between the Elbe and the Saale rivers, their state being called White Serbia. The remnants of the Lusatian Serbs (Sorbs) recall this name down to the present day.

Additional evidence for the Sarmatian origin of the Croats and the Serbs may be found in Constantine Porphyrogennetus's *Book of Ceremonies*.[2] In describing how the princes of the Cau-

---

[1] Pliny the Elder in his *Natural History* (Book VI, 19), which was written in the first century A.D., located the "Serbi" in the region between the Sea of Azov and the Caucasus. In the second century, Ptolemy's *Geography* (Book V, 8, 13) located the "Serboi" between the lower Volga and the Caucasus. Jireček, the main authority on Serbian history, has questioned the correctness of this reading; but the critical edition of Pliny by C. Mayhoff and that of Ptolemy by C. Müller preserve the expressions "Serbi" and "Serboi."

[2] Book II, Chap. 48, p. 688 (Bonn edition). Up to now, this passage seems to have been overlooked by most scholars who have studied the problem of the origin of the Croats and the Serbs. D. Obolensky drew my attention to it. The passage is mentioned only in Vivien de Saint Martin's *Études de géographie ancienne* (Paris, 1850, 1852), vol. II, pp. 244 ff. Cf. also J. Saint-Martin, *Mémoires sur l'Arménie* (Paris, 1818–1820), vol. II, p. 310. A. Rambaud (*L'empire grec au Xème siècle* [Paris, 1870], pp. 510, 525, 526) identifies the tribes mentioned by the imperial writer with the Serbs

casian region should be addressed in Byzantine diplomatic correspondence, the imperial writer speaks of the Prince or Archon of the Krevatades as "He who is called Krevatas." Then he mentions the Archon-Prince of the Sarban, "who are located between Alania and Tsanaria." If we could identify the Krevatades and Sarban with the Croats and Serbs, then we could conclude that some of the Croats and Serbs were driven by the Huns towards the Caucasus, where they continued to live under their own princes recognizing a kind of Byzantine protectorate.

There are grounds for believing that the Croats, when pushing towards the north, had acted with the connivance of the Antês. The author of *The History of the Origins of the Langobards* says explicitly that when the Lombards were moving, in the fifth century, from the Elbe into modern Austria, they forced their passage through Anthâib — evidently the land of the Antês. According to our source, the Anthâib can be only the country occupied at that time by the Croats. This identification of the land of the Croats with that of the Antês can be explained if we admit that the Antês imposed a form of political overlordship over the Croats. If this is so, we can speak of a loose Antic empire extending from eastern Bohemia to the middle Dnieper, the Black Sea and the Don.

In any case, even if we hesitate to go as far as that, it seems established that almost all the Slavic tribes recorded in the

---

and Croats. The "Servotioi," who are called "black children," located by Constantine Porphyrogennetus on the confines of Armenia (*ibid.*, p. 687) were identified by J. Marquart (*Osteuropäische und ostasiatische Streifzüge* [Leipzig, 1903], pp. 36 ff.) with the Sevortioi (Sevordik), a Magyar tribe. They are the "Black Hungarians," whose name was transformed in Armenian, by popular etymology, into Sevordik, which means "black children." H. Grégoire ("L'origine et le nom des Croates et leur prétendue patrie caucasienne," *La Nouvelle Clio* IV [1952], p. 323, V [1953], p. 466 ff.) identifies the Krevatades with the Kabardinci, a Czerkess tribe now living on the upper Terek. This identification cannot be accepted because the Kabardinci migrated to this region only in the fourteenth or fifteenth century, after expelling the Mongols. Neither can the Sarban be identified with the Sirvan, a suggestion rejected already by Reiske, the editor of *De Ceremoniis*. We are not entitled to correct wilfully the reading of the only manuscript of this work.

Russian Primary Chronicle, with the exception of the Northern
ones, were under strong cultural, and perhaps also political, influence from the Antês and Sarmatians.

8

So far, we have followed the slow progress of Slav penetration
into the part of Europe which was later to be called Russia. But
at the beginning of our era the Slavs started migrating through
the Moravian Gates and the Carpathian Mountains, entering
what is now Hungary in the direction of the Danube and the
Roman frontiers.

It is known that in modern Croatia between the rivers Drava
and Sava and in the so-called Banat between the lower Tisza
(Theiss) and the Danube certain places (Vuka, Vrbas, Vučica)
have borne Slavic names from the second century onwards.
This first Slavic penetration was sporadic and isolated. A more
systematic movement started in the third century. The map
called Peutinger's *Tabula*, one of the oldest maps of Europe,
describing the Roman Empire of the third century, places the
Venedi Sarmatae in Dacia and the Venedi proper somewhere in
Bessarabia. We learn from several Roman writers — notably
Ammianus Marcellinus — that in about A.D. 334, the Sarmatian
Iazyges who, as previously mentioned, had dwelt in Hungary
between the Danube and the Tisza rivers since the second half of
the first century, were defeated by a people who were subject to
them — the *servi Sarmatorum*. These could have been only the
Venedi — Slavs — whom Peutinger's map calls Venedi Sarmatae.
These Venedi mixed with the Sarmatian Iazyges and for a considerable period lived peacefully with their nomadic Sarmatian
masters, who were glad of the products of the agricultural arts
which the Venedi practised. Later, when their numbers had
multiplied and the rule of their masters became intolerable, the
Venedi revolted.

The Slavs also seem to have remained in Hungary during the
Hunnish occupation of that country. This appears to be con-

firmed by the records of Priscus, a member of the Byzantine embassy to the Huns in 448. He reports that he found in the region between modern Belgrade and Budapest a people who were neither Gothic nor Hunnish, but who recognized Hunnish political supremacy. They offered their Byzantine guests a beverage made from honey, which the Greek ambassador calls "medos" and which was evidently a Slav speciality in the way of liqueur.

Jordanes has preserved another detail which confirms the presence of the Slavs in Hungary under Hunnish supremacy during Attila's reign. He describes the burial feast which was held at the grave of Attila in the year 453, somewhere on the middle Tisza, and refers to it as "strava" — a word which sounded strange to him. It is evidently a Slav word for a funeral feast, still preserved in the Slavic languages, partly also with its ritual meaning. Its adoption by the Huns to designate the burial feast testifies that the Slavic subjects in Hungary had begun to influence their masters and that a kind of mixed Huno-Slavic culture was being formed.

This situation did not last, because the presence of the Huns in Central Europe was of short duration. We know that in the early days of their domination of Central and Southeastern Europe, the Huns imitated the Visigoths in their attitude towards the Roman Empire. Like the Visigoths, they became first *foederati* and then invaders. Attila excelled in organizing and carrying out acts of depredation in the Illyrian provinces. In A.D. 450, when the Emperor Marcian refused to pay tribute and began instead to mobilize his forces to deal with his unaccommodating neighbor, Attila preferred to follow the way chosen by those other faithless federates, the Visigoths, and, accompanied by his Alanic and other German subjects, he invaded Gaul. He was less fortunate than he expected; yet, though he was defeated by Aetius near Campus Mauriacus in Gaul, he was still able to invade Italy and menace Rome. Then he died in 453.

With Attila's death came the end of the Hunnish power in Central and Eastern Europe. The German tribes in the Danubian basin, which had been subjugated by the Huns, revolted and, possibly supported by the Emperor Marcian, utterly defeated their Hunnish overlords in Pannonia. After their defeat the Huns retired in the direction of the Black Sea, only one section of them finding a refuge within the Empire.

It must be admitted that the short-lived Hunnish empire rendered some service to European civilization by retarding the dismemberment of the Roman Empire by the Germans. In point of fact, the Huns for many years kept under control those Germanic tribes beyond the Danube who constituted the gravest danger to the Romans. Moreover, the Huns provided the Roman Empire with a considerable number of auxiliaries for use in the struggle against the Germans. It was also evident that the victorious Germanic nations were less valuable as *foederati* than the Huns had been, although the Emperor tried hard to make the best of the new situation. He particularly favored the Gepids, who established themselves firmly in the former Dacia. The Ostrogoths received settlements in Northern Pannonia, as federates of the Empire. The Rugians found a new home opposite Noricum on the north bank of the Danube, while the Scirians and the Heruls settled in regions further east.

For a short period it looked as if Central Europe, and especially the Danubian basin, would become a Germanic land. But the new state of affairs consequent on the defeat and disappearance of the Huns was not destined to last for long. The first of the Germanic nations to disappear from their new-found home were the Rugians. Odoacer, a Scirian or a Rugian, and the actual ruler of Italy, made an end of the Rugian kingdom and stopped the frequent incursions which this Germanic tribe had been making into Roman territory.

The Ostrogoths were the second of the Germanic nations to vanish from the Danubian region. Their presence in Illyricum became very menacing to the imperial power and in order to get rid of them, the Emperor Zeno invited their king, Theoderic, to overthrow Odoacer, ruler of Italy, and then to rule that country himself under the imperial authority. Theoderic agreed to the bargain and after defeating Odoacer (A.D. 489) and establishing his people as Roman federates in Italy, he ruled it as a deputy-governor of the Emperor. This Gothic power in Italy was not broken until the Emperor Justinian (527–565) took the administration into his own hands and, with the aid of his famous generals Belisarius and Narses, drove out the foreigners who had established themselves in the midst of the Latin population.

There were left in the Danubian basin only the Lombards and the Gepids. The Lombards had come from the Elbe and settled, as we have seen, in upper Pannonia, which is now Austria, in the second half of the fifth century, and the Gepids had been established by Emperor Marcian in the former Dacia. The Slavs who had survived the Hunnish occupation continued to live in the Danubian basin together with the Germans.

The Lombards seem to have been responsible in some way for the migration of the Marcomanni and the rest of the Quadi from what is now Moravia and Bohemia to the lands east of the Lech and southwards towards the Brenner, the river Inn and the upper Danube. The inhabitants of the regions now occupied by the Marcomanni and the Quadi referred to the newcomers as the men (vari, vares) coming from the parts which, centuries ago, had been occupied by the Celtic Boii — thus, Bojuvari, Bojuvares; and in this way the new home of the Marcomanni received the name of Bajovaria. It is curious to note that the Celtic Boii have given their name to two countries in Central Europe, Bohemia and Bavaria.

9

The migrations of the Germanic tribes towards the south had created a kind of vacuum in the region of the middle and lower Elbe, but this was rapidly filled by the Slavs. They began to move from their primitive homeland towards the west and soon occupied the territories vacated by the Germans. An ancient treatise on the rivers, attributed to Vibius Sequester (fourth to sixth century), describes the Elbe as the frontier between the Germans — "the Svabians" — and the Slavs — "the Cervelii" — evidently the Sorabs or Sorbs (Serbs). During the sixth century the Slavs crossed the Elbe in large numbers and, while the Germans concentrated their attention upon Gaul, then in the hands of the Germanic Franks who were trying to conquer all the Germanic tribes, the Slavs pushed towards the North Sea and also to the west and the south. They occupied the territory where the cities of Hamburg, Lüneburg, Magdeburg, Erfurt and Gotha now stand, advancing as far as the river Saale. From there they moved in the direction of modern Bamberg and reached the Danube near Ratisbon.

The Slavs established between the Saale (Solava) and the Spree (Spreva) — the Sorbians (Sorabians, Serbians), the Milčani (in the vicinity of the modern Bautzen) and the Lužiči in Lower Lusatia — forced the Germanic Thuringians to move further west. The northerly neighbors of the Sorbians were the Vilci (Veletians), whom Ptolemy in his famous map located on the lower Vistula, whence they had travelled as far as the Elbe to occupy the territory between that river and the Varnava. These people have also been called Ljutici, because of their exceedingly wild character — *ljuty* meaning "wild." The modern Mecklenburg was held by the Obodrites, Holstein by the Vagrians, and Lüneburg by the Dreviane. The Baltic coast from the estuary of the Oder to the mouth of the Vistula was settled by the Pomeranians, who formed at the same time a transition between all these tribes, the Polabians, the Baltic Slavs and the Poles.

During the fifth century and at the beginning of the sixth a new wave of Slavs pressed forward, probably from the upper Oder and the Vistula, to occupy the regions which were being left empty by the Marcomanni and Quadi — although it is not unlikely that sporadic penetration of that territory by Slavs had been going on for some time before the withdrawal of the Germanic tribes.[1] Thus the Slavs took final possession of Bohemia

---

[1] Recent archaeological discoveries made in Czechoslovakia, especially in Moravia and Slovakia, show that the Slavs were in possession of this country in the fifth century. Before the fifth century, Slavic archaeological finds

and Moravia, while other Slavic tribes closely akin to them moved into modern Slovakia as far as the Danube. Slavs from Moravia also pushed towards the Danube, crossed it and moved into Hungary as far as Lake Balaton (Blatno).

The withdrawal of the Germanic populations from Central Europe was the signal for other Slavic peoples to move into the territories which they had vacated. Ancient Pannonia and the greater part of ancient Raetia were gradually overrun by Slavic tribes — mostly the Slovenes of today.

10

At the beginning of the same century, other Slavic peoples pushed towards the lower course of the Danube. It seems that these were the first Slavs to come into contact with the eastern part of the Roman Empire, and it is likely that they formed some important settlements in modern Wallachia on the Danube. According to the Byzantine historians and chroniclers, they started to cross the river after 517 with the object of raiding Macedonia, Thessaly and Epirus, and these Byzantine writers have placed on record many impressions of numerous Slavic incursions into the imperial territories during the reign of the Emperor Justin (518–527).[1] In view of the fact that Justin's successor Justinian (527–

---

in this region are not numerous. Their existence proves, however, that Slavic infiltration into these parts must have started before this date. This seems to accord with the report of the Byzantine writer Procopius (*De Bello Gothico* II, chap. 15, Bonn edition, p. 205) who says that the Germanic Heruls, after being defeated by the Lombards, decided to return to their old home in Denmark and were given free passage by the Slavs through their territory in 508–514. The Heruls might have followed the course of the river Tisza and reached the river Vistula through the Dukla Pass. They could also have reached the Vistula through the Moravian Gates after switching from the upper Tisza to the Danube and after following the course of the river Morava and of its tributary the Bečva. It is improbable that they passed through Bohemia, as the passage through the forests to reach the Elbe would have been more difficult.

[1] See the review of historians' appreciations of Slavic invasions during the reign of Justin in A. A. Vasiliev, *Justin the First* (Cambridge, Mass., 1950), pp. 302–312.

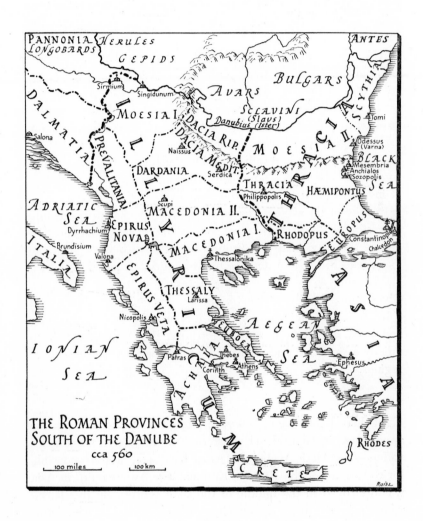

PANNONIA
LONGOBARDS
HERULES
GEPIDS
ANTES
Sirmium
Singidunum
AVARS
BULGARS
SCYTHIA
DALMATIA
MOESIA I.
DACIA RIP.
Danubius (Ister)
SCLAVINI
(Slavs)
THRACIA II.
Tomi
Salona
PREVALITANIA
DACIA MEDIT.
Naissus
MOESIA II.
Odessus
(Varna)
DARDANIA
Serdica
THRACIA
BLACK
Mesembria
Anchialos
Sozopolis
ILLYRICUM
Scupi
MACEDONIA II.
Philippopolis
HÆMIPONTUS
SEA
ADRIATIC
SEA
Dyrrhachium
EPIRUS
NOVA
RHODOPUS
EUROPUS
Constantinop
Chalcedon
ITALIA
Brundisium
Valona
MACEDONIA I.
Thessalonika
ASIA
EPIRUS VETA
THESSALY
Larissa
Nicopolis
AEGEAN
SEA
IONIAN
SEA
ACHAIA
Patras
EUBOEA
Thebes
Athens
Corinth
Ephesus

THE ROMAN PROVINCES
SOUTH OF THE DANUBE
cca 560
100 miles   100 km
RHODES
CRETE
Raisz

565) assumed the title of "Anticus," it seems likely that he must have scored some important victories over these Slavic raiding parties. We find that in fact the Antês were obliged to follow the same course as the Goths and play a part as federates of the Empire.

At the beginning of the sixth century Slavic tribes had entered Illyricum and started their push in the direction of Dalmatia. In A.D. 536 they reached the shores of the Adriatic, and the famous Dalmatian city of Salona, the ruins of which were discovered and excavated by the late Mgr. F. Bulić, the Croatian archaeologist, heard with terror the war cries of the Slavs. By the year 548 they had moved to Dyrrhachium (Durazzo). The Byzantine writers Procopius and Theophanes give many details of invasions of Illyricum by the Slavs in 549, 550 and 559.

In spite of the violent character of these Slavic incursions into Byzantine territory, there were some signs to show that the contact of the Slavs with the Empire might have become, in time, more peaceful. The Antês, the best organized group of the Slavs, had become, as we have seen, federates of the Byzantine Empire. Given time, the Byzantines might have persuaded other Slavic tribes to follow their example, and it is probable that, if the Slavs had been settled in Byzantine territory, they could have been quietly assimilated and civilized by the superior culture of these regions.

11

All these hopes were, however, dashed to the ground by the appearance in Central and Eastern Europe of new Asiatic invaders — the Altaic Avars, who, as we have seen, were responsible for the arrival of the Huns in Europe. The Avar empire in Asia was destroyed in the middle of the sixth century by the Turks, whose primitive home was to the north of Mongolia. The Turks had actually been subjugated by the Avars, but had revolted and overthrown the empire of their masters. The Avars, being probably of the Mongolian race, were akin to both the Turks and the Huns. After the overthrow of the Avar power in Asia by their

Turkic subjects, some of the Turkic tribes, namely the Uigurs, Mongolian and possibly Manchu clans, moved westwards in the direction of Europe. It should be observed that they were not actually Avars, but that they had merely acquired the name of their former masters through having lived for a long time under their domination.

About the middle of the sixth century, the new "Avars" crossed the lower courses of the Volga and defeated the Turkic Bulgars, who then controlled the region on the east coast of the Sea of Azov, between the rivers Kuban and Don. The greater part of the defeated Bulgars accepted the rule of the conquerors, but the remainder fled westwards, finding a refuge in the territory of the Lombards.

Although the Avars came into contact with the eastern fringe of the Byzantine Empire, they did not halt their advance. The lowlands beyond the Carpathian Mountains attracted their no-madic instincts, as they had those of the Huns. In due course a good opportunity to seize this desirable region was presented to them by the Lombards, the jealous neighbors of the Gepids, who, by this time, were settled in the former Dacia. The Gepids, assailed from all sides — by the Lombards and the Avars — were overwhelmed and exterminated. The Lombards realized too late that their new neighbors scarcely represented a change for the better and, shaking the dust of Pannonia from their feet, they followed the example of the Ostrogoths and established them-selves in Italy.

By the time they made this move, the ranks of the Lombards had been considerably strengthened by the inclusion of the rem-nants of several other Germanic peoples in Central Europe, in-cluding a large contingent of Saxons. They moved into northern Italy in the year 568, not as federates, but, for the first time, as an invading enemy. As a result of their speedy victories the Lom-bard kingdom in Italy was founded and Italy itself was divided into an imperial province and a Germanic kingdom. And so the Lombards wrote the last pages in the history of the Roman Empire in the West.

The Khagan of the Avars, whose name was Baian, occupied the territory vacated by the Lombards. The whole of modern Hungary became Avar and formed the center of the new empire, whose sway in Central Europe was destined to be less brief than that of the empire of the Huns. Indeed, it seemed that the Avar empire was taking ever firmer root and thus developing into a very grave danger to the eastern part of the Roman Empire as well as to the new Frankish kingdom in Gaul which was being welded together under the direction of the Merovingian dynasty, especially under King Clovis.

The establishment of the Avars in the Danubian basin was of the utmost importance for the future history of the Slavs. Instead of becoming federates of the Byzantine Empire most of the Slavs became subjects and federates of the Avars. Some Slavic tribes — especially in Bohemia, on the Elbe, and in Poland — must have joined the Avars voluntarily when they battled with the Franks on the Elbe in 561–562 and in 566–567. The Slavic tribes in Wallachia and Pannonia, Noricum and Illyricum, Moravia and Slovakia, had to acknowledge the supremacy of the Avars.[1]

The only opposition came from the Antês. We learn from contemporary Byzantine sources that the Antês collaborated with the Byzantines in order to check the mounted warriors from Asia. The Khagan Apsich was forced to organize a special campaign against them in A.D. 602 and he defeated them in what is now known as Bessarabia. This was the end of the first would-be Slav empire and the name of the Antês disappears completely from history. When we remember that the Antês were a leading element in a confederation of Slavic tribes and naturally did most

[1] Avar domination seems to have extended from its center in Pannonia, in the northeast over modern Slovakia, southern Moravia and part of modern Austria. It should, however, be stressed that recent archaeological researches carried out in southern Moravia have failed to reveal evidence of the prolonged presence of Avars in that country in the sixth and seventh centuries. A few tombs with Avar character found in this country have to be dated from the eighth century. They are located in burial grounds of a marked Slavic character and seem to contain the bodies of Slavic chieftains who have adopted Avar customs. The Slavs in Bohemia and northern Moravia appear to have entered freely into alliance with the Avars.

The Antes, White Croatia and White Serbia before the invasion of the Avars cca.560

of the fighting, their disappearance is easily explained by their annihilation in battle. Subsequently in south Russia we encounter only some separate Slavic tribes, which, as we have seen, probably formed the main body of this earlier so-called confederation.

The tribes in modern Rumania and Yugoslavia, on the other hand, seem generally to have accepted the leadership of the new masters quite gladly. Their pressure in the direction of the Adriatic and their incursions into Roman territory by no means diminished after their subjugation. It is, indeed, surprising to observe how quickly these Slavs adapted themselves to the military tactics of the Avars, even to the extent of adopting their types of armament. During the later half of the sixth century and the whole of the seventh, the Slavs were constantly multiplying their attacks against the imperial provinces, acting both on their own aggressive initiative and as auxiliaries of the Avars.

The Slavs, however, changed their tactics in one respect. When they invaded a territory, they did not limit themselves to devastating the countryside and withdrawing with their booty, as did the Avars; they exerted themselves to establish firm settlements. Two Syriac writers provide evidence of the fact that the Slavs first made a settlement on Greek soil in the year 581. The situation worsened rapidly during the first years of the reign of the Emperor Maurice (582–602) after the important imperial city of Sirmium (now Srěm in modern Croatia) was forced to capitulate to the Avars and their Slavic auxiliaries. By A.D. 578 the Slavs had penetrated as far as the Peloponnese, and Slavic colonies established in this province were considerably strengthened by the arrival of new tribes after 587. The Milingues and the Ezerites settled on both slopes of the Taygetus Mountains.

In the years 587 to 589 the Slavic colonies in Greece were further strengthened; and famous cities of the Greek classical period — Thebes, Demetrias and Athens — had to suffer the presence of barbarians in their vicinity. In 597 even Thessalonica had a narrow escape when the city was menaced by a combined force of Avars and Slavs. The Greeks believed that it was only through the intervention of its patron saint Demetrius that the city was saved.

The eastern part of the Roman Empire was hard pressed to deal with the new invaders. Already weakened by the Germanic invasions, it had also to fight an even more dangerous enemy in the East — the Persians. The Emperor Maurice could only send his generals Priscus and Peter against the Avars and the Slavs after defeating this new enemy. When the Slavs across the Danube were crushed and the Avars were twice roundly defeated by the Roman armies, the Avars showed a willingness to make peace, and for the last time in history the frontier between the Empire and the newcomers was fixed on the Danube.

However, the Empire was unable to continue its campaign against the Avars and the Slavs and the situation became critical again in the reign of the Emperor Phocas (602–610). Moreover the Slovenes, who were now firmly established in Pannonia and Noricum, began to push towards the Adriatic. In the years 592, 600 and 602, they made a series of devastating raids into Istria and Venetia, making their way as far as the banks of the Tagliamento in Italy and Dreiherrenspitze, Dachstein and Hallstadt in the Alps. In the seventh century the whole of Dalmatia to the rivers Sava and Danube was occupied by numerous Slavic tribes. The Byzantine Empire, preoccupied by its struggle with the Persians, could keep only the most important cities on the Adriatic — Zara, Trogir, Spalato (Split), Ragusa (Dubrovnik), Cattaro (Kotor), Dyrrhachium (Durazzo) — and some of the islands off the coast, but other islands were occupied by the Slavic tribe of the Narentans (Neretvans), who settled on the coast between the river Narenta (Neretva) and Cetinje. This tribe was the most important of all those settled on the rivers Lim, Drina, Piva, Tara, Ibar, Morava and the Adriatic shores — i.e. the Dukliane, the Travuniane, the Konavliane and the Zachlumiane.

The remaining parts of the Balkans were completely transformed by the Slavs. The Roman provinces of Moesia, Dacia, Dardania and Macedonia were entirely occupied by them. Epirus had large Slav settlements, while others were established even in Thrace and Greece proper. During the first half of the seventh century, Slavs even penetrated to some of the islands of the Aegean including Crete and raided the coasts of Asia Minor.

All these Slavic tribes which had established themselves in the whole of the territory stretching from the Alps to the Adriatic and to the Dobrudja on the Black Sea were very similar. Their idioms, at the same stage of evolution, were, in fact, dialects of one common language. If they had been able to find a common political center, they would have formed one immense nation of which all branches would have spoken the same language. All these tribes called themselves Slovenes, which the Latins transcribed as Sclavini, Sclavi, Slavi, and the Greeks as Sklavenoi (Sthlavenoi), Sklavoi. Owing, however, to the different political and national evolutions of the Southern Slavs, only the Slovenes of today have preserved the ancient name; the others have acquired the designations of those tribes under whose leadership they came — such as the Serbs, the Croats and Bulgarians.

12

The establishment of the Slavs in southern Europe was of the greatest importance for the evolution of Europe as a whole, and for that matter, for the history of all mankind. The Slavs, unlike the Germans, took possession of these parts of the Roman Empire not as federates, but as conquerors. The Avar hordes displayed an extreme ferocity, destroying everything with which they came into contact. All the Latin cities in Pannonia, Noricum, Illyricum and Dacia disappeared as the Avar and Slav waves engulfed them and the same fate overtook the Greek cities in Dardania, Praevalis and Scythia. On the Dalmatian coast, in Epirus, in Macedonia and Thrace, only a few towns escaped destruction and many priceless monuments of the classical and early Christian periods were utterly destroyed. Christianity, which had been flourishing in those parts of the Empire ever since the fourth century, was almost completely uprooted.[1] It is, indeed, of the

[1] The evolution of Christianity in Illyricum and in Pannonia is well outlined

SLAVIC SETTLEMENTS
south of the Danube - VII century

greatest interest to follow the fate of the many episcopal sees in these regions during the troubled years of the Slavic occupation. One after another they disappeared, most of them forever. This whole immense territory suddenly became a pagan land once more, and "terra missionum."

The destruction of Christianity in this vast region of the Roman Empire called Illyricum, which included all the provinces mentioned above, from the Alps to the Peloponnese — with the exception of Thrace — had another important consequence which has never been pointed out before. This territory came under the jurisdiction of the Roman See, which had established the metropolitan of Thessalonica as a special apostolic vicar for Illyricum. It was, moreover, in this region that Latin and Greek populations were intermingled, living peacefully together and forming a bridge between the Latin West and the Greek East. If the Christian civilization in Illyricum had not been destroyed by the Avars and the Slavs, the Western and Eastern Churches would, by virtue of this "bridge," presumably have remained in contact and their evolution would never have proceeded in the contrary directions which they actually followed. Because this bridge between the two Churches was wrecked by the new occupants of Illyricum and because the Arabs gained control to a great extent over the Mediterranean Sea, communication between East and West became extremely difficult.[1] The Byzantines

---

by the French specialist J. Zeiller in his works: *Les origines chrétiennes dans la province romaine de Dalmatie* (Paris, 1906); *Les origines chrétiennes dans les provinces danubiennes de l'Empire romain* (Paris, 1918). On the destruction of Christianity in these regions, see the chapter on Illyricum in F. Dvornik, *Les légendes de Constantin et de Methode vues de Byzance* (Prague, 1934), pp. 248 ff.

[1] H. Pirenne, when formulating his famous theory on the consequences of the Islamic expansion on the economic and cultural evolution of medieval western Europe, overstressed the importance of the Islamic expansion. His theory, expressed especially in his monograph on *Mahomet and Charlemagne* (London, 1936), encountered many criticisms. An almost complete review of Pirenne's ideas and of the objections raised by his critics will be found in Anne Riising's study, "The Fate of Henri Pirenne's Thesis on the Consequences of the Islamic Invasions" (*Classica et mediaevalia, Revue danoise de philologie et d'histoire* XIII [1952], pp. 87–130). Most of the criticism

were forced by the Persians and Arabs to look more and more towards the East, when the vital danger threatened. Having lost almost all the European provinces, they were bound to increase their reliance upon the eastern provinces, especially those of Asia Minor. A slow Orientalization of the Empire and of the Church was a natural consequence.

On the other hand, Christianity in the western part of the Roman Empire lost many of its old Roman traditions and customs on account of the Germanic invasions. In order to win over the Germans, the Church had to respect and accept those of their traditions which were not directly anti-Christian. The two Churches thus followed different lines of development. For centuries both of them had to fight on different fronts and they could not easily communicate to one another their experiences and the new methods they devised for dealing with peoples so widely different. Only Illyricum could facilitate such intercourse and the de-Christianization of this province rendered that impossible. Then, eventually, when the Churches did recover some of their strength and energy and triumphed over the new peoples in the ninth century, they met in Illyricum as rivals who, by dint of their long separation, had become almost strangers to one another.[1]

Thus Illyricum, instead of being a bridge between West and East, contributed most to the estrangement of the two Churches. It finally became the battlefield on which the two forces of Christianity waged the first great struggles which led to that complete separation so fateful for the whole of Christendom and all mankind.

---

is well founded. Pirenne and his critics have, however, completely neglected the consequences which the destruction of Illyricum had for the further estrangement between the Byzantine East and the Frankish West. Pirenne's theory, although not well founded in the arguments advanced by its author, appears in most respects true in the consequences analyzed by him. The disappearance of the "Illyric bridge" between the East and the West supplies the missing link for which his critics seek with such eagerness.

[1] See below, pp. 118 ff.

2

Primitive Slavic Civilization

The main sources on Slavic civilization — Common Iranian and Slavic religious conceptions — Main Slavic deities and their Iranian counterparts — Iranian influence on Slavic burial customs — Commercial intercourse and its influence on the life of the primitive Slavs — Gothic and Roman cultural influences — Biskupin a Slavic settlement? — Primitive social organization of the Slavs — The Sarmatians and the political evolution of the Slavs.

The rarity of references to the Slavs in classical Greek and Roman literature is also responsible for the lack of a more profound knowledge of primitive Slavic civilization. The earliest written observations on this subject date from the sixth century and are made by Procopius and Jordanes. A seventh century treatise on strategy, attributed to the Emperor Maurice, gives some valuable details on the military tactics of the Slavs. The *Russian Primary Chronicle* reproduces some genuine documents of the tenth century — texts of several Russo-Greek commercial treaties — and provides some interesting information on the religious and social life of the Eastern Slavs before their official conversion to Christianity. The first Novgorod *Chronicle* is also of some importance in this respect.

Latin sources dealing with the Polabian and Baltic Slavs date from the eleventh and twelfth centuries only — the chronicles of Thietmar of Merseburg, of Adam of Bremen, and of Helmold. The details they give are supplemented by Saxo Grammaticus in his *History of the Danes* and by the biographers of St. Otto of Bamberg, apostle of the Pomeranians.

The pagan Slavic temples were mostly completely destroyed and it was thought that in the earliest period of their evolution, the Slavs had produced very little in the way of art or architecture. Recent excavations, especially in the territory of the Baltic and Polabian Slavs and elsewhere, have shown that this view is not well-founded.[1] More complete results must, however, be awaited before a definite judgment on this subject can be formed. Meanwhile we must depend on philological investigations and on archaeological finds in tombs and old settlements, which are becoming more and more numerous. In this respect, a considerable advance has been made in recent years, although many problems still await a solution.

2

Marked progress was made recently in the study of Slavic religious ideas, thanks mainly to the comparative method used by Slavic philologists. It has been established that until the end of the first millennium, the differences between the Slavic dialects were negligible. A study of the words used by the different Slavic groups in pagan religious worship also reveals a considerable uniformity. All this leads to the general conclusion that the primitive Slavs had the same cult and religious belief. A comparison of the Slavic religious vocabulary with that of other Indo-European peoples further discloses a rather striking similarity with the Indo-Iranian nomenclature. This is the more remarkable since, in this field, the Indo-European languages display in general marked differences of development. It is not easy to say when this similarity of Slavic and Iranian religious conceptions was achieved, but since some of this vocabulary is also found in the Baltic languages, it seems that this evolution must have started in prehistoric times when the Balts and the Slavs formed one linguistic group. Other words and beliefs, however, appear to have been borrowed by the Slavs from the Iranians at a much later period.

It is known that the Iranians did not follow the other Indo-European peoples in the use of the symbolic name Diēus —

[1] See, for example, Thede Palm, *Wendische Kultstätten* (Lund, 1937).

"worshipped sky" — for the Divinity.[1] Not only did they substitute the term "cloud" for "sky" but they also used the cognate form Deiwas (changed to Daêva) to designate not God but the demoniac being who was hostile to God. The Slavs followed the Iranians in both these respects. The Iranian Daêva corresponds to the Slavic Divŭ and, in some Slavic languages, to the name for "she-demon" (*diva, divožena*). The Slavs, like the Iranians, used a word to designate God which means not only wealth but also the giver of wealth, the Slavic Bogŭ, corresponding to the Iranian Baga.

This observation is supported by Helmold, who describes the Slavs as worshipping good and evil divinities. This shows that the Slavs followed the Iranians in accepting a sort of dualistic mythology. Like the Iranians, they had a special religious term — *věra* (faith) — for the choice between good and evil, which recalls the Indo-Iranian *var*, meaning "choice."[2]

3

In the names of Slavic deities many Iranian influences can also be detected. Procopius tells us that "the Slavs recognize one god, author of lightning, the only master of the universe, and they bring him sacrifices of cattle and different birds." Helmold also says that the Slavs believed in a kind of divine monarchy, one supreme god ruling in heaven over the others. This is a type of pagan monotheism and some features in this belief are common to all Indo-European primitive religions.

The supreme god, god of lightning and of the storm, was called Perun by the Eastern Slavs. He has the same function as the Vedic Parjanya and his existence and worship can also be traced among other Indo-European peoples. The Lithuanians called him Perkunas and the oak was his sacred tree. The West-

---

[1] On the religion of Indo-European nations see the recent work by G. Dumézil, *Les dieux des Indo-Européens* (Paris, 1952).

[2] Cf. A. Meillet, "Le vocabulaire Slave et Indo-Iranien," *Revue des études slaves* VI (1926), pp. 170 ff.

ern Slavs must also have known him, as is shown by the name of a god venerated by the Baltic Slavs in oak groves — Pron, a distorted name for Perun, and the Slovak curse Perom or Parom. Moreover, Thursday was called Peründan by the Polabian Slavs, while the Poles used the word *piorum* as an appellation for thunder and lightning. Perun's name is also reflected in the ritual of the rain charm used by the Southern Slavs and in their toponymy.

Another god venerated by the Eastern and Northwestern Slavs was Svarogŭ, whose name still survives in Czech and Slovak as *rarog, rarach* — the devil. This Slavic deity has many features which connect him with the Iranian Verethragna. Like this Iranian deity, Svarogŭ was also credited with being able to appear in different animal and bird forms — as a falcon, a golden-horned aurochs, a horse, a bear, or even as a whirlwind. The Slavs also connected Svarogŭ with fire, as the Iranians did with Verethragna. Svarogŭ, like Verethragna, was a warrior god, a giver of virility and strength. This virility — Slavic Jędrŭ, which is reminiscent of the Indian Indra — had various manifestations, a fact which the Polabian Slavs symbolized by providing their idols with several heads. The names Sventovitŭ, Jarevitŭ, Porovitŭ and Ruevitŭ, given to the deity by the Polabian Slavs, are possibly best explained by this.

Like the Iranian Verethragna, the Slavic Svarogŭ is represented as generating the heat and light of the sun, called Xŭrsŭ Dažĭbogŭ by the Slavs. These words have survived in some old Polish and Serbian proper names. Xŭrsŭ (Chors) is obviously borrowed from the Iranian expression Xuršīd, designating the personified sun; Dažĭbogŭ is reminiscent of the Old Persian Baga and the Vedic Bhaga, meaning giver of wealth.

We find in the Kievan pantheon a god called Simargl, who should evidently be identified with the Iranian Bird-Dog, Senmurv. In the Sarmatian mythology, this winged monster was believed to be the guardian of the tree which supplied the seed for every plant.

The Eastern Slavs and the Czechs also knew a god called Veles, who was the god of flocks. According to the *Russian Primary Chronicle*, Russians took the oath in his name when promising to observe the conditions of the commercial treaties concluded with the Byzantines.

Only one goddess appears to have been admitted to the pantheon of the Eastern Slavs. Her name was Mokoš, which means "moist." This divinity seems to survive in popular Russian tradition as the personified "Mother-moist-earth" (*Mati syra zemlja*). Some scholars consider that this goddess was a Russian equivalent of the oriental Ashtarte and the Greek Aphrodite; but it seems more probable that we have here a further example of borrowing from the Iranians, who venerated the goddess Anahita. In the later Persian tradition she formed, together with Ahura Mazda and Mithra, a kind of divine trinity and was called Ardvi Sura Ana-hi-ta. The word *ardvi* means "moist" — which makes it more probable that Mokoš is a Slavic counterpart of the Iranian Anahita.

The Eastern Slavs knew another divinity called Stribogŭ, a name which also seems to be derived from an Iranian root and which means "the distributor of wealth." [1] This would bring him into line with Amsa, the partner of the Vedic Bhaga, giver of wealth. The personified winds — *větrŭ*, reminiscent of the Indo-Iranian Văta — are called in the first Russian epic, the *Tale of Igor's Campaign*, grandsons of Stribogŭ. [2]

Moreover, a considerable number of words in the Old Slavonic vernacular, originally connected with worship or religious practices, can be traced back to Iranian words or ideas. The word for "holy" (*svent*) is similar to the Iranian; the Slavic *mir* — "peace," "community," "agreement" — is apparently associated with Mithra. Other words of this kind are similar to Iranian

[1] Cf. also S. Pirchegger's study, "Zum altrussischen Götternamen Stribogŭ," *Zeitschrift für slavische Philologie* XIX (1947), pp. 311–316. He derives the Slavic word from the Iranian Sribaga, designating Ahura Mazda as god of the firmament.

[2] See R. Jakobson's commentary in "Les geste du Prince Igor" (H. Grégoire, R. Jakobson, M. Szeftel) *Annuaire de l'Institut de philologie et d'histoire orientales et slaves* VIII (1945–47), pp. 354 ff.

terms, for example: to worship (*žrěti*), to wail (*vŭpiti*), to practice divination (*gatati*), to chastise (*kajati*), to fear (*bojati se*), to invoke (*zŭvati*), fire (*vatra*), chalice (*čaša*), burial mound (*mogila*), to cure (*goiti*), shame (*sramŭ*), guilt (*vina*). Furthermore, the Slavic word for paradise (*rai*) is directly borrowed from the Iranian *ray*, which means beatitude and heavenly radiance.

How receptive the primitive Slavs were in this respect is well illustrated by the following example. The Eastern and the Balkan Slavs recognized another divine being called Trojan. The admission of this god into the Slavic pantheon is a sign of the Slavic intercourse with the Latin world; for this god is none other than the Emperor Trajan. It seems that Trajan's victories over the Dacians so impressed the peoples who were involved in the results of his conquests that the Emperor became a legendary figure.[1] Not only did the Eastern Slavs elevate him to their gallery of mythological personalities, but Balkan folklore also enshrined him among its most important figures. This evolution is understandable if we remember that the Romans deified Trajan after his death.

Besides these main divinities, the Slavs venerated other beings of a lesser order who were credited with supernatural powers. Procopius describes this cult as follows: "Besides that they venerate rivers and nymphs and some other demons. They bring sacrifices to all of them and when bringing them they make divination (in order to know the future)." Because our information about the religion of the primitive Slavs is so scanty and incomplete, it is impossible to reconstruct the whole hierarchic system of the Slavic pantheon, but further studies in Slavic mythology will clarify many problems, especially when the specialists follow the newly discovered road of this Slavo-Iranian affinity in religious beliefs.

---

[1] V. Čajkanović (*O srpskom vrchovnom Bogu* — On the supreme god of the Serbs — [Belgrade, 1941], pp. 58 ff.) presents Trojan as a god with three heads.

4

Further Iranian influences on the life of the Eastern Slavs can be traced in the burial practice which some of their tribes adopted. At the beginning of their history the Slavs used to cremate their dead, collect the ashes and deposit them in special urns which were then buried, and over the graves they erected mounds, this kind of burial being similar to that of the Lusatian and Venedian cultures. The cinerary urns were sealed with an inverted dish, but in all early burials a hole was carefully bored in the walls of the urn, and this seems to be another sign of belief in a future life; for the hole was provided to permit the ghost to escape. In the case of the Lusatian culture, the shape of the cinerary urn was invariably bi-conical. Sometimes a barrow was raised over the tomb, but in all cases the graves form regular cemeteries. Numerous burial rites and customs intended to protect the living from the dead, or to help them on their way to the place of the dead, testify to the belief of the Slavs in a future life.

But even in this respect we can see the influence of Sarmatian practices; for we know that the Sarmatians observed the practice of inhumation. It is curious to note that, although those East Slavic tribes which were far from the center of Sarmatian influence — the Kriviči and those in the neighborhood of Novgorod — remained faithful to the old Slavic form of cremation, the Vjatiči, the Radimiči, the Dulebi, the Drevljane and the Dregoviči, on the other hand, adopted the Sarmatian practice of inhumation. The same seems to have been done by the Poljane and the Severjane, who returned to cremation in the tenth century. This seems to be of definite importance, because it confirms the fact that Iranian influences on the primitive Slavs were strong not only in the prehistoric period but also when the Sarmatians had replaced the Scythians as the dominant race in the steppes of southern Russia.

5

It is difficult to say anything more precise on the relationship between the Scythians and the primitive Slavs. Although it seems that in the pre-Scythian period most of the words relating to religious actions and concepts were borrowed from the Iranian, this influence might very well have continued when the Scythians were neighbors of the Slavs. Very little is known of the Scythian language, but commercial intercourse certainly went on, because the Scythians were intermediaries between the Greek colonies on the Black Sea and the Baltic, and the find of blue glass beads, most probably of Egyptian provenience, in the settlement of Biskupin which was established in the later period of the Lusatian culture in Polish Pomerania (700–400 B.C.) confirms the existence of this kind of commercial exchange. Even if we hesitate to locate the Slavs so far north at that time, we must at least admit that the highway of commerce led through territory occupied by Slavs. If the tribe of the Neuroi and the "Scythians practicing agriculture," mentioned by Herodotus, were really Slavs, then they certainly came under strong Scythian influence. Amber and stone instruments which were certainly not indigenous, found in the territory north of the Carpathian Mountains, testify that this commercial highway was used from the neolithic period onwards.

Nevertheless, the Slavs do not seem to have profited from this commercial intercourse as much as the Scythians and Sarmatians did, and their civilization does not seem to have been greatly advanced by these exchanges. They were familiar with the principal metals — gold, copper, silver, tin and iron; they had primitive forges and workshops and fabricated the implements necessary for the cultivation of the soil and weapons for hunting and fighting. Their main occupations were cattle-raising, agriculture, hunting, fishing and bee-keeping, but they were not nomads, although they frequently changed their habitat in search of fresh lands to till. If we bear this in mind, we can accept the evidence of Byzantine and other writers who state that their dwellings were built of light materials. They could be easily abandoned when the tribe moved on or when, at the approach of some hostile band, the tribe fled to the protection of the dense forest or to the special fortifications which were set up, preferably in some almost impenetrable marsh.

This also helps to explain the slowness with which the primitive Slavs penetrated from the upper Bug towards the Dnieper, the Dniester and the lower Danube, or through the plains of modern Hungary towards the approaches of the Roman Empire. The Slavs, accustomed to agricultural pursuits, could not move as rapidly as the nomads. The dense forests provided them with game and furs and the waterways with fish; but cattle-raising and agriculture — they seem to have been particularly skilful in the production of vegetables — were still their main source of sustenance. This explains why they were left unmolested by the Goths and other Germanic tribes which preceded and followed them on the way to the shores of the Black Sea and also shows why alien, warlike races — the Iranian Sarmatians, the Goths, the Huns, the Avars — were so easily able to dominate them.

6

It would be natural to suppose that, after the Iranian Sarmatians, the Goths would have exercised the greatest influence over the civilization of the primitive Slavs. The Goths dominated some Slavic tribes on the Baltic for about two centuries; they came into contact with Slavs on their way to the Black Sea and they became the overlords of the Slavs once again after the defeat of the Antês, particularly during the short-lived empire of Ermanarich. And yet the Gothic influence on the Slavs in general, and on the Eastern Slavs in particular, must not be overrated. It should be stressed that not one single Germanic term connected with spiritual matters is found in the Old Slavonic language. This is the more remarkable when we take into account the many expressions from the religious and spiritual field which the Slavs had borrowed from the Iranians. Gothic influence on the Slavs is noticeable only in the field of material culture and is illustrated mainly by some Slavic words which have been borrowed from the Gothic. They include a number of military terms, such as helmet, armor, sword, some commercial expressions — glass, kettle, plate, vinegar, earring, purse, debt, usury, buy — and a few words concerned with agriculture — plough, vineyard, donkey, fig, bread. Some of these words had been borrowed by the Goths from the Latins. All this not only reveals the nature of the influence exerted by the Goths on the Slavs, but also shows that this influence was still effective when the Goths were in close touch with the Roman Empire.

Archaeological evidence clearly shows that Roman influence began to reach the Slavs only when the Romans reached the Danube and started to penetrate beyond that river, and that this influence was due to the Roman merchants who followed the victorious Roman legions, the second and third centuries of our era being especially important in this respect. Roman exports now also began to reach the tribes beyond the Carpathian Mountains, and, at that period and for a time afterwards, the Slavs confined themselves to accepting Italian merchandise without attempting to produce for themselves any of the goods which they thus acquired. It was only in the making of pottery that Roman patterns were introduced and eventually became predominant. Apart from this particular craft, it was not until the Slavs were firmly established in their new homes that Roman and Byzantine influences upon their civilization became really marked.

7

If we could definitely establish that it was a Slav people who constructed the fortified settlement on the lake of Biskupin in Polish Pomerania, the ruins of which were unearthed by Polish archaeologists after 1930, we should be able to piece together a much clearer picture of primitive Slavic civilization. The settlement was constructed between the years 700 and 400 B.C., and was abandoned when the level of the lake rose and the waters flooded the site. Thanks to a thick deposit of sand and mud, the foundations of the fortifications and the dwellings, together with many objects of the greatest archaeological interest, have been preserved intact.

The settlement must have been inhabited by a peaceable people, seeking to protect themselves from the raids of their neighbors, who were probably of Baltic stock. The construction of the walls and, indeed, the whole planning of the settlement testify to a well-developed architectural technique which, if not invented by the Slavs, was at least adopted by them, because it is the technique which was used in Poland during the 2,500 years following the building of this fort, right down to the present day.

The plan of the settlement and its construction suggest that the inhabitants were a well-disciplined body of men who submitted to the authority of one leader. In his turn, this leader must have exercised his authority in quite an energetic and intelligent way. The archaeological finds made on the site also throw considerable light upon the civilization of the people living there. The pottery shows that they were not without artistic tendencies, as some of the specimens found are encrusted with a white substance or are painted with red ochre, and two of them are decorated with figures of horsemen chasing stags. Luxury objects are represented by numerous pins, a few bracelets, some small rings, beads and buttons. That the inhabitants were an agricultural people is shown by finds of celts with sockets, sickles, hammers, a primitive wooden plough, a wooden wagon wheel made of a single block of wood, fossilized grains of corn, wheat, barley, millet and pea and fibers of flax. There was some raising of domestic animals, while hunting and fishing were also practiced. A find of blue glass beads indicates — as mentioned above — that some kind of commercial exchange must have gone on, the beads having most probably originated in Egypt. Some form of primitive industry existed, because molds for making pins, necklaces and other objects have been found. Their arms consisted of bows and arrows, spears and bronze swords.

Many of the features of the civilization of the people who lived at Biskupin are similar to those of the primitive Slavs. This civilization is, in fact, a good illustration of the late Lusatian culture, but we have already seen that archaeologists are still doubtful about attributing this culture to the primitive Slavs. It is, however, not impossible that in the years between 700 and 400 B.C., the Slavs had already reached the neighborhood of Biskupin, even if they had not been settled there from time immemorial. In this case, we may suppose that they adopted the main features of the Lusatian culture, especially the socketed celt, which was characteristic of it and marked a great advance upon the common contemporary form of axe. But a definite solution of this and similar problems awaits the finding of further archaeological evidence.

8

The basis of the social organization of the primitive Slavs was the same as that of the other Indo-European peoples. The foundation of society was the family, in which the father was the undisputed master. Related families lived in collective settlements and their joint affairs were directed by a council of the family chiefs presided over by the oldest or otherwise most prominent among them. The land was the common property of the whole community, all members being engaged in its cultivation and its products were their collective possession; this regime was known by the name of *zadruga*. Private property existed, but was limited only to those things which the individual member of the community required in his day-to-day life — the tools necessary for his share in the tilling, his weapons, some jewelry and similar objects. Only at the end of the pagan period did the individual acquisition of what had been common property begin. This process advanced but slowly, and echoes of the primitive conception of collective possession are to be encountered among the Southern and Eastern Slavs even in modern times.

In addition to the free members of the clan, primitive Slavic society also had its slaves, chiefly members of some conquered population or prisoners of war. Historical records show that the slaves were generally well-treated and were regarded as being members of the family albeit with certain restrictions upon their rights.

Among the Polabian Slavs and the Eastern Slavs, the free tillers of the soil were called *smerdi*. The Polabian Slavs also had a third class of the population called *vitiezi*, who appear in historical times as a kind of petty military aristocracy, performing their military service on horseback.

The etymology of these names is still disputed, but the fact that the class of *smerdi* appears only among the Slavs who, as we have seen, were organized politically by the Antês and Serbs, is often taken as an argument for the theory that this social organization was of foreign, i.e. Sarmatian, origin.[1] The same suggestion has been made about the origin of the word *župan*, which among the Polabian and Southern Serbs and Croats designated a governor of a group of tribes or of a district or districts. Moreover, the ruler of the Croats, later representing the king, is called *banus*. It is true that we encounter this information concerning the Croats only in the tenth century writings of Constantine Porphyrogennetus, who, as will be seen, describes their migration to the south; but we are fully entitled to suppose that the Croats had a similar organization when they were living northeast of the Carpathian Mountains.

However, the Sarmatian origin of these words cannot be ascertained. The word *vitiez* is shown to have been derived from the Germanic word *Viking*.[2] The word *smerdi* seems to be formed from an old Indo-European root. The same can be said about the words *župan* and *ban*. The Czechs and the Poles did not

[1] For example, B. D. Grekov (*Krestjane na Rusi s drevnejšich vremen do XVII veka* [Russian peasantry from the earliest period to the XVIIth Century] S.S.S.R. Academy [Moscow, 1946], pp. 15–17) reviews the different attempts at the etymology of this word. He derives the word from the Iranian *mard* (man) and thinks that, in the later evolution, popular etymology associated the word with the Slavic *smerdetŭ* (to stink).

[2] See the study by O. Hujer in *Listy filologické* [Philological Bulletin] XXXI (1904), pp. 104 ff., XL (1927), p. 304.

possess these two terms, but they have the word *pan* to designate a master, and it might have been formed from the same common root.

9

As we have seen, the Slavs had a very loose social and political structure, and we learn from Byzantine sources that, although their military qualities were high, their armament was poor and consisted mostly of bows, arrows and shields. Their military organization, based upon the social structure of family and clan, was also poorly developed. These facts, together with the primitive Slavs' predilection for cattle-raising and agriculture, explain why it was always so easy for nomadic invaders in the form of a seasoned body of well-armed cavalry — the Sarmatians were especially notorious in this respect — to gain control over the Slavic tribes. These were usually only too happy to be left to their peaceful pursuits and often welcomed protection against other possible invaders.

The fact that the Slavs had a very loose social and political organization is confirmed by the Byzantine writers of the sixth and seventh centuries. The Byzantine historian Procopius describes their political organization as follows: "The Slavs do not live under the regime of one man, but in democracy and that from old times. Therefore all profitable or damaging things are common to them."

In those circumstances it is no wonder that the Sarmatians were the first to give the Slavs a firmer political structure. The state of the Antês was monarchic, with a king at the head surrounded by a numerous retinue. And we learn, again from Byzantine writers, that the Slavs quickly gleaned from their masters the secrets of military tactics and imitated the Sarmatians and the Avars so well that the Roman armies could not resist the skill and fury of their attacks. It seems that the Antês constituted only the ruling class and were organized on a military basis. A similar organization was introduced by the Croats among the Slavs who came under their domination.

3

The Franks, Byzantium
and the First Slavic States

*Samo's Slavic empire — The Croats and Serbs liberate the Southern
Slavs — Khazars, Bulgars and Byzantines — Advance of the Franks —
First attempts at political union of the Southern Slavs — Charlemagne
and the Western Slavs — Imperial ideas and Frankish missionary methods among the Slavs.*

At the end of the sixth century, the Avar Empire comprised
practically the whole of Central Europe and a great part of the
Balkans. Their political influence extended from the middle
course of the Elbe and the Oder to the Alps of Styria and Carinthia, from the Carpathian Mountains to the Adriatic and south-
eastwards as far as the Sea of Azov.

The position of the Avars in the heart of Europe made them a
terrible menace not only to the Byzantine Empire, but also to
all the Slavic and Germanic tribes surrounding them, while they
directly threatened the new Frankish Empire. In their attempt
to penetrate further west, the Avars, with their Slavic allies, attacked the Franks in 562. Although King Siegebert, who met
their second attack, was defeated and captured in A.D. 567, he
was able to come to a friendly agreement with them. In spite
of that, the Avars, perhaps called in by their Slavic allies for
help against the Franks, invaded Thuringia in 595.

However, an important Avar reverse had an immediate effect
upon the situation. We learn from the chronicle of Burgundian
origin attributed to Fredegar [1] that, about the year 623, the Slavs

---

[1] The problems concerning the origin and the authenticity of this chronicle
are discussed by G. Labuda in his Polish work, *Pierwsze Państwo Słowiańskie,
Państwo Samona* [The first Slavic State, the State of Samo] (Poznan, 1948),
pp. 52–93, 296–320. The author comes to the conclusion that the work was

in the neighborhood of the Frankish empire revolted against
the Avars and that the rebellion was led by a Frank named
Samo. This revolt, which seems to have started in Moravia, apparently enjoyed the support of the Franks, and Samo, a Frankish nobleman, whose name appears to be Celtic rather than Germanic, was sent to the insurgent Slavs to negotiate with them and
to assure them of Frankish support. He probably saw that the
most important asset which the rebels lacked was good leadership. He therefore took over the direction of operations and
after the final victory was recognized as ruler of the liberated
territories.

A lively discussion is still going on among specialists about
the extent of Samo's empire. Probably it comprised Moravia,
Bohemia, Lower Austria and, from 631 onwards, White Serbia
also. It is most unlikely that Samo's power extended as far as
Carinthia, as is often supposed.

The Franks claimed supremacy over the liberated Slavs because their new-won freedom was achieved with Frankish support. Samo, although himself a Frank, refused to submit to
King Dagobert and in the conflict which ensued with the Franks
(in 631) he was able to uphold his claim to complete independence.

This second Slavic state — the first being that of the Antês —
did not last. Samo died about the year 659 and his empire seems
to have disintegrated, though remnants of a political organization
among his Slavic subjects may have survived. This seems to be
confirmed by the fact that the next attempt to build a solid or-

---

composed about 660 at St. Jean-de-Losne (Latona) near Chalon-sur-Saône,
the ancient capital of Burgundy. The whole compilation, together with the
original chronicle describing the events from 585 to 643, should be regarded
as the work of the same author. Labuda's study, which also gives abundant
bibliographical notes on the period, should be consulted by historians interested in the relations between the Avars, Franks, Slavs and Byzantines at
this time. A long summary of his work in French, with critical remarks, may
be found in V. Chaloupecký, "Considérations sur Samo, le premier roi des
Slaves," *Byzantinoslavica* XI (1952), pp. 223–239.

ganization of the Slavs came once more from Moravia, in the
ninth century.

It is quite possible that not only the Franks but also Byzantium had a part in supporting this Slavic revolt and we may assume that Byzantine diplomacy employed every means at its
disposal to reduce the Avar danger. The revolt occurred at a
time when Constantinople itself was menaced by the Avars, who
were about to conclude an alliance with the Persians in the hope
of capturing the city. We read in the chronicle of Fredegar that
Dagobert, King of the Franks (628–638), and the Emperor
Heraclius (610–641) exchanged embassies and concluded a
treaty of friendship. These negotiations are dated by the chronicler in the years 626 and 629, but may have been started earlier.
The treaty could have been directed only against the common
enemy — the Avars.

2

Most probably about the same time, a section of the Serbs
migrated from White Serbia — according to Constantine Porphyrogennetus — and asked Heraclius for permission to settle
on imperial soil. This report has been rejected by most historians
as legendary; but Fredegar's statements about the negotiations
between the Franks and Heraclius can be invoked to support
Constantine's evidence. Like White Croatia, White Serbia
escaped coming under the authority of the Avars; but after the
Franks' conquest of Thuringia, which bordered on White Serbia,
the Serbs (Sorbs) could not free themselves from Frankish
sovereignty. Frankish pressure, dissensions among their leaders,
and the knowledge that Heraclius was looking for allies against
the Avars would have been enough to justify the migration of
part of the Serbs to Byzantium. But Heraclius seems also to have
sent an embassy to the Croats, offering them a new home in Illyricum after they had expelled the Avars from that province.
The Croats — accompanied by some other Slavic tribes — eager
to settle their own account with the Avars, welcomed the Em-

peror's advances and sent a body of well-seasoned troops on to
Byzantine soil.[1] There, together with the small army of the Serbs,
and with the support of the Byzantine navy and of the refugees
from the destroyed cities who had settled in the surviving cities
on the littoral and on the islands, they commenced their operations against the Avars from the south. They liberated first
Dalmatia, then the rest of Illyricum and finally the territory between the Drava and the Sava rivers.[2]

The Avars continued to control Hungary, but they do not seem
to have regained Bohemia and Moravia after the death of Samo.
The Croats and Serbs were settled by the grateful Emperor in
the liberated lands, where they took over from the Avars the
leadership of the Slavic tribes which had been in occupation of
present-day Yugoslavia from the end of the sixth century. The

[1] The Serbs and the Croats must have taken the old route beyond the
Carpathian Mountains following the course of rivers they knew well. The
Serbs were first settled by Heraclius in "the theme of Thessalonica." There
they seem to have founded a colony at Serbište in Greece, at the foot
of Mount Olympus. It is difficult to imagine how they could have travelled
through the center of Avar territory. Constantine's account of the liberation
of Illyricum from the Avars is, from the military standpoint, perfectly sound
and logical.

It seems that the Croats who migrated to the south on the invitation of
Heraclius were the tribes which were settled in western Galicia, round
Cracow and the upper Vistula, although some Slavs, still bearing their name,
may have stayed in their old home and seem to be mentioned in the founda-
tion charter of the bishopric of Prague in the tenth century. The Croats of
Bohemia and of eastern Galicia did not follow their *confrères* of the Vistula,
because they are mentioned in documents of the tenth century — in the
foundation charter mentioned above and in the *Russian Primary Chronicle*.
Constantine Porphyrogennetus says that the ancestor of the prince of the
Zachlumjans came to the south during the Croat migration, from the river
Vistula. This seems to indicate that some other Slavic tribes had joined the
Croats on their way towards the south. The imperial writer presents the
events in a Byzantine way, stressing that the initiative for the migration
came from the Croats, who had solicited the Emperor's protection. This
presentation of the facts seems tendentious, having the aim of strengthening
Byzantine claims over the territory occupied by the Croats and the Serbs.

[2] The revolt of Greek prisoners concentrated by the Avars in the strip of
land between the Danube and the rivers Sava and Drava, mentioned in the
Miracles of St. Demetrius, seems to have been connected with the victorious advance of the Croats towards the Sava river.

Emperor naturally still claimed to be the overlord of this territory and, according to Constantine Porphyrogennetus, asked the
Pope Honorius to send missionaries to the Croats and Serbs, evidently recognizing Roman jurisdiction over ancient Illyricum.

The Slovenes of Carinthia were also set free by the Croats,
and there are indications that the expulsion of the Avars from
Carinthia was achieved by the followers of Kosentzes, one of
the men who, according to the imperial writer, had led the
Croats into Dalmatia.[1] In the Middle Ages the existence of free
peasant families called *Kasanz* or *Edelinge* (aristocrats) can be
traced in many parts of that country. They probably formed
originally an aristocratic class deriving its origin from the liberators who settled among the Slovenes as their new masters.

3

The liberation of the rest of the Slavs from the Avars was
achieved by the Bulgars and the Khazars. The Bulgars, who
settled north of the lower Danube, were fortunate in escaping
Avar domination when their chieftain Kovrat drove the Avars
away in a northeasterly direction between the years 635 and
641. It seems that this enforced withdrawal of a race which had
hitherto carried practically everything before it was in fact the
beginning of the end of Avar domination over the south of
modern Russia.[2] We have no evidence of Avar domination over
these regions during the seventh and eighth centuries. Their
dominant position was probably destroyed by a revolt of the
Slavic tribes settled there, who were aided by the Khazars, a new

---

[1] Constantine names five brothers — Klukas, Lobelos, Kosentzes, Muchlo,
Chrobatos — and two sisters — Tuga and Buga — as the leaders of the
Croats who had left White Croatia. The names may also designate different
tribes. Many scholars think that Kosentzes is a Germanic name. If this is
so, it would show that one Gothic tribe had joined the Croats when they fled
before the Hunnish onslaught.

[2] It is not surprising that the Emperor Heraclius, who was looking everywhere for allies against the Avars, maintained friendly relations with the
Khagan Kovrat.

Turkic race, akin to the Bulgars, who followed in the footsteps of
the Avars.

The Khazars, who thus emerge on the scene in southeastern
Europe, had formed, with other Turkic hordes, an immense
Turkic empire extending in the sixth century from the steppes of
Central Asia to the boundaries of China. After the dismemberment of this empire, the Khazars followed the Avars along the
historic way trodden by all the nomadic invaders of the West.
They first established their center at Balandjar in the Caucasus
region, to the north of the famous Pass of Derbent. From there,
in the years 685 and 686, their khagans subjugated Georgia,
Caucasian Albania and Armenia, and the collapse of the rest of
the Avar power between the Carpathian Mountains and the Sea
of Azov must probably be ascribed to their intervention.

The empire of the Khazars was in no way ephemeral, and
after 720 they transferred their political center to Itil on the
Caspian Sea, near the Volga delta. They had already extended
their domination as far as the Crimea, where their lands bordered
on the remnants of the Byzantine possessions, and for a considerable period even Kiev was under Khazar domination. The Slavic
tribes which formed the nucleus of the Antês confederation had
to await the arrival of the Scandinavian Russians before they
were freed from the Khazars and were able to form the first extensive Russian State.

The Khazars were also partially responsible for the arrival of
the Bulgars in modern Bulgaria; for, in order to evade their
pressure, Asparuch (Isperikh), son of the Khagan Kovrat, moved
westwards from the Caucasus region into Bessarabia and later
turned towards the south and appeared on the Danube about the
year 679. Frightened by the approach of yet another barbarian
tribe which threatened vital provinces of the Byzantine Empire,
the Emperor Constantine IV (668–685) sent an army against the
Bulgars. But Asparuch's forces evaded a decisive battle by taking to the marshes of the Danube delta. Thence, after negoti-
ating the crossing of the river, he was able to march against
Varna.

He was welcomed by some Slavic tribes which dwelt in these regions; Byzantine sources mention especially the Severjane. Other tribes were forced to submit and to pay tribute.[1] In any case, in time, a kind of understanding followed between the Bulgars and the Slavic tribes on the right bank of the Danube. The Bulgars under Asparuch were not numerous, but they formed a well-organized standing army and possessed a sense of discipline which the Slavs lacked. Thus with his boyars Asparuch was quickly able to form the embryo of a solid political organization among the Slavs and in this way the foundations of future Bulgaria were laid.

The only power which could oppose the formation of the first new empire in the Balkans was Byzantium. Unfortunately, at the time when Asparuch was disciplining and organizing the Slavs, Byzantium was going through a period of grave internal troubles. Thus it happened that Terbel (Tervel), Asparuch's successor (701–718), was even given the opportunity of intervening in the internal affairs of the Byzantine Empire. The help which he gave to the Emperor Justinian II (685–695, 705–711) in his campaign to regain his throne was rewarded by the conferment on Terbel of the title of Caesar and by the cession to him of a province called by the Slavs Zagorje (Beyond the Mountains). This period of weakness in Byzantium enabled the Bulgars to strengthen their position and ultimately to survive the difficult years which followed.

After the extinction of the Asparuch dynasty, the boyars naturally worked to increase their influence in public affairs. Two parties were formed in Bulgaria; the one pro-Greek and anxious to remain on good terms with Byzantium by tolerating its growing influence in their own country; the other, national and advocating the necessity of opposing Byzantium in all matters. The nationalists won the day, towards the end of Khagan

[1] It was generally believed that the Bulgars concluded a pact with the Slavs for common defense against the Byzantines. This does not seem sufficiently warranted. It appears that the Bulgars had to force some of the Slavic tribes to submit to their rule. Cf. I. Dujčev's study, "Protobulgares et Slaves," *Seminarium Kondakovianum* X (1938), pp. 145–154.

Kormisoh's reign (739–756). Their victory meant war with Byzantium. Thus in 755, the great and glorious Emperor Constantine V (741–775) began a series of successful campaigns in Bulgaria. A rapid succession of khagans followed, some installed by the victorious Byzantines, the others being replacements brought about by the constant revolts of the nationalists.

At last the Khagan Telerig (769/70–777) was able to arrest the Byzantine push just as it threatened to annihilate the first new empire in the Balkans. Constantine V died during his ninth campaign (775), and his death ended Byzantine intervention in Bulgarian affairs for some time. The Khagan Kardam (777?–803) at first concluded an armistice with the Empire and then in 792 inflicted a terrible defeat on the Byzantines.

The Bulgars were thus firmly established in the land which still bears their name and no other power could wipe them out. The most terrible of the pagan Bulgarian khagans, Krum (803–814), consolidated the gains of his predecessor. To put an end to the interference of the boyars, he re-established the hereditary succession to the Bulgarian throne and instituted new legislation with the most drastic sanctions and penalties. Not only was he able to take advantage of the disappearance of the Avar empire and threaten the very existence of Byzantium, but he was also able to stop the advance into the Balkans of a new and important factor in European affairs — the Franks.

4

The Frankish Kingdom made immense progress after the accession of Clovis to the throne, and his conversion to Christianity in 496 greatly facilitated the consolidation of his rule and the fusion of the conquerors with the ancient Gallo-Roman population. Clovis not only erased the remnants of the Roman Empire in Gaul but also destroyed the power of the Visigoths and dissipated forever their dream of a Visigothic empire extending from Belgium to Gibraltar. His sons Clothar and Childebert, after conquering Burgundy in 532–534, attacked Germany proper, which in the sixth century was seriously embarrassed by the advancing Slavs who had pushed far to the west beyond the Elbe and the Böhmerwald.

In addition to the Alamanni, who had been subjected to the Franks since 496, the Thuringians, Angles, Saxons, Frisians and Bavarians had to acknowledge Frankish supremacy. It seems that even the Lombards, when in Pannonia, had to accept Frankish overlordship until 568. Encouraged by all these successes, the Franks began to cherish ideas of pushing beyond the Alps into Italy, but the realization of this dream was frustrated first by the Byzantines under Justinian I and then by the Lombards, who moved southwards and founded their own kingdom on the banks of the River Po.

The decline of the Merovingian power which followed the great successes of the dynasty checked any further Frankish adventures for a considerable time, Dagobert being the last great ruler of this dynasty. The Avars were now able to consolidate their power in Central Europe. The wars of the Franks with the Lombards and a variety of difficulties ensuing on the overthrow of the Merovingian dynasty by Pepin (752), founder of the Carolingian house, gave the Avars a further breathing space, but their fate was already sealed.

Charlemagne (771–814) and his son Pepin disposed of the Avars forever. After several expeditions the last and decisive blow was delivered against them by Pepin in 796. Their chief fortification, situated somewhere in the interior of Hungary, was stormed and razed to the ground, and all the Avar treasure, the loot of countless pillaging expeditions which had been amassed there, was captured by the victorious Franks. It was complete disaster for the Avars. Their broken armies fled in all directions, while remnants of them professed their willingness to embrace Christianity and settle where the victor would permit them. They were allotted territories in southern Pannonia, but their defeat was so decisive that they never rose again. They have disappeared completely from history and we do not even know how the remnants of them were absorbed by other populations.

The destruction of the Avars must have made a profound impression on the Slavs. We find a reference to it in the *Russian
Primary Chronicle*, which was written in its final form about
1111. Commenting on the end of Avar power, the chronicler
exclaims: "God destroyed them. They all perished and not one
Avar survived. There is to this day a proverb in Rus which runs,
'they perished like the Avars.' Neither race nor heir of them remains."

The Slavic tribes between the Danube and the Sava rivers
were delighted to escape the Avar danger forever. They had
already developed a kind of political organization and were
ruled by a prince named Vojnomir, who joined the Franks with
an army, but was obliged to recognize Frankish sovereignty, and
his territory was called Pannonian Croatia. The Franks also extended their sway over the Slavs of ancient Noricum — modern
Carinthia and Styria in the Alps.

Thus Charlemagne, who in 788 had restored Frankish supremacy even over the Bavarian duke, was complete master of
an immense territory comprising the Alps and the whole of ancient Pannonia to the rivers Danube and Sava. The consequence
of his conquests was disastrous for the rest of the Byzantine possessions in Istria. Even this territory became Frankish, and Byzantium could preserve only Venice, which acquired a very particular quasi-independent position. In this way the foundations
were laid for the later glorious and astonishing rise of Venice in
the Middle Ages.

All these newly acquired territories were allotted to the
Friulian March. It was the traditional policy of Charlemagne to
erect "marches" or "marks" in the conquered countries and to
transform them into springboards for fresh conquests. The Friulian March was designed to be a spearhead for the conquest of the
Balkans, but the first attempt to subjugate the Croats of Dalmatia failed and the Margrave Erich was killed while besieging
Tarsatika, the modern Rijeka (Fiume).

The Frankish push towards the Balkans and the Adriatic was
a direct threat to the interests of Byzantium. The sword had to

decide which of the two rival powers was to dominate these countries. Attacks were renewed upon the Croats of Dalmatia until the Peace of Koenigshofen settled the dispute. By its terms the Franks definitively received Istria and the whole of Dalmatia with the exception of Venice and the coastal cities and islands. A show of force by the Byzantine navy in the Adriatic in 812 frustrated the attempt of the Franks to claim the cities of the coast.

5

Thus the Franks became masters of all the territories occupied by the Slovenes and the Croats and were looking forward to conquering even the lands where the Serbs and other Slavic tribes had settled. But then their plans were upset by the first attempt to form a Yugoslav empire. This attempt was made by Ljudovit, prince of the Pannonian Croats, who in 819 revolted against the Franks. At first he met with great success and was able to rally to his side the Slovenes from Carinthia and Styria and Isonzo, and even the Slavic tribe on the river Timok in the ancient Roman province of Moesia joined him. In addition, Ljudovit forced the Croats of Dalmatia to throw in their lot with him after he had defeated their prince, Borna. Moreover, the Byzantines encouraged his revolt to the utmost of their power. Finally, Ljudovit established his capital at Sisak, near the modern Zagreb. The emperor, Louis the Pious, himself had to intervene in order to cope with this dangerous development. After several expeditions had been led against him, Ljudovit in 822 found himself in a desperate situation. He took refuge among the Serbian Slavs and then in Dalmatian Croatia; but he was murdered at the instigation of his enemies. Thus the first attempt to unite the Yugoslavs into one empire was thwarted. The Croats saw their Frankish overlord restored; but the Croats of Dalmatia were at least permitted to elect their own prince.

Then another new and unexpected factor emerged — the Bulgarians. They made an attempt not only to arrest the Frankish

push into the Balkans, but also to group as many of the Slavic
tribes as possible around their new empire. Their khagan, Krum
(803–814), had already extended his authority over the Slavic
tribes in Thrace and Macedonia, and after the Avars had been
disposed of by Charlemagne, he incorporated in his territories
a large part of modern Hungary, from the Carpathians to the
river Tisza. Krum pushed even as far as modern Serbia, forcing
the tribes of ancient Moesia to recognize his suzerainty. He
secured his empire against any threat from Byzantium and had
the grim satisfaction of drinking the health of his boyars on
special occasions from the skull of the unfortunate Emperor
Nicephorus — mounted on silver to form a cup — who had fallen
in battle against him in 811.

His successor Omortag (814–831) was able not only to maintain what Krum had gained, but also to intervene with authority
in the attempt of the Franks to exploit their success over Ljudovit. He first of all restored Bulgarian authority over the Slavic
tribe on the Timok and asked the Emperor to give him back
some other territory occupied by another tribe which had originally been under Bulgarian domination but had subsequently
joined the rebels. Not receiving full satisfaction, he simply occupied the contested territory and then invaded Pannonian
Croatia.

The division of the Friulian March into four separate marches
and the trouble which arose out of the partition of the Carolingian Empire enabled the Bulgarians to obtain a firm foothold
in the plains of Slavonia proper and in the region of ancient
Sirmium (now Srěem). For some years even the whole of Pannonian Croatia had to acknowledge the supremacy of the Bulgarians. The Pact of Paderborn (845) gave back to the Franks
the greater part of this territory, but Omortag's successor, Malamir (831 or 836?–852), retained his rule over the remainder, including Sirmium. The Bulgarians thus frustrated the Frankish
hopes of bringing the major portion of the Balkans under their
control.

In the middle of the ninth century, therefore, three powers were jealously watching each other's moves in the Balkans: Byzantium, Bulgaria and the Frankish empire. The Slovenes and the majority of the Croats were under Frankish authority, while the majority of the Slav tribes which were to be called Serbians were under that of Byzantium. Their position became almost completely independent as the Byzantines, having lost Crete and Sicily to the Arabs, were unable to enforce their authority in those regions.

6

The collapse of the Avar domination and the reorganization of the Frankish Kingdom led to changes in other parts of Central and Eastern Europe also. The Slavic tribes, which were settled under Avar domination in ancient upper Pannonia around Lake Balaton (Blatno), and extending to the Danube, had to accept the Franks as overlords. Here the Franks seem to have ruled in rougher fashion than they did in Pannonian Croatia, but still through the medium of native princes.

The Slavs in Bohemia, Moravia and modern Slovakia, after the death of Samo, avoided the danger of renewed subjection to the Avars thanks to the victories of Charlemagne, whom they aided against their former masters, but Frankish suzerainty over those territories seems to have been less effective than it was between the Danube and Sava rivers. What was known as the Ostmark, created by Charlemagne in 803 and destined many years later to grow into the Duchy of Austria, faced the Moravian Slavs.

Further to the northeast, the Franks, having reasserted their supremacy over the Bavarians (788) and crushed the Saxons in a series of fierce and bloody battles (772–804), came up against the Polabian Slavs. Towards these people, commonly called Wends by the Germans, Charlemagne had a policy of his own. He was anxious to preserve from further Slav incursions the territories which the Franks had consolidated or had newly conquered. He therefore founded several marches on the borders of his Empire in order to protect it. Against the Sorabians, settled between the Saale and the Elbe in modern Saxony, he created the Thuringian March, called also the *Limes Sorabicus*. Further towards the north the small Marches of Magdeburg, Fells, and Bardewyk had to keep watch on the notoriously wild Vilci, and the *Limes Saxonicus*, or the March of Saxony, faced the Obodrites.

But Charlemagne was content to respect the natural frontiers in those parts. Generally he did not intend to extend his domination beyond the Elbe or to incorporate the Slavs of those lands into his Empire. He treated as his subjects all the Slavs scattered on the left bank of the Elbe but did not even attempt to Christianize their fellow-tribesmen on the other bank of the river. Naturally some exceptions were necessary because of the frequent incursions of the Slavs into Frankish territory, but that was the chief tenet of Charlemagne's policy and it was followed, generally speaking, by all members of the Carolingian dynasty. It was only in the tenth century, with the arrival to power of the Saxon dynasty, that a drastic change occurred in those lands.

Nevertheless, the consolidation of the Frankish power on the left bank of the Elbe by the Carolingian dynasty had considerable importance for future developments. Ever since the fifth century, the Franks had arrested the westward push of the other Germanic tribes. By conquering these marches on the Elbe they had also consolidated the Germanic forces and stopped any further Slavic advance to the west of that river. The initiative of the Franks forced the Germans not only to halt their own westward expansion but to turn round and seek room for expansion in the east.

The Franks also paved the way for the success of this expansion by Christianizing and ecclesiastically reorganizing the German territories and their ecclesiastical administration. The Christianity of Saxony, for example, was rude and primitive and recovered only very slowly from the wounds inflicted upon it during the bloody struggle which raged between the Franks and the Saxons in the last decades of the eighth century; but its solid foundation remained and was strengthened during the ninth century. The episcopal sees of Osnabrück, Verden, Bremen, Paderborn, Minden, Halberstadt, Hildesheim and Münster in Saxony and of Ratisbon (Regensburg), Passau, Freising and Salzburg in Bavaria were to become important bulwarks against the pagan Slavs as well as springboards for German political and cultural influence over the Slavs beyond the Elbe, and beyond the Böhmerwald and the Danube.

7

The influence which the Carolingian Empire was to exercise over the future evolution of the nations and tribes with which it came into contact was enhanced by two important factors. During Charlemagne's reign, the Empire was not only consolidated and reorganized; it also became a universal empire, the heir to the Roman Empire in the West. This idea of a universal empire necessarily entailed ideas of conquest and of the subjugation of all nations to its sway. Conquest had to be directed against those nations and states which could offer the least resistance and these were, principally, the Slavs in northeastern, central and southeastern Europe.

This new empire claimed the heritage of ancient Rome, but it was not pagan. Christianity gave it not only great strength and union but also a special right to conquest. The emperors, extending their power towards the East, proclaimed that they were acting as the special protectors of the Christian faith and in the eyes of other Christian peoples they were offering those nations the greatest gift of all, the Christian faith and Christian civilization. The Church could not oppose but only bless their push towards the East.

Unfortunately, the Church in this Frankish Empire could not escape the entanglement of secular with ecclesiastical affairs. The feudal system, a specially Germanic institution, was applied even to religious establishments, and during the rule of the Merovingian dynasty and that of Pepin and Charlemagne, it became very deeply rooted in the ecclesiastical life of the West.

Abbots and bishops became powerful landlords, dependent upon the will of the king. They became the strongest supporters of the royal and imperial idea, but were at the same time completely entangled in the secular affairs of the Empire. At first controlled by the State, the Frankish Church rapidly gained an immense influence, until, by the end of the ninth century, it was itself controlling state affairs.

This situation could not fail to be reflected in the missionary activities of the Frankish Church. So at the beginning of the Carolingian period the conversion of pagans and foundation of churches had become a highly lucrative investment for the German landowning aristocracy, which thus acquired an economic stranglehold over the newly conquered lands. According to the primitive Christian usage, churches built by both rulers and faithful came under the jurisdiction of the bishops who appointed the ministering clergy, while the revenues of the churches and monasteries remained the property of the clergy or the monks. This was consonant with Greek and Roman notions of private property. But Roman missionaries never succeeded in making this idea acceptable to the Germanic nations whom they evangelized. The Germans had a notion of private property which was different from that of the Romans and much more individualistic. This made the churches the private property of their founders, whose business it was to provide the priest and to pay him, in consideration of which they claimed possession of all contributions made by the faithful.

In the later period when the Church became more powerful and began to take the business of gaining converts into its own hands, the German clergy, who were often as hungry for land as the lay feudal lords, could not overlook the lucrative aspect of evangelizing the pagan nations which could pay good tithes and provide good workers to till the Church lands. Thus it can be explained why the missionary activity of the Frankish, and later of the German, Churches so often had an excessively worldly aspect and why missionaries so often called armed forces and colonists to their assistance to hold the territory which they were "evangelizing." The example of Charlemagne, who completed the conversion of the Saxons by force and terror, was a fatal precedent.

The Wends on the Baltic and on the Elbe were to experience those same methods of evangelization in a later period, between the tenth century and the thirteenth. The Slavs of Moravia, Bohemia, the Alps and Pannonia were evangelized by Frankish missionaries during the first period, from the end of the eighth century to the middle of the ninth. Charlemagne devoted himself especially to encouraging the Christianization of the Slovenes in ancient Noricum (Styria and Carinthia) and in upper Pannonia as far as the Danube and to promoting Christianity among the Croats in Pannonia and Dalmatia. The gentle Alcuin, Charlemagne's "Minister of Culture," who had a nobler conception of evangelization than many of his contemporaries, was particularly interested in this work. Charlemagne, acting as always on his own initiative, elevated the See of Salzburg to an archbishopric intended to replace all the episcopal sees of Pannonia and Noricum, which had disappeared during the barbaric invasions. Regensburg, Freising and Passau had to work further to the northeast.

Very little information is available on the progress of Christianity among the Croats. According to Constantine Porphyrogennetus, "the Emperor Heraclius sent to Rome to find priests (for them). From them he chose an archbishop, bishops, priests and deacons through whom he baptized the Croats. And the Croats had at that time Porga as their prince." Constantine's words cannot be interpreted as if the Croats had their own hierarchy in the seventh century, although there must be some truth in his statement. Most probably Constantine had in mind the ecclesiastical reorganization of the coastal region, which had escaped the Avar and Slav upheaval and had remained in Byzantine possession. This had to be done in accord with the Pope because the whole of Illyricum was still under the jurisdiction of the Patriarch of Rome.

If we could take the Emperor's statement literally, we should conclude that Heraclius had promoted Spalato, heir of the ancient Salona, to an archbishopric and had created bishoprics in some other coastal cities, namely in Zara and Cattaro. Local tradition attributes the elevation of Spalato to a metropolitan status to this period. Traditionally the first archbishop was John of Ravenna. But many scholars think that there is some doubt about this, and that John of Ravenna is actually the Pope John IV, a native of Dalmatia, or Pope John X, who reorganized the hierarchy of Dalmatia and Croatia and subjected the whole country to Spalato (about 925).

In any case the Christianization of the Croats must have started from the coastal cities and Spalato must have played a certain role in it. This first evangelization must have shown some success. In 641–642 Pope John IV sent the Abbot Martin to Dalmatia to recover the relics of saints from the destroyed churches. The Abbot travelled freely in the country and fulfilled his mission successfully. In 680 Pope Agathon mentioned in his letter to the Emperor Constantine Pogonat that there were Roman missionaries working among Slavs, which can only mean among the Croats. It seems that, thanks to his Christianizing activity, peaceful relations between the new masters of Dalmatia and the coastal cities were established. It is difficult to say how successful this missionary activity was. We can, however, suppose that already during the eighth century churches were built in Croatia for the new converts. Christianization must have progressed quickly during the period when Dalmatian Croatia was under Frankish supremacy. Vyšeslav, Prince of Dalmatia (mentioned about 800), was probably Christian before he recognized Frankish supremacy. Rome seems, however, to have continued to show a particular interest in Croatia and the influence of the coastal cities on the Croats did not diminish. All this explains why Frankish methods of evangelization did not take root in Dalmatian Croatia.

The consequences of this rivalry between the Franks, Rome and the Latin coastal cities subject to Byzantium were most fortunate for the Croats of Dalmatia. They obtained an independent bishopric at Nin, the residence of their ruling princes. The foundation was perhaps accelerated by Rome when the Franks got control of Dalmatian Croatia. The bishopric is mentioned already in 852, but must have existed for some time before that date because Rome was not willing to lose the results of its work in Croatia and therefore the bishopric was made directly dependent upon the Roman See. The Franks had to accept this, although they would have liked to attach the Croats more closely to their own ecclesiastical provinces of Aquileja or Salzburg. It is not known whether these first attempts at Christianization reached Pannonian Croatia, where the activities of Frankish missionaries must have been more systematic. Their first success was the conversion of Vojnomir, Prince of the Pannonian Croats.

Frankish methods of evangelization were also applied in full force in ancient Noricum and in upper Pannonia, round Lake Balaton (Blatno), countries in which Frankish colonization started very early. Allotments of land were made to bishops, abbots and great lay nobles, who imported settlers from Bavaria, the lower Main and the middle Rhine, though many of these immigrants were of servile status. The feudal and ecclesiastical aristocracy which directed the colonization soon had complete control over the whole territory. Even the Slavic nobility in these lands quite readily accepted the language and customs of the new masters and adapted itself to the feudal system, which was in many ways favorable to their material interests.

Meanwhile, the Archbishop of Salzburg was extending his influence even to the left bank of the Danube. We know that about 833 he consecrated a church at Nitra in modern Slovakia, which was very probably built for a Frankish colony there, as the local prince, Pribina, was still a pagan at the time. Here, in the shadow of the Carpathian peaks, Frankish expansion reached its northeasterly limit.

Frankish missionaries also achieved some success in Bohemia and Moravia, and about 845, fourteen Czech nobles accepted baptism at Regensburg. The Prince of the Moravians, Mojmir, who succeeded in uniting all the Slavic tribes in Moravia under his rule, did not oppose the activities of these missionaries among his people, for he was nominally under Frankish authority. It is also known that Rastislav, who succeeded him, was certainly a Christian.

4

The Moravian Empire
and Its Greek Apostles
SS. Constantine-Cyril and Methodius

Franco-Bulgarian and Moravo-Byzantine alliances — Careers of Constantine-Cyril and Methodius — Eastern and Western attitudes towards national liturgies; consequences of Moravo-Byzantine alliance — East Frankish Church and papal policy — Confirmation of Slavic liturgy, metropolis of Sirmium and East Frankish opposition — Pope John VIII, Methodius and Svatopluk of Moravia — Methodius's visit to Constantinople; ruin of his work in Moravia.

At the beginning of the second half of the ninth century a very energetic reaction arose in Moravia against the Frankish brand of Christianity and Frankish political influence, and this reaction was so sudden, so violent and so well organized that it upset all the Frankish plans of penetration and conquest in those regions. The consequences of this reaction were not confined to the political side; they were even more revolutionary in the ecclesiastical and cultural fields and here two new factors came into play: Byzantium and the Papacy, both of which had scarcely been heard of before in those lands.

Mojmir, the founder of the Moravian State, although he did not oppose directly the Frankish penetration among his subjects, was yet well aware of the danger which it represented for the independence of his realm. He particularly disliked the Frankish push into the territory of Pribina, since it was part of an encircling movement. Acting very swiftly, he attacked the pro-Frankish Pribina, drove him out of Nitra and annexed his territory to his own Moravian realm (between 833 and 836). Pribina took refuge with the Frankish Margrave Radbod, his neighbor, and after accepting baptism and being later rewarded with the gift of a holding in lower Pannonia, became a zealous supporter of the Frankish missionaries. Frankish colonists were encouraged and made especially welcome in the region around Lake Balaton (Plattensee, Blatno), and here Pribina built himself a stronghold called Mosaburg. In order further to reward his zeal and the services which he had rendered to the Franks, Louis the German, King of the East Franks (843–876), gave him this territory in 847 as his hereditary property.

In chasing Pribina from Nitra, Mojmir arrested for centuries the Frankish push on the left bank of the Danube towards the Carpathian Mountains. His successor Rastislav (846–869) was able to extend his power as far as the Tisza, where his realm became contiguous to the Bulgarian Empire. His growing power aroused the jealousy of both the Franks and the Bulgars, and in order to crush him forever, Louis the German offered a pact to the Bulgarian prince Boris. The latter, afraid both of Rastislav and of Byzantium, gladly accepted the offer and even promised to receive Christianity from the hands of the Frankish missionaries, who seemed to him less dangerous than their Byzantine confrères.

But Rastislav was not unaware of this new development. He seems to have enjoyed very good relations with the Bulgarians at the beginning of his reign when the khagans were in conflict with the Franks; but he rapidly changed his policy and reacted to the move of Louis the German with a surprising counter-attack. He was himself looking for an ally; and now he offered an alliance to the Byzantine Emperor Michael III. Consequently, sometime in 862, the population of Constantinople had the pleasure of greeting within the walls of the city "guarded by God" a strange embassy coming from the far Northwest where none but a few Byzantine traders and missionaries had ever penetrated.

Rastislav's counter-move has seemed so surprising and improbable to many historians that until very recently some of them have strongly doubted whether a semi-barbarian prince was capable of so brilliant a stroke of diplomacy. I have been able to establish, however, in a special study,[1] that the Moravian ruler did actually make such a move. Knowledge of Byzantium and of its glories was being spread even in such distant regions by traders who never ceased to maintain contact with the countries on the Danube and its tributaries. The Avars, especially in the last period of their existence, seem particularly to have encountered the influence of Byzantine civilization.

The Emperor Michael III would have preferred to receive an embassy from the Bulgarians, who were then in the center of the interest of Byzantine policy; but he and his counsellors were able immediately to grasp the importance of a Moravo-Byzantine alliance possibly developing into an encircling movement directed against the Bulgarian Khagan Boris, who, though still a pagan, appeared to prefer to accept his impending conversion from the Franks rather than from the Byzantines. Thus a Moravo-Byzantine alliance was concluded, the aim of which was to facilitate the cultural expansion of Byzantium. Rastislav, who dreaded the influence of the Frankish missionaries, besought the Emperor to send him Greek missionaries who could speak the Slavic language.

In the year 863, Rastislav in his "formidable fortress," as the Frankish annalists called his residence, probably situated somewhere on the lower course of the river Morava, received a diplomatic and "cultural" mission sent to him by Byzantium. At the head of the mission were two brothers from Thessalonica (Slavic Solun'), Constantine-Cyril and Methodius, worthy representatives of the cultural revival which was taking place in the Byzantine Empire in the ninth century.

2

The two brothers were sons of a high-ranking officer (*drungarios*, a rank corresponding to that of colonel) attached to the command of the governor (*strategos*) of the province

[1] See especially F. Dvornik, *Les légendes de Constantin et de Méthode vues de Byzance* (Prague, 1933), pp. 212 ff.

(*thema*) of Thessalonica. Methodius was born about the year 815 and Constantine in 826 or 827. Methodius chose an administrative career and — according to his biographer — was appointed by the Emperor to "the government of a Slavic principality." Constantine was interested in scholarship and his biographer relates that, invited in a dream to select the most beautiful girl in a contest, he chose Sophia — Wisdom. After his father's death, the Prime Minister Theoctistos himself took charge of Constantine's education at the University of Constantinople, which had trained thousands of officials for the imperial service. At that time also he became the favorite disciple of Photius, the greatest humanist of the age, and eventually succeeded him at the university, when Photius took over the direction of the imperial chancery, and he also seems to have accompanied Photius when the latter was sent as ambassador to the Arab Khalif Mutawakkil. It was Photius who seems to have reconciled the brothers with the new regime after Theoctistos had been murdered by Bardas, uncle of the Emperor Michael III. Fearing that this upheaval and the changes which followed might have unfortunate consequences for him as a favorite of the murdered Prime Minister, Constantine left the capital and joined his brother in his monastery at Mount Olympus in Asia Minor.

Methodius seems to have chosen the monastic life on his own initiative. In the "canon" or liturgical panegyric in honor of St. Methodius,[1] there is an interesting passage which gives us some new and surprising details concerning him. The Saint is apostrophized: "Holy and most glorious teacher, when you had decided to leave your family and your native country, your spouse and your children, you chose to go away into the wilderness in order to live there with the Holy Fathers." If this information is reliable, then it must be concluded that Methodius was married and had decided to become a monk, probably by mutual agreement with his wife — an arrangement which was not uncommon in Byzantium. The "canon" insists upon the free decision of the

---

[1] Published by P. O. Lavrov, *Materialy po istorii voznikovenija drevn. slav. pismennosti* (Leningrad, 1930), pp. 122 ff.

Saint, a circumstance which excludes any kind of political pressure.

It was in this monastery that the new Emperor Michael and the new Patriarch Photius found the two brothers and persuaded them to accept an important religious and diplomatic mission to the Khazars in 860. A long report on this mission is to be found in Constantine's biography. After their return from the Crimea, Methodius became abbot of the monastery of Polychron, while Constantine accepted the post of professor of philosophy at the patriarchal school which was being reorganized by Photius in the church of the Holy Apostles.[1]

Such were the men whom the Byzantine government was preparing to send as ambassadors to Moravia. Both accepted the new mission.

3

Constantine-Cyril was one of the finest polyglots and grammarians of the Middle Ages. Possessing a perfect knowledge of the Slav dialect of Macedonia — a fact which in no way reflects upon his Greek origin — he set to work to invent a special alphabet to express all the significant features of the Slavic language, and he brought this alphabet — known as glagolitic — to the Moravians as a special gift from the Emperor. Then, with his brother Methodius and his disciples, he started to translate the Holy Scriptures and the liturgical books into Slavonic.[2]

The Byzantine missionaries were warmly welcomed in Moravia and were easily able to out-manoeuvre the Franks, whose mission-

[1] For details see F. Dvornik, "Photius et la réorganisation de l'Académie patriarcale," *Analecta Bollandiana* LXVIII (1950), pp. 108–125.

[2] The dialect of the Macedonian Slavs was thus promoted to be a literary language and was adapted to the needs of the Slavs first in Great Moravia and later in other regions. It is customary to call the common literary language "Slavonic" or "Church Slavonic" and in its oldest version — from the ninth to the eleventh centuries — "Old Church Slavonic." Henceforward in this book the word "Slavonic" will be employed for all works written in the Macedonian dialect, the literary language of all Slavs in the oldest period of their cultural evolution.

ary methods the Slavs had grown to fear and hate. Thus the foundations of a new Slavonic Church were laid. Its characteristic sign was a mixture of the Byzantine and Roman liturgies. At first the newcomers probably used the Greek rite, but discovering that the Roman rite for the Mass was more widely known in Moravia, they adopted it, after translating it into the Slavonic tongue.[1] In many other respects, however, they followed eastern liturgical practices, and translations of holy books were also made from both Greek and Latin.

This happened at a time when the other European nations from the shores of Ireland to the Elbe, the Alps and the Adriatic were already Christians and had been, often for centuries, incorporated in the Latin and Roman cultural world. In those countries, only one language — Latin — which had nothing in common with their vernacular, was considered suitable for transmitting and developing the cultural treasures inherited from ancient and Christian Rome.

When the Slavs first came into contact with Christian culture in the ninth century, only the Anglo-Saxons had succeeded in securing for their native tongue a place second to the Latin. But they were situated far away from the valleys of the Morava and the Danube, where a Slavic political center was coming into being. King Alfred knew about the Moravians and, indeed, knowledge of this part of Europe seems to have been more extensive in Alfred's England than it was in later days. But the Anglo-Saxon example could not inspire the Slavs any more than it impressed the recently converted Franks, Saxons and Germans, although the last named were converted by Anglo-Saxon missionaries. So overwhelming was the impact of Roman culture and memories upon the Franks that when Charlemagne decided to revive the glory that was Rome and adopt the imperial title, he deemed no language but Latin worthy of his renovated

[1] It is possible that the brothers were familiar with a Greek version of the Roman liturgy known as the "Liturgy of St. Peter." This Roman liturgy in the Greek translation seems to have been used in some places by the Eastern Church. Cf. below, p. 166.

Empire. Personally, Charlemagne was not averse to the use of the Frankish language; but his wholesale introduction of the Roman liturgy and customs and his infatuation with Roman traditions contributed most to the final victory of the Latin language, at the expense of the national languages and literatures.[1]

In the meantime, while the new Slavonic Church was being established in Moravia, the military and political clauses of the Moravo-Byzantine alliance came into operation. Louis the German was preparing a large-scale campaign against Rastislav and as this new adventure appeared to be of the first importance, he asked the blessing of the Pope Nicholas I. His new ally, Boris of Bulgaria, was requested to come to Tulln to discuss the details of the proposed campaign and of the alliance in general. But in spite of all these imposing preparations, Louis had to embark upon his campaign in 864 alone, and he waited in vain for Boris to launch his expected attack upon Moravia from the other side.

An explanation of this is to be found in the works of some Byzantine writers, who speak somewhat confusedly of an armed Byzantine intervention in Bulgaria in 864, which apparently took Boris completely by surprise. While preparing his own campaign against Moravia, he had to capitulate to the Byzantine forces. After this he promised to abandon the Frankish alliance and received baptism at the hands of Byzantine priests, and his country was placed under the jurisdiction of the Patriarch Photius. It was a great triumph for both the Byzantine Empire and the Church. The Byzantines were so anxious to detach the Bulgarians from the Franks that the Emperor gave his god-child, Boris-Michael, a small territorial concession as a baptismal present in 865.

[1] The only instance in which the Anglo-Saxon example might have had some influence on the continent was the composition of the Saxon religious poem "Heliand." But it would never have occurred to anybody in the West, not even to an Anglo-Saxon, to have his holy liturgy in the native tongue. The Franks, who fancied themselves as the heirs of the Romans, especially from Charlemagne's time onwards, were the least tolerant in this respect. Cf. F. Dvornik, *The National Churches and the Church Universal* (London, 1945).

This Byzantine intervention against the Bulgarians probably saved the Moravian Empire from complete destruction. Rastislav was able to hold out against Louis the German only with the greatest difficulty and in the end he had to acknowledge Frankish supremacy in his lands. Had the Bulgarian threat materialized, Rastislav could scarcely have avoided utter extinction. Later in 866, when the son of Louis the German unsuccessfully rebelled against his father, Rastislav supported him.

4

The fight continued in the ecclesiastical field and was, indeed, no less fierce. The East Frankish bishops did not like the work which the Greek missionaries were so successfully carrying out in Moravia, and the Bishops of Regensburg and Passau, in particular, considered that their interests were being injured because their sees were the chief centers of propaganda in Moravia and Bohemia. Moreover, as has already been stated, the introduction of the Germanic custom of proprietary churches into the newly conquered lands made the conversion of pagans a very lucrative enterprise for the bishops and abbots who had become powerful landlords. A particularly busy evangelizing and colonizing activity was being directed in ancient Pannonia in the ninth century by Frankish bishops and barons. It was natural that the Frankish hierarchy should see a great danger to the expansion of its influence in the new missionary methods introduced into Moravia by Byzantine missionaries.

On the other hand, however, Pope Nicholas I had long watched with suspicion the growing ambitions of Salzburg and the other Bavarian sees. He was aware that an East Frankish or German Church was rising in the eastern part of the Carolingian Empire and that if it were allowed to assume great importance, it would prejudice the rights of the Roman See, as he conceived them.

Nicholas I (858–867) had a very high conception of papal supremacy. Under him the medieval Papacy emerged, for it was his letters and decrees which gave the medieval canonists the

material upon which they were to build the doctrines of the
supremacy in all respects of the spiritual over the secular power.

This thesis, first developed by Gregory VII and his canonists
in the eleventh century, was brought to fruition by Innocent III
(1198–1216). It was defined in the most categorical terms by
Boniface VIII (1294–1303) in his struggle with Philip the
Fair, King of France. The whole evolution of the relations between the Church and the State in the Middle Ages was influenced by these theses of the canonists which were so fiercely
opposed by secular lawyers at different periods.

It must be said that Nicholas I very greatly enhanced the
ascendancy of the Papacy in the eyes of his contemporaries. He
was, without doubt, a noble figure. Not only did he defend
the indissolubility of Christian marriage against King Lothair
of Lorraine with the greatest courage and perseverance, but
he also tried to maintain complete control over all Christian
Churches. He did not succeed in the East, where his attempts
to intervene were unfortunately timed owing to his lack of
knowledge of the actual situation and the successful opposition
of the Patriarch Photius. Nicholas, however, registered complete
success in the West, as the weakening of the Carolingian Empire
after its partition in 817 greatly helped his efforts, and the
Emperor Louis II (855–875), third successor of Charlemagne,
proved to be a weak partner.

Thus Nicholas, having strengthened his authority over the
Italian bishops, crushed every attempt of the West Frankish
Church to obtain a degree of ecclesiastical autonomy. This is
the real meaning of his struggle with Hincmar, Archbishop of
Rheims. Nicholas once more claimed direct Roman jurisdiction
over the whole area of the former province of Illyricum, which
was in great part occupied by Slavs: Slovenes, Croats, Serbs and
Bulgarians. He had to let the Franks send their missionaries to
their pagan neighbors, but, while blessing their Christianizing
activity, he was determined to seize the first opportunity to
secure the direct submission of the newly converted peoples to
the Roman See.

As will be shown in more detail,[1] Nicholas succeeded in sup-
planting Frankish missionaries in Bulgaria with priests sent from
Rome and in subordinating Bulgaria, at least for the time being,
directly to Roman jurisdiction. When all this is borne in mind,
it can be understood that it was impossible for Nicholas to remain
indifferent to the activities of Frankish and Byzantine missionaries in Moravia and Pannonia. It is therefore not surprising to
learn from the biographers of Constantine-Cyril and Methodius
that the Pope invited the Greek brothers to come to Rome.

It is not known in what circumstances this invitation was
made, but Methodius's biographer (Chap. VI) attributes the
initiative to Nicholas I. Constantine's biographer (Chap. XV),
however, seems to indicate that the papal invitation reached the
two brothers in Venice, after they had left Moravia "in order to
have their disciples ordained." [2]

There is nothing surprising in the brothers' acceptance of the
Pope's invitation to visit Rome as at that time there was no
animosity towards Rome in the East. Moreover, the two brothers
were well aware that the Slavic lands where they had worked
were a part of the patriarchate of Rome and it would have been
only natural if they had intended to stop there — even if they
were on their way to Constantinople.

On their way to Venice, the brothers registered another suc-
cess: Kocel, the son of the Slavic Prince Pribina, who ruled in
Pannonia under Frankish supremacy, had not only received the
Greeks well as they passed through his country, but, preferring

[1] See below, Chap. VI, p. 119.
[2] It seems probable that the two brothers intended to return from Venice
by sea to Constantinople in order to report to the Emperor and to the
Patriarch on the result of their work and to have their disciples ordained.
After receiving the invitation from Nicholas I, they changed their minds
and went to Rome. It is, however, also quite possible that the Greek
brothers intended to reach Constantinople by way of Rome. The fact that
they had with them some of the relics believed to be those of Pope Clement
I, the third successor of St. Peter, which they had discovered during their
stay in Kherson in the Crimea during their mission to the Khazars, suggests this. They might have intended to leave the relics in Rome. We know
that they left some of them in Kherson and others in Constantinople.

their method to that of the Franks, had given them about fifty young men to be instructed in Slavonic letters.

It was Nicholas's successor, Hadrian II, who received them with every mark of goodwill in 868, approving their innovations and the Slavonic liturgy and himself ordaining their disciples. It was the Pope's policy which explains his attitude towards the Greek missionaries; for after a short period of vacillation at the beginning of his reign, Hadrian followed very closely the policy of his energetic predecessor. As he also was determined to defend the rights of the Roman See among the newly converted peoples, it is not surprising that the Greek brothers from Moravia aroused such great interest on his part.

5

The concessions he made to the new Slavonic Church in Moravia — especially the solemn confirmation in a special bull, of the use of a Slavonic liturgy — were intended to weaken the influence of the Frankish Church. Constantine died unexpectedly in Rome on February 14, 869 (he became a monk on his deathbed and assumed the name of Cyril) and this seemed a serious setback to the Pope's plans,[1] but when Kocel sent a special messenger to Rome requesting the Pope to join his territory to the new diocese planned for Moravia, Hadrian saw that the moment had come for speedy action. Methodius was therefore sent forthwith to Pannonia so that he might confer with the

[1] According to Constantine's biographer (Chap. XVIII) Methodius was determined to return to Constantinople with his brother's body. There might be some truth in this report, especially if we are authorized to surmise that both had intended to return to Byzantium via Rome. Methodius must have learned in the meantime of the political upheaval in Byzantium — the assassination of Michael III by Basil I and the replacement of Photius by Ignatius on the patriarchal throne. It is possible also that he wanted to return to his monastery in order to escape from such complications, or that he thought he needed a fresh authorization for his mission from the new regime. Kocel's request seems to have made him change all such plans. F. Grivec's monograph on Kocel (Slovenski knez Kocel, Ljubljana, 1938) was not available to me.

interested parties on the spot. When he returned to Rome to report, Hadrian decided to restore the ancient Metropolitan See of Sirmium (Srěm) for Methodius and to attach to his diocese not only Pannonia, but also the lands of the Moravian State. In 870 the news was received in Rome that the Bulgarians, who had accepted the jurisdiction of Rome in 866, had now returned to that of Byzantium. This fact may have influenced Hadrian's decision.

In any case it was a very bold stroke and from the outset invited conflict with the rising Frankish-German Church. This new development caused the Bavarian bishops to abandon their ambitious and carefully laid plans, and when they learned of the Pope's intentions, they protested by sending a memorandum to Louis the German, their King — and perhaps also to the Emperor Louis II. In spite of some distortion of historical facts, this document, entitled "The Conversion of the Caranthanians and Bavarians," is very important for the study of the Christianization and colonization of the former Pannonia and Noricum.

Then, unfortunately, just as the Pope was sending out Methodius as Archbishop of Sirmium with the confirmation of all these unprecedented privileges, the political situation in Moravia suddenly changed and Louis the German became temporarily master of the whole country. Meanwhile Rastislav's nephew Svatopluk,[1] impatient to become ruler of all these lands, made an alliance with the East Franks, who after deposing Rastislav blinded and imprisoned him in a Frankish monastery. Svatopluk had to acknowledge East Frankish supremacy and also became, for a time, a prisoner of Louis the German.

And so it happened that while Methodius was returning to take up his duties, he was arrested by Bavarian troops and tried by a local synod of sorts, presided over by the Archbishop of Salzburg, on charges of being an impostor and a usurper of episcopal rights. He was threatened by Hermanrich, Bishop of Passau, with being horse-whipped, and condemned to be locked

---

[1] The old Slavonic form of his name was Svįętopl'k'. German chronicles called him Sventobold.

up in a Bavarian monastery.[1] Nicholas's fear of the growing power of the Bavarian bishops was plainly not unfounded. Svatopluk appears to have been present at the synod, powerless to undo what his own mischief had created.

While Methodius was trying to send news of his plight to Rome, there was anxiety there about the result of his mission, and when Bishop Anno of Freising paid a visit to the Pope, he was asked for news of Archbishop Methodius. Bishop Anno replied that he had never heard of him, and it was not until three years later that Pope John VIII learned what had happened; he immediately despatched Paul, Bishop of Ancona, as a messenger to the Bavarian bishops and to King Louis the German, demanding the release of Methodius. The letters which the legate carried were couched in forceful terms; in the Pope's opinion, the audacity shown by the Bavarian bishops out-topped the clouds, nay, heaven itself! If one were to weep over such tyrannical depravity, the Pope wrote to Hermanrich of Passau, all Jeremiah's tears would not suffice. All the responsible bishops were temporarily suspended and severely lectured on canon law. King Louis the German and his Carloman were not spared either. It was stated that the rights of the Holy See were inalienable and that only the barbarian invasions had prevented Rome from claiming direct jurisdiction over Pannonia.

6

John VIII stood fast. He tried to contact Kocel directly and addressed an invitation to the Serbian Prince Mutimir, who ruled over what had been Moesia Inferior, to acknowledge the new Metropolitan See of Sirmium as reorganized for the new

[1] H. W. Ziegler in his study "Der Slawenapostel Methodius im Schwabenlande" (*Jahrbuch des Histor. Vereins Dillingen a.d.D.* LII [1950], pp. 169–189) concludes that the Moravian archbishop was imprisoned in Ellwangen in the Black Forest. The synod was probably held in Freising. See F. Grivec's "Quaestiones Cyrillo-Meth." in *Orient. Christ. Period.* XVIII (1952), pp. 113–118, and S. Sakač's "Bemerkungen," *ibid.* XX (1954), pp. 175–180.

titular, the Greek Methodius. Only in one particular did the Pope make a concession to one of the main grievances of the Frankish bishops — he forbade the use of Slavonic in the liturgy. It may be that a copy of the memorandum addressed to Louis the German by the Bavarian episcopate in 870 had found its way to Rome. There this accusation may be read against Methodius: "With his new-fangled philosophy and his recently invented Slavonic letters he undermines the Latin language, the Roman doctrine and the official Latin writing; he vilifies before the whole people [in Slavic countries] the Mass, the Gospel and the ecclesiastical office of the priests which [so far] they have celebrated in Latin."

The words well express the Frankish clergy's shocked bewilderment at this new method of missionary activity and illustrate the Latin complex that had developed since Charlemagne and was more characteristic of western and eastern Francia than of Rome itself. Making the concession did not greatly trouble the Pope so long as he could placate the Bavarians; but it was a matter in which Methodius could scarcely have been expected to concur. All his success among the Slavs was mainly due to the use of a Slavonic liturgy. So he paid no heed to the papal injunction and, together with his disciples, carried on as before in the interest of the Church. The legate himself may have seen the difficulty of acting otherwise, and Methodius hoped to explain the matter personally to the Pope before a definite decision was reached; for he was asked to report in person to Rome after two years, when the Pope proposed to make a final decision on the whole affair.

Methodius felt all the easier about it because the political situation in Moravia had altered again in his favor. The Moravians revolted against the Frankish nobles who were administering the territory during Svatopluk's exile in East Francia, and Svatopluk volunteered to placate the population. Instead, he joined hands with the rebels and under his leadership they annihilated the Bavarian army. He defeated every Frankish contingent sent against him and remained undisputed master of the Moravian State. The Franks accepted the inevitable and signed a peace treaty in 874.

There followed a period of wide expansion. The Bohemian Duke Bořivoj and the Sorbs of modern Saxony joined the new Slavic federation. They were followed by the Slavs on the Vistula, whose capital was Cracow. The *Vita Methodii* states (Chap. XI) that the Archbishop tried in vain to convert "the mighty prince on the Vistula" and prophesied to him that he would be defeated, captured and baptized in a foreign land. The prophecy came true. This passage may justifiably be interpreted as a reference to Svatopluk's conquest of the former White Croatia. So it came about that Svatopluk's empire extended from the Elbe and the Saale to the upper Bug and the Styr, and in the east and south to the Tisza and the Danube — with fair prospects of annexing Pannonia.

A great Slavic empire — Constantine Porphyrogennetus called it "Great Moravia" — was thus in process of formation in the heart of Central Europe that seemed likely to absorb the other Slavic tribes to the north and south and to stop forever the progress of the Franks and the Germans towards the east. Its Slavic culture, rooted in Byzantium and combined with Western and Latin elements, gave it the essential condition of permanence and displayed in its Slavonic liturgy a mixture of Byzantine and Roman rites.

Why then did Svatopluk support Methodius only half-heartedly and show greater favor to the Frankish clergy? When Methodius was accused of disobedience and heretical teaching, he went to Rome, accompanied by a Latin priest named Wiching, who worked in Moravia and was a favorite of Svatopluk. There he cleared his character and the Pope proceeded with the organization of Methodius's metropolitan diocese; but at this point an unfortunate concession had to be made to Svatopluk, who requested that Wiching be made the Bishop of Nitra. Methodius felt that this appointment would handicap his work; but in giving way he hoped to find a compensation in the fact that henceforward accusations against him would cease and that the Pope would again approve the use of the Slavonic liturgy.[1]

Scholars have tried with little success to explain Svatopluk's attitude towards Methodius. It is generally thought that Methodius upbraided Svatopluk over his private life; but whether true or not, this does not explain everything. The Greeks were as a rule excellent diplomats and always knew just how far they could go when dealing with potentates or princelings. There must have been some other reason, and it can probably be found in the different ways in which Greeks and Franks defined the rights of rulers over the churches they built.

To judge from the memorandum composed in 870 by the Bavarian bishops, the Germanic system of proprietary churches had prevailed in Pannonia. Frankish missionaries had also introduced this system into Moravia, and it was bound to appeal to a ruler of Svatopluk's type. Greek missionaries certainly objected to it as being alien to their conception of canon law, and in this Methodius had the support of the Pope, since in the ninth century Rome did not know of any other system of ecclesiastical property other than that in force in the Eastern Church. This was conceived in the old Roman spirit, which in the eleventh century was to inspire Gregory VII during the Investiture contest with the Emperor Henry IV. It seems, then, that the ninth century witnessed in Moravia the prelude to the gigantic Investiture struggle which was to end so tragically in the disruption of Western Christianity at the Reformation. Things might have shaped differently had the Roman Church been able to keep the Slavonic Church under its immediate control, since it was free from this restriction of Germanic canon law, but with Svatopluk's partiality for the Frankish system, this was not possible.

An additional reason explaining Svatopluk's liking for German clergy and customs may be found in his political ambitions.

---

[1] In his letter to Svatopluk the Pope writes: "It is not against the faith or against doctrine to sing the Mass in the Slavonic tongue, or to read the Holy Gospel or the divine lessons of the New or Old Testament well translated and interpreted, or to sing the other hours of the holy office."

Owing to his military success he added to his empire a major part of Frankish Pannonia. This fact and the declining power of the Carolingian dynasty in East Francia — modern Germany — may have emboldened him to plan to extend his domination over Bavaria, and even to replace the Carolingians in the eastern part of the Frankish Empire. He may have thought he had found in Wiching an able agent who would be helpful in the realization of his far-reaching political plans. Of course, the first condition for winning the support of the Bavarian clergy for his plans was to favor German customs and Latin liturgy in his lands.

Relying on Svatopluk's favor, Wiching carried on his intrigues against the metropolitan and pretended that Methodius had sworn in Rome not to use the Slavonic tongue in the liturgy. Svatopluk was at a loss to know what to do; but Methodius appealed to the Pope for a formal denial of Wiching's statement. This was granted and sent to Moravia.

7

The author of the *Vita Methodii* (Chap. XII) says that Methodius received an invitation from the Emperor Basil I to visit him in Constantinople. This invitation reached Methodius, according to the *Vita*, at a time when his adversaries were spreading rumors that "the Emperor was hostile to him and if he got hold of him, he would not escape alive." It has been suggested [1] that this Byzantine animosity towards Methodius was caused by his partisanship for the Latins, and that because he obeyed the Pope, he was regarded as a traitor in Byzantium.

This interpretation ignores, however, the peaceful atmosphere which reigned between Byzantium and Rome after the reconciliation of the Patriarch Photius and the Pope in 880 — the rumors mentioned by the *Vita* are supposed to have circulated in Moravia after this date.[2] If the Byzantines surrendered Bulgaria in 880 to

[1] See E. Honigmann, "Studies in Slavic Church History," *Byzantion* XVII (1945), pp. 163–182.

[2] See F. Dvornik, *The Photian Schism, History and Legend* (Cambridge Univ. Press, 1948), pp. 159–236.

Roman jurisdiction, how can it be asserted that they regarded Methodius as a traitor, since Constantinople had never made any serious claims to the land in which he worked?

Another theory has been advanced [1] in order to explain the feelings of hostility towards Methodius in Constantinople. Having been reinstated in the patriarchate, Ignatius is said to have ordained, after 870, another archbishop for Moravia in place of Methodius, who was a partisan of his rival Photius. This was Agathon whose name is mentioned in the Acts of the Council of Reconciliation of 880. This course not only was too dangerous for Ignatius, who had been reinstated by the help of the Pope, who was an ardent supporter of Methodius; he also appears to have accepted, for patriotic reasons, Photian clergy in Bulgaria, in spite of the condemnation of Photius and his followers by the Council of 869–870. Why then should he have ordained a rival prelate for distant Moravia?

Such initiative on the part of Ignatius could be explained only if the Moravians, after learning of Methodius's disappearance, had asked Constantinople for another archbishop. In such a case Ignatius's action would have no anti-papal or anti-Photian bias. When we take into consideration that in 870 Moravia was in the hands of Louis the German and governed by German counts — Svatopluk being held under surveillance in Bavaria — it is hardly conceivable that the Moravians could have taken such a step, unless we surmise that, in preparing a revolt against Louis the German, they had asked Byzantium for help. There is, however, no evidence for such a supposition.

[1] See E. Honigmann, *loc. cit.* Honigmann's thesis that Agathon of Moravia is identical with Archbishop Agathon, member of a Byzantine embassy to Germany in 873, does not appear to be adequately demonstrated. It is true that Agathon of Moravia is listed among metropolitans and archbishops in the Acts of the Council of 880, but it is highly doubtful whether this may be taken as a proof of his higher ecclesiastical rank. In this respect the list is not reliable. Other bishops are mentioned among prelates of higher rank (e.g. the bishops of Apro, Keltzene, Ilion) and prelates of higher rank among bishops (e.g. the metropolitan of Neai Patrai, the archbishop of Arcadiopolis). It is better to remain on firmer ground and to regard Agathon as archbishop or bishop of Moravia in modern Serbia. See below, p. 164, for further details of this ecclesiastical foundation.

If there was any foundation for the spreading of rumors that the Emperor Basil I was hostile to Methodius, the latter's attitude towards the Croats and the Pope's attempt to extend Methodius's jurisdiction over the territory of the Serbian Prince Mutimir — nominally subject to Byzantium — might have given Methodius's enemies in Moravia the pretext for circulating rumors that he had lost the support of his countrymen.

In order to explain Methodius's journey to Constantinople, which took place about the year 882, historians have often inferred that the persistent opposition of the Franks and Svato-pluk's vacillations forced Methodius to look to Byzantium for support. The authenticity of this report is simply denied by other historians, who were shocked by the idea that a man canonized by the Western Church should have had any dealings with the Patriarch Photius because, despite his reinstatement and recon-ciliation with Rome by the Council of 879–880, he had been re-excommunicated by the Pope.

But all these difficulties vanish if it is remembered that there never was any second excommunication of Photius. Once his true character has been established, there will be no objection to the historical validity of Methodius' journey to Constantinople. But whether he travelled simply to visit his mother's grave, or, more probably, to report to the Emperor and the Patriarch Photius, an intimate friend of his late brother Constantine-Cyril, who had given his blessing to the brothers' missionary activities in Moravia, Methodius's journey, undertaken in the peaceful atmosphere of reconciliation between Rome and Constantinople, could only promote the interests of Pope John VIII — a stout supporter of Methodius who had welcomed the reconciliation.

When it is recalled that Methodius's diocese touched Bulgaria and perhaps even comprised a portion of the Serbian territory mentioned above, which was technically under Byzantine suzerainty, then the Moravian archbishop had every reason to go to Constantinople, whether at the Emperor's invitation, as the legend has it, or even without it.

Basil I and the Patriarch Photius received Methodius cordially

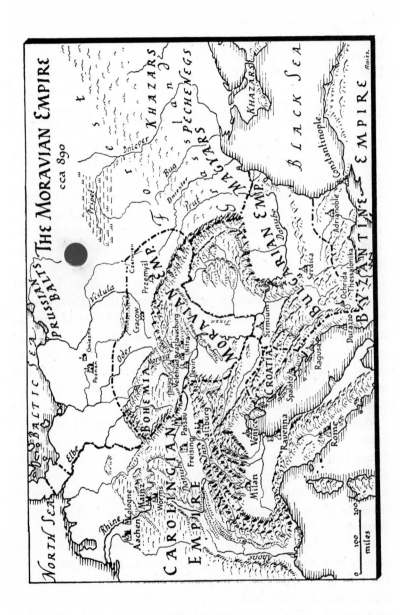

The Moravian Empire cca 890

and he had the satisfaction of learning that his innovations in Moravia were approved by his fellow-countrymen, who manifested their intention to use them in the interest of their own Church. This is confirmed by the account of this incident in the *Vita* which states that at the Emperor's request Methodius left a priest and a deacon behind in Constantinople with various Slavonic books. These formed the nucleus of a Slavonic center in the capital which may have been destined to supply the Bulgarians with Greek writings and Slavonic translations.

Byzantine support may have impressed Svatopluk, but it did not put a stop to the hostility of the Franks and their representative Wiching. The climax came in 884, the year of Methodius's death (April 6, 884). As a precaution to ensure that his work would be perpetuated, he recommended as his successor his disciple Gorazd, a native of Moravia and one well schooled in Slavonic, Greek and Latin letters.

But before Gorazd had time to secure his succession, Wiching hastened to Rome where he produced some forged documents to convince Stephen VI that John VIII had forbidden Methodius to use Slavonic for the liturgy, that Methodius's orthodoxy was suspect and that he had acted illegally in appointing his successor. Thereupon Wiching was made administrator of the metropolis, the use of the Slavonic liturgy was prohibited and Gorazd was summoned to Rome.

Wiching lost no time in getting his own way in Moravia, where Svatopluk, although surprised by the speed with which Rome had changed its attitude, placed him in charge of the diocese. Then, taking advantage of Svatopluk's absence on a military expedition, Wiching proceeded to harass the favorite disciples of the late metropolitan. Those among them who were Byzantine subjects were either sold into slavery or exiled.

We learn from the *Life of St. Naum* that he was rescued from slavery by a representative of the Emperor Basil I in Venice, and the *Life of St. Clement*, a biography of another disciple, states that he was roughly handled by his military escort of German mercenaries. The exiles crossed the Danube and made for

Belgrade, which was then in Bulgarian hands, and were well received by Boris-Michael, Khagan of Bulgaria. Thus the work of the two Greek brothers was saved; for the Bulgarians handed on the fruits of their labors to the Serbs and the Russians. Other disciples of Methodius fled to Bohemia, possibly to Cracow and probably also to Dalmatia, where the Slavonic liturgy has survived to this day.

Later, things took a more hopeful turn in Moravia. On the outbreak of hostilities between the Moravians and the Franks, Svatopluk decided that he had had enough of Wiching's intrigues and expelled him from the country. He realized too late the futility of his political ambitions in East Francia.

Svatopluk's premature death changed the whole situation, however, and his successor, Mojmir II, had to defend his rights against the claims of his two brothers. The Franks took advantage of this state of affairs to weaken their dangerous neighbor. They succeeded also in winning over the Czechs and the Sorbs, who made peace with them and recognized their supremacy. The Moravian Empire, exhausted by the struggles, thus found itself much reduced in size, but Mojmir II, who eventually defeated his brothers, proved to be an able ruler. His first preoccupation was to reorganize the Church in his country. When he applied to Rome for bishops, John IX sent a legate to consecrate a new hierarchy in Moravia, with results which are not known for certain.

In 906 the Germans called upon the Magyars to help them to destroy this rising power in Central Europe and the invaders swept into Moravia through the Carpathian passes. Mojmir II fell in battle and his capital was so thoroughly destroyed that its very site is still a topic of debate. It does seem, however, that a few bishops in Cracow and modern Slovakia were able to survive the catastrophe.

Such was the end of a noteworthy attempt to set up a political and cultural power in Central Europe; but the disaster left its mark upon the subsequent history of the whole continent. What Europe needed at the time was direct contact with Byzantium, the storehouse of Greek and Hellenistic culture. Access by sea had been almost cut off by the Arabs; but the Danube valley and the Balkans were kept open by the Moravians and the Greeks so that Roman and Byzantine cultures could meet in Central Europe. Had this situation lasted, Western Europe would have evolved along different lines. But the opportunity was lost and centuries were to elapse before the treasures of Constantinople were re-discovered in circumstances which were not so happy.

5

After the Destruction of the Moravian Empire. Germany and the Rise of Bohemia and Poland

Consequences of the Moravian catastrophe — The two Bohemian dukedoms — Bohemia, Bavaria and the new Saxon dynasty — The first wave of the "Drang nach Osten"; St. Wenceslas of Bohemia — Otto II, the Magyars and the Slavs — Mieszko I of Poland, Boleslas I of Bohemia — St. Adalbert, Bishop of Prague; Poland and the struggle between the two Bohemian dynasties.

The Moravian catastrophe proved to be an important turning point in the evolution of the Slavs and in the history of Central Europe. A new foreign element had appeared in the Danube basin and separated the Western from the Southern Slavs, who now had to adapt themselves to a new situation and find fresh outlets in their political and cultural life.

What were the immediate effects of the destruction of Moravia on those Slavs who had been incorporated in the Moravian Empire? It seems that the Magyars limited themselves to wiping out the center of Moravian power in the valley of the Morava and in the territory between the river Dyje (Thaja) and the Danube. After the archaeological discoveries recently made at Staré Město, there can now be little doubt that one of the main centers of Moravian power — perhaps the fortress which had astonished the writer of the *Annals* of Fulda — lay in the valley of the lower Morava. This center was completely destroyed at this time and a similar fate befell other Moravian fortified settlements. But in Slovakia the Magyars seem to have done no more than subjugate the native population. We learn from the *Annals* of Sázava, the Czech abbey of the Slavonic rite, that in the eleventh century the Slavonic monks expelled from this Abbey took refuge in Hungary. This evidence shows that priests of the Slavonic rite must have survived the Magyar invasion and that Christian settlements continued to exist in Slovakia and perhaps also in Pannonia. This was due to the fact that the victorious nomads were not interested in the mountainous regions and they needed the agricultural products of the natives. There is evidence which strongly suggests that a most important Christian and Slav center existed in Esztergom (Ostĕrgom᾽) on the middle Danube and it was from there that the Christianization of the Magyars started in the tenth century. Other similar centers, it seems, continued to exist, and in the eleventh century they formed a bridge between Bohemia (with its surviving Slavonic clergy), Kievan Russia and the Croats.

In the other parts of the former Moravian Empire, Cracow and the rest of former White Croatia were most probably spared. This region may have recognized a kind of Magyar overlordship; at least it appears to have lived on friendly terms with them. Constantine Porphyrogennetus, in his report on the White Croats, asserts that their prince made a "matrimonial alliance and friendly treaties with the Turks," i.e. with the Magyars. As will be shown, the Slavonic liturgy survived in Cracow and this city may also have become the refuge of two Moravian bishops who had survived the destruction of their metropolis.

2

Bohemia and White Serbia had both drifted away from the Moravian Empire, torn as it was by dissensions between Svatopluk's successor, Mojmir II, and his brothers. The only course open to them now was to accept the overlordship of the Franks. The *Annals* of Fulda report that after the death of Svatopluk the Sorbs sent a mission to Arnulf to assure him of their loyalty, thus signifying the submission of White Serbia. The same annalist further reports that in 895 two Czech Dukes, Spytihnĕv and Witizla (Vitĕslav), accompanied by numerous nobles, appeared at the Reichstag of Regensburg where they were received with full honors by King Arnulf and with the customary handshake renewed their allegiance to the Frankish Empire as represented by the Duchy of Bavaria.

The fact that two dukes are specially mentioned indicates that Bohemia was divided into two dukedoms, which coincides with what we know from other sources about ancient Bohemia. The presence of Croats in eastern Bohemia is attested by King Alfred and by the foundation charter of the bishopric of Prague. On the other hand, an old Czech tradition attributes the foundation of the Czech dynasty to Přemysl. Bořivoj, the first known Christian Duke of Bohemia, who was baptized by St. Methodius, governed the western part of Bohemia including Prague. It is probable that eastern Bohemia was annexed by Svatopluk of Moravia when he conquered the whole of White Croatia, which included that region. The western dukedom became part of Moravia after the submission of Bořivoj and the short symbiosis of the two parts of Bohemia within a common empire appears to have brought them close together. The Bohemian Croats joined the Přemyslide part of Bohemia and from 895 onwards the two dukedoms remained closely allied. At the Reichstag of Regensburg, Spytihněv represented the Přemyslide part of Bohemia and Witizla (Vitěslav) that of the Croats. Vitěslav's dynasty is known in history as the dynasty of Slavnik, after the best known member of this family. The subjection of other tribes in Bohemia was concluded by both dukedoms at the beginning of the tenth century.

3

The common Magyar danger naturally drew Bohemia and Bavaria closer together. Spytihněv's successor, Vratislav (915–920/21), probably died while defending his country against a Magyar invasion. He was succeeded by his son Wenceslas I (920–929), who was still a minor, and so the regency was exercised by his mother Drahomira. She, however, found her authority undermined by her mother-in-law Ludmila, a very pious lady who had great influence with the young Duke. So, Drahomira, counting on the support of a semi-pagan reaction, had her put to death, but the Christian party overthrew the mother and proclaimed the young Wenceslas as reigning prince.

So it happened that the Czechs acquired their first martyr, St. Ludmila, a circumstance of great importance, because it impressed on their German neighbors that they were good Christians. The Duke of Bavaria was one of the first to learn about the new Saint and, afraid that the change on the throne might also mean a change in the attitude of the Czechs towards Bavaria, he made a journey to Bohemia. There he was assured by the young Duke that everything would remain unaltered. To placate the Bavarian Duke, Wenceslas even promised to dedicate the cathedral he proposed to build in Prague to St. Emmeram, patron saint of Bavaria and of Regensburg, to which Bohemia was now ecclesiastically subordinated.

It is interesting to note that in spite of this promise, which is attested by the Slavonic legend of St. Wenceslas, the Duke actually dedicated the new cathedral to St. Vitus (Guy), patron saint of Saxony.

This substitution of one patron saint for another was symbolic of a very important political change which Germany, formerly East Francia, had meanwhile undergone. After the extinction of the eastern branch of the Carolingian dynasty, the German Dukes, faced by the constant Magyar danger, decided to elect a king. After the death of Conrad of Franconia in 919, Henry the Fowler, Duke of Saxony, the most outstanding duke in Germany, became king. This year marked the birth of medieval Germany. Bavaria, which was certainly more civilized than Saxony, also claimed the leadership of the German nation, or *Regnum Teutonicorum*, as it was already called in this period, and Henry had great difficulty in getting Arnulf of Bavaria to acknowledge his royal authority. As a result, the Saxons were determined to undermine the position of Bavaria in Germany as much as possible. It seems probable, therefore, that, in his determination to weaken the influence of Bavaria, Henry I tried to supersede it in Bohemia.

He succeeded only too well; for Wenceslas and his counsellors, preferring to have as their overlord a distant Saxon instead of a nearby Bavarian, transferred their allegiance to the King and Duke of Saxony. This was the beginning of the decline of Bavarian influence in Germany. The later course of events shows that it would have been better for Germany and for Europe as a whole if Bavaria, which was more cultured and nearer to the West, had assumed the leadership in the *Regnum Teutonicorum*. For it was from Saxony that the "Drang nach Osten" started — the push towards the East which ultimately produced Prussia and the Prussian spirit of domination.

4

Henry I initiated this new policy of eastward expansion which Germany was to pursue for the next thousand years and which culminated in 1942 on the Volga river. After successfully stemming the terrible invasions of the Magyars and completing the military organization of Saxony and Thuringia, Henry I launched the first big Saxon drive beyond the Elbe in the winter of 928. His army crossed the Elbe and the frozen marshes of the Havel river and took Brunabor, the principal town of the Havelians. Thus the foundation stone of the history of Brandenburg was laid and Brunabor became the first important milestone in the German drive towards the East. There followed the submission of the Veletians (Ljutici or Vilci), who had to promise to pay tribute. The same fate overtook the Obodrites and marked the beginning of the history of modern Schleswig-Holstein and Mecklenburg.

The triumphal march of the Saxon armies through Slavic territories ended, probably in the spring of 929, with the subjugation of the Sorbian tribes between the Saale and the Elbe rivers, and on the site of Jahna, the conquered capital of the Daleminci, the new city of Meissen was founded to become the second important Saxon outpost.

It was believed by historians that these victories over the

Polabian Slavs were crowned by the conquest of Bohemia, then ruled by Wenceslas; but in fact Wenceslas remained loyal to Henry I throughout his life, as is attested by his biographer Christian, and by the chronicler Thietmar. The murder of Wenceslas by over-zealous followers of his brother Boleslas cannot be invoked as a proof that his pro-Saxon policy was resented by the Czechs. His murder and the change on the ducal throne of Prague were the results of internal strife and domestic jealousy. Wenceslas led a pious life, and seems to have married only under pressure from his counsellors; but having produced an heir, he separated from his spouse, devoting himself to works of piety. This and the growing influence of the clergy on public affairs were resented by many, and the party of opposition to Wenceslas's religious policy was lucky enough to enlist the support of his brother, the energetic and ambitious Boleslas.

Henry I, it is true, was alarmed by the change in Prague and, accompanied by Arnulf of Bavaria, he made an appearance in Bohemia. The King and the Duke soon realized, however, that Boleslas had no intention of altering his country's policy towards Germany and, as the Saxon chronicler Widukind has it: "He remained faithful and useful to the Emperor as long as he [Henry I] lived."

5

The reorganization of the subjugated countries in the East was accomplished by Henry's son, Otto I (936–973), who concentrated his attention on the region between the Saale and the Elbe, as it was an important link between Saxony, Bavaria and Bohemia. He extended to this country the military system, invented by his father, of fortified castles at strategic points and entrusted its government to the notorious count Gero, whose ruthless methods extended German power as far as the rivers Neisse and Bober. Gero was long remembered by the Slavs and his deeds earned him a place in the most famous German heroic epic, the *Nibelungenlied*. After Gero's death (965) Otto I divided the territory into several marks, including Ostmark,

Lausitz and Meissen, and undertook the Christianization of the newly conquered Slavic territories. Instead of repeating the old missionary methods, he started founding bishoprics — Oldenburg, Havelberg, Brandenburg, Merseburg, Zeitz and Meissen — which became the seats of German bishops, following in the spirit of the German ecclesiastical system. All Slavic lands, according to Otto's grandiose plan, were to be under the new metropolis, Magdeburg, his own favorite foundation. Pope John XII accepted this idea in 962 and gave Otto the right to establish bishoprics in all Slavic territories, as and where it seemed expedient.

So it appeared that German political and ecclesiastical supremacy over all Slavic lands east of the Elbe was firmly established; but very soon two new and important factors began to retard German political and cultural penetration — the Bohemia of Boleslas I and Poland.

There is some evidence to show that Boleslas had difficulty in dealing with Otto I at the beginning of the latter's reign, probably because one of Boleslas's vassals had tried, unsuccessfully, to transfer his allegiance to Otto. But this dispute was settled amicably and henceforth Boleslas continued to recognize the overlordship of the Saxon. With his contingent of troops he took part in the famous battle on the Lechfeld (955) in which Otto I finally crushed the military might of the Magyars, forcing them to settle down to a more peaceful life. Boleslas not only occupied Moravia, which at that time still included the whole of modern Slovakia, but also Silesia and the rest of the former White Croatia including Cracow, and it looked as though Bohemia would become the heir of Great Moravia. This idea certainly inspired Boleslas and was not objected to by Otto I, because both Bohemian Dukes owed allegiance to him not only as Emperor (from 962 onwards) and head of western Christendom, but also as King of Germany.

It was only to be expected that this new version of the Moravian Empire would try to expand towards the north into the former White Serbia.

6

The other important factor emerging at this period was the Polish Duke Mieszko I. He is introduced into the annals of history by the chronicler Thietmar of Merseburg and by the contemporary Arab writer Ibn Jakub. According to these two authors, Mieszko — of the dynasty founded by Piast — was a mighty ruler commanding a standing army of 3,000 men whom he paid in minted money. He appears to have been master of a strong federation of Slavic tribes known since then as Poles (Polane) after the most powerful among them, and the center of his realm was Gniezno (Gnesen).

The sudden appearance of a powerful Slavic prince on the political scene of Central Europe about the middle of the tenth century has mystified many historians and, to solve this difficulty, they invented the theory that Mieszko was a Scandinavian Viking who had imposed his rule on the Slavs on the Oder and the Vistula. There is no evidence whatsoever for the view that the Piast dynasty was of a non-Slav origin. If it is recalled that Mieszko ruled over the territory which may have been the center of the primitive habitat of the Slavs — or which, at least, was in Slavic possession from after 500 B.C. — then the appearance in the tenth century of a powerful confederation in these regions ceases to be mysterious. Mieszko's state was the result of a long evolution under the leadership of an energetic Slav dynasty, an evolution which remained unrecorded because there was no chronicler to record it for posterity.

When the first Polish duke attested by history appeared on the political scene, he was about to annex the Pomeranian Slavs to his own state. Observing that the Germans also had their eyes upon this region, especially its western part including Stettin (Sczeczyn), Mieszko made a rather clever deal with Gero in 963, and in order to avoid complications with the Germans, Mieszko promised to hold the western part of Pomerania with Stettin, which he was about to conquer, as a fief of the Empire. It was an ingenious move, which allowed Mieszko to complete

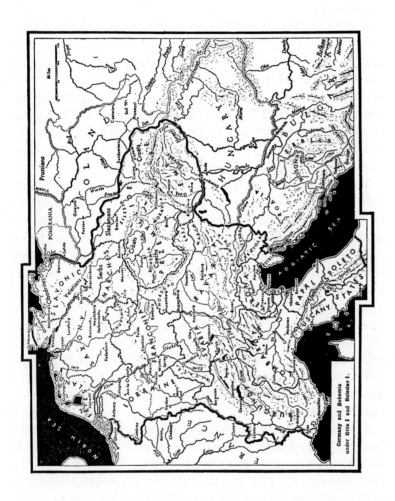

Germany and Bohemia
under Otto I and Boleslav I.

his conquest of western Pomerania without coming into conflict with the Germans. There is no evidence that Mieszko declared his whole country to be a fief of the Empire, nor was there any need for this.

But Otto's plans for Magdeburg and the Christianization of the Polabian and Baltic Slavs had opened Mieszko's eyes to another danger. He saw that it was necessary for him and his country to become Christian and to remove forever any danger of German intervention in his lands under the plea of spreading the Christian faith. Once again he made a clever move, turning not to Otto I but to Boleslas I, the Christian Duke of Bohemia. Boleslas gave Mieszko his daughter Dubravka in marriage and sent him the first Christian missionaries.

The Bohemian and Polish Dukes went even further and, probably in 966, addressed to Pope John XIII (965–972) a request that they might establish bishoprics in their countries. It was again a request which Otto could not oppose. So it came about that the Polish bishopric of Poznań (Posen) was founded about 968 and was made directly subject to Rome and not to Magdeburg. The bishopric of Prague did not come into being until 973. Otto did not oppose its foundation, but in order to gain more influence over Boleslas II, who succeeded his father in 967, he created two bishoprics, one for Prague and one for Moravia, reserving for himself the investiture of both bishops. And, again continuing the policy of his father, he subordinated the Czech bishoprics not to Salzburg, the Bavarian metropolis, but to Mainz.

So it happened that Otto's ingenious project of making Magdeburg the metropolitan see for the whole of the Slavic East could be only partially realized. Owing to further developments in the lands between the Elbe and the Oder, however, Otto's ecclesiastical foundations became almost a dead letter for at least two centuries. When in 983 the news reached the Elbe that Otto II, who had succeeded his father in 973, had been defeated by the Arabs in Calabria and had died, all the newly conquered Slavs between the Elbe, the Oder and the Baltic rose against the

CENTRAL MICHIGAN
UNIVERSITY LIBRARY

Germans and their God. Hamburg was captured, Havelberg sacked, Zeitz razed to the ground, and Brandenburg destroyed. When the tornado of this bloody revolt had passed, the Germans held only Holstein in the north and the lands of the Sorbs, and the whole work of Christianization was undone. New ways had, therefore, to be found and this task fell upon the young Emperor Otto III.

Another change of great consequence was brought about by Mieszko in the east. After consolidating his position among the Pomeranians and the tribes on the Oder and the Vistula, Mieszko began to annex the Slavic tribes of ancient White Croatia. He seems to have occupied after the defeat of the Magyars what is today Eastern Galicia, the Red cities and Přemysl, and his growing power attracted the Slavs of Silesia and of the Cracow region and impressed even the Slavniks, whose country had long ago belonged to White Croatia. Boleslas II proved less competent than his father, and seizing his opportunity, Mieszko annexed Silesia and the region of Cracow.

Thus at the end of the tenth century there emerged in Eastern Europe a mighty Slavic state which was bound soon to expand to other Slavic lands, and Otto II, engrossed in difficulties in Italy, could not intervene to change the situation. To ensure for himself the protection of the Papacy, the greatest spiritual power in Europe, Mieszko I dedicated the whole of his kingdom, from Stettin to Gdansk and from Gnesen to Cracow, to the Holy See before his death in 992. It was a clever move and Mieszko thereby initiated a tradition which was to be followed by Poland for many centuries to come.

7

The results of the rise of Poland were inevitably felt in Bohemia. That country, as has been mentioned, was divided into two dukedoms united by free consent of the two ducal families — the Přemyslides and the Slavniks. At first this partnership was very successful and the cooperation between Boleslas I and

CARNEGIE INSTITUTE
OF TECHNOLOGY LIBRARY

Slavnik led to the conquest of Moravia, Silesia and the region of Cracow. This agreement continued to operate when Boleslas II succeeded his father in Prague. The first Czech bishop of Prague, after the death of the German Dietmar, was a member of the Slavnik family, Adalbert-Vojtěch, who had been educated at Magdeburg. Adalbert was a saintly man and zealous in the missionary work of his large diocese and, owing to his intervention, the Pope consented to the suppression of the bishopric of Moravia after the death of Vracen, the only known titulary. This fulfilled an old dream of Boleslas II, who wanted the realm which he administered in association with the Slavniks to be subjected to a single bishop residing in Prague.

This peaceful collaboration between the two leading families of Bohemia was disturbed after the Polish conquest of Silesia and Cracow. When Boleslas II declared his intention of attacking the Poles to win back the lost territories, he was opposed by Soběslav, the reigning duke of the Slavnik dynasty, Adalbert's brother. This first disagreement between the two Dukes cost Adalbert the support of Boleslas II and, realising that the break between his brother and the Duke of Prague made it impossible for a Slavnik to administer the Czech Church successfully, Adalbert left Prague, intending to go on a pilgrimage to Jerusalem. The Abbot of Monte Cassino, where he stopped on his way, dissuaded him from his plan, arguing that it was not by pilgrimages but by leading a saintly life that salvation was to be won. Adalbert then resolved to enter the Greek monastery founded by St. Nilus, but in the end he became a monk in the Abbey of SS. Alexius and Boniface in Rome.

Boleslas II attacked the Poles but, lacking the support of the Slavniks, he was defeated. His prestige sank very low and he saw that the only way out of his difficulties lay in a reconciliation with his former allies. Their first condition, of course, was the restoration of the See of Prague to Adalbert, who consented reluctantly to return in 992. But this agreement lasted for only three years. New difficulties arose and Adalbert left Prague again; for it was evident that the Slavniks preferred to be allied with the Poles rather than with the Přemyslides. Boleslas II, who lacked his father's diplomatic talent, foresaw that the defection of the Slavniks would probably entail the loss of Moravia and modern Slovakia, and in desperation he decided to follow the advice of his counsellors and rid himself of the whole rival dynasty by assassination. In 995, when the Slavnik Duke Soběslav was in Germany with his army helping the Emperor to subdue a new revolt of the Slavs, Boleslas II, in spite of his promise not to take any action inimical to the Slavniks during the Duke's absence, treacherously attacked Libice, the main castle of the Slavniks, and massacred all its inhabitants, man, woman and child. This bloody act united the whole of Bohemia under the exclusive rule of the Přemyslides. Soběslav was unable to undo what had been done and took refuge with his troops in Poland. The new Polish Duke Boleslas the Great, called Chrobry (The Brave) by the Poles, welcomed him and together they awaited an opportunity for revenge against Prague.

6

The Southern Slavs, the Franks, Byzantium and Rome

Slow Hellenization of the Slavs in Greece — Byzantine, Frankish and Roman interests clash in Bulgaria; foundation of the first Slav national Church — Byzantium, the Franks, the Papacy, Serbs and Croats — Political aspirations of Symeon the Great of Bulgaria — Political union of Dalmatian and Pannonian Croatia — Evolution in Serbia, the coastal cities and Venice — The Bogomils and the disintegration of Bulgarian power — End of the first Bulgarian Empire.

While these states were emerging among the Western Slavs, other developments were ensuing among those Slavs who had penetrated into Greece, those who had mingled with the Bulgars and the Croats, and among the Slavs of modern Serbia.

The political and military weakness of Byzantium in the seventh century, when the Empire was attacked by the Persians and then by the Arabs, had given the Slavs the opportunity to settle permanently in the former province of Illyricum and in Dalmatia, and also to penetrate deeply into the interior of Greece.[1] Later the situation improved owing to the reforms introduced by the Emperor Heraclius (610–641) and brought to their full effect by the iconoclastic emperors of the Isaurian dy-

[1] On the Slavs in Greece, see the most up-to-date study by M. Vasmer "Die Slaven in Griechenland" (*Abhandl. d. Preuss. Akademie, Phil.-hist. Kl.*, Berlin, 1941). The author gives useful bibliographical notices on the subject and analyzes in an unbiased way the Slavic place names in Greece and on the islands which testify to the presence of the Slavs in those places for some time after the Slavic invasions.

On the great victory won by Justinian II in 688 over the Slavs in Greece, see the study by A. A. Vasiliev, "L'entrée triomphale de l'empéreur Justinien II à Thessalonique en 688," in *Orientalia Christiana periodica* XIII (1947), pp. 355–368. This Byzantine success was decisive for the further evolution of Greece. Justinian II also transported a great number of captive Slavs to Asia Minor where they formed an important military colony.

nasty (717–780). The whole Empire was divided into *themes*, each governed by a *strategos*, in whose hands all civil authority and military command were vested. The Empire was, of course, deprived of its eastern possessions, which were occupied by the Arabs, but it retained a firm hold on Asia Minor, the center of its economic and military resources. The position of the Empire in Macedonia, Greece and the Peloponnese was considerably strengthened during the eighth and the first part of the ninth centuries. The Slavs in Macedonia and Greece were successfully brought to heel in 783 under Constantine VI (780–797), and Irene (797–802) crushed a Slavic revolt in Greece, thereby influencing the complete Hellenization of the Slavs of this part of the Empire. The Hellenization of the Slavs in the Peloponnese started at the beginning of the ninth century, when an attempt by them to besiege Patras was frustrated after 805. Hellenization here, however, took much longer than it had in Greece, and important Slavic settlements could be found in the region of the Taygetus Mountains as late as the fifteenth century.[1]

The Christianization and Hellenization of the Slavs in Macedonia, Thrace and Epirus — at least in those parts of these provinces which remained under Byzantine rule — were pressed on with vigor during the first half of the ninth century, and it is interesting to follow the different stages of the ecclesiastical reorganization of those regions after Christianity had been utterly destroyed there. This meritorious activity of the Byzantine Church reaped its best harvest under the Patriarch Photius.

[1] For the Slavs in the Peloponnese see the recent study by A. Bon, *Le Péloponnèse byzantin jusqu'en 1204* (Paris, 1951), pp. 27–74; cf. also P. Charanis, "The Chronicle of Monembasia and the Question of the Slavonic Settlements in Greece," *Dumbarton Oaks Papers* V, 1950. Several problems concerning Slavic settlements in Greece are still debated as is shown by the controversy about the capture of Corinth: cf. Kenneth M. Setton, "The Bulgars in the Balkans and the Occupation of Corinth in the Seventh Century," *Speculum* XXV (1950), pp. 502–543; P. Charanis, "On the Capture of Corinth by the Onogurs and its Recapture by the Byzantines," *ibid.* XXVII (1952), pp. 343–350; Kenneth M. Setton, "The Emperor Constance II and the Capture of Corinth by the Onogur Bulgars," *ibid.*, pp. 351–362.

But the growing influence of the Roman See under Nicholas I was felt at an early date even in the Balkans. This territory formed the major part of the old Roman province of Illyricum, which up to the year 731 was ecclesiastically directly subject to the Roman See. Leo III, the first iconoclastic emperor, detached Illyricum from the jurisdiction of Rome and subordinated it to the patriarch of Constantinople, and although the decrees against the worship of images issued by the Emperor and his iconoclastic successors were later rescinded, the Byzantines refused to return this territory to the direct jurisdiction of Rome. Nicholas I made fresh and energetic attempts to regain at least the jurisdiction over the Slavic population of the former Illyricum, but as has been shown, the Franks were also anxious to extend their political and religious influence over the new Slavic states which were rising in the Balkans, and Bulgaria was the land where the interests of these three powers clashed most vehemently.

2

Thanks to their alliance with Great Moravia, the Byzantines were able to effect a military and cultural encirclement of Bulgaria and force Malamir's successor, Boris (852–889), to enter the cultural sphere of Byzantium. This was a great success; for it put a stop to Frankish penetration into the Balkans. But complications soon arose. The first Christian khagan of the Bulgarians, Boris-Michael, was an astute ruler who perceived very quickly that there was a chance for him to profit from the competition between the Byzantines and the Franks for influence in Bulgaria, and also that the interest which was being shown in his country by the Papacy, a new power in the West, could eventually be turned to his own advantage.

He accepted Byzantine religious supremacy; but he was very jealous of his own influence over the Church and disliked the leading part which the Byzantines were playing in the religious affairs of Bulgaria. Desiring more independence, he asked the Byzantines to give him a Patriarch, but all he received in reply (in 865) was a beautifully written and lengthy screed from Photius explaining all the most important doctrines of the Church and containing a list of the names of all the heretics who had been condemned by the holy councils in the past centuries. This was accompanied by a treatise on the duties of a Christian ruler. Boris, whose way of life was primitive and simple, did not appreciate all these platitudes, and Greek dialectics were more than his untutored intelligence could grasp. He therefore decided to ask the Pope for a patriarch and the Franks for missionaries.

This request from the Bulgarian ruler caused great rejoicing in Rome. Nicholas I seized this opportunity of bringing Bulgaria completely under Roman influence. With perfect understanding of the simple Bulgarian mind, he lost no time in sending Boris a letter, which still remains a masterpiece of psychology and pastoral theology. At the same time, he sent to Bulgaria two bishops and a number of missionaries with the object of forestalling the Franks.

Nicholas's initiative was crowned with success. Boris was so delighted to have found someone who explained to him that the Bulgarians did not commit mortal sin by wearing their trousers even after baptism — for such were the problems that troubled the primitive Bulgarian Christians — that he dismissed not only the Greek missionaries but also some Franks who had arrived in response to his own invitation. Thus, the former province of Illyricum, which could have become the bridgehead connecting West and East, became instead the battlefield of two Churches.

This Roman success naturally provoked the greatest indignation in Constantinople. The Byzantines, however, had their day in 870 when Boris, disappointed by the Pope's refusal to give him a patriarch or at least an archbishop of his own choosing, turned again to the East and accepted bishops and priests from Byzantium. Then Ignatius, who became Patriarch after the removal of Photius, is said to have sent an archbishop and some bishops to Bulgaria.

So in 880, Bulgaria became once more the object of bargaining between Rome and Byzantium when, after Ignatius' death Pope John VIII succeeded in coming to an understanding with the new Patriarch Photius and then it was agreed that Bulgaria was to be left to Roman jurisdiction. This was the price which Byzantium had to pay for the Roman See's recognition of Photius as a legitimate Patriarch.

So greatly did the Byzantines value reconciliation with Rome that they accepted this condition and the Patriarch Photius surrendered jurisdiction over Bulgaria.[1] It seems, however, that he asked Rome to leave the Greek priests there and not to replace them by Latin clergy, as had happened when Nicholas gained his temporary foothold in Bulgaria.

Contrary to the opinion of most historians of this period, this arrangement was a perfectly sincere one. There was no attempt on the part of the Byzantines to deceive Rome nor was there any re-excommunication of Photius by the Roman See. Thenceforward, until the eleventh century, peace reigned between the two Churches which had formerly quarrelled so bitterly over the jurisdiction of this part of ancient Illyricum. Nevertheless, Bulgaria did not return to Rome.

The explanation of this is to be found in the policy followed by the Khagan Boris-Michael for a number of years. This primitive but astute ruler perceived that the rivalry between Rome and Byzantium offered him his best chance of securing ecclesiastical independence for his country. He cleverly evaded all the invitations from the Pope to send an embassy to Rome to settle the details of the new agreement by which the Roman supremacy was recognized. He neither refused nor accepted anything but simply thanked the Pope for his solicitude, assured him that he and his people were in good health and expressed the cordial hope that all was well in Rome. At the same time he retained

---

[1] This concession was all the more important because the Bulgarian State comprised not only a great part of Macedonia, which belonged to Illyricum, but also a part of Thrace, which was outside this province and under the jurisdiction of the Patriarch of Constantinople. This problem is treated in F. Dvornik, *The Photian Schism, History and Legend* (Cambridge Univ. Press, 1949), pp. 210 ff.

the Greek bishops and kept them very much under his control.

Thus the quarrel between Rome and Byzantium over ancient Illyricum laid the foundations of the first national Church to arise among the peoples who had only recently been converted to Christianity. It is permissible to surmise that the Greek clergy rather encouraged Boris-Michael in his attitude of compromise. Then he was greatly favored by fortune; for Pope John VIII died and a rapid succession of three other Popes between 882 and 885 prevented any further Roman intervention in Bulgaria.

The year 885 presented Boris with another unexpected opportunity. As has been seen,[1] many of the most prominent disciples of Archbishop Methodius took refuge in Bulgaria when they were driven from Moravia, and Boris readily realized that the Slavonic alphabet and liturgy which they offered could be of great value to him in completing his ecclesiastical scheme. He also perceived that by favoring the Slavic element in his realm and in the Church, he would find the popular support necessary for his attempt to break the powerful class of the boyars who opposed his autocratic tendencies. He received the refugees from Moravia, therefore, with every honor and gave them every opportunity to continue their activities in Bulgaria. At a later date, Symeon appointed their leader, St. Clement, to the bishopric of Velica, near Ochrida.

His see became an important center of the Slavonic liturgy and Slavonic literature. By this time the Bulgarians were gradually being completely Slavicized and most of the differences which had existed between the Turko-Bulgar ruling class and their Slavic subjects were now disappearing. In Bulgaria, the disciples of Methodius naturally returned to the Greek rite translated into the Slavonic language, because this was the rite in common usage in their new home and one of them even adapted the Slavonic alphabet invented by Constantine-Cyril (later called Glagolitic), bringing it closer to the Greek alphabet. This new alphabet, which later received the name Cyrillic, is still used by all Orthodox Slavs.

[1] See above, pp. 100 ff.

It was thus in Bulgaria and not in Moravia that the first Slavonic Church was firmly established. Boris did not dare to proclaim the complete and formal independence of this Church, being quite content with at least a measure of genuine independence. The formal foundation of a special Patriarchate of Bulgaria was reserved for his son and successor, Symeon the Great, about 925. The initiative of the Bulgarian khagan was, however, of the greatest importance; for not only did his idea succeed, but it survived for centuries after having been accepted by the Serbs, the Russians and the Rumanians. It would be difficult indeed to find in all history another example of a newly converted prince so effectively influencing the evolution of Christianity.

3

In the meantime, Byzantine, Frankish and Roman interests were clashing in other parts of the Balkans and in Croatia. Among the tribes which were later to form the great Serbian nation, the most dangerous were the Narentanes, who were settled near the delta of the river Neretva (Narenta). From there this tribe occupied a number of important islands in the Adriatic — Meleta (Mljet), Korkura (Korčula), Issa (Vis), Pharus (Hvar), Barzo (Brać) — and developed into a kind of Slavic Vikings who threatened the safety of the sea route through the Adriatic from Venice to Byzantium. The Venetians therefore were most anxious to secure the friendship of the Narentanes, or at least to render them harmless. At last in 830 envoys of the Narentanes, exhorted by the Doge John, consented to be baptized in Venice. In spite of this favorable beginning, however, the Narentanes were again at war with Venice in 840. The Venetians were also alarmed at the growing maritime power of the Dalmatian Croats, who had equipped a small flotilla to defend their territory against the frequent raids of the Arabs, and in order to secure a maritime monopoly, the Venetians concluded a treaty in 840 with the Emperor Lothair I (840–855), son of

Louis I, the Pious, the conditions of which provided for the defense not only of Istria but also of the Italian coast against Arab incursions.

The Croats of Dalmatia, although nominally still under Frankish supremacy, could hardly escape the influence of the coastal cities, which were under Byzantine suzerainty. There is no information about Borna's successor, Vladislav (821–about 835), but Mislav (about 835–845) and Trpimir (845–864) were in friendly contact with the coastal cities and they granted many privileges to religious foundations there. They also transferred their residence to Klis, near Split (Spalato), in order to be nearer this center of the last Byzantine possessions on the Adriatic. The friendly relationship between Dalmatian Croatia and Byzantium was illustrated by the fact that when Zdeslav, Trpimir's heir, was deprived of the succession by Domagoj (about 864–876), he took refuge in Constantinople, where he awaited his opportunity to return to his native land.

The Byzantines were still nursing the hope of regaining control over the whole of ancient Dalmatia and their prestige grew considerably in those parts when, in 867, the Emperor Basil I (867–886) succeeded in relieving Ragusa (Dubrovnik) which had been besieged and cut off by the Arabs. The Slavic tribes of modern Serbia, with the exception of the Narentanes, recognized Byzantine overlordship and a special mission of priests headed by a high imperial official succeeded in reintroducing Christianity among them. The Serbs and the other tribes were, however, able to preserve a large measure of autonomy in the management of their own affairs.

A further Byzantine success was registered in 870. The imperial fleet attacked the coast of Dalmatian Croatia while the Croatian navy was supporting the attempt of the Emperor Louis II to capture Bari in Italy from the Arabs. As a result of this Byzantine victory even the Narentanes had to acknowledge Byzantine supremacy. Then in 874, an attempt was made to provoke a *coup d'état* in Croatia against Domagoj.

Domagoj, taking advantage of the troubles which followed the death of Louis II in 875, refused to accept the supremacy of Carloman, son of Louis the German, who according to a previous agreement was supposed to take over Bavaria with its Slavic vassals. Carloman's army, led most probably by Kocel of Upper Pannonia, was defeated (876) by Domagoj's successor, his son Jljko. Kocel, the unfortunate son of Pribina, lost his life in this battle, and afterwards it seems that Upper Pannonia was ruled by Prince Brasla (Braslav).

Once Byzantine prestige in the coastal cities had been restored and the Slavic tribes in modern central and southern Serbia were under Byzantine supremacy, the time was judged to be propitious for the realization of Byzantine aspirations in Dalmatian Croatia, and in 878, Zdeslav invaded and defeated Jljko, son of the usurper Domagoj. The situation seemed extremely grave for the Croats and for the Latin Church. If the Byzantines and their ally Zdeslav could confirm and consolidate their hold over Dalmatian Croatia, Byzantine political influence, Byzantine culture and perhaps also the Greek rite would be extended, possibly forever, over the whole of the Balkans and over Dalmatia and ancient Pannonia. The Eastern Church would have extended its influence to the very gates of Italy and Germany, and there would never have been any difference between the Croats, who belonged culturally to Western Europe, and the Serbs, whose civilization was essentially Eastern.

But Western influence was already firmly established among the Croats and the situation was saved by the Croat Church. The elected Bishop of Nin, Theodosius, was jealous of the growing influence of Spalato, whose bishop was claiming jurisdiction over the whole of Dalmatia as heir of the Metropolitan of ancient Salona and realized that his power would be broken if the Byzantines were victorious. So he became leader of the anti-Byzantine opposition and worked steadily to prepare for the downfall of Zdeslav. The national Croat party rallied round Branimir, who is of unknown origin, and Zdeslav, ill-supported by Byzantium, was defeated and killed in 879.[1] Branimir (879–

[1] Professor R. Jakobson notes that the Slavic hagiographical tradition con-

892) became ruler of the country, but after his death the old dynasty of Trpimir was reinstated on the Croatian throne. The narrow escape which the Western Church had in Croatia was of the utmost importance for Western civilization and in spite of occasional fluctuations in later years, the boundary between East and West remained forever at the gates of Croatia.

The importance of these events is enhanced by the fact that soon afterwards, or perhaps at the same time, the Slavonic liturgy in use in Moravia began slowly to penetrate through Pannonia and Pannonian Croatia, into Dalmatian Croatia. This time, it was the liturgy of the Roman rite, which was also in use in Moravia. The history of this penetration is not known, but it was slow and pacific and it can best be understood if it is recalled that Pannonian Croatia was a part of the diocese of Sirmium, which was formed for the Archbishop Methodius.[1] What this would have meant had Byzantium won the day in Dalmatian Croatia can be gauged by what happened in Bulgaria.

The Slavonic liturgy took firm root in Dalmatia, where it sur-

---

nects the downfall of Zdeslav with the intervention of Methodius. (See the "Short Life of Methodius" published in the *Fontes Rerum Bohemicarum* I, p. 75.) This tradition seems to be based on some facts; unfortunately the evidence quoted is slender and confused. Methodius was in Moravia during the Croatian crisis and he went to Rome in 880, summoned by the Pope, who was alarmed by accusations launched against the Moravian Metropolitan. It seems that the Pope was informed about these accusations by the priest John of Venice, who was the Pope's agent at the courts of the Slavic princes and who played a role in the Croatian reversal. This does not seem to warrant the above tradition. Methodius may, however, have visited Dalmatian Croatia on his return from Rome, perhaps at the request of the Pope John VIII, who was anxious to attach Croatia more closely to Rome. It is possible that the Slavonic liturgy, approved by the Pope in 880, started to spread in Dalmatia at that time and that the Pope used Methodius's influence and the Slavonic liturgy to detach the Croats from Constantinople. In this way we can explain how it happened that Methodius's name was mentioned in connection with Zdeslav's downfall.

[1] We have very little information on the spread of the Slavonic liturgy in Pannonian Croatia and only a few writers have dealt with this problem. For more details see the study by F. Fancev, "The Oldest Liturgy in Pannonian Croatia" (*Zbornik Kralja Tomislava* [Zagreb, 1925], pp. 509–553), written in Croat with a résumé in French.

vived for many centuries and is still in use in some places along the Dalmatian coast [1] as a curious reminder of the struggles between the Franks, the Slavs, Byzantium and Rome for political and cultural supremacy in Central and Southeastern Europe in the ninth century.

There is one other fact that deserves special mention and that has not yet been noticed by historians. It is curious to note in the letters of the Popes of this period — Nicholas I, Hadrian II and John VIII — addressed to the Slavic princes of Moravia, Croatia and Bulgaria, that the writers particularly stress the fidelity of these princes to St. Peter. This is the first stage in the development of the theocratic theory later emphasized by so many Popes of the Middle Ages, especially Gregory VII and Innocent III, for as early as the second half of the ninth century, Rome was trying to bring the new realms under its special protection and to make them the instruments of its policy.

4

Thus it happened that Byzantium failed to realize all its political aspirations in the Balkans. It did, however, win a great cultural victory in eliminating the Franks and the Papacy from Bulgaria and in securing a firmer cultural hold over the Slavs of modern Serbia. Boris of Bulgaria eventually became a very good Christian and resigned his throne in 889 in favor of his son Vladimir to become a monk. Only once did he leave his solitary retreat and that was when Vladimir began to support a pagan reaction in his country. Boris then exchanged his monk's garb for the accoutrement of the soldier. He called his faithful boyars together, defeated the rebels, punished his son by putting out his eyes, and returned to his monastery to continue his meditations, conscious of having completed an act of much piety.

---

[1] The best known specialist on Slavonic liturgy and literature in Dalmatia is J. Vajs, Professor at Charles IV University in Prague. See his bibliographical data in *Slovanské Studie*, published in Prague in 1948 by J. Vašica.

But the new khagan, Symeon (893–927), Vladimir's younger brother, proved to be much more dangerous to the Byzantines than Boris had been. His pious father had planned an ecclesiastical career for him, and to this end had had him educated at the patriarchal academy in Byzantium. He became, indeed, a distinguished Greek theologian and it is of no small interest to study the letters which the learned Patriarch Nicholas Mysticus exchanged with him at the time when the Tsar was pounding at the gates of Constantinople.

Already in 894 the Byzantines had to experience the consequences of the change in the Bulgarian political situation. Symeon, complaining that the Byzantines had violated the commercial treaty with Bulgaria, invaded the territory of the Empire and routed the imperial army. Seeing that they were unable to bring Symeon to a halt by their own resources, the Byzantines persuaded the Magyars — who at that time were established in the steppes of southern Russia — to attack the Bulgars in the rear. This sudden onslaught, combined with the dangerous manoeuvres of the Byzantine army and navy, was formidable; but Symeon withstood it. He concluded an armistice with the Byzantines and with the help of the Turkic Pechenegs (Patzinaks), the new invaders of southern Russia, he inflicted such heavy losses on the Magyars that they retired and did not return. This reversal seems to have induced them to invade Moravia and to settle down in Hungary. They also occupied the lands between the river Tisza and the Carpathian Mountains, a territory which had belonged to Bulgaria since the time of Krum, but in which the Bulgars had never shown any particular interest.

After dealing with the Magyars, Symeon turned against the Byzantines and cut their army to pieces. In the peace treaty of 896, the Byzantines promised to pay a yearly tribute to the young Bulgarian ruler.

From that time onwards, Symeon's power grew steadily and he extended his influence over almost all Serbian tribes and his lands prospered. His reign inaugurated the golden age of Greco-Slavic civilization when Slavonic literature flourished in Bulgaria, and under Symeon's inspiration numerous important Greek works on theology and history and other sciences were translated into Slavonic. His capital Preslav was embellished by many churches and palaces, imitations of Byzantine art and architecture.

Symeon, however, did not intend to content himself with his splendid Bulgarian residence. During his studies in Byzantium the young prince had become almost a Greek. He was deeply imbued with the Byzantine political conception, according to which the Emperor of Constantinople was the only representative of God on earth and the supreme ruler of the Christian commonwealth. Symeon's greatest ambition was to transport his capital from Preslav in Bulgaria to Constantinople itself and there to supplant the Byzantine emperors.

At first, Fate seemed to favor his plan. In 912 the Emperor Leo VI died and his brother and successor Alexander refused to fulfill the stipulations of the peace treaty of 896. Symeon, now at the height of his power, welcomed this opportunity to reopen hostilities. The debauched Alexander died in June, 913, and taking advantage of the disorders which followed at Byzantium, Symeon invaded Thrace. A military revolt had deprived the government of the means to oppose the Bulgarians and the way to the capital thus lay open. Shortly afterwards the gates of the city "guarded by God" shook to the triumphant shouts of Symeon's soldiers.

The situation seemed desperate for the Byzantines. The new Emperor Constantine VII Porphyrogennetus, the legitimate heir, was still a mere child and the Patriarch Nicholas Mysticus, who presided over the Regency Council, thought it necessary to enter into negotiations with the victorious Bulgarian in order to save the city and secure the throne for the young Emperor. Symeon knew well that, without a navy, it was hardly possible to take the city by assault and was, therefore, ready to negotiate. The agreement that followed arranged that the young Emperor should marry Symeon's daughter and that Symeon should be crowned as co-emperor.

The Bulgarian Empire under Tsar Symeon (893–927)

The coronation ceremony was performed in the imperial palace by the Patriarch in the presence of the young Emperor and the members of the Regency Council. Contrary to what many historians say, it was not a mock ceremony, but a genuine coronation [1] and the Bulgarian monarch became thus Basileus. The question is whether the Byzantines had acknowledged, on that occasion, Symeon as the Basileus of Bulgarians only, or of the Bulgarians and of the Romaeans, as the Byzantines called themselves, thus stressing that they were Rome's heirs.

Symeon seemed to be at the threshold of the realization of his ambitious dreams; for as co-emperor and Basileopator — the Emperor's father-in-law — he would be able to direct the policy of the Empire. Then, loaded with rich presents, the new Basileus returned to his residence in Preslav.

Unfortunately, his luck did not last. By the intervention of an ambitious and proud lady the possibility of a peaceful amalgamation of Bulgaria and the Byzantine Empire was prevented forever. Zoe, Constantine VII's mother, who had been removed from the palace by Alexander, came back to power and took the Regency into her hands. She was horrified at the idea that her son should marry a "barbarian" princess, and repudiated the agreement made by the Patriarch with Symeon.

Symeon, greatly disappointed by this turn of events, invaded the Empire, but in 917 the Byzantines then prevailed upon the Turkic Pechenegs to attack Wallachia and as a result the Bulgarians lost all their possessions on the left bank of the Danube, which were, however, of little importance to them. Because of a lack of agreement between the imperial agent who was leading the Pecheneg hordes and the admiral Romanus Lecapenus, who had to transport them into Bulgaria proper, the worst was averted for Symeon and he was able to inflict two subsequent crushing defeats on the imperial army. The Byzantines created

[1] Cf. G. Ostrogorsky's and F. Dölger's studies dealing with this problem published in the *Bulletin de l'Institut Archéol. Bulgare* IX, 1935 ("Die Krönung Symeons von Bulgarien," pp. 276–286; "Bulgarisches Cartum und Byzant. Kaisertum," pp. 57–68).

a diversion by urging the Serbs to rise against Symeon but, in the end, their attempts proved vain. If Symeon had appeared before Constantinople in 918, when the power of the Empress was crumbling because of the disastrous military defeats and when the city was on the brink of anarchy, he might have achieved his aim with the help of the Empress's enemies. However, for unknown reasons, Symeon missed this opportunity and the Regency was taken over by a new upstart, the Armenian peasant Romanus Lecapenus.

Refusing to accept the new situation, Symeon continued his bloody invasions hoping to enforce the deposition of the new rival who, in the meantime, married his daughter to the young Emperor and became the reigning Emperor. The exhortations addressed to Symeon by the Patriarch and by the Emperor himself were all in vain and the Bulgarian continued to use the title "Basileus and autocrator of Bulgarians and Romaeans." In this mood he established the independence of the Bulgarian Church about 925 by the foundation of a special Bulgarian Patriarchate. Symeon's negotiations with the Fatimid Calif of Africa to secure the help of the Arab fleet against Constantinople were luckily checkmated by Byzantine diplomacy and money. But not even after his interview with the Emperor and the Patriarch under the walls of Constantinople in 924 was Symeon reconciled to the evil change in his fortunes.

It has been suggested by F. Šišić and V. N. Zlatarski, the leading Croatian and Bulgarian historians, that Symeon finally turned to Pope John X with the request for recognition of his imperial title, asking the Pope to send him a crown and scepter and to confirm the establishment of an independent Bulgarian Patriarchate. There is no evidence for such a *démarche* from Symeon's side. It is true that John X had sent his legates — whose main function was to investigate the religious situation in Croatia and to preside at the Synod of Spalato — to Bulgaria in order to promote peace between the Tsar Symeon and the Croat King Tomislav. Symeon, anxious to secure his western frontier before launching his final attack against the Byzantine Emperor, had

132 EARLY SLAVIC CIVILIZATION

sent an army against the Croats, then the Emperor's allies. His army, however, suffered a major defeat and Symeon was preparing a new campaign. The Pope feared that the new war would compromise Rome's interests in Croatia, then being ecclesiastically reorganized under the primate of Spalato. He himself took the initiative and sent his legates to Symeon. According to the Acts of the Synod of Spalato, their intervention met with success and peace was concluded between Symeon and Tomislav.

There is, however, no contemporary evidence that Symeon on this occasion addressed a request to the Pope for recognition of his imperial dignity, or for a crown and a scepter. Symeon, who was so deeply imbued with Byzantine political ideas, could hardly have thought of addressing such a request to the Pope. The only argument brought forward in favor of such a supposition — the letter of Kaloyan (from the year 1204), the founder of the second Bulgarian Empire, to Pope Innocent III [1] — is not conclusive. In the thirteenth century, when the papal theory of the supremacy of the spiritual power over the temporal was universally recognized, the situation was quite different, but ideas which were current in the thirteenth and fourteenth centuries must not be transferred to the tenth century. Symeon would have gained nothing from the recognition of his dignity by the Pope and he never took any steps to seek it.

Fate denied Symeon the realization of his ambitious dreams. Before he was able to organize a new campaign for the conquest of Constantinople, he died in 927 and when the news reached Constantinople the whole Empire gave a long sigh of relief. The Byzantines could now happily forget the humiliating scene

---

[1] Kaloyan claims in his letter that, after carefully examining the writings dealing with the reigns of his predecessors Symeon, Peter and Samuel, he found that they had all received their crowns from the Roman See. This is in contradiction to his previous letter in which he says simply that Peter and Samuel had the imperial title, without mentioning Symeon or Rome. The astute prince exaggerates in order to curry favor with the Pope. There is certainly no evidence that the Tsars Peter and Samuel received the crown from the Pope. Why should his statement concerning Symeon be accepted literally?

which had taken place in the imperial palace in 913 and, in order to cover up the fact and to save the honor of the Empire, the rumor was circulated that Symeon's coronation was not a valid one, because the Patriarch had deceived Symeon by placing on his head, instead of the imperial diadem, only the cover of his head-dress. Symeon the Logothetes, followed by Skylitzes, recorded this rumor in his *Annals* and led many historians into error.

5

It was inevitable that the swift rise of Bulgaria under Symeon should influence the development of Croatia and Serbia, and the Croats benefited considerably by the decline of East Frankish (German) power at the end of the ninth century. At the same time the Dalmatian Croats became independent and it was thought that the propitious moment had arrived for the Croats to create a political union of Dalmatian and Pannonian tribes. This was achieved by the Duke of the Dalmatian Croats, Tomislav (910–928), the successor of Mutimir (892–c.910), and during his reign Pannonian and Dalmatian Croatia were welded into one. The motive of the Pannonian Croats in desiring the union was most probably dictated by the Magyar danger. Tomislav assumed the title of King of the Croats and, in 925, he was recognized as such by the Pope John X. It was an important turning point in Croat history.

In Serbia proper — a territory generally called Raška in the Middle Ages — there reigned the dynasty of *župans*, founded by Višeslav about the year 780, and after the death of his third successor, Vlastimir (about 835–860), the country was governed by Vlastimir's three sons, Mutimir, Strojimir and Gojnik. Mutimir was the prince who had been exhorted by Pope John VIII to join the metropolis of Sirmium, founded for St. Methodius. He governed alone after driving his brothers from the country, a usurpation of power which was responsible for long dynastic struggles after his death (about 890) between his brothers' sons and grandsons. These struggles were cleverly exploited for their own ends by Serbia's neighbors, especially Bulgaria and Byzantium. The most energetic of these later princes was Peter, son of Gojnik (891–917), who extended Serbian domination over the Narentanes. But when Peter agreed to a Byzantine proposal that he should attack Symeon of Bulgaria, the latter, warned of the plan by Michael, Prince of Hum (Zachlumje, modern Herzegovina), swiftly placed another pretender on the Serbian throne. Further Serbian intrigues with the Byzantines resulted in the complete occupation of Serbia proper by Symeon of Bulgaria. Only the Prince of Hum preserved his independence, first as an ally of Bulgaria and then as a supporter of Byzantium.

During the Bulgaro-Byzantine wars there was a dangerous possibility that the Bulgarians would advance as far as the Adriatic and conquer the Dalmatian cities which were still in Byzantine hands. Unable to check this menace alone, the Emperor Romanus I (919–944) ceded all the towns and islands of Dalmatia to the Croat King Tomislav in order to secure his neutrality in the struggle with the terrible Bulgarian. Tomislav was given the title of proconsul and was supposed to rule over the "theme of Dalmatia" as the Emperor's representative.

This new situation found its expression and confirmation in the first important provincial Council of the Croat Lands, held in 925 at Spalato. Some of the Serbian princes, driven from their own territory by the Bulgarians, were present at the meeting, together with all the Dalmatian bishops and abbots headed by the Bishop of Nona (Nin) and King Tomislav himself. This was the first Serbo-Croatian demonstration ever to be held in Dalmatia. At this meeting the Archbishop of Spalato was proclaimed Metropolitan of the whole Adriatic seaboard from Istria to Cattaro and three years later another Council held at Spalato confirmed this decision by suppressing the first Croat bishopric of Nona.

Bulgarian pressure on Serbian territory and its princes diminished after the death of Symeon in 927. In 931, the prince of Serbia proper, Česlav, revolted and, with the help of the Byzantines, the Croats and the Prince of Hum, regained his independence under nominal Byzantine sovereignty. Taking advantage of troubles in Croatia after the death of Tomislav, he was even able to extend his possessions by occupying Bosnia, which, until then, appears to have formed part of Croatia.[1] The Narentanes on the Dalmatian coast began their sea-borne raids once again. Venice had to take up arms against them and eventually defeated them in 948.

The complications which followed the death of Tomislav resulted in the loss of direct political control of the theme of Dalmatia by his successors, the legendary Trpimir II (about 928–935), Kresimir I (about 935–945), Miroslav (945–949), and the imperial proconsul of Zadar (Zara) took over the administration.

The prestige of Croatia began to rise again under King Kresimir II (949–969), who regained Bosnia and restored good relations with the coastal cities, and his son Stephen Držislav (969–997), who succeeded him, brought the realm to a new high level of strength and power. Byzantium could not remain blind to this fact and did not hesitate to acknowledge it. In 986 the Emperor Basil II sent the royal insignia to Držislav and restored him to the governorship of the Dalmatian theme. The Croat King then became *eparchos* and received the high-ranking title of Patricius and for the first time the King officially described himself as "Rex Croatiae et Dalmatiae."

But Dalmatia had long been coveted by another power rising on the Adriatic — Venice. Under the leadership of the doges of the Orseolo family, Venice grew more and more conscious of her power and in 996 Peter II Orseolo (991–1009) refused to pay the annual tribute due to the King of Croatia. Taking advantage of the fact that Držislav's sons and successors, Svetoslav (997–1000), Kresimir and Gojslav, who should have shared the throne,

[1] The territory called Bosnia at that time comprised only the upper valley of the river Bosna to the middle Drina. I am dealing with the problems of Croatian and Serbian history to the eleventh century more thoroughly in the commentary to chs. 27–36 of Constantine Porphyrogennetus' *De Admin. Imperio* in the forthcoming second volume of the edition by Gy. Moravcsik and R. J. H. Jenkins.

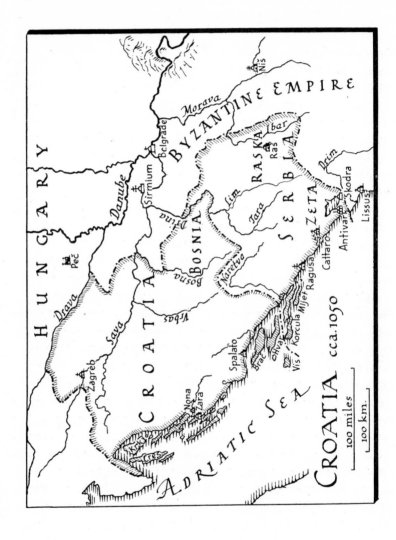

had started to quarrel among themselves, Venice concluded an agreement with Byzantium by which the Emperor ceded to her his nominal sovereignty over the Dalmatian towns and islands, and in the year 1000 the Doge Peter II occupied the whole Adriatic seaboard, taking the title of "Dux Dalmatiae."

Years of rivalry between Croatia and Venice were the result, both parties striving to hold or to reconquer the Adriatic coast. King Kresimir III (1000–c. 1030), who made his brother Gojslav (1000–1020) co-regent, having concluded a peace treaty with Venice, renounced the tribute which the Republic had refused to pay and agreed that the Doge should assume the title of "Dux Dalmatiae." His son received Orseolo's daughter in marriage (1008). But in spite of these concessions the struggle for Dalmatia went on.

In 1018 even Croatia acknowledged the supremacy of Byzantium when Basil II, after destroying the Bulgarian Empire, stood on the frontiers of Croatia. As Patricius of the Byzantine Empire — the title was given to him by the Emperor — Kresimir III thought perhaps that he was entitled to occupy the theme of Dalmatia when the Orseolos were driven from power in Venice, but he was mistaken. The Byzantines intervened and from 1024 onwards the coastal cities again came under the direct supremacy of Byzantium and were governed by the imperial proconsul of Zadar (Zara). Further attempts made by Kresimir III and his successor Stephen I (about 1030–1058) to regain control over these cities, with the help of the Hungarian king St. Stephen, were not successful.

Only Peter Kresimir IV (1058–1073) met with any success. He extended Croatian sovereignty once more over the whole Byzantine theme of Dalmatia. This happened probably about 1069, when the Emperor Romanus IV (1068–1071), hard pressed by the Seljuk Turks in Asia and fearing that the Normans from Sicily might get a foothold on the Adriatic, consented to the incorporation of the small Dalmatian theme into the Croatian kingdom. Kresimir IV extended his power as far as the Narenta. He ruled in the coastal cities not as proconsul or imperial repre-

sentative — as Kings Tomislav and Držislav had done — but as
sovereign, and in his royal charters he proudly called the Adriatic "nostrum Dalmaticum mare." Croatian power was at its
height.

6

Byzantium was not especially concerned in interfering with
the growth of Croatian power. The country was too far from
the Empire's immediate interests to warrant any particular anxiety. But Bulgaria was close at hand and her power was still
redoubtable. Here, the Byzantines were favored by fortune.
Symeon's son and successor, Peter (927–969), was a pious man,
but lacking his father's energy and ambition. He was granted
the title of "Basileus of the Bulgarians" and married the Emperor's granddaughter. He made peace with Byzantium and
Greek influence began to grow strong once more in Bulgaria.
This unpopular move provoked a new insurrection of the national
party in Bulgaria.

Popular discontent with the growing Greek influence at the
Bulgarian court found a curious expression in the rise of a new
heretical sect, the Bogomils, whose teaching was a development
of the dualistic doctrine of the Manichaeans of Persian origin and
their heirs, the Paulicians. The latter were very numerous in
the border districts between the Arab and the Byzantine Empires
in Asia Minor. In the eighth century thousands of Paulician
families had been transferred by the Byzantine emperors from
Asia Minor into the Balkans. This was done in order to break
their power, which was dangerous not only to Orthodox doctrine
but also to the State on account of their alliance with the Arabs.
While the Paulicians mixed naturally with the Slavic peoples
in their new habitat, a considerable number remained faithful
to their old creed. The Bogomil sect rose to power in the tenth
century owing to the activities of a sectarian leader called Bogomil.

The Bogomils believed that the visible world was created by
Satanael, the first son of God, who had been rejected — with his

angels — by his father because he revolted against him. Satanael created also the body of man; but the soul was a product of God the Father. In order to save the human race, God the Father sent his second son — the Word — into the world. He entered into the body of the Virgin Mary through the ear, was born, and taught men how to defeat the world and its creator. Through his apparent suffering and death — he could not suffer in reality, being God's son — he liberated man, deprived Satanael of his divine nature — henceforth the latter is called only Satan — and took his place at the right side of God-Father.

The sectarians rejected the Mass, the Sacraments, all images and the Cross, because they were connected with *materia* which was the work of Satan. They also opposed marriage and taught civil disobedience. They accepted only the New Testament and the Psalms, claiming that the Old Testament was the work of Satan. Details of their origin and their beliefs are not thoroughly known. There is still some mystery about the way the sect spread through the Balkans and about its influence on the origins of the Albigensians or Catharists of Albi, who became so well known in northern Italy and southern France in the twelfth and thirteenth centuries.

The Bogomils played an important role in Balkan history. On occasions they succeeded in gathering round them the national and popular opposition to the Greeks, the official Church and the nobility. All this greatly weakened the Bulgarian State, which also suffered considerably at that time from the incursions of the Magyars and Pechenegs.

The Byzantines followed this development with the keenest interest. It has already been shown how in 931 they had secretly supported the revolt of the Serbian prince Česlav (d. 960), and the Emperor Nicephorus Phocas (963–969), infuriated with the Tsar's request for the payment of tribute — or, rather, of the dowry of the Tsaritsa Mary-Irene, a Byzantine princess, which was to have been paid in instalments from 927 but ceased after her death in 965 — decided to break the Bulgarian State, which was still regarded as dangerous. He was able to persuade the adventurous Russian prince Svjatoslav (962–972)[1] to invade Bulgaria. This took place in 967 when the Russians from Kiev crossed the frontier near the Danube delta and occupied the eastern part of Bulgaria. Svjatoslav intended to keep this territory forever and even to transfer his capital to Perejaslavec (Little Preslav). But the sudden and violent attack launched by the Pechenegs on Kiev forced him to abandon this plan and depart from the lands he had conquered (968).

He returned, however, in the next year when he had routed the Pechenegs and destroyed the Khazar empire. Then the new Bulgarian Tsar, Boris II (969–972), had to go through a very difficult period; for the whole of the western part of his realm refused him obedience, the remainder was overrun by the Russians, and he was taken prisoner by the invading army. Svjatoslav, emboldened by success and greedy for yet more spoils and tribute, rejected the peace offer of the Byzantine Emperor John Tzimisces (969–976) and attacked the army of Byzantium, but he was defeated and in 971 the Emperor expelled the Russians from eastern Bulgaria. After a desperate and futile attempt to escape with his army from Dristra (Dorostol, Silistria), the last fortress besieged by the Byzantines, Svjatoslav had to acknowledge final defeat. He had to evacuate eastern Bulgaria, which became a Byzantine province, and to content himself with a commercial treaty with the Empire. On his way back to Kiev he was cruelly murdered by his old enemies the Pechenegs.

The Byzantines won the cooperation of the Bulgarians against their common enemy only because they posed as the liberators of Bulgaria, but in point of fact, after the defeat of the Russians, the whole eastern part of the country was occupied by Byzantine forces and Boris II was taken to Constantinople where he was obliged to provide a spectacle for the triumphal procession of the Emperor. Even the Bulgarian Patriarchate, the seat of which had been probably transferred according to the stipulations of the treaty of 927 to Dristra (Dorostol) was completely destroyed.

[1] On Svjatoslav, see below, pp. 202–204.

7

Only the western part of the Bulgarian Empire, comprising Macedonia, southern Albania and western Moesia, continued to exist as an independent country. Its first ruler was Nicholas, formerly a provincial governor, who drifted away from the rest of Bulgaria, probably after the death of Peter. He was followed by his sons, David, Moses, Aaron and Samuel. After the death of his brothers — Aaron died in 987 — Samuel ruled alone as tsar from c. 996 to 1014. The Bulgarian capital was transferred from Prespa to Ochrida and this city represented the national aspirations of all Bulgarians. A Patriarch, Gabriel or Germanos, was established, first at Sofia and Prespa, while his successor, Philip, resided at Ochrida. The Tsar Boris II and his brother Romanus looked to this territory as the sole hope of their nation, and when they succeeded in escaping from Constantinople, they fled to join Samuel. Boris lost his life at a spot near the frontier, and his brother, having arrived safely, was obliged to surrender all his rights to his host.

The aspirations of Samuel were certainly significant. It was his intention to unite all the Balkan Slavs under the leadership of Bulgaria and to use this combined force to crush Byzantium, the only power which could stand in the way of the realization of his dream. The situation seemed to favor his plans; for Byzantium was having to fight the Saracens in Asia and in Sicily, while in Italy she was faced with the pretensions of the German Emperor Otto II. Samuel's initial successes can, indeed, be explained by these Byzantine difficulties; for his first invasion of Byzantium swept all opposition before it. He pushed as far as the Peloponnese and defeated Basil II (976–1025), when the Byzantine Emperor attempted (in 986) a drive towards Sofia. Then Samuel started upon his campaign for the reunion of the Southern Slavs.

He invaded Serbia proper, defeated Vladimir, Prince of Dioclea,[1] overran Bosnia and the region of Srem, and reached

[1] Prince Vladimir of Dioclea seems to have been an ally of the Emperor

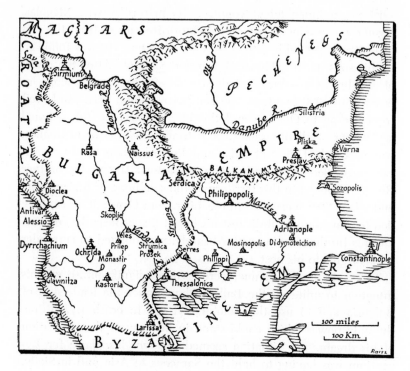

The Bulgarian Empire under Tsar Samuel (976–1014)

the Adriatic coast south of Cetinje. He occupied present-day Herzegovina and put an end to the temporary independence of Dioclea and Trebinje. Even the fierce Narentanes had to bow to the Bulgarian yoke. All these victories were great achievements, and there were times when the realization of the old dream of reuniting all the Balkan Slavic peoples under one leader seemed very near.

But all was in vain. The Byzantines were slowly but surely gathering their strength. Samuel's ambitions could not be extended to Croatian territory; for his attention was once more absorbed by events on the Byzantine frontier.

The great Emperor and general Basil II succeeded in bringing hostilities in Asia Minor to a conclusion and after the year 990 he was ready to deal with any threat from Bulgaria. A long and bitter struggle commenced, brutal and bloody and conducted mercilessly on both sides, each in turn exhibiting Oriental and Balkan fury and cruelty. The different epic phases of the struggle have been depicted in a masterly fashion by the French scholar G. Schlumberger, who did so much to revive Byzantine studies. There were scenes in this terrific conflict which surpassed anything which the genius of a Shakespeare could have imagined in the way of ghastliness and ferocious cruelty. There are few more horrible deeds in history than the blinding of 15,000 Bulgarian prisoners by the merciless victor, who spared one eye of one man in every hundred so that he might lead his helpless comrades back to the court of the unhappy Tsar. This happened in 1014, after the terrible and overwhelming defeat of the Bulgarians near Thessalonika. Well did Basil II merit his notorious

---

Basil II. A Serbian embassy to the Emperor is mentioned in an Act of Mount Athos (G. Ostrogorsky, "Une ambassade serbe auprès de l'empéreur Basile II," *Byzantion* XIX [1949], pp. 187–194). It may be that Basil II had entrusted the prince with the administration of Durazzo, as suggested by Ostrogorsky. The embassy should be dated between 990 and 992. The envoys went by sea and were surprised on a small island near Lemnos by Arab pirates, were captured and freed through the intervention of the Emperor. The occupation of Dioclea should thus be dated not in 986, but about 993. Vladimir was reinstated in Dioclea by Samuel as his vassal.

Kingdom of Dioclea *cca.* 1080

See page 282

title — *Bulgaroctonos,* Killer of the Bulgarians. At the sight of his blinded army, the Bulgarian leader fell dead (October 6, 1014).

The struggle continued under his successors Gabriel-Radomir and John-Vladislav. Yet hate, treachery and murder within the Bulgarian royal family all served to help the Greeks. In 1018 the campaign was definitely concluded. The Bulgarian Empire was annexed, together with all the lands once conquered by Samuel, and, as has already been pointed out, Byzantine supremacy was extended, at least nominally, over Croatia. In the following year the aged Emperor entered the Golden Gate of Constantinople in triumph, surrounded by vast loads of spoils and captive Bulgarians, sons of a state once so powerful, now brought so low.

Thus Bulgaria became a Byzantine province and was divided into several themes, or administrative units. At the same time, the independent ecclesiastical organization of the country was terminated. The Patriarchate of Ochrida vanished; but in the early days of their rule over Bulgaria, the Byzantines wisely refrained from depriving the Bulgarians of their language and national institutions. Basil II suppressed the Patriarchate; but Ochrida remained an independent archbishopric under the Patriarch of Constantinople and was granted important privileges.[1] Its jurisdiction extended over all bishoprics existing on the territory of the former western and eastern Bulgaria, but the appointment of the archbishop was reserved to the Emperor. Basil II's successors manifested, however, less statesmanship than the great Basileus. All Bulgarian and even the Serbian bishoprics were handed over to Greek priests. Nevertheless, in spite of some attempts to suppress it, the Slavonic liturgy survived this national disaster.

As the grip of the Byzantines over Bulgaria grew tighter from 1037 onwards, a number of insurrections broke out. The most

[1] Cf. J. Granić, "Kirchenrechtliche Glossen zu den vom Kaiser Basileus II dem autokephalen Erzbistum von Ochrida verliehenen Priviligien," *Byzantion* XII (1937), pp. 395–415.

dangerous occurred in the years 1040 and 1072. Many events conspired to prevent the Byzantines from reaping the full benefit of their occupation or enjoying the fruits of their conquest in peace and also hampered the natural evolution of Bulgarian national life. These were the invasions of the Pechenegs, the Hungarians and especially the Turkic Cumans (1064); the invasion of the Normans under Robert Guiscart (1081–1085); another Norman invasion under Boemund of Tarento in 1107; and troubles caused by the increased influence of the Bogomils. Not until the end of the twelfth century did Bulgaria emerge again as an independent country.

Old Slavonic Culture and Literature
and Their Byzantine Background

*Byzantine cultural influences in Moravia — Cultural and political evo-
lution of the Croats — Main features of early Bulgarian civilization —
Social and religious organization of the Serbs — Literary activity
of SS. Constantine-Cyril and Methodius — Achievements of Old
Slavonic literature in Bohemia — Traces of Moravian culture in Poland
and Pannonia — Slavonic liturgy and letters in Croatia — St. Clement,
founder of the Slavonic school of Ochrida — The school of Preslav and
some Slavo-Byzantine literary problems — Historical literature in Bulgaria — Literary activity of the Bogomils.*

It was only to be expected that the first attempts to rise to a
higher cultural level which were made by the Slavic nations,
newly converted to Christianity by Byzantine missionaries,
should be under strong Byzantine influence. In the case of
Moravia, however, Byzantine influence, especially in art and
architecture, has been generally underestimated. It was thought
that the main inspiration in these fields came from the Carolingian Empire; but in the light of new archaeological evidence this
opinion should now be thoroughly revised. Excavations made
recently in southern Moravia reveal that this part of the country
formed the political and religious center of the Great Moravian
Empire. Remnants of important settlements with fortifications
were discovered on the banks of the river Dyje (Thaya), a
tributary of the Morava, and in the region between the Dyje and
the Danube. This region, now divided between Moravia and
Lower Austria, was an important part of Great Moravia. Another prominent outpost was the fortified settlement at Děvín —
Dovina of the German annals — at the confluence of the Morava

and the Danube, near modern Bratislava. The excavations made near Staré Město, on the middle Morava, yielded particularly rich archaeological material.

It seems that the basis of Moravian political power was formed by the union of four Slavic tribes, governed by tribal chiefs, under the leadership of one of them, the founder of the Mojmir dynasty. An analysis made recently by Czech archaeologists of the pottery found in different regions of Moravia and in Austria helps to locate the four tribes with precision. Each had its fortified places and its centers of political and religious life. This unification was effected under the threat of the growing expansion of the Franks towards the Danube and beyond it, which started at the end of the eighth century.

No information is available concerning the political organization of this Slavic State. It can, however, be supposed that the different Moravian tribes preserved, at first, their primitive organization. With time, the unification made further progress, and during the ninth century the differences between the tribes were rapidly disappearing. The newly conquered territories — Bohemia, the former White Croatia, White Serbia and Pannonia — seem to have continued to live under their tribal chiefs, owing allegiance to the Moravian ruler. There was not enough time left for the Mojmir dynasty to effect a more centralized government.

The constant danger of invasion from the west induced the Moravian Slavs to develop a solid system of defense. The existence of fortified places with earthworks and wooden walls, mostly in heavily wooded country or marshy tracts where, according to the old Slavic custom, the population used to take refuge in the event of invasion, is now proved by archaeological findings. It has not yet been possible to locate with any degree of exactitude the "formidable fortress" of the Moravian rulers. The Frankish annalists were impressed by its appearance, but failed to give us a more precise description of it. It could be identified with the large Slavic settlement at Staré Město, but the settlements on the river Dyje (Thaya) seem also to have been of great importance. Only further archaeological discoveries will help to solve this problem.

Contrary to what has hitherto been asserted, the civilization of the Moravian Slavs was hardly influenced by the Avar and Teutonic cultures. They seem to have fallen, before the arrival of the Avars, under the influence of the decadent Roman culture. This is particularly evident in their products of pottery. Nor does it appear that the Moravian and Pannonian Slavs had been attracted by Avar jewelry nor by other products of Avar domestic industry adorned with reproductions of fantastic beasts and plants, so popular among the nomads. The origin of this art should be sought in the workshops on the north side of the Black Sea, which continued to maintain the artistic traditions developed by the Scythians and the Sarmatians. After the Avars had settled down in modern Hungary, Byzantine workshops started to produce this kind of merchandise for export to the nomads, and Avar artisans continued to manufacture objects in the spirit of the old tradition.[1]

Some objects of this sort have been found in Slavic tombs from the eighth and ninth centuries, evidently a proof that Byzantine export to the north did not cease after the destruction of the Avar empire. Soon, Byzantine industry accommodated itself to the better taste of its new customers, as is shown by the great number of pieces of jewelry, often of considerable value, found recently in tombs in Moravia from the ninth century. Bracelets, rings, silver and golden earrings, buttons and necklaces were discovered in quantity. They reveal new designs and finer ornamentation, including filigree work and enamel. Silver crosses of Byzantine making and a silver dove — a Christian symbol — were also found. Most of these imports came from Byzantium, although the workshops of the Black Sea may also have continued to export their wares. There are some indications that native artists started to imitate the imported articles.

[1] The short study by J. Eisner, "Pour dater la civilisation avare" (*Byzantinoslavica* IX [1947–48], pp. 45–54) gives a succinct review of recent publications concerning the Avar culture.

Objects of western or Frankish origin found so far are few. This seems to indicate that commercial intercourse with the Franks was not lively. This is easily explained by the hostile relationship which existed between the Franks and the Moravians. More frequent may have been commercial exchanges between Moravia and Venice. A beautiful scabbard of a dagger found in a tomb at Staré Město seems to be of Lombard origin. The fact that some of Methodius's disciples were sold into slavery and were found in the slave market in Venice testifies to a commercial intercourse with this city and shows at the same time what kind of merchandise was mainly exported from Great Moravia. The *Legend of St. Naum* which contains this information gives us to understand that Jewish merchants were engaged in these transactions. The unfortunate disciples were liberated by a high Byzantine official in Venice who bought them and sent them to Constantinople, where they were provided for by Basil I.

The mining of iron ore and a primitive iron smelting industry also flourished in Moravia. The old Slavic blacksmiths showed a certain originality. They excelled in the manufacture of a new type of axe — which seems to have been the standard weapon of Moravian warriors — and of agricultural implements. This was important because agriculture, together with cattle-raising, was the main occupation of the Moravians.

There have been other remarkable archaeological finds, and the discovery of the foundations of two churches within the settlement of Staré Město came as a great surprise to archaeologists. Until then the specialists had thought that the first churches in Moravia and Pannonia were built of wood. The churches found at Staré Město, however, were built of stone. They were of rather small dimensions (8.50 metres by 7.25 metres; 18.50 metres by 8 metres) and had an apse. The more spacious of the two had also a narthex.[1] The remnants of a stone church with three apses were also recently discovered at Zalevar, near

[1] See the preliminary report by V. Hrubý and F. Poulík of the discoveries in the Czech archaeological review *Archeologické rozhledy* I (1949), pp. 109 ff.; II (1950), pp. 12 ff.

Lake Balaton in Hungary.[1] This can only be the church built about 850 by Pribina or, later, by his son Kocel, in their residence, Mosaburg.

There are strong indications that this church architecture was introduced into Bohemia also. No precise information is available on the church built by the first known Czech Christian Duke Bořivoj at Levý Hradec, but Wenceslas's biographer Christian says it was dedicated to St. Clement by the priest Kaich, who was sent to Bohemia by St. Methodius, probably before 880. The church built by the same duke in Prague seems, however, to have been of a pattern similar to the Moravian churches. The excavations made in 1950 on the emplacement of the Castle of Prague [2] resulted in the discovery of the foundations of a small stone church (8.15 metres by 6.65 metres) with an apse. It was the church of Our Lady constructed by Bořivoj and restored by his son Spytihněv, whose tomb was discovered with that of his wife inside. We can deduce from this that the church at Levý Hradec was also of stone and of the same kind. The residence of the Slavniks, the other ducal family in tenth century Bohemia, had also a stone church of similar pattern with an apse but in addition a transept. Its foundations were unearthed in 1949 at Libice in Bohemia.[3]

Specialists are still debating the origin of this architecture. It may be that the primitive Slavic architects had followed the pattern of early Christian [4] or Byzantine provincial architecture.

[1] See D. Derseny, "L'église de Pribina à Zalevar," Études slaves et roumaines I (1948), pp. 85 seq.

[2] See the description of the church made by the excavator I. Borkovský in Archeolog. rozhledy II (1950), pp. 188–198; III (1951), pp. 3–6.

[3] See the reports of R. Turek in Archeolog. rozhledy II (1950), pp. 93–98; III (1951), pp. 191–202. The church was more spacious (27.60 metres x 8.60 metres; transept 20 metres x 18 metres).

[4] For example, the foundations of an early Christian basilica of similar pattern with an apse were found in 1938 at Szombathely in Hungary on the emplacement of the old Roman Pannonian city of Savaria. Cf. S. Paulovics, "Basilica ad Scarabeteusem portam di S. Quirino in Savaria," Atti del IV Congresso Internat. di Archeol. Christ. (Citta del Vaticano, 1948), pp. 49–63. Cf. also the study by E. Dyggve ("Le type architectural de la Cámara Santa d'Oviedo et l'architecture asturienne," Cahiers

Its simplicity appealed particularly to the inexperienced architects of the newly converted nations.

From the tenth century on we find, in Bohemia, another characteristic feature in ecclesiastical architecture. Numerous churches were constructed in circular form with domes and usually with one or more apses. Rotundas seem also to have replaced churches constructed in the older pattern. This appears to have been the case, at least, in Levý Hradec. Several rotundas, constructed during the oldest period of the Přemyslide dynasty, still exist in Prague and Bohemia. This style of church architecture spread over the whole area of the Přemyslide State and was introduced into Austria, Poland and other neighboring lands.

The origins of this architecture are still subject to dispute. Was it of Carolingian origin, an imitation of the rotunda of St. Guy built on a Carolingian pattern by St. Wenceslas in Prague at the beginning of the tenth century? Did it develop from the primitive architecture introduced by the Byzantine mission? Was it imported from Italy or is it simply an imitation of the church of the Holy Sepulchre in Jerusalem? The problem is not yet definitely solved.[1]

2

It is interesting to note that similar examples of primitive Moravian and Bohemian architecture can be found also in Dalmatian Croatia: the churches of St. Donatus, St. Peter, St. Vit

archéologiques VII [1952], pp. 125–133) on a striking similarity between early Dalmatian and Catalan architecture. Some plans of Dalmatian churches are reproduced in this study.

[1] The problem was studied by J. Cibulka, "Václavova rotunda sv. Víta" (Wenceslas' rotunda of St. Guy), published in Svatováclavský Sborník (Prague, 1933), with a résumé in German. He came to the conclusion that the rotunda of St. Guy was inspired by Carolingian architecture and that other similar churches were built in imitation of the church of St. Guy. Detailed information with abundant bibliographical data on the religious architecture of this period will be found in H. Weidhaas' study "Zur Frage der Przemyslidischen Rundkirchen," in Kyrios II (1937), pp. 279–312. Many of the author's suggestions, although they differ from those mentioned above, deserve to be carefully studied by art historians.

and St. Ursula in Zadar (Zara); the churches of the Cross and of St. Nicholas in Nin; the church of St. Barbara in Trogir; the church of the Holy Trinity in Split (Spalato); the churches of St. Luke and St. Mary in Kotor (Cattaro). All these small churches were built during the ninth and tenth centuries. Numerous others were erected in other parts of Dalmatian Croatia, especially in the region of Knin and that of Split, between the ninth and eleventh centuries, but were destroyed during the Turkish occupation.

This early Croat architecture is completely different from the monumental architecture predominating in contemporary Europe. It presents a considerable variety of forms — rectangular with a cupola, of one, two or three naves, mostly with apses, round with six apses, covered with groined or barrel vaulting. It has little in common with the contemporary Byzantine architecture and the simplicity of construction indicates that these churches were built by native craftsmen. It seems that early Croatian architecture should be studied in connection with the remnants of architecture discovered recently in the former Pannonia, in Moravia and in Bohemia.[1] Perhaps further archaeological finds will help the art historians to explain this interesting evolution.

From the second half of the eleventh century onwards, Croatian architecture reveals a growing affinity with the monumental art of the rest of Western Europe. This coincides with the new period in Croatian history inaugurated by King Peter Krešimir (1058–1073). The more intimate relations with Rome opened the way to artistic influences coming from Italy. The protagonists of this new style were the Benedictine monks of Monte Cassino, who started to build — in their own fashion — numerous abbeys and churches in Dalmatia, and from that time onwards Croatian architecture and art developed on lines parallel with the evolution in the rest of Western Europe.

[1] The study by J. Böhm, "Deux églises datantes de l'Empire de Grande Moravie découvertes en Tchechoslovaquie" (*Byzantinoslavica* XI [1950], pp. 207–222) gives an idea of how complicated are the problems connected with these new archaeological finds and their connection with Byzantine art.

The decorative art of the early Croatian period also presents many original features. Numerous sculptures in bas relief have been preserved with typical interlaced designs in stone. Geometrical patterns, crosses and other Christian symbols, figures of birds and animals, rosettes, spirals, interwoven arches, stars, symbolic plants and other representations are executed with remarkable precision and skill on pillars, church walls, sarcophagi, baptismal fonts and pulpits. The character of this art is symbolic, expressing some Christian ideas — especially those concerning the holy Eucharist — with surprising originality. One of the oldest monuments of this nature is the baptismal font of Duke Vyšeslav, which dates from the end of the eighth century, and the little church of the Holy Cross in Nin was decorated with numerous sculptures of this character. This kind of decoration was in great vogue during the early period of Croatian history, and one of the finest specimens of this art is the plaque in relief representing the eucharistic star in a very original way. It decorated the pulpit given about 1070 by King Peter Kresimir to the cathedral at Split. Another monument preserved in the cathedral of Split — a bas relief on the baptismal font — combines this kind of decoration with the representation of human figures. The figure of a Croat king is sculptured in a rather rough fashion and the technique combines Byzantine and Frankish artistic traditions.

From Dalmatian Croatia these artistic tendencies spread also over Pannonian Croatia, although in this region, owing to the political conditions, artistic activity was never as lively as in Dalmatia.

The question arises, from where did the Croats obtain this peculiar artistic inspiration. Was it from Italy? We find similar tendencies in decorative art in Venice and Lombardy from the eighth century onwards.[1] It is, however, remarkable that this decorative art appears in Croatia almost at the same time as it

---

[1] The main protagonist of the theory of the Italian origin of early Croatian art is L. Karaman ("Notes sur l'art byzantin et les Slaves catholiques de Dalmatie," *L'art byzantin chez les Slaves* II [Paris, 1932], pp. 332–381).

does in Italy. It is executed by native artists who give proof of more skill and originality in decoration than in architecture. The symbols sculptured by them and the decorative figures often reveal a striking similarity to the symbolic motifs current in oriental Christian art. No wonder some art historians — L. Jelić, J. Strzygowski, U. Monneret de Villard, for example — believed that they had discovered Iranian and Sarmatian elements in them and thought that this artistic tradition should be traced back to the Sarmatian Alans of the fifth century, who had penetrated into Dalmatia with the Goths and might have stayed there. Perhaps the theory of the Sarmatian origin of the primitive Croats will eventually help art historians to find a way of solving this problem.[1]

There are in Dalmatia only a few reliefs of Byzantine origin. For example, in the cathedral of Rab (Arbe) there is a relief of Christ upon a throne, while reliefs of Our Lady are preserved in the church of St. Symeon in Zadar (Zara) and in Biskupija, near Knin. Specimens of minor arts imported from Byzantium are more numerous.[2]

In painting and in engraving Byzantine influences were felt in Croatia from the eleventh century onwards, but rather through the mediation of Italy. The school of Monte Cassino, which effected an interesting blend of Anglo-Saxon, Carolingian and Byzantine practices in engraving, left particularly deep influences in Croatia.

Byzantine jewelry was imported into Croatia, as is shown by numerous finds in old Croatian cemeteries. In this respect, however, native goldsmiths and silversmiths were soon to develop

[1] In this respect, interesting but rather daring suggestions are made in the short study by P. S. Sakač, "Symboles eucharistiques dans l'ancien art croate (VIIIe–XIIe s.)" in the Croat review Osoba i Duh (Person and Spirit) IV (Madrid, 1952), pp. 209–232. The author wrote several studies on early Croat history which are listed in the article. The Iranian character of early Croatian art should not be exaggerated. It is not known how strong the Iranian element was among the Croats when they took possession of modern Croatia.

[2] Cf. M. Abramić, "Quelques reliefs d'origine où d'influence byzantine en Dalmatie," L'art byzantin chez les Slaves II (Paris, 1932), pp. 317–331.

their own technique. Split (Spalato) became particularly famous in this field from the eleventh century onwards.

Thanks to their contact with the Latin cities on the coast, the civilization of the Croats made good progress and they advanced also in other directions. Not only did they obtain their own bishopric, but other religious foundations made their appearance in Croatia much earlier than they did in Bohemia and Poland and the first Benedictine abbey was founded in Klis by Trpimir as early as 850.

In Croatia the Church also developed on different lines from those followed in Central Europe. The Croats of Dalmatia did not know the Germanic system of proprietary churches. In old Croatia there was no feudalism and no investiture. The Church regulated its internal affairs by special synods or local councils which used to meet in Spalato, the seat of the archbishop in Dalmatia.

Moreover, the power of the duke, later the king, of Croatia was not as absolute as in some other countries. He was obliged to take advice from his council and in important matters he was expected to convoke a national assembly. The Dalmatian cities had, of course, their city councils, the presidents of which were locally elected and then confirmed, first by the Byzantine emperor and subsequently by the Croatian king. The fact that from the beginning of their political evolution the Croats realized the importance of cities in the life of a nation was of great significance for their whole history. It should be remembered that cities began to play a part in the evolution of Germany only from the twelfth century onwards. So, in this respect, the Croats had a two-centuries' start on the other nations of Central Europe.

Many peculiarities can be observed also in the administration of the Croat realm. The representative of the duke, later king, was the *banus* and under him were the *župani*, who administered the different "counties." Constantine Porphyrogennetus gives a very accurate account of the fourteen *županije* of Dalmatian Croatia and the territory of the Narentanes. The western title of Count — *comes* [1] — was given first to those *župani* who occupied different posts at the royal court; at the later stage in this development, it was given also to the provincial *župani*.

Only members of the highest nobility could become either *župani* or any of the court functionaries. There was no court nobility, as there was among the Western nations. This particular feature of Croat history can best be explained if it be recalled that the semi-slavicized Croats had taken over the government of the Slavs who had been liberated from the Avars, and therefore the kernel of the Croat aristocracy was formed of the descendants of the chiefs who commanded the tribes, organized on a military footing, who had accepted the invitation of the Emperor Heraclius and had migrated from White Croatia to the south. Moreover, in addition to this high ranking nobility, the Croats also had lesser nobles, who seem to have formed the nucleus of the Croat army.

The chief of the Croat State had at his court officers for his own service and others who were entrusted with the administration of the country. They were members of the ducal or royal council, which assembled also for judicial purposes. The first officer was the *jupanus palatinus*, and the second, the *jupanus camerarius*, a kind of finance minister. Others were in charge of the armory, the horses and the provender. The number of minor officials increased in the eleventh century and among them was the *dvornik*, who was probably superintendent of the buildings. Some of these offices developed on the western pattern; others, on the eastern. As was customary in Central Europe, the office of the royal chancellor was generally held by a bishop and was one of the duties of the Bishop of Knin, a see founded in 1040.

3

In Bulgaria, Byzantine influences in art and architecture were, of course, manifest from the time when Christianity was first in-

---

[1] From this Latin word was borrowed the Slavonic term "K'met'."

troduced. It appears, however, that the primitive Turkic Bulgars had their own artistic traditions of a rather oriental character, which had nothing in common with Byzantium. The two palaces of which ruins were discovered near the village of Aboba on the site of Pliska, the ancient capital of the Bulgar khagans, were bold constructions, built of large hewn stones, which in their style and execution showed a striking similarity to Persian architecture of the Sassanian period. A similar style can be detected in the construction of the oldest fortified walls in Preslav and Tirnovo. The small fortress of Madara, founded during the oldest period of Bulgar history, was another example of this kind of architecture.

The oriental spirit of the Turkic Bulgars showed itself also in the numerous monumental inscriptions in the vernacular Greek used by the remnants of the native population on the soil occupied by Slavs and Bulgars. Most of them are from the first half of the ninth century and celebrate in Babylonian or Persian fashion the deeds of the khagans. The most impressive example of this kind of monument is the "rider of Madara," a large relief carved on the rock face near Madara, representing the Khagan Krum on horseback, returning from a successful hunt. The Greek inscription which accompanies the relief glorifies the main deeds of Krum's eventful reign and the whole composition and execution are strongly reminiscent of similar rock reliefs in Persia.

The objects known as "Attila's treasure," which are kept in the Museum of Vienna, also have an oriental character. Specialists have ventured the opinion that the precious vessels of the treasure were brought by the Bulgars from their original home. There is also a strong oriental character about the few slabs with animal and other reliefs, from the seventh and eighth centuries, found at Stara Zagora and in the church of Drenovo.

All this shows that the primitive Bulgars possessed a certain degree of civilization, a fact which may have helped them in subduing the Slavic population. The primitive civilization of the Bulgars was formed by traditions which originated in the ancient Near East.

In spite of that, Byzantine influences started to be felt in Bulgaria at an early period — they are visible also in Pliska — and increased substantially when the country became Christian. They were very strong during the reign of Symeon. The capital was transferred to Preslav either by Symeon — or perhaps by his father, after he had deposed Vladimir. There, to rival the capital of the Byzantine emperors, the churches and palaces were built by Symeon on the Byzantine pattern. We have an eloquent description of the splendor to be beheld in Preslav, from the pen of John the Exarch, a prominent Bulgarian writer of the period. After trying to describe in the most glowing terms the beauty of the many buildings, John confesses at the end: "It is impossible to tell of the splendor, beauty and orderliness, and each of you must see it for yourselves." Of these buildings only ruins remain today. The remnants reveal a strong Byzantine influence, but some oriental elements are still apparent. A characteristic is the use of glazed ceramic tiles of which interesting specimens have been found in the ruins of a monastery near Preslav. This shows that there were attempts to introduce some oriental and native patterns into the Byzantine style.[1] It is a pity that only foundation walls remain of the first Christian basilica built in Bulgaria, near Pliska.

A similar tendency to combine the native traditions with Byzantine style and technique is apparent in the architecture and decorative art which flourished during the reign of the Tsar Samuel. The old Bulgar traditions can be traced in the ruins of the fortress of Ochrida and in marble slabs from the church of St. Sophia there. The main architectural monuments are the church of St. Achilles in Prespa and that of St. Sophia in Ochrida, both executed in the Byzantine fashion.

The political and social evolution of the first Bulgarian Empire differed in some ways from that of other Slavic countries. As the

---

[1] The excavations at Pliska and Preslav were re-started in 1945. The results will be published under the auspices of the National Museum in Sofia. See the preliminary report made by V. Ivanovna in the *Byzantinoslavica* IX (1947–48), pp. 315–323 ("Les fouilles du Musée National de Sofia à Preslav et à Pliska").

state was founded by a Turkic tribe, the non-Slavic elements in Bulgarian political life were naturally more prominent. It should be stressed once more that the primitive Bulgars were superior to their Slavic subjects not only in the military but also in the cultural sphere and that the assimilation of the ruling minority by its numerous Slavic subjects was not as rapid as has often been thought.[1]

In political organization the predominance of the Turkic element was, of course, most prominent. The chief of the state was called *khan*, or *khagan*, the Greeks giving him the title of *archôn*. From the second half of the eighth century, Bulgarian inscriptions, written in Greek by Greek artists, add to the title *archôn*, the words "by the grace of God." Symeon adopted the title of *tsar* in Greek *basileus* (but he also used *samodr'ž'c*, the Bulgarian version of *autocrator*) and seems to have adopted the purple robe and purple shoes of the Byzantine emperors. It is not known if the first Bulgarian khagans used a throne or a crown, but a scepter as an emblem of royalty was used only during the second Bulgarian Empire.

The hereditary dignity of khagan was vested in one family and was never shared, as was sometimes the case in other Slavic states. The Turko-Tatar conception of the supreme power being concentrated in the hands of one chieftain was reflected also in the fact that the state was never divided among several members of the family as was often done in other Slavic lands.

The chief of the state was, above all, the supreme commander of the army, because the military organization of the Turkic tribes who took over the leadership of the Slavs was not only the main feature of the new state, but also the principal source of its power. The khagans were surrounded by their boyars, the most valiant of the military commanders. This was in accordance

---

[1] In this respect, the discovery of an inscription at Preslav, from the beginning of the ninth century (published by I. Venedikov, *Bulletin de l'Institut archéol. bulgare* X [1946], pp. 146–160), is of some importance. The inscription is written in Greek characters, but in the proto-Bulgar language. It indicates that the proto-Bulgar language, a Turkic idiom, was still used in the period preceding the conversion of the Bulgars.

with a Turkic custom that developed in the steppes during the nomadic existence of the tribes. Traces of this primitive social and political organization are to be found in the ruins of the first residence of the khagans, Pliska, which has been excavated near the village of Aboba. Pliska was a great military camp, protected by the khagan's boyars against any surprise attack.

In the beginning the boyars were completely dependent upon the khagan. During the eighth century his absolute power was, however, disputed by them, but in spite of a temporary success, the boyars failed to replace the hereditary system by an elective one and Krum and Boris finally broke their opposition.

In addition to those boyars who comprised the high aristocracy, the Bulgars also had boyars of lesser ranks who could not boast as much property as their superiors. The khagan selected the court functionaries and the governors of the different provinces from both classes. It appears that the boyars in command of the frontier posts were the most important in rank. The boyar classes, originally exclusively of Turkic origin, were gradually increased by the addition of Slavic chiefs, who in time mingled with the Turkic families and eventually formed one class which took on a completely Slavic character. Dignitaries of various kinds usually had Turkic titles — *kopan, tarkan, boilas,* etc., the meanings of which are still debated among specialists.[1]

Bishops and abbots were regarded as being the equals of the boyars, and the higher clergy and their property enjoyed many privileges. The number of Bulgarian bishoprics grew considerably and under Tsar Peter reached as many as forty. Among the numerous monastic foundations, that of Ryla, founded by Tsar Peter, was the most important.

On the territory which they occupied the Bulgars found many urban foundations dating from the Roman period, and from the remnants of the subjugated population they learned of the im-

---

[1] An attempt has been made to explain some of these titles in the author's edition of two Bulgarian inscriptions from Philippi: F. Dvornik, "Deux inscriptions gréco-bulgares de Philippes," *Bulletin de correspondence hellénique* LII (Paris, 1928), pp. 125–147.

portance of cities in a nation's life. New Bulgarian cities sprang
up around the fortresses which were built either for the defense
of the country or as administrative centers. The appearance of
the cities, moreover, demonstrated to the Bulgarians the importance of commerce in the national life. From the beginning
of the eighth century, we hear of Bulgarian merchants, and from
that time onwards the conclusion of commercial treaties with
Byzantium figures prominently in Bulgaro-Byzantine relations.

Among the peasantry there existed free peasants and others
who were settled on seignorial estates. The number of free
peasants, however, gradually diminished. Unable to pay their
taxes and to render the services imposed upon them by the state,
they started to look for protection to the boyars and the higher
clergy and became their subjects, designated by the Greek term
paroikoi.

A thorough Byzantinization of Bulgarian administration and
political life, which had started under Symeon the Great, was
completed during the occupation of Bulgaria by Byzantium.
Then the old Turkic titles disappeared to be replaced by Byzantine titles. This Byzantinization was to become a prominent
feature of the second Bulgarian Empire.

4

The civilization and social organization during the early
period of the evolution of those Slavic tribes who were to
be called the Serbs are less well known than those of the Bulgars.
According to Constantine Porphyrogennetus, these Slavs were
governed by *župani,* called by the Greeks *archontes.* Their
function was hereditary and their territory was regarded as a
family patrimony. Unlike the Bulgarian system, the members of
the *župan* families received their share of the territory of their
župa. Under Byzantine and Bulgarian influence, the system of
individual succession was started, but it did not become the rule
until during the twelfth century.

The main function of the *župan* was a military one. Originally the Serbs did not have a proper aristocracy, with the exception, perhaps, of the Narentanes. An aristocracy in the western sense of the word originated on Serb territory much later, and was formed of such free men as distinguished themselves by amassing riches. According to Constantine Porphyrogennetus, the župans resided in castles round which settlements — primitive towns and cities — formed.

Very little is known about the religious organization of the Serbs. Basil I must have done something in this direction; but we do not know anything certain about it. It may be that provisions for the Serbs were made as early as 870, when the Bulgarians had returned to Byzantine obedience. It is known that the Patriarch Ignatius consecrated an archbishop and several bishops and sent them to Bulgaria. The bishopric of Belgrade was then founded. In 878 the Pope John VIII mentions in his letter to Boris of Bulgaria Bishop Sergius of Belgrade and protests against his elevation by George, probably the Bulgarian archbishop consecrated by Ignatius.

In the Acts of the Photian Council (879–880) there is registered among the assisting prelates the name of "Agathon of the Moravians." If this prelate can be identified with the Archbishop Agathon mentioned in the *Annals* of Fulda as a member of a Greek embassy to Louis II in 873, it can be concluded that Basil I had established, after 870, another independent missionary archbishopric for the Slavs on the river Morava, the neighbors of Serbia proper. This territory, which was the object of a fierce contest between the Franks and the Bulgarian Khagan Omortag and of another between the Serbian Župan Vlastimir and the Khagan Malamir, was situated on the confines of the last Byzantine possessions in northern Macedonia and was particularly suited to be an advance post for Christian propaganda. The erection of an independent archbishopric in this region, subject only to the Patriarch, would be in line with the general trend of Byzantine policy, because it would weaken Bulgarian influence over this country.

However, as mentioned above,[1] the evidence concerning the high ecclesiastical rank of Agathon is not conclusive. He may have been only a bishop and if his see was an independent archbishopric, this arrangement did not last. When Symeon the Great of Bulgaria had extended his sway over all Serbia and had created, about 925, the Bulgarian Patriarchate, he introduced profound changes in the ecclesiastical organization of these countries. It may be that at that time the see of Morava was already reduced to a bishopric and united with the See of Braničevo. The former status was, however, still recalled in the privilege given by Basil II to Ochrida and in the lists of Bulgarian bishoprics from the eleventh, twelfth and thirteenth centuries.[2]

Probably in about 925 Symeon of Bulgaria founded for the Serbs the bishopric of Rasa (Ras, Raška, modern Novi Pazar). It was incorporated in the new Patriarchate of Bulgaria and is listed among Bulgarian bishoprics existing during the reign of the Tsar Peter (927–968). After the suppression of the Bulgarian Patriarchate, the Serbian bishopric of Rasa remained — together with that of Morava-Braničevo — under the jurisdiction of the Archbishop of Ochrida.

The Bulgarian Church was more interested in expansion in Macedonia where several sees were founded anew or the existing ones affiliated to the Patriarchate. No new foundations were made by the Bulgarians for the Slavic tribes on the Adriatic.

The Slavic tribes in the coastal region, the Narentanes, the Zachlumjans, Trevunjans and the Dioceans, had to content themselves, at first, with the ecclesiastical organization existing in the coastal cities, namely, in Spalato, Ragusa, Cattaro and Dyr-

[1] See above, page 97.
[2] For details see H. Gelzer, "Ungedruckte und wenig bekannte Bistümerverzeichnisse der orientalischen Kirche," *Byzantinische Zeitschrift* I (1892), pp. 256 seq.; II (1893), pp. 40–66. The eleventh century Archbishop of Ochrida, Theophylactus, speaks in one of his letters of a bishop "ho Morobou," evidently bishop of Morava or Braničevo. Lambert of Hersfeld mentions Morava in his *Annals*. In 1059, on his pilgrimage to Jerusalem, he spent Christmas "in civitate Morouwa, in confinio sita Ungeriorum et Bulgariorum" (M.G.H.S. V, p. 160).

rhachium (Durazzo), but at the famous Synod of Spalato it was decided to create a new bishopric in Stagno in order to promote Christianity in Zachlumje. This foundation was confirmed in 928 by Pope Leo VI and this seems to have been the only effort made by the Latins to strengthen their influence among the Slavic tribes on the coast.

It seems that the metropolitans of Dyrrhachium were the most active in this respect. Of the four bishoprics which remained under their jurisdiction after the upheaval caused by the invasions, that of Alessio (ancient Lissos) was the nearest to the Diocleans. It seems that the christianization of the Dioclean Slavs was completed by missionaries from Dyrrhachium and new episcopal foundations were made on the coast from this center. Towards the end of the eleventh century Dyrrhachium claimed jurisdiction over the following new episcopal foundations: Dioclea, Scutari (Skadar), Drivasto, Pulati and Antibari, all of which were in the territory of the Dioclean Slavs. Antibari, however, was predestined to play an important role in the further evolution of the Diocleans.

This illustrates the important position of this Byzantine metropolis among the coastal Slavic tribes. Dyrrhachium, moreover, extended its claims over several bishoprics in the interior which were incorporated in the archbishopric of Ochrida. It thus appeared that the Slavs of the small principalities, or *županije*, near the coastal region would be definitely incorporated in the ecclesiastical system of the Byzantine Church, and Durazzo was about to take over the spiritual leadership of this part of future Serbia. Political evolution, however, changed the situation and the hopes of the metropolitans of Durazzo were dashed to the ground.

5

The greatest cultural achievements of the Slavs in this early period of their evolution were in the literary field, thanks to the Byzantine missionaries, SS. Constantine-Cyril and Methodius.

It will be useful therefore if, before examining the influence of their literary heritage on Bohemia, Bulgaria and Croatia, a short survey of the literary work of the two brothers is given.

As has been seen, Constantine-Cyril began his literary work for the Slavs in Constantinople, before leaving for Moravia. The Byzantine *Evangelistarion*, the book of the liturgical lessons from the Gospels, was the first work to be translated into Slavonic. The dialect chosen was that of southern Macedonia, which thus earned the distinction of becoming the literary language of the Slavs.

After reaching Moravia, Constantine-Cyril translated, according to his biographer (Chap. XV): "the whole ecclesiastical office, Matins, the Hours, Vespers, Compline and the Mass." Experts are still not in agreement as to which Mass formulary he used for his translation but it seems natural to surmise that both brothers used the Byzantine liturgy when they arrived in Moravia. A Roman Mass formulary, used in Moravia, has been preserved in part in the fragments of the Old Slavonic Missal brought to Kiev from Palestine. It has been thought that it was based upon the *Sacramentarium* or Mass formulary of St. Gregory the Great. A version of it, recently discovered at Padova, appeared the most likely prototype; but according to a more recent discovery [1] it seems that the Slavonic text preserved in the *Leaflets of Kiev* is a supplement to the Liturgy of St. Peter, a Mass formulary which was a Greek translation of the Roman liturgy of St. Gregory. This liturgy seems to have been used in some places in Byzantium, perhaps also in Thessalonica, the native city of the two brothers, and in Greek monasteries in Rome. Numerous Greek manuscripts have preserved its text, sometimes enlarged by additions from the Byzantine liturgy. The Liturgy

---

[1] J. Vašica, "The Slavic Liturgy of St. Peter," *Byzantinoslavica* VIII (1939–46), pp. 1–54, in Czech with a résumé in Latin. For more ample information see the edition by M. H. W. Codrington, "The Liturgy of St. Peter," *Liturgiegeschichtliche Quellen und Forschungen* (Münster, 1936), and J. M. Hanssen's study, "La liturgie romano-byzantine de Saint Pierre," *Orientalia Christiana Periodica* IV (1938), pp. 235–259; V (1939), pp. 103–150.

of St. Peter seems to be mentioned in the *Vita Methodii* (Chap. XI), and this is an additional argument in support of the above conclusion.

Constantine also wrote three works in Greek: an account of "The discovery of the relics of St. Clement," which were found by him during his stay in Cherson when on the Khazarian mission, a panegyric and a hymn to St. Clement. Unfortunately these writings have been lost as well as the Latin translation made by Anastasius of the story and the panegyric combining excerpts from all three works, but there exists an Old Slavonic text dealing with the same subject. It might be a translation of the Greek original, made probably by Constantine himself. There exists also a "Sermon on the Right Faith" (*Napisanie o pravei vierie*) dating from the Old Slavonic period, which is ascribed to Constantine-Cyril.

Constantine-Cyril was also a poet. Evidence exists that he composed a panegyric on St. Clement in Greek verse. It thus seems natural to suppose that he was also the author of some of the short religious poems in Slavonic. Some attribute to him the composition of a prayer in alphabetical acrostic and the introduction to a translation of the Gospel.[1] There is no doubt that he composed a *pochvala*, a short panegyric in honor of St. Gregory [2] quoted in the *Vita Constantini*. Most specialists agree that the two Slavonic biographies of the Saints contain some short passages in verse. Clement's *pochvala* on St. Cyril, which was probably written in Moravia, is also highly praised for its poetic quality. There is no probability in the claim that Constantine was the author of a liturgical panegyric in honor of St. Demetrius, the patron saint of Thessalonica.[3] This was written by St. Methodius and was not in verse, but in prose.

[1] See R. Jakobson, "The Beginning of National Self-determination in Europe," in *Review of Politics* VII (1945), pp. 29–42.

[2] E. Georgiev, *Dve proizvedenija na sv. Kirila* (Sofia, 1938).

[3] Jordan Ivanov, "Novi Vesti za Kirila i Metodija," *Zora*, No. 5404 (June 3, 1937), p. 7. Cf. also the short study — with a rich bibliography — by I. Dujčev, "Zur literarischen Tätigkeit Konstantins des Philosophen" in *Byzantinische Zeitschrift* XLIV (1951), pp. 105–110.

According to his biographer, St. Methodius is said (Chap. XV) to have translated the whole of the Old and the New Testaments with the help of two of his disciples and this in the short space of eight months. There is a good deal of truth in this report, although it may have been that Methodius only finished a translation commenced by Constantine, taking over the work after his brother's death. This translation is only fragmentarily preserved in different manuscripts; but experts now generally agree that there did exist, in the Moravian period, a complete translation of Holy Writ. This certainly was a great achievement. Only one homily which can be attributed to St. Methodius seems to have been preserved. It appears to have been addressed to Svatopluk and his councilors on the occasion mentioned by the *Vita* (Chap. XI). Methodius defends Church prescriptions concerning marriage.[1]

In addition, Methodius is said to have translated a collection of the sayings of the Holy Fathers and a collection of canon law. It is debated among specialists which Byzantine collection he followed, as works of this type were very common in Byzantium. It seems most probable that what he translated was a Greek collection called the *Book of the Holy Fathers* (Βίβλος ἀγίων Πατέρων),[2] while as regards the collection of canon law, experts generally are of the opinion that Methodius translated the Collection of Sixty Titles edited by John Scholasticus.

The translation of the canon law has a short treatise on the primacy of the Roman See, in which the author explains the decision of the Council of Chalcedon in favor of Rome. No Greek copy of this scholion has ever been found. It may have originated

---

[1] See A. Vaillant, "Une homelie de Méthode," *Revue des études slaves* XXIII (1947), pp. 34–47. Cf. also F. Grivec, "Duo sermones s. Methodii" (*Orient. Christ. Period.* XVI [1950], pp. 440–448).

[2] This is the result of N. van Wijk's studies of the problem. See the résumé of his several studies in *Slavische Rundschau* X (1936), pp. 6–9 ("Der grossmährische Erzbischof Method als Übersetzer der Erbauungsliteratur"). This collection — called the *Paterik* by the Slavs — was very popular. Van Wijk's commented edition of this work is to appear posthumously in Leiden.

in one of the numerous Greek monasteries in Rome, where Methodius or one of his disciples discovered it and added a translation of it to the Church Slavonic edition of the Byzantine canon law.

To the Moravian period should also be ascribed the important original writings of the *Legends* of Constantine and Methodius. The *Vita Constantini* may have been the work of Methodius or of one of his disciples who accompanied him and wrote under his supervision. It has all the characteristics of Byzantine hagiographical literature, especially of semi-secular biographies, so abundant in the ninth century. Its reliability can no longer be questioned and it is one of the best original writings of that period both in East and West.

There are also typically Byzantine passages in the *Vita Methodii*, the introduction being such an example. Less elaborate than the *Vita Constantini*, it was probably written by St. Clement, a disciple of Methodius and a Byzantine Slav, or by Gorazd, shortly after their master's death, as the author seems to be conscious at the end of the *Legend* of dangers lying in wait for the disciples. It is noteworthy that no copy of this *Legend* existed among the Southern Slavs, although they possessed copies of the *Legend of Constantine-Cyril*.

The Byzantine mission in Moravia seems to have laid a solid basis also for the further evolution of civil legislation among the Slavs. A detailed analysis of the oldest Slavic legal work, the *Zakon sudnyj ljudem* (Judicial law for laymen), made recently by J. Vašica,[1] shows a marked linguistic affinity between this work and the writings of St. Constantine-Cyril. We are thus entitled to add also this first Slavic law book to the list of works composed by him. The law collection is based on the Greek handbook, the *Ecloga* of the Emperor Leo the Isaurian, which was replaced by the *Procheiron* under Basil I. There are, however, some prescriptions which are not derived from the *Ecloga*, but from the Roman Law as it was known in the West.

---

[1] J. Vašica, "Origine Cyrillo-Méthodienne du plus ancien code slave dit 'Zakon sudnyj ljudem,'" *Byzantinoslavica* XII (1951), pp. 153–174.

6

Such are the works which constitute the basis of Slavonic letters. The destruction of the Moravian Empire dealt a grievous blow to the achievement of the two Greeks; but it did not spell the end of Slavonic culture in Central Europe. Many of the Slav priests fled to Bohemia, where the Slavonic liturgy and letters had been introduced in Methodius's lifetime by one of his converts, Duke Bořivoj. They flourished at Bořivoj's court and were under the patronage of his widow Ludmila. At this time St. Wenceslas, who is said to have been able to read Slavonic besides Latin and Greek, had the church in his residence administered by Slavic clergy, but as he was under Saxon suzerainty, he dedicated the principal church of his capital to St. Vitus, the patron saint of Saxony. Later SS. Ludmila and Wenceslas were claimed as patron saints by the Slavic clergy, and there is positive evidence extant that at the beginning of the tenth century a Slavonic *Legend of St. Ludmila,* recording her saintly life and martyrdom, was written in Prague. The first biography of St. Wenceslas, who was murdered in 929 at his brother's instigation, was also written in Slavonic and is rightly regarded as the prelude to Czech national literature. A Slavonic hymn, paraphrasing the *Kyrie Eleison,* an invocation which is often recited in Eastern liturgy, also belongs to this period and is still sung in Czech churches.[1]

The Slavic clergy defended their national language with the pen and curiously enough they wrote in Latin. The introduction to the Latin *Life of St. Wenceslas,* written in the second half of the tenth century in Bohemia by Christian, a member of the second reigning family of Bohemia, the Slavniks, is nothing less than a plea in Latin for Slav letters. There, too, evidence is to be

---

[1] The credit for showing definitely that this hymn — *Gospodi pomiluj ny* — originated in Bohemia in this period must go to Prof. R. Jakobson. See his latest publication on the subject in *Ramovšev Zbornik, Slavistična revija* III (1950), pp. 267–273 ("O stichotvorenych reliktach rannego srednevekovja v českoj literatyrnoj tradicii" — On poetical remnants of Early Middle Ages in Czech literary tradition).

found that the cult of SS. Cyril and Methodius was not forgotten in Bohemia.

There must also have been some monasteries of the Slavonic rite on the territory of what was once the Moravian Empire. We know of one for certain — the Abbey of Sázava, founded by St. Procopius in the eleventh century. But there must have been similar institutions in what is now Slovakia, since Sázava and northern Hungary were in normal contact with one another. These relations became easier after 955, when the Magyars were defeated by Otto I and forced to settle down to a peaceful life. The first missionaries among the Magyars seem to have been priests of the Slavonic rite coming from modern Slovakia, and Ostrĕgom' (Esztergom) appears to have been one of their centers.

It was in such places as this that Slavonic letters were cultivated, old manuscripts of the Moravian period copied and new translations made from the Latin. Recent discoveries have made it possible to trace these translations and to gather an idea of these activities.[1] There is no doubt that a Latin *Legend of St. Vitus* was translated into Slavonic in Bohemia.[2] There also exists a translation of a Latin *Vita S. Benedicti*, which points to the Abbey of Sázava as its most likely place of origin. Other interesting works of this kind are: an account of the martyrdom of St. Apollinaris of Ravenna, a work translated in Bohemia; the *Martyrdom of Pope St. Stephen*; a sermon by Gregory the Great and other sermons, which may have been written by St. Clement, Methodius's disciple, in Bulgaria.

Of special interest is a Slavonic version of the Latin *Life of St. Wenceslas*, written by the Bishop of Mantua, Gumpold, at the request of the Emperor Otto II. The original has been considerably enlarged in the translation, which gives details of Wences-

[1] Cf. R. Jakobson, "Kernel of comparative Slavic Literature" in *Harvard Slavic Studies* I (1953), pp. 1–71. More details about these original works and translations are given below, pp. 239–241. Most of them were preserved in Russia, whither they were conveyed in the eleventh century.

[2] Cf. the most recent short study by J. Vašica, "Staroslovanská legenda o sv. Vítu" (The Old Slavonic Legend of St. Vitus) published in *Slovanské Studie* (Prague, 1948), pp. 159–163.

las's career that could not have been known to the Italian bishop.

Besides these works, some Slavonic prayers are known which were composed in Bohemia in the eleventh century and which contain allusions to native and also Western saints, such as the Anglo-Saxon Botulf, the Abbot of Ikanhoe.

All the above works were written in Old Slavonic, based on a Macedonian dialect; but philologists have detected in them many new forms which are alien to the primitive Church Slavonic. It seems as though the Czech writers have tried to bring the language up to date by the use of Czech words and idioms. The same process became popular later in Croatia, Serbia and Russia, and helps the reader to fix the date and origin of the changes.

7

Two fragments of the Slavonic liturgy — the *Leaflets* of Kiev and of Prague — reveal in this way that they were, if not composed, at least copied, on territory which used to be part of the Moravian Empire.

Moreover, Slavonic letters penetrated as far as Cracow and the lands of the Vistulanians, which in the distant past belonged to White Croatia and were annexed by Svatopluk and added to his Moravian realm. It is even possible that one or two Moravian bishops, who had been consecrated by the papal legate at the beginning of the tenth century, survived in Cracow. An old local tradition tells of the existence of two such bishops, Prochorus and Proculphus, before the foundation or the revival of the see in the year 1000.

Another point indicating a more intimate connection of the Cracow region with Great Moravia is the cult of Gorazd, a disciple of St. Methodius, which apparently existed in this part of Poland. Gorazd's name is found in a Polish calendar of the fourteenth century, fragments of which have been recently discovered,[1] and this calendar seems to have been in use at Wiślica, a

[1] It was found by J. Zathey during the last war on the binding of a manuscript from Wiślica. Cf. J. Zathey, "O kilku przepadłych zabytkach

town in Little Poland or western Galicia. The manuscript is most probably a copy of a calendar which was in use at an earlier period. Gorazd is venerated in the Orthodox Church with the other disciples of St. Methodius and his feast was celebrated by the Poles on the seventeenth of July. The appearance of his name in a Polish Roman Catholic calendar can be explained only by the connection of Poland with the Slavonic liturgy and culture which had penetrated into the region of Cracow in the ninth century from Great Moravia and in the tenth century from Bohemia.

It should be recalled in this respect that this corner of the former Moravian Empire seems to have kept a certain independence from the Magyars, and that after the Magyar defeat it was annexed by Boleslas I to the state of the Czech Přemyslides. It remained in Czech hands for some decades and then passed to the first known Polish prince, Mieszko I. He was baptized through the instrumentality of his wife, the Czech Princess Dubravka, who brought with her to Poland priests of the Slavonic rite. This Slav invasion under Mieszko I must have strengthened the Slavonic elements which had survived from the time of the missionary work of Methodius in southern Poland. This explains why Mieszko's son, Boleslas the Great (Chrobry, the Brave) issued coins bearing a Slavonic inscription and why Anonymus Gallus, the first Polish chronicler, listed among the mourners at Boleslas's death Polish peoples of both Latin and Slavonic rites. Later, his son Mieszko II was praised by the German Mathilda of Swabia for being able to worship in Slavonic, Latin and Greek.

Slavonic letters must also have survived for a time in Pannonia, a country which was in close contact with the Franks, although this point has not yet been fully elucidated. It is, however, worthy of note that in Freising (Frisinga) in Bavaria and in Klagenfurt in Austria some short Slavonic texts have been preserved which are translations from Latin formulas and from ninth cen-

rękopiśmiennych Biblioteki Narodowej w Warszawie" (Remnants of some lost manuscripts in the National Library in Warsaw), published in *Studia z dziejów kultury polskiej* (Warsaw, 1949), pp. 73–86, ed. H. Barycz, J. Hudlewicz.

tury German [1] and which betray a familiarity with the Slavonic language as it was spoken in old Moravia. There are indications that the Slavonic rite survived in the former Noricum to a much later date, but this requires confirmation.

8

The Slavonic liturgy and Slavonic letters probably reached Croatia and Dalmatia from Moravia before the end of Methodius's mission, if not earlier. Some of Methodius's disciples might have fled to Croatia after the destruction of Moravia, but after the defeat of the Magyars frequent contact seems to have been made with the remnants of Slavism in the Czech lands by the second half of the tenth century.[2] It was then that the Croats received a copy of the Slavonic *Life of St. Wenceslas* and incorporated the feasts of SS. Ludmila and Wenceslas into their calendar. There are also some Slavonic texts of purely Croat origin.

It might have been expected that the princes of Dalmatian Croatia, who had succeeded in recovering their independence, would favor the Slavonic liturgy as a powerful factor of national appeal to those Croats settled between the Drava, the Sava and the Danube in Pannonia, who were still under Frankish sovereignty. Yet, although Dalmatian Croatia had its own bishop in Nin, there is no indication that the Slavonic rite was in general use in his diocese, a fact which still puzzles historians.

[1] Published by V. Vondrák, *Frizinské památky* (Prague, 1896). For a more complete and more recent bibliography concerning the many problems connected with these texts, see the short study by A. V. Isačenko, "Nachträgliche Bemerkungen zur Frage der ältesten deutsch-slavischen literarischen Beziehungen" in *Zeitschrift für slavische Philologie* XIX (1947), pp. 303–311. Cf. also his study in Slovak, *Jazyk a pôvod Frizinských pamiatok* (The language and the origin of the records of Freising), (Bratislava, 1943) and his article "Začátky vzdelanosti ve Velkomor. Ríši" (Beginning of intellectual life in Great Moravia), in *Jazykovedný Sborník* I (Bratislava, 1946–47).

[2] Cf. M. Weingart, "Hlaholské listy vídeňské" (Glagolitic Leaflets of Vienna) in the Czech review for modern philology (*Časopis pro mod. filol.* XXIV [1938]).

There is an explanation. The one ambition of the princes of Dalmatian Croatia was to gain control over the Latin cities of the littoral, especially over Zara, Spalato (Split) and Ragusa, which were remnants of the Latin-speaking province of Dalmatia, and which owed their survival, after the Slavic onslaught, to their geographical position and their uninterrupted contact by sea with Byzantium. This coastal province of Dalmatia had maintained its independence, and its culture made a greater appeal to the Dalmatian Croats, because of its contact with the surrounding Slavic world, than did that of the Franks. Its cities, which clung to their Latin culture, spoke a Latin dialect and were proud of their Latin past, also represented wealth, commerce and access to the outer world, that is to say, to Venice and Byzantium.

From the beginning of the tenth century, the bishops of Split had been trying to gain ecclesiastical jurisdiction over the whole of Dalmatia, on the grounds that they were the successors of the bishops of Salona, the old metropolis of Dalmatia which had been destroyed. Anxious to curry favor with them, the princes of the Dalmatian Croats tolerated their claims, although these conflicted with the rights of the new national bishopric of Nin; and since the Splitans favored the Latin liturgy, the priests of the Slavonic rite could not rely upon their princes for protection.

But this situation forced the Croat bishops of Nin to stand up for their rights. As has been shown, the conflict came to a head at the Synod of Split in 925 when Pope John X sided with the Archbishop of Split. The decrees of the Synod state that the Pope forbade the use of the Slavonic liturgy and that the Synod confirmed his prohibition. It is often said that the Bishop of Nin vetoed this decision and thereby saved the Slavonic liturgy, yet without furthering its spread in the country. There are, however, scholars who think that the Bishop of Nin was defending not the Slavonic rite, but only his right to jurisdiction over the whole of Croatia and that the synodal decrees forbidding the Slavonic liturgy are interpolations of the eleventh century.[1]

[1] See, for example, the study by J. Srebrnić, "Odnošaji pape Ivana X prema Bizantu i Slavenima na Balkanu" (The Relations of Pope John X

In any case, the timely intervention of a legend assured its survival through the Middle Ages. As St. Jerome was a native of Dalmatia and an Illyrian by nationality, he was credited with the invention of the glagolitic letters and the introduction of the Old Slavonic into the liturgy. He was a Saint and a Father of the Western Church. His supposed deed commanded respect and was confirmed by several decisions of the popes in the thirteenth and fourteenth centuries. So, whether he was willing or not, St. Jerome became the patron saint of the Slavonic liturgy.

This incident shows how the memory of SS. Cyril and Methodius was gradually fading into oblivion in the West and that the suspicion of heresy cast upon their activities by the Frankish clergy — especially on St. Methodius — had done its work. It was dangerous to claim the patronage of such questionable saints; but St. Jerome saved the situation.

In the twelfth century, when the Slavonic liturgy flourished in Macedonia, some intellectual intercourse can be detected between Macedonia and Croatia which favored the survival of glagolitic writing.[1] In Dalmatia it has actually survived, through many vicissitudes, down to the present day. It is still in use along

---

with Byzantium and the Balkan Slavs), published in *Zbornik Kralja Tomislava* (Zagreb, 1925), pp. 128–164, with a résumé in French. I also think that the said passages are interpolated. John X was anxious to bring Dalmatia into closer relationship with Rome. The price which the metropolitan of Spalato asked was the suppression of the national Croat bishopric of Nin. This was a great sacrifice on the part of the Croats. To forbid the Slavonic liturgy used in many parts of Croatia would have been too great a risk as it would certainly have strengthened the opposition of Croat nationalists against Spalato. The Acts of the Synod were most probably interpolated towards the end of the eleventh century when Roman reformists started their campaign against national liturgies. This campaign is responsible also for the suppression of the Slavonic liturgy in Bohemia.

[1] When comparing some linguistic peculiarities contained in glagolitic texts of Croatian origin with texts which originated in Moravia and in Bulgaria, Slavic philologists are more and more inclined to admit that contact between Croatia and the Macedonian centers of Slavonic culture must already have existed in the tenth and eleventh centuries. Cf., for example, the short study by K. Horálek in *Slavia* XIX (1950), pp. 285–292 ("Kořeny charvatsko-hlaholského písemnictví" — Roots of Glagolitic Literature in Croatia).

the littoral and on the Adriatic islands of Krk (Veglia), Cres (Cherso), Lošinj (Lussin), Rab (Arbe), and in the neighborhood of Zadar (Zara). In Croatia, the Old Slavonic introduced by Cyril and Methodius has undergone alterations with the introduction by copyists of old manuscripts of words and idioms of the Croat language, while the glagolitic letters have become more angular in shape.

9

Just as in Moravia, Bohemia and Croatia, the West influenced Slavonic literature, although substantially it remained Byzantine, so Byzantium influenced Slavonic literature in Bulgaria. The *Vita S. Clementis* tells about the introduction of Slavonic letters into that country. This work was written in the eleventh century by the Greek Archbishop of Bulgaria, Theophylactus, who must have read the Slavonic Life — now lost — of this same saint, written in the tenth century. It is learned from this source that the Moravian refugees were cordially received by the commander of the fortress of Belgrade, then a Bulgarian stronghold. The *Life* makes particular mention of Clement, Naum, Laurentius and Angelarius as being among the refugees. They stayed for a while at the court of Boris in Preslav and then about the year 886, Clement was sent by the Khagan to evangelize Kutmitčevica, in the extreme southwest of Macedonia. Boris's successor, Symeon the Great (893–927), made him Bishop of Velica, near Ochrida. Later Naum carried on Clement's work and this part of Bulgaria became the cradle of the Slavonic liturgy and letters in the Balkans.

This great work was due to the initiative of Clement himself, who first of all made a number of additions to the series of short homilies which had been brought out of Moravia. To him also are attributed homilies for all the feasts of Our Lord and Our Lady and in honor of St. John the Baptist, together with lives of the prophets and the Apostles, discourses on martyrs and Fathers, and hymns in honor of Our Lady and other saints. He also completed the Slavonic translation of the *Triodion*, a collection of church hymns. But it is difficult to estimate exactly the number of his translations and original compositions, as the manuscripts of Bulgarian, Serbian and Russian origin are not in agreement on their authorship.

To this first period of Old Slavonic literature in Bulgaria also belong the *Vita S. Naumi*, a short, original composition written in the spirit of Byzantine hagiography, and a *Defense of Slavonic Letters*, by an anonymous author called Chrabr, or as translated "The Courageous." In Bulgaria in Clement's time, another translation was also made of a Byzantine collection of canon law, the *Syntagma in Fourteen Chapters*.

10

Symeon's reign is rightly called the Golden Age of Slavonic Letters. It was he who ordered the translation of the extracts from St. John Chrysostom's works, called *Zlastostruj*, or the Golden Stream. Also due to him is a collection which is a kind of Byzantine chrestomathy containing quotations from many Greek Fathers and including the questions and answers of Anastasius of Sinai. This very rich collection also contains a short chronograph from Augustus to Constantine Porphyrogennetus and an interesting chapter by George Choiroboskos "On images," discussing tropes and figures of speech. This work was copied in 1073 for the use of the Kievan Prince Svjatoslav and is known as the *Izbornik* of Svjatoslav.[1]

The most prominent writer of the school of Preslav was John the Exarch, who by translating part of St. John of Damascus's famous treatise on the *Source of the Faith* endowed the young Bulgarian Church with a handbook of dogmatic theology. This book together with a theologico-philosophical treatise on the creation of the world in six days *Šestodnjev* (*Hexaemeron*) was

---

[1] See the detailed description of the *Izbornik* given in the catalogue of MSS. kept in the Library of the Holy Synod (A. Gorskij, K. Novostruev, *Opisanie slav. rukopisej* II, 2 [Moscow, 1859], pp. 365–405).

based on Byzantine writings, parts of which were simply translated. There are also some sermons attributable to this writer.

The priest Gregory is known only as the translator of the Penta-
teuch and of the Books of Joshua, Judges and Ruth. Another
representative of the same school, Bishop Constantine, translated
the sermons of Athanasius of Alexandria, but parts of his collection of Sunday sermons are original. This Bishop also wrote some
exquisite poems based on Greek models, but not without a touch
of originality. He is also believed to have composed in acrostic a
"canon" or short panegyric in honor of St. Methodius.[2]

The same school was also responsible for the adaptation to the
Bulgarian idiom of the Old Slavonic translation of the Holy Writ
which was attributed to SS. Cyril and Methodius. The Psalter
and the Book of Prophets were adapted or "modernized" with
special regard to their use in Bulgarian churches, and it was in
this school that glagolitic writing was replaced by the so-called
Cyrillic writing, which was more akin to the Greek uncial, simpli-
fied matters considerably and is still used by the Orthodox Slavs.

This is only a brief summary of the development of Old Slavonic in Bulgaria, but many problems of interest to Byzantinists
and Slavonic scholars alike must be solved before a clear
picture can be obtained of the literary activity which, under
Byzantine inspiration, stirred Eastern and Western Bulgaria in
the tenth century. It must, for instance, be established which
version of the Holy Writ was used by the Slavonic translators of
the Bible. The most popular text in Constantinople in the ninth
and tenth centuries seems to have been that of Lukianos, though
it is curious to note that the translation of the Book of the
Prophets used in Eastern Bulgaria was based upon the so-called
Alexandrine or Hesychios's text of the Septuagint. The West
Bulgarian school of Ochrida added to the Old Slavonic translation of the Moravian period the commentary on the Psalms by

---

[2] Two studies have recently been devoted to Constantine of Preslav as a
poet of old Bulgaria — that of J. Pović in *Bogoslovska Smotra* XXIV
(Zagreb, 1936), pp. 59–86 and that of D. Kostić in *Byzantinoslavica*
VIII (Prague, 1937–38), pp. 189–211.

Hesychios of Jerusalem. The Slavonic text of the Psalms published by the East Bulgarian school of Preslav differs in many respects from the Moravian and Ochrida edition and is accompanied by the translation of the Greek commentary written by Theodoretos of Kyrrhos.

This may be a minor detail; but its bearing on the literary tradition of the Septuagint text and on Byzantine religious life at this period has its importance. It seems evident that the Slav translators must have chosen the texts that were most popular in Byzantium; for instance, the Alexandrine text composed about the year 290, which was popular at least in those monastic circles in which Symeon the Great had moved before he became Tsar of Bulgaria.

There are similar problems associated with the translations of other scriptural and apocryphal books. It is known that the so-called *Book of the Mysteries of Enoch* has been preserved only in a Slavonic translation.[1] Three separate versions of this translation are known in Russian, Serbian and Bulgarian manuscripts; but the original translation seems to have been made in Bulgaria during Symeon's reign.

Another thing which throws light upon the religious life of Byzantium in the ninth, tenth and eleventh centuries is the choice of homilies translated by Slav writers. Here again, they must have selected those Fathers who were most popular in Byzantium — St. Basil, St. John Chrysostom, Cyril of Jerusalem, St. Gregory of Nazianzus, the favorite saint of Constantine-Cyril, Epiphanius, Ephraemus of Syria and others. The Old Slavonic "Codex Suprasliensis" contains a homily by the Patriarch Photius.

Whoever is interested in Greek hagiography and wishes to trace the manuscript tradition of the Greek collections of the Lives of the Saints, should study the Slavonic translations of the Greek *Menaea*, or readings from the Lives of the Saints for each month.

---

[1] See the German translation with bibliographical indications by G. N. Bonwetsch, "Die Bücher der Geheimnisse Henochs. Das sogenannte slavische Henochbuch," *Texte und Untersuchungen zur Geschichte d. altchrist. Literatur* 44 (Leipzig, 1924).

A better knowledge of the Byzantine origins of Old Slavonic literature would also be fostered if the editions of Slavonic texts were accompanied by the Greek texts from which the Slavonic translations were made. Such an edition does exist at least for one important Old Slavonic text, the *Euchologium Sinaiticum*, made in 1933 by F. Frček, in the *Patrologia Orientalis* (R. Graffin, vol. 24).

11

Public taste in historical matters had an effect on the choice of Greek historical works to be translated and the first Slavonic work of this kind was the translation of John Malalas's *Chronicle* from the time of ancient Egypt to the year 563. This was a popular Byzantine chronicle addressed to ordinary people and written in a popular style, and was just the kind of book a Bulgarian translator of the tenth or eleventh centuries would choose in order to give his countrymen an idea of the earliest history of the world. The first translation made in Bulgaria has been lost and it is known only by Russian copies, but it was well known in Bulgaria and Russia, where it became a favorite source for chronicles.

More popular still was the translation of the Greek chronicle by George the Monk or Hamartolos (the Sinner), which is a history of the world from Adam to the year 843. It was supposed until recently that this chronicle was translated in Bulgaria in the tenth or eleventh century. The translation was known by the name of *Vremenik*. It seems, however, that the translation was made not in Bulgaria, but in Kiev, in the eleventh century, probably with the collaboration of South Slavic and perhaps also Czech translators.[1] This was also one of the main sources of the *Russian Primary Chronicle*. A second translation of Hamartolos's chronicle was made in Bulgaria in the fourteenth century and called

---

[1] This seems to emerge from the detailed studies by N. Durnovo and P. A. Lavrov of the text of the translation (published in 1920 in Petrograd, by V. M. Istrin) in *Slavia* IV (1925–26), pp. 446–484; IX (1930–31), pp. 801–815.

Ljetovnik, which was used by Serbian chroniclers. There also existed a translation of the chronicle of the Patriarch Nicephorus, giving a short account of events from Adam until after the reign of the Emperor Michael III in the ninth century and this is preserved in a Russian manuscript of the thirteenth century. There is also a translation of the short ninth-century chronicle composed by George Syncellus and one of a Byzantine history of the world by an unknown writer. This chronicle was added to the Sunday sermons published by the priest Constantine.

The collection called *Hellenic and Roman Chronograph*, which is preserved in four different editions and was much read in Russia, seems also to have been translated and compiled in Bulgaria during the Golden Age of its literature. It contains several remnants of the original Bulgarian historiography, and includes the names of some old Bulgarian khagans and some old Bulgarian words. It seems that some Bulgarian annals must have existed, for the Tsar Kaloyan mentions them in his letter to Pope Innocent III in 1202;[1] but unfortunately nothing, so far, save the remnants referred to have come to light.

The Slavic *Paleia*, an abbreviated version of the Bible with many extracts from apocryphal literature which was very popular at a later date among the Russians, probably also originated in Bulgaria before the twelfth century. That popular handbook of natural science of the Middle Ages, the Greek *Physiologus*, was another work translated into Slavonic in Bulgaria in the same century.

There are no traces of Old Slavonic translations of Greek philosophical and classical works, but this does not mean that the Bulgarians, or at least the Bulgarian educated classes, were not acquainted with them. Symeon the Great and many other prominent Bulgarians of this period had been educated in Byzantium, and were familiar with the classical lore which was the basis of Byzantine intellectual life. In his *Šestodnjev* John the Exarch, for example, gives a short account of the teaching of Plato, Aristotle and some other Greek philosophers, but in their literary

[1] See above, page 132.

activity the Bulgarian intellectuals were primarily interested in popular works intended for the majority of people, who had no Greek training. Although some of the translations were made for the intellectual *élite*, it is to be supposed that more works of a scholarly nature would have been translated at a later stage in Bulgaria's cultural progress, had this not been interrupted by political events.

Bulgarian literary activity naturally reflects some characteristic features of Byzantine literary production and this explains why so many collections of excerpts from Byzantine authors were translated into Old Slavonic. The Byzantines of this period had a great fondness for encyclopedias and collections of extracts from classical and patristic writing. Constantine Porphyrogennetus gave a new impetus to this tendency, a circumstance which explains why Russian literary activity of the Kievan period continued to develop, in great measure, along these lines.

It should be stressed that, in spite of the lack of direct translations of classical philosophical works, Church Slavonic has a very rich philosophical terminology.[1] The Old Slavonic writers developed it when translating some of the Fathers such as St. John Chrysostom, St. Basil and especially John the Damascene. The Slavonic philosophical terminology is, of course, based on the Greek. Later, the Russians continued to build on these foundations, and even the modern Russian language is in this respect mainly indebted for its rich vocabulary to the work of Old Slavonic writers in Moravia, Bulgaria and Kiev.

12

Another kind of early Bulgarian literature owes its origin to the appearance of the Bogomil heresy, as the heretics liked to spread their ideas in various apocryphal writings, which were translated from the Greek and very popular. Bogomil himself was said to have composed several apocryphal treatises, but, it seems,

[1] See on this matter R. Jakobson's study "Etymological Dictionaries" in *Slavic Word* I (1953).

that this kind of literature was introduced into Bulgaria not by Bogomil, but by the priest Jeremiah who is often identified with him. This identification seems unwarranted, and the writings attributed to the priest Jeremiah do not show any traces of Bogomil doctrines, at least not in their Old Bulgarian version.

This is particularly true of a book entitled *The Legend of the Cross*, a compilation of legendary stories from the Old Testament and Apocryphal episodes from the life of Christ made up of: "How Christ was made a priest" — "How Christ plowed with the plough" — "How Christ called Probus His friend," etc. Also Jeremiah's compilation entitled *Falsehood and Fever and Other Illnesses* contains some Christian apocryphal legends (the story of St. Sisinius and the twelve daughters of Herod) made up with certain elements of pagan magical lore, but there is nothing which indicates that the author of the compilation was a Bogomil. Bogomil tendencies which are apparent in a later Russian version of *The Legend* show, however, that the Bogomils used Jeremiah's writings to popularize their doctrines.[1]

There is only one apocryphal writing which is an important Bogomil document — the legend of *The Sea of Tiberias*. Other apocrypha, translated from the Greek, — for example, the *Vision of Isaiah*, the *Book of Enoch*, the *Apocalypse of Baruch*, the *Elucidarium*, the *Story of Adam and Eve* and the *Gospel of St. Thomas* — are of non-Bogomil origin, although they may have been used by the Bogomils for the spread of their doctrine.

The most well known Bogomil piece of literature was the *Secret Book* or *Liber Sancti Johannis*, which claimed to contain the answers of Our Lord to questions which John the Apostle had addressed to Him at the Last Supper. The compilation was taken to Italy in the twelfth century by a prominent Bogomil and became, in its Latin translation, an important holy book of the Italian *Paterenes*.

---

[1] This has been clearly shown by D. Obolensky in his book, *The Bogomils* (Cambridge, 1948), pp. 271–274 (The Pope Jeremiah). For more details on Bogomil literature, see the book of J. Ivanov, *Bogomilski knigi i legendi* (Sofia, 1925).

The most prominent defender of Orthodoxy against the new heresy was the priest Cosmas, a contemporary of Tsar Samuel, and his book entitled *Discourse Against the Recent Heresy of Bogomil* is one of the most important sources for the study of this religious movement.[1] He was helped in his efforts by the monk Athanasius of Jerusalem, who wrote a book called a *Discourse on the Tree of Knowledge of Good and Evil.*

The date of the composition of the apocryphal works mentioned above is not yet certain, but most of them seem to have been written during the eleventh and twelfth centuries, though an earlier date should not be ruled out. The same should be said about other popular apocryphal writings. Some of them were ascribed to John the Apostle, to St. John Chrysostom, Gregory the Theologian and Basil of Caesarea. Other very popular works were the *Descent of the Holy Virgin into Hell,* apocryphal stories on *Adam and Eve,* on *Daniel, Samson,* on *Christ's Infancy,* and on *Solomon and Kitovras* (Centaur).

The Byzantines also gave the Bulgarians material for their epic literature. The book of Pseudo-Kallisthenes on Alexander the Great, which is the source of the *Romance of Alexander* so well-known in medieval Europe, must have been translated into Bulgarian during the first Bulgarian Empire, and the Old Slavonic translation of the chronicle of Malalas — from the tenth century — contains the *Legend of Troy* which is based on the Greek text of Pseudo-Dictys.

The Greek romance about *Digenes Akritas,* celebrating the exploits of this Christian hero in his fight with the Musulmans in Asia Minor, was also translated [2] into Old Slavonic but, according to recent research in Russia, and not, as was hitherto thought, in Bulgaria. The Byzantine romance, *Barlaam and Josaphat,* which is a Christian adaptation of the Life of Buddha, was translated

---

[1] See H. Ch. Puech, A. Vaillant, *Le traité contre les Bogomiles de Cosmas le Prêtre, traduction et étude* (Paris, 1945, Travaux de l'Institut d'Études Slaves XXI). Cf. *ibid.,* pp. 128 ff. Puech's judicious remarks on the Apocrypha, the authorship of which is attributed to Bogomil.

[2] Cf. H. Grégoire's work in modern Greek *Ho Digenes Akritas* (New York, 1942).

in Bulgaria and the romance of *Tsar Sinagrip and his Minister Akir*, which was taken from the famous Arab cycle, *Thousand and One Nights*, was also translated into Old Slavonic from a Greek adaptation and also became popular in Russia. The Greek text has not been preserved.

13

All these writings show that the cultural level of the first Bulgarian Empire was high. This fact explains why it happened that this new Slavo-Christian culture made its first conquest by influencing profoundly the subsequent history of a non-Slavic nation — the Rumanians. The latter, called also Vlachs, were established on the territory occupied by the Bulgarian Slavs, from the end of the third century. They were settled there by the Romans when the latter had evacuated not only their legions but also the half-Romanized Dacian population from their province of Dacia. The romanization and christianization of the Dacians was completed in their new home — the Latin provinces, Dacia Ripensis, Dacia Mediterranea and Dardania.

The former home of the Dacians became a kind of no man's land, which was successively occupied by the Sarmatians, Germanic Gepids and Goths, the Huns, the Avars and other barbarian hordes. From the sixth century onwards, the Roman provinces on the right bank of the Danube were fought over by many invaders, the populations suffering terribly at the hands of the Huns and the Avars. Christian centers and monuments were destroyed and, when the Slavs took possession of the country, the Daco-Illyrian native population was reduced to an inferior status. The Latinized former Dacians, now called Vlachs, took refuge in the mountainous terrain, leading a half nomadic life with their herds of goats and sheep, but their language was profoundly influenced by the Slavic idiom. Besides 2,600 words of the old Latin stock, the modern Rumanian language has 3,800 Slavic terms in addition to some Albanian words. In spite of that, the Vlachs were not Slavicized.

When, after the destruction of the Avar Empire, the Bulgars occupied ancient Dacia — modern Transylvania — the Vlachs started to cross the Danube, taking possession once more of the ancient home of their ancestors. The *Russian Primary Chronicle* (year 6406; 898) is probably well informed in stating that the Magyars, when invading modern Hungary, had to fight not only the Slavs, but also the Vlachs: "The Ugri (Magyars) . . . . struggled across the great mountains and began to fight against the Vlachs and the Slavs in that region. For the Slavs had settled there first, but the Vlachs had seized the territory of the Slavs. The Ugri subsequently expelled the Vlachs, took their land and settled among the Slavs, whom they reduced to submission. From that time this territory was called Hungarian (Ugor'ska)." [1]

The symbiosis of the Vlachs with the Slavs had interesting consequences for both nations. The Vlachs were Christians from the fourth century onwards and the first knowledge of Christianity should thus have penetrated to the Slavs from the native Vlach and Illyrian population. If it should be true that the Slavic word for church, *cerŭky*, is not derived from the Greek word *kyrikon* but from the Rumanian word *biserica* [2] (from the Latin *basilica*), it would be found to be an interesting instance of Rumanian influence on the Bulgarian Slavs.

The cultural growth of Bulgaria under Symeon the Great soon started to exercise a profound influence on the Vlachs and although they had been first evangelized by Latin missionaries, they now accepted the Eastern liturgy in the Slavonic language. The Slavonic alphabet was adopted by them and Slavonic literature became also one of their cultural assets. The Bulgarian

[1] S. H. Cross's translation of this passage is not correct. Instead of "Ugri" he puts "Huns." In spite of their subjection to the Magyars, the number of Vlachs grew in Transylvania; it is probable that the Hungarian kings made repeated appeals to them to colonize this country, threatened by the Pechenegs and the Cumans. It seems also that the two other Rumanian provinces — Wallachia and Moldavia — between the Carpathian Mountains and the Danube and the Pruth started to be colonized by the Vlach-Rumanians from Transylvania.

[2] See for details, G. Gunnarsson, *Das slavische Wort für Kirche* (Uppsala, 1937).

Church took over their Christian education and Ochrida became the cultural center from which both Slavs and Rumanians received their spiritual guidance and cultural inspiration.

This situation lasted not only during the reign of the Bulgarian Tsars Symeon the Great, Peter and Samuel, but also after the suppression of the Bulgarian Patriarchate and the destruction of the first Bulgarian Empire. A special bishopric for "Vlachs of all Bulgaria" figures among the sees placed by Basil II under the jurisdiction of the Archbishop of Ochrida. So it came about that the Rumanians, formerly Christianized by the Latin Church, became dependent on the Patriarchs of Constantinople through the influence of the Bulgarian Patriarchs and then of the autonomous Archbishops of Ochrida.

The Slavonic language and liturgy were naturally adopted by all Rumanians and were in use for centuries, not only among the Bulgarian and Transylvanian Rumanians, but also in the new Rumanian principalities of Wallachia and Moldavia, which emerged in the thirteenth and fourteenth centuries. It was only then that the Rumanian Church came into being, but it continued to use the Slavonic liturgy and writing until the end of the seventeenth century.[1]

[1] For a rapid review of the main problems concerning the origins of the Rumanians see F. Lot, *Les invasions barbares* (Paris, 1937), vol. I, pp. 278–300, where the main bibliography is given. On the Slavo-Rumanian relations, see the short but clear and well-written study by G. Nandriş, "The Beginnings of Slavonic Culture in the Rumanian Countries" (*The Slavonic and East European Review* XXIV [1946], 160–171). See also his study, "The Development and Structure of Rumanian," *ibid.* XXIX (1951), pp. 17–39.

The Russia of Kiev

I. History   *The Eastern Slavs, the Volga Bulgars, the Khazars —
Scandinavians discover the river route from the Baltic to the Near
East — Origin of the name Rus — Discovery of the route from the
Baltic to Constantinople; Norsemen and Slavic confederates — Askold
and Dir of Kiev accept Christianity — Oleg, founder of the Russian
State; Commercial treaties with Byzantium — Baptism of Olga, her
relations with Byzantium and Germany — Svjatoslav and the Bulgars
— Vladimir and Byzantine Christianity — Roman or Bulgarian origin
of the Russian hierarchy? — Special features of Russian Christianity —
Jaroslav the Wise — Vladimir Monomach, the decline of Kiev.*

II. Civilization   *Commercial intercourse between East and West
the basis of Kiev's greatness — Importance of cities in Kiev's growth,
their "veče" a democratic institution, the boyars, the ducal officers —
Beginning of feudalism? — Byzantium's legacy in art — The Bulgarian
and Moravian literary legacy — Original Russian literary works in
prose — Russian Belles Lettres in the Kievan period.*

III. Kiev, the principalities, the West and Byzantium   *Literary
relationship between Bohemia and Kiev — The Cult of Western saints
in Kiev — Religious contact between Kiev, Germany and Bohemia
after the schism — The Kievan State and Western Europe — Kiev's
relations with the Byzantine Emperor — Kiev, an intermediary between Byzantium and the West? Lost possibilities — Western influences in Galicia, Volynia and Novgorod — The Principality of Suzdaľ,
and expansion towards the east — The Tatar invasion and Novgorod's
survival.*

Before the problems connected with the formation and development of the mighty political organization of the Eastern
Slavs centering in the city of Kiev are surveyed, the political,
cultural and racial situation in the eastern territories occupied
by the Slavs must be examined. Successive waves of invaders had

followed one another across the steppes of southern Russia —
Scythians, Sarmatians, Goths, Huns, Turkic Bulgars, Avars, and
Khazars. Each of these invasions left its mark on the lands over
which it rolled, a mark which could not be ignored by the Slavic
tribes which had made it clear from the beginning of their penetration eastwards that they intended to stay there for good. Then
the sudden appearance of the Huns came as a warning, a red
light for the whole of Eastern Europe, indicating that from the
human reservoir in the Asiatic steppes, teeming with fierce, nomadic tribes, a new deluge might at any time sweep over the
grassy plains of southern Russia and submerge all Central Europe. Two of the floods of invaders which followed were particularly dangerous, not because of their dynamic fierceness, but
because they had stopped on the fringes of the Slavic lands and
because the peoples which these great waves from Asia brought
with them settled securely on the boundaries of the Slav territories at a time when the Slavic masses had not yet found a
strong form of leadership. The two peoples concerned were the
Bulgars and the Khazars. As has been related the Turkic Bulgars
had settled on the middle Volga and the Kama river and different
branches of that nation extended their sway over the Russian
steppes as far as the Danube. Their empire suffered a serious setback when the Avars appeared; but the Avar invasion removed
the danger which threatened Central Europe from the Bulgars.
Like all other invaders from Asia, the Bulgars pressed instinc-
tively towards the frontiers of the Roman Empire. Indeed, a
section of the Bulgars not only reached the Danube but, with
the eventual help of the Slavs, founded a solid state in Macedonia
and Thrace, that had once been flourishing imperial provinces.

The Bulgars who had established themselves on the Volga consolidated their state and soon a prosperous era opened for them.
It was to be expected that their expansion from the Volga would
be directed westwards into the lands which the Slavs were gradually occupying.

The Khazars, of the Turkic linguistic family, after establishing
themselves in the Caucasus region in the second half of the sev-

enth century, were destined to play an even more important role among the Eastern Slavs than the Bulgars had done. They replaced the Avars as overlords of the Slavs on the Dnieper, and Kiev became the western outpost of their empire, the center of which was transferred, some time after the year 720, to Itil on the Volga delta.

The danger which threatened the Slavs from these two Turkic empires was the more pressing in that neither the Volga Bulgars nor the Khazars were totally lacking in culture. Each had a close relationship with the empire of Bagdad, where the Abbasid dynasty of khalifs had brought the power of the Arabs to new heights. Art and culture flourished at the court of Bagdad and the influence of this Arab renaissance was felt as far as Constantinople, especially in the first half of the ninth century. The Caspian Sea and the Volga river gave the Arabs easy access to the interior of modern Russia and even to the Baltic coast. These waterways were also a channel for Islamic propaganda among the Turkic tribes there. This propaganda was, indeed, so successful that the Volga Bulgars embraced the religion of Mohammed, probably during the ninth and early tenth centuries. Islam also penetrated into Khazaria and it is said that in the ninth century the khagan of the Khazars lent an ear to Christian, Jewish and Mohammedan missionaries alike.

Here was a serious danger for the whole of Europe. Had the Islamic civilization from Khazaria and Bulgaria reached the pagan Slavic tribes, which were drawing nearer and nearer to the Volga and the lower Don, the frontiers of Europe would have been fixed somewhere on the Carpathian Mountains. At this time, Russia was on the verge of becoming a part of the Moslem world of Asia.

The danger was averted thanks to a new factor which entered the Eastern Slavic scene: the appearance of the Scandinavians and the Byzantines. The Scandinavians came first, making their appearance among the Eastern Slavic tribes just in time to weld them into a firm political bloc, which proved able to withstand and obstruct the westward rush of the Asiatic hordes and even to contribute in the long run, thanks to the intervention of Byzantium, to the expansion of European civilization eastward, far beyond the Volga and the Ural Mountains.

2

The appearance of the Scandinavians on the Baltic shore and in the interior of modern Russia is only one of the exploits of the daring sons of the fabulous Scanza in the ninth and tenth centuries. They regarded the whole continent of Europe as a field to be exploited and colonized. The deeds of the Danes and Norsemen in Frisia, in the valleys of the Seine and Loire, in Normandy and England, in Ireland and the isles of the North Atlantic, and those of the Swedes and Norwegians among the Finns in the Baltic region and among their Slavic neighbors — all these represented the last wave of the Germanic migratory movement. The settlement of the Scandinavians among the Eastern Slavs was destined to become one of the most important and decisive events among the achievements of the Germanic migratory period.

The story of their advent among the Slavs is long and fascinating and many details of it are still hotly debated by specialists. Their explorations along the east coast of the Baltic brought them into contact with the Baltic and Finnish populations settled there. Through these peoples they heard of the existence of two flourishing empires on the Volga and of the brisk trade which the Khazars were carrying on with the Arabs of Bagdad. It was not difficult to discover the easy artery provided by the Volga for these commercial transactions. In the second half of the eighth century, if not earlier, the Scandinavians were on the middle Volga. Direct relations between Swedes and Khazars began about 800. The discovery of the Volga route was most probably made, not from the Gulf of Riga and the provinces of Dvinsk, Vitebsk, Kovno and Pskov, where little evidence of Scandinavian occupation has been found, but from the Gulf of Finland which offered an easy access to the Volga via Lake Ladoga and Beloozero and where it was a comparatively simple matter for them to haul their boats over the portage. There was another route from Ladoga *via* Lake Ilmen, which the Slavs had already reached in the ninth century.[1] The country between Ilmen, the Volkhov river and Ladoga is apparently the wooded and marshy island on which some Arab writers located the original habitat of the "Rus." On these routes, two important Scandinavian colonies were founded — Beloozero and Novgorod, their establishment being attributed to Rurik (Roersk) and his brothers.

How can the sudden interest of the Norsemen in commercial intercourse with the Eastern world be explained? Here we must return to those facts which H. Pirenne attempted to set down more or less convincingly.[2] Trade with the Levant had become indispensable to Western Europe ever since Roman civilization had reached it. The products of the Near East used to find their way to the West by way of the Mediterranean; but the Arab conquest of the Near East, North Africa, Sicily, Spain and a part of southern Italy drastically changed the situation. The Arabs then had control over this easy maritime route between the Near East and the West. Moreover the consumption of eastern spices and other luxury merchandise in the Arab empire grew in direct ratio to the increasing refinement of its civilization. This left little of these wares over for export to the West. Furthermore in the ninth century Arab pirates made sea communications between the East, Byzantium and the West almost impossible. There was an urgent need to find new routes to the Orient and it was this which encouraged the Norsemen in their exploration of the eastern end of the Baltic Sea. The memory of commercial intercourse between the Baltic, the Crimea and the Near East was

[1] Besides archaeological evidence — gathered by T. J. Arne, *La Suède et L'Orient* (Stockholm, 1914) — important philological material allows us to trace the presence of the Norsemen on the Baltic and on the Volga and the Dnieper with precision. See for details, M. Vasmer "Wikingerspuren in Russland" (*Sitzungsberichte d. Preus. Ak. Phil. Hist. Kl.*, Berlin, 1931). Vasmer's findings also show that the Volga route was discovered first.

[2] In his book *Mohammed and Charlemagne* (London, 1940). See above page 44. Cf. especially the criticism of Pirenne's theories made by R. S. Lopez ("Mohammed and Charlemagne: a Revision," *Speculum* XVIII [1943], pp. 14–38).

still fresh in the minds of the peoples on the Baltic coast and by following up these clues the Norsemen found a new way by which the Near Eastern countries could be reached.

3

The native population found a strange name for the new-comers and many theories have been advanced to explain how it came about that they were called Rus — Russians. The most plausible theory is that the origin of Russia's name comes from the Scandinavians themselves and the Finns. Certainly the name shows an affinity with the Old Swedish word *rodi* or *rodhsi* — in modern Swedish, *ro, ros* and *rod* — meaning "rowing" or "sculling." There is a part of Sweden — probably the first part with which the Finns became acquainted — which is called "Roslagen," or in older documents "Rodslagen" and it is natural to suppose that the first Swedes to come into contact with the Finns came from this part of Sweden. The Swedes are still called "Ruotsi" by the Finns and "Rootsi" by the Estonians; and it was this name which was apparently given by the Finns to the first Swedish settlers amongst them. The Slavs have transformed the name, according to their phonetic pattern, probably as early as the eighth century, into Rus, Rusi. The Byzantine form, Rhôs, is possibly an adaptation from the Septuagint version of the Holy Scriptures, where, in the prophecy of Ezekiel, a people called Rhos is erroneously mentioned.[1]

4

The Norsemen soon became well known on the Volga, among the Bulgars and in Khazaria, and they ventured across the Caspian Sea and reached Bagdad. Rich finds of Arab coins in

---

[1] The Norsemen were also called *Varyagi* by the Slavs and *Varangoi* by the Byzantines. The word is a Slavic derivation from the Nordic, *vaering*, *varing*, denoting a member of a kind of brotherhood formed by a number of the Norsemen for a military expedition or commercial enterprise. The men forming the brotherhood — *družina* in Slavic — were bound to each

Sweden and on the Baltic coast still testify to the lively commercial intercourse which was carried on between Scandinavia, the Baltic countries and Bagdad.

But of even greater significance for the future was the Norsemen's discovery of a route from Novgorod *via* the Dnieper and the Black Sea, to Constantinople. The region of the upper and middle Dnieper was already a Slavic country when the Norsemen reached it; but commercial traffic on the river was controlled by the Khazars, masters of the Dnieper Slavs and of Kiev, its important trading center. A strong detachment of Norsemen, led by Askold and Dir, reached Kiev (c. 856–860), and as the Khazars were unable to provide the Slavs with adequate protection against bands of nomads marauding in southern Russia — the presence in the ninth century of the Magyars amongst others is proven — the Poljane or Slavs of Kiev and the middle Dnieper welcomed the newcomers and willingly accepted them as overlords in place of the Khazars. Constantine Porphyrogennetus gives some important details, in his book on the administration of the Empire, concerning the kind of relationship which existed between the Slavs and the Norsemen. On two occasions he refers to the Rhôs and their Slavic "confederates." This clearly indicates that the occupation by the Norsemen of various Slavic settlements was not carried out by force, but that in many cases the Slavs accepted the Scandinavians and concluded protective treaties with them.

In this way, the Norsemen took over control of the trade between the Baltic and the Black Sea as successors of the Scythians, the Sarmatians and the Khazars. There were still Greek cities in the Crimea, now under Byzantium, and numerous settlements of Jewish merchants, which had survived for many centuries. Their citizens still made their living by trading with Byzantium, Asia Minor, the Near East and the interior of modern Russia; but the Norsemen were not content to deal only with the Greeks of

---

other by a special oath. Cf. also what H. Paszkiewicz (*The Origin of Russia* [London, 1954] pp. 1–25, 107–132) says on the origin and meaning of the word "Rus."

the Crimea. Peaceful trading had revealed to them the wealth
of Constantinople, and with their Slavic subjects and confederates
they formed a bold plan to seize these treasures by a surprise
attack.

In the early summer of 860, when the Emperor Michael III and
his uncle Bardas were leading an expedition against the Arabs in
Asia Minor, a large fleet manned by hitherto unknown barbarian
invaders appeared before Constantinople, having laid waste the
shores of the Black Sea. The city "protected by God" went
through some exciting moments while it watched the newcomers
burning the suburbs and preparing their final assault from the
sea. But Byzantium was saved even before the Emperor and his
fleet, summoned in the nick of time by the commander of the
city and the Patriarch Photius, had returned. The danger had
been so great, however, that future generations were wont to
speak of the miraculous intervention of Our Lady brought about
by the prayers of the holy Patriarch.

5

This first Russian attack upon Constantinople had great consequences for the subsequent history of the Eastern Slavs. In order
to protect themselves against another surprise of this kind, the
Byzantines hastened to strengthen their friendship with the
Khazars. The embassy which was dispatched to Khazaria via
the Crimea for this purpose was headed by Constantine and
Methodius, the future apostles of the Slavs. From the *Vita
Constantini* valuable details may be learned concerning the
nations inhabiting the Crimea and the religious propaganda carried on among the Khazars by Jews, Christians and Mohammedans.[1]

[1] It is known that the khagan of the Khazars and many of his subjects
had yielded to the Jewish propaganda coming mainly from the numerous
Jewish colonies in the Crimea. They accepted the Jewish creed — the
first case of a large part of one nation becoming Jewish at such a late
period. The Khazars were otherwise a very tolerant nation. They are probably to some extent the ancestors of the eastern Jews. Driven by the Cumans

The sealing of the friendship between Byzantium and the Khazars had its effect upon the Russian Slavs of Kiev. They soon yielded to the cultural influence coming from Byzantium and asked to be baptized and the Patriarch Photius had the satisfaction of sending missionaries to them and of establishing, some time about the year 864, a bishopric at Kiev. This first phase of Christianity did not last very long. About 878–882, Kiev was conquered by the Russian Prince Oleg (Helgi), who came from Novgorod. The Russians and the Slavs under his sovereignty were, naturally, pagan and they were bitterly jealous of the prosperity of the colony at Kiev. Because of this, Christianity in Kiev was quickly exterminated.

This was a great pity, for the whole future of Russia would undoubtedly have developed very differently had Christianity survived in Kiev. It was at that time that other Slavic nations, the Moravians and the Bulgars, were being won for the Christian faith by Byzantium but Russia had to wait another hundred years before becoming a Christian country.

6

Oleg is the real founder of the Russian state. It was he who united North and South in one political unit and from Kiev brought almost all the eastern tribes under his sovereignty. He

---

and the Mongols from their homeland, many of the Jewish Khazars were settled in Poland by the Polish kings. There they mixed with western Jews. On the conversion of the Khazars, see F. Dvornik, *Les Légendes de Constantin et Méthode vues de Byzance* (Prague, 1933), pp. 148 ff. A complete bibliography on the Khazars to the year 1933 will be found in this book. A more recent critical bibliography has been compiled by A. Zajączkowski in "Ze studiów nad zagadnieniem Chazarskim" (Studies on the Khazar problem), published in the *Memoirs of the Oriental Commission of the Polish Academy* (No. 36, Cracow, 1947), with a résumé in French. The author thinks that the letters of Khazar history allegedly from the tenth century are apocryphal, probably dating from the twelfth century, but that they are based upon a national Jewish tradition. Their compiler used quite precise geographical and historical information given by Islamic writers. They are documents which are not to be neglected. On the fate of the Khazars after the eleventh century see H. von Kutschera, *Die Chazaren* (Vienna, 1909), pp. 162 ff.

conquered the Drevljane about 883, the Severjane in 884 and the Radimiči in 885. He put a definite end to Khazar supremacy over the Slavic tribes and protected his subjects effectively against enemy incursions. He also inaugurated a period of friendly relations with the Byzantines which may have occurred after a more or less successful show of force during the second Russian attack on Constantinople in 907.[1] His new state received a kind of international recognition in 911 with the conclusion of a commercial treaty with Byzantium.

Oleg also applied his statesmanship successfully to the task of fusing the Scandinavian upper class with the Slavic elements and his name therefore deserves to rank with those of two other great Norse conquerors who altered the course of European history — William the Conqueror and Robert Guiscard.

There was a temporary rift in the good relations between the Russians and the Byzantines during the reign of Oleg's successor Igor' (Ingvar), who organized an expedition against Constantinople in 941. The *Russian Primary Chronicle* describes the attack, which ended in disaster for the Russians. The same source refers to another expedition which led in 944 to the conclusion of a further commercial treaty but the report of the chronicler should be read with caution. One thing does appear to be clear, however: that peaceful relations between Igor', and the Byzantines were restored, and that the Russian Prince renewed the commercial treaty concluded by his predecessor. But if the text of this new treaty, as given in the *Russian Primary Chronicle* is compared with that of the old one,[2] it becomes clear that the rights of the Russian merchants were curtailed because of Igor' 's defeat by the Byzantines. There is no provision in Igor' 's treaty for the

[1] The historical authenticity of this attack, recorded in detail in the *Russian Primary Chronicle*, is still questioned by many specialists. For details and bibliographical notices see A. Vasiliev, "The Second Russian Attack upon Constantinople," published in *Dumbarton Oaks Papers* VI (1952), pp. 161–225.

[2] A new edition of the text of the Russo-Byzantine treaties was published, with commentaries and bibliographical data by A. A. Zimin in *Pamjatniki prava Kievskago gosudarstva* (Legal documents of the Kievan State) I (Moscow, 1952), pp. 1–70.

Russian merchants to be excused from customs duties, nor, under
this treaty, were the Russian traders allowed to move about freely
on Byzantine territory. The Russians had to promise to repatriate
slaves escaping from Greece and were prohibited from intervening in affairs concerning Byzantine possessions in the Crimea.
They were allowed to fish near the mouth of the Dnieper; but
were denied permission to spend the winter there. Both treaties
give a very impressive picture of social and economic conditions
in Kievan Russia and show that trade with Byzantium was the
main source of the steady economic and cultural progress of that
state. It seemed that the Scandinavians had at last found the
new way to the riches of Byzantium and the Near East, the way
which Western Europe had been seeking since the Arabs had
obtained control over the maritime routes in the Mediterranean
Sea.

7

It was Igor' 's widow, Olga (Helga), who took over the regency
after his death in 945, during the minority of their son Svjatoslav.
She first of all crushed the revolt of the Drevljane, who were responsible for the death of her husband. Olga enforced the unity
of her vast realm and through wise administration strengthened
its economic basis. This energetic and intelligent woman
quickly realized the importance of Byzantium to Russian progress
and she decided to link her country even more closely with the
Empire by introducing Christianity into the regions over which
she ruled. It was only to be expected that friendly intercourse
between Russia and Byzantium would prepare the way for the
penetration of Christianity into Russia. We learn from the *Primary Chronicle* that in 945 there was a church of St. Elias in Kiev,
where the Russian Christians confirmed by oath their resolve to
abide by the stipulations of the commercial treaty with Byzantium. This Christian community had grown up on the ruins
of the first Christian center, which had been destroyed when
Kiev was conquered by Oleg. It consisted mainly of Russian

traders who had become acquainted with the Christian religion when they were quartered near the church of St. Mammas in Constantinople. It was in this small Kievan center that Olga first encountered Christianity, and it would thus be quite natural to suppose that she herself was baptized there. According to the old Russian tradition, preserved in the *Primary Chronicle*, however, she went to Constantinople for this rite. It is known that her voyage to Constantinople in 957 is an historical fact, because her reception there was described in some detail by Constantine Porphyrogennetus in his *Book of Ceremonies.*

Specialists in early Russian history still debate whether this traditional story should be accepted. Most of them have decided that Kiev was the place of her baptism, arguing that the imperial writer describes only Olga's reception and not her baptism and that the Russian chronicler places her baptism in the year 955, that is, two years before her visit to Constantinople. In spite of these views, the tradition of the *Primary Chronicle* should not be lightly dismissed. The chronicler's dates for this period are generally regarded as unreliable and should not therefore be quoted as an argument. As for Constantine Porphyrogennetus, he described in his *Book of Ceremonies* only those events which were likely to recur at the court of Constantinople. It could well be expected that another Russian prince might visit the city, and the masters of ceremonies were therefore given a record of all the details to be observed on such an occasion, were it to be repeated. But it could hardly be taken as likely that Russian princes, once Christianity had been accepted in their country, would make a habit of visiting Constantinople in order to be baptized. Therefore, Constantine limited himself to describing only the ceremonies performed during Olga's reception at the court.

Moreover, Olga's baptism in Constantinople is also mentioned in the Byzantine chronicle of Cedrenus, which was based on that of Scylitzes, not yet published, and by the continuator of the Latin *Chronicle* of Regino. This last source is important. The report in it was written by the German envoy to Kiev, of whom more will be heard presently, and should thus give a true impression of

Kiev in the tenth century. We should, therefore, date Olga's baptism in the year 957 and place it, not in Kiev, but in Constantinople. One thing cannot be contested: that Olga's conversion was the work of the Byzantine missionaries who administered the church of St. Elias in Kiev. The fact that Olga received the baptismal name of Helen, which was the name of the Byzantine empress who was her godmother, also points to the conclusion that the Byzantines were responsible for her conversion.

But how is Olga's action in requesting Otto I of Germany to send a bishop to Kiev to be explained? This fact is reported by the continuator of the *Chronicle* of Regino, most probably Adalbert, the very bishop whom Otto sent at Olga's request. This has seemed so extraordinary to many Russian historians that they simply refused to admit the authenticity of the annals which reported it. It can, however, be quite easily explained. We can see here that Olga's bold action in accepting Christianity did not apparently win the unanimous approval of the Russian aristocracy. The Scandinavian boyars were suspicious of Byzantium's political and religious influence. Many of them still remembered Igor' 's expedition against Byzantium, on which they had accompanied him, and they could not reconcile themselves to the sudden change brought about by his widow. Olga tried to allay their apprehensions and to neutralize Byzantine influence by forging a closer link with the mighty German king, whose deeds against the Magyars had won him great respect in the eyes of the fierce Scandinavian warriors at Olga's court. There is no need to suppose that Byzantium had refused the new convert an independent religious organization and that she had therefore turned to the German ruler to obtain it. In fact, there is no evidence to support such a theory.

Olga's request appeared to Otto as a godsend, for he dreamed of making Magdeburg into a mighty metropolis for all the Slavic lands in the East and his plan seemed to be well on the way to realization. He sent Bishop Adalbert to Kiev; but a great disappointment awaited him. Probably even before Otto's envoy had reached Kiev, Olga had been forced to hand over all effective authority to her son Svjatoslav, who had no use for either Byzantine or Western Christianity. This is fresh proof of the strong anti-Christian reaction in his Kievan retinue.

8

Svjatoslav (964–972), the first Norse ruler of Kiev to be known only under a Slavic name,[1] was a true Viking at heart, adventurous, reckless, courageous and mainly interested in battle and booty. This is the conventional picture of Svjatoslav drawn by most historians. Recently, however, Russian historians have tried to portray Svjatoslav in brighter colors. B. D. Grekov,[2] for example, sees in him not only a great warrior but also a ruler of international renown, who by his deeds profoundly influenced the history of the Moslem world and of Byzantium.

It must be acknowledged that Svjatoslav gave proof of considerable political vision when concentrating his efforts at the beginning of his reign on Russian expansion towards the East. It is difficult to establish the exact dates of Svjatoslav's eastern campaigning, as the information given in the *Russian Primary Chronicle* and by the Arab writer Ibn Haukal is slightly confused. One of the results of Svjatoslav's expeditions was the subjugation of the Vjatiči, the last Slavic tribe still subject to the Khazar khagans. Thus, the unification of all Eastern Slavs in one empire was completed. Svjatoslav's lasting achievement was the destruction of the Khazar empire, brought about probably in two campaigns (963 and 968–?), and instead of the Khazars the Russians of Kiev became the masters of the Ossetians in the lower Don Basin and of the Circassians in the Kuban area. Svjatoslav saw, however, clearly that, if he wanted to rid his realm for good of the Khazar danger, it was imperative for him to control the middle and lower Volga and this led him to an expedition against

[1] He seems to have had a Scandinavian name also. A. Stender-Peterson, "Die Varägersage als Quelle der altruss. Chronik," *Acta Jutlandica* VI (1934), p. 15 thinks that Svjatoslav's Scandinavian name was Sveinald.

[2] In his work, *Kievskaja Rus* (The Russia of Kiev) (Moscow, 1944, 4th ed.), pp. 263 ff.

the Volga Bulgars. Probably about the year 965 he broke their resistance and sacked their capital Bulgar. This finally sealed the fate of the Khazar empire and Svjatoslav's troops looted the Khazar capital Itil.

For the first time Russia extended its domination to the Volga, the Caspian Sea and towards the Caucasus and it seems that Svjatoslav's influence was also strongly felt in the Crimea. All this was a great success which might have become decisive for Russia and Europe, because in the middle Volga among the Bulgars and in Itil the Russians came into direct contact with Islam. When it is recalled what a profound impression Svjato- slav's victories had made on the contemporary Moslem world — Ibn Haukal testifies to that — it can be imagined that the Arabs would have made a great effort to win over this new and power- ful ruler. For Moslem missionaries had succeeded in converting the Bulgars and in penetrating into Khazaria. As the Varyags and their Slavs were still pagans, there was a danger that the fas- cinating civilization of the khalifs might outshine that of By- zantium and that instead of Christianity in either the eastern or the western form, Islam would have crossed the Volga, the Dnieper and the Dniester to take firm root on Russian soil. Had this happened, it might then have crossed the Carpathian Mount- ains to find a warm reception among the nomad Magyars.

The danger was averted by the Byzantines, who persuaded Svjatoslav to march against the Danubian Bulgars. Here the prince showed his adventurous nature; for instead of consolidat- ing his new conquests in the east, as would seem logical to any statesman, he accepted the offer from Byzantium. Perhaps the secret hope that once firmly established in Bulgaria he could realize the dream of his predecessors — to conquer Constantinople — influenced his decision.

There is some evidence to indicate that Svjatoslav had far- reaching plans once he was established in the eastern part of Bulgaria. The *Russian Primary Chronicle* attributes to Svjatoslav the intention of transferring his residence from Kiev to Pereja- slavec (Little Preslav) in Bulgaria: "Svjatoslav announced to his mother and boyars, 'I do not care to remain in Kiev, but should prefer to live in Perejaslavec on the Danube, since that is the center of my realm, where all riches are concentrated, — gold, silks, wine and various fruits from Greece, silver and horses from Hungary and Bohemia, and from Rus furs, wax, honey and slaves.' "

This is an interesting declaration. If it can be taken at its face value, then we have to conclude that Svjatoslav planned to found a great Slavic empire which would comprise not only Kievan Russia but also a great part of the Balkans. The reaction of the Byzantines shows that they were well aware of the new danger and when the Pecheneg diversion engineered by them failed to deter Svjatoslav from reentering Bulgaria, the Byzantines concentrated all their efforts against the Russian Prince. After defeating him, they annexed Eastern Bulgaria and Svjatoslav's imperial dreams were shattered for ever. All that he got out of his Bulgarian adventure was a new commercial treaty with Byzantium. On his way home he met his death at the hands of the new invaders of southern Russia, the Pechenegs (Patzinaks).[1]

9

The fate of the Kievan State was finally decided by Vladimir (Volodimer, Valdimar?) (c. 980–1015), Svjatoslav's son. After fleeing from Novgorod to Sweden, Vladimir defeated his brother Jaropolk of Kiev with the help of a detachment of Norsemen, whom he brought from there. Vladimir then consolidated the State by once more uniting Novgorod with Kiev and affirming his authority over some recalcitrant tribes — the Vjatiči and the Radimiči. He then opened a new gate to the West by adding to his realm the Red cities and Přemysl, territories which formerly had been part of White Croatia, and had then been occupied by the founder of the Polish State, Mieszko I.

Vladimir's most important act was the introduction of Chris-

[1] See above, page 140.

tianity into Russia, and the *Russian Primary Chronicle* gives a vivid account of his conversion. According to this, he was solicited by the Mohammedan Bulgars, the Jewish Khazars, the Germans representing the Pope, and the Byzantines, each of them pressing him to embrace their respective religion. Then Vladimir decided to send envoys to the different countries to investigate their religious practices and faiths. His representatives showed no enthusiasm for the religions of the Bulgars, the Khazars or the Germans; but when they came to the Greeks, they were full of admiration. "We knew not," they confessed, "whether we were in heaven or on earth. For on earth there is no such splendor or such beauty, and we are at a loss how to describe it . . . We cannot forget that beauty." On the strength of their report, Vladimir decided to accept the Greek version of Christianity.

The account is, of course, legendary; but it reflects certain historical facts. It shows first of all that the Mohammedan danger from the Bulgars, which we mentioned above, was a reality. This influence is moreover attested by archaeological finds showing that Arab culture penetrated into Kievan Russia in its early history.

Secondly, it is known that Jewish influence in southern Russia grew stronger after the conversion of the Khazars to Judaism. It was natural for Jewish merchants to be interested in such an important commercial center and a Jewish colony certainly existed in Kiev. Mention also of the Germans in the account above may be an echo of the short episode of Olga's reign, but the stress laid by the chronicler on Byzantine propaganda and on the deep impression made by the Byzantine liturgy reflects the prolonged peaceful penetration of Greek Christianity into Russia from Askold's and Igor''s times.

The Russian chronicler goes on to describe how Vladimir was baptized by the Bishop of Kherson, a city which he had conquered from the Greeks when he realized that they were delaying the fulfillment of their promise to send him a Byzantine princess, "born in the purple," for a wife.

The facts reported by the Russian chronicler — that Vladimir was baptized by the Greeks and that the organization of the Russian Church was the work of Byzantium — are questioned by some scholars who believe that the baptism was carried out by Scandinavian missionaries and that the establishment of the Russian hierarchy was due to the initiative of Rome. Others think that credit should be given to the Danubian Bulgars and the Patriarch of Ochrida.

The defenders of the Scandinavian theory think that Scandinavian priests had acquainted Vladimir with the principles of Christianity and that Olaf Tryggvason finally prevailed upon him to embrace the Christian faith. But it is well known that Christianity made very slow progress in Novgorod, where the Scandinavian influence was most marked, and it is to be expected that if the Scandinavians had shown such a missionary zeal their work would have left its deepest impression there. Olaf Tryggvason was in close contact with Vladimir; but his Christian influence should not be overrated. Before he recovered his throne in Norway, this Scandinavian hero was far more interested in plundering the British Isles than in preaching the Christian faith in Russia. We have no evidence that the Scandinavians, who had only recently been converted to Christianity and who certainly did not have a superabundance of priests, had developed any missionary activity at such an early stage.

Moreover, it appears that the Scandinavians were under a strong influence from Byzantine civilization. The names of the merchants mentioned in the Russo-Byzantine treaties are all Scandinavian. Trade with Byzantium was thus in their hands and most of the Russian merchants living in the quarter of St. Mammas in Constantinople were Scandinavians. They were touched by Byzantine religious propaganda. We have thus to admit that the Scandinavians were mainly responsible for the spread of Byzantine civilization and religion in the Kievan state.[1]

---

[1] Cf., for example, what A. Stender-Peterson (*Die Varägersage,* op. cit., pp. 84 ff., 120 ff., 237 ff.) says about strong Byzantine influences on the origin of some Scandinavian "sages."

10

The partisans of the Roman theory argue that later Russian historical documents — the *Chronicle* of Nikon and the *Stepennaja Kniga* (Book of Degrees) — state that while Vladimir was in Kherson, an "ambassador from Rome came to Vladimir and brought him relics of saints." They argue that this embassy was sent to Vladimir at his own request and had as its purpose the establishment of the Russian hierarchy in the Kievan State, after the Byzantines had refused to cooperate in this matter. But when it is examined closely, this theory is found untenable.

The Roman embassy to Vladimir at the time when he became a Christian must be regarded as an historical fact. Pope John XV, however, had very little to do with it. This embassy was sent by the Empress Theophano, widow of Otto II, who was at that time in Rome,[1] and who had special reason to be interested in Vladimir's baptism and in his marriage. It was not difficult for Theophano to get information from Constantinople about the request sent by the Emperor Basil II to Vladimir for help against Bardas Phocas, a pretender to the imperial throne, but in order to explain this request, the Russo-Byzantine treaties of 945 and 971, by whose terms the Russian prince undertook to help the Emperor with auxiliaries whenever asked to do so must be recalled. Vladimir was pleased to oblige and, at the same time, to get rid of the Norsemen whom he had brought from Scandinavia to assist him against Jaropolk and who were growing very tiresome in their idleness. As a compensation, however, he asked for the hand in marriage of a Byzantine princess, "born in the purple," and promised to receive baptism. The princess who was chosen to become Vladimir's wife was Anne, daughter of the Emperor Romanos II. She was Theophano's cousin and it seems that at one time it was Anne whom Otto I wished his son Otto II to marry. All this makes the interest which Otto's widow took in the fate of her cousin far more comprehensible.

[1] On the two other embassies to and from Russia during Vladimir's reign see F. Dvornik, *The Making of Central and Eastern Europe*, pp. 179 ff.

The Byzantine princess did not relish the idea of marrying Vladimir and it is not to be wondered at that the Greeks tried to "forget" their commitment. The poor princess had, however, to make the best of it and to find consolation in the knowledge that for her sake her husband had dismissed his five other wives and 800 concubines — an extravagant number even for a Viking, but a figure probably improved upon by the chronicler anxious to demonstrate the transformation which baptism could bring about in a pagan soul. Theophano knew by experience what it meant to be married to a semi-barbarian and her sympathy for her cousin was extreme. Hence she sent her some saintly relics and some words of consolation. If the Pope had anything to do with the embassy, it was only to send his blessing to the bride and her husband and to endorse the message sent by the Empress Theophano. It certainly did not dawn upon him to establish a hierarchy in so distant a region.

It is true that in Russian Christianity in Vladimir's time there were some Western usages, particularly the tithe, a Frankish invention, and certain canonical customs; but these could have penetrated from the West in a perfectly natural way. Intercourse with Germany was free and open. We learn, for example, that Vladimir's predecessor, Jaropolk, had sent an embassy to Otto I in 973. The *Annals* of Lambert refer to the presence of Russian envoys at the Reichstag of Quedlinburg in that year. After Vladimir had opened another gate to the West through his occupation of the Red cities, Western influences could penetrate peacefully into Russia from Bohemia.[1]

As for the theory concerning Ochrida, there is no evidence for the assertion that the Patriarch of Ochrida had provided Kiev with a metropolitan, although Bulgarian cultural influences on Russian Christianity must be admitted. Let us remember that

[1] According to the *Russian Primary Chronicle* and the *Chronicle* of Nikon, the relations between Bohemia and Vladimir's realm were lively. Among Vladimir's wives were two of Czech birth, and embassies sent to him by the Czech Duke "Andrich" (Oldřich) are mentioned. See for details A. V. Florovskij, *Čechi i Vostočnye Slavjane* (Czechs and Eastern Slavs, Prague, 1935), pp. 14–44.

after the death of the first Archbishop of Ochrida, John, who was a Bulgarian, the see was occupied by Greeks.[1]

The best solution of the puzzle regarding the establishment of the Kievan hierarchy will be found by taking into consideration Vladimir's policy in the Crimea and following the lead given by the *Primary Chronicle*. We know that Vladimir took a lively interest in the Crimea, which was an important link between Kiev, Byzantium, the Varyago-Slav colony of Tmutorokan'[2] on the Taman' peninsula, the Khazars and the Near East. He surrendered Kherson, which he had occupied, to the Greeks as a token of friendship; but he was determined to keep in close touch with this eastern outpost of Byzantium. As this was also in the interests of the Emperor, it seems that a compromise was reached by establishing the Archbishop of Kherson as a kind of supervisor of the young Russian Church. An allusion to this fact is found in the statement of the *Primary Chronicle* that the first priests sent to Kiev were from Kherson. Moreover, at the ceremonies marking the translation of the relics of SS. Boris and Gleb, the first Russian saints,[3] it appears that the Archbishop, named John, who presided, did not reside in Kiev but came there for this special purpose. This seems to indicate that he was the autocephalous Archbishop of Kherson.

11

This compromise was perhaps unusual in Byzantine practice, but in the light of the circumstances, it seems perfectly natural and logical that the Byzantines should prefer to entrust the supervision of the young Russian Church to a prelate who was on good terms with Vladimir, whom he had baptized, and who was

[1] Recently V. Nikolaev tried to defend the "Ochrida theory" in his book *Slavjanobolgarijat faktor v christijanisacijata na Kievska Rusija* (Sofia, 1949, Bulg. Academy). He brought forward no new evidence for his thesis. See the detailed review in French of his book by B. Zástěrová in *Byzantinoslavica* XI (1950), pp. 240–254.

[2] On the theories concerning the origins of this colony see F. Dvornik, *The Making of Central and Eastern Europe*, pp. 312 ff.

[3] Cf. below, p. 212. The translation took place in 1020 or 1026.

also in direct communication with both Russia and Byzantium. This state of affairs lasted until the reign of Jaroslav the Wise, on whose initiative Kiev was raised to metropolitan status.

It was Vladimir then who laid the foundation of Kievan Christianity. The *Primary Chronicle* describes with great satisfaction the more spectacular manifestations of his Christian zeal — the beating of the statue of Perun by twelve muscular men and the mass baptism of the people in the Dnieper river. These spectacles were doubtless also organized to reassure the Byzantine princess that his feelings towards her were most laudable. Vladimir also had a new cathedral built in Kiev for the first bishop.

Although the methods chosen by Vladimir to implant Christianity were somewhat forceful, he encountered really stubborn opposition only in Novgorod. It may be that the introduction of the Slavonic liturgy in the new Church — thanks to the presence of Bulgarian priests, who brought Slavonic books with them — helped considerably to spread the new faith across the Russian lands. In spite of that, many pagan practices survived among the people as we can judge from complaints voiced in sermons of that time. Special embassies sent by Vladimir to the main Christian shrines made the fact that Russia had entered the Church known to the whole Christian world.

The introduction of the Slavonic liturgy also helped considerably in bringing about the amalgamation of the Varangian and Slavic elements. The Varangians were, of course, at a disadvantage when this transformation took place, and the political influence of the Varyag aristocracy decreased in proportion as the Prince derived increasingly powerful support from the Church and its clergy. All this explains how it came about that despite the important role they had played at the beginning of Russian history, the Scandinavians were unable to influence the evolution of the Russian language, and why words of Scandinavian origin in Old Russian are few. It is interesting in this respect to observe in the Kievan State an analogous development to that noticed in Bulgaria after the christianization of the country and the introduction of Slavonic liturgy and letters. There also these factors helped Boris to reduce the power of the aristocracy of Turkic origin. The Slavonic liturgy contributed also to a closer unification of the many tribes of Eastern Slavs. Thus a great new Slavonic national Church was formed which was destined to become of immense importance for the growth of national sentiment among the Eastern Slavs. From now on, the dynastic links created by the unifying action of the Varangian princes to hold the many tribes together were strengthened by new cultural and religious ties, which would prove in future even more effective than the idea of a single dynasty for the whole of Russia.

The fact that for several decades most of the Russian bishops were Greeks [1] did not interfere with this unification. On the contrary, the alien bishops were not interested in the local feuds between members of the reigning family, but only in the unity of the Church which they were governing. This unity was, of course, also in the interests of the Byzantines. Thus it happened that the Church, although under Greek supervision, rendered a great service to the Russian nation as a whole, maintaining the principle of the unity of all Russian lands.

12

Among Vladimir's successors two dukes deserve special mention — Jaroslav the Wise (1036–54) and Vladimir II Monomach (1113–1125). Jaroslav was the only survivor of the fraternal strife between Vladimir's sons lasting from 1015 to 1036 — a struggle which threatened to ruin the work of Oleg and Vladimir and which was a bad omen for the future. Two of the brothers,

---

[1] D. Obolensky suggests that, according to an agreement concluded by the Russians with the Byzantines — probably under Jaroslav the Wise — the Metropolitan See of Kiev was to be held alternately by Greek and Russian prelates. If a native was elected, he had to be consecrated by the Patriarch of Constantinople. This suggestion is very plausible, although conclusive evidence is hardly available. Another suggestion advanced by D. Obolensky that Vladimir, when he married the Byzantine princess, was distinguished by a high Byzantine court title, perhaps even the title of Basileus, is probably correct. Both suggestions deserve detailed study.

Boris and Gleb, became victims of Svjatopolk and were afterwards venerated as martyred saints by the Russians.

Jaroslav's reign was one of the most brilliant periods of Kievan
Russia. He was a great church builder, and a study of Kiev's cultural achievements will show how great a part he played in the
literary and artistic development of his country. He proved also
to be a wise lawgiver, and following the example of his father,
who had tried to secure the frontiers against the raids of other
nations, Jaroslav tried to protect the northern part of his realm,
which was menaced by the Balts and the Finnish Estonians who
were trying to extend their territories. The foundation of Juriev
(Dorpat or Tartu) in the first half of the eleventh century was
intended to put an end to the Estonian colonization of Russian
lands, and Jaroslav's expedition of about 1040 against Lithuania,
in which he cooperated with the Poles, was also designed to
arrest the Balts.

The only expedition which ended in disaster for him was that
against the Byzantines in 1043. This was probably provoked by a
disagreement which had broken out between Russian and Greek
merchants in Constantinople. It was often said that this conflict
induced him to undo some of his own work, *i.e.*, the agreement
reached with the Emperor and the Patriarch concerning the reorganization of the Kievan Church. According to this agreement,
Kiev was to be the see of a metropolitan, who would be the head
of the whole Russian Church. The metropolitan was to be consecrated and sent to Kiev by the Patriarch. He would then ordain
bishops for other cities, the nominations being made in accordance with the wishes of the princes. The first Metropolitan of
Kiev, Theopemptus, was sent to Russia from Constantinople
about the year 1039.

It has hitherto been thought that the metropolitan would always have been Greek and that this stipulation was infringed in
1051 when Jaroslav caused a Russian, the learned Ilarion, to be
elected Metropolitan of Kiev. There is, however, no evidence of
such a rift between Byzantium and Kiev ensuing from this incident. Jaroslav's move can best be explained on the basis of the

UNITED THEOL.
THEOLOGY LIBRARY

above-mentioned suggestion concerning a special arrangement which allowed for the See of Kiev to be occupied alternately by a Greek and a Russian prelate. It may be that there is a connection between this agreement and Jaroslav's attack on Constantinople in 1043 and the peace treaty concluded between Kiev and Byzantium which followed. But subsequently Jaroslav settled the whole dispute between Kiev and Byzantium by arranging a marriage between his son Vsevolod and a Byzantine princess.

In order to preclude feuds among his successors, Jaroslav established a new order of government. He gave to each of his five sons a principality as a kind of appanage, reserving for the eldest, Izjaslav, the cities of Kiev and Novgorod. The Prince of Kiev had to guard his pre-eminence over the others, but it appears that the old Scandinavian and Germanic influences made themselves felt again in Kiev in determining the order of succession. Jaroslav seems to have adopted the Germanic system of "tanistry," which hitherto, however, had been followed only by the Vandals in Africa.[1] According to this system, the father is not succeeded by his son but by his younger brother, and the youngest brother is followed on the throne by the eldest of his nephews.

At first, this system was observed with some regularity. Izjaslav I (1054–1073) was followed on the throne of Kiev by his brothers Svjatoslav (1073–1076) and Vsevolod I (1078–1093). Then the succession fell to Izjaslav's son Svjatopolk II (1093–1113) and after him to Vsevolod's son Vladimir II Monomach (1113–1125). The changes on the throne were, however, disturbed by incidents of ill omen for the future. Izjaslav failed to establish the superiority which belonged to him as the senior prince holding Kiev. He had to share his authority over the whole of Russia with his brothers Svjatoslav and Vsevolod. Then Vseslav, the Prince of Polock, great grandson of Vladimir the Great, and Rostislav of Novgorod, resenting their exclusion by Jaroslav the Wise from participation in the joint rule over Russia, started to make trouble.

[1] This system was followed also in Scotland until the eleventh century, when it gave rise to the struggle between Duncan and Macbeth and was finally ended by the sons of Duncan's son Malcolm III and St. Margaret.

CARNEGIE INSTITUTE
OF TECHNOLOGY LIBRARY

Rostislav occupied the principality of Tmutorokan, but because this move threatened Byzantine interests in the Crimea, he was poisoned by a Byzantine agent from Kherson. Vseslav, who in 1068 was proclaimed Prince of Kiev by the Kievan population who were in revolt against Izjaslav,[1] was captured treacherously by the three brothers and expelled from Kiev by the Poles whose help Izjaslav had implored. Izjaslav, who was himself driven away from Kiev in 1073 by his brothers, asked the Pope Gregory VII for help, offering Kiev as a papal fief; but no help came [2] and he was able to return to Kiev only after Svjatoslav's death in 1076.

13

Vladimir Monomach was called to the throne of Kiev by rebellious citizens who were disgruntled at Svjatopolk's social and financial policy. He owed his popularity to his display of energy and valor during the campaign against the new invaders of southern Russia, the Cumans, called the Polovci by the Russians. Their invasions started in the sixties of the eleventh century and were devastating, though quarrels among the ruling princes facilitated their initial success. Eventually, in 1103 Svjatopolk and Vsevolod's son Vladimir joined forces and crushed the invading hordes. The victory was crowned in 1111 by a great Russian raid deep into the steppes, and the hero of this campaign was the young Vladimir. This popularity won him the favor of the Kievans, and the rights of Svjatopolk's brothers and Svjatoslav's sons to succeed in Kiev were thus ignored.

Monomach started his reign with some legislative measures in favor of the lower classes and throughout his reign he showed a deep understanding of social problems. In his *Poučenie* — "Admonition" to his sons — he left a kind of "mirror of a good prince" for his successors. The document shows, at the same time, how

---

[1] Vseslav survived in the Russian epic tradition as a prince-werewolf. See R. Jakobson's and M. Szeftel's study, "The Vseslav Epos" in *Russian Epic Studies* (Memoirs of the American Folklore Society, Vol. 42, edited by R. Jakobson and E. J. Simmons, Philadelphia, 1949), pp. 13–86.

[2] For details see below, pp. 275, 276.

profoundly Christian principles had penetrated the Russian soul.

Because of his popularity, Monomach was able to leave the Kievan throne to his eldest son Mstislav I (1125–1132), whose mother was Gyda, daughter of Harold II, the last Saxon king of England. Together with his brother Jaropolk, Prince of Perejaslavl', Mstislav I made a serious effort to secure the northern and southern borders of the Russian lands, menaced by the Finnish Estonians and the Cumans.

It seemed now as if the dynasty of Monomach would stay firmly established in Kiev. After Mstislav's death, his brother Jaropolk II succeeded him (1132–1139). Unfortunately a quarrel that broke out among the members of Mstislav's family for the possession of the principality of Perejaslavl' weakened Jaropolk II's position. As a result his brother Vjačeslav, who should have succeeded him, was driven away from Kiev by a descendant of Svjatoslav, Vsevolod II (1139–1146). A prolonged struggle between the dynasties of Monomach and Svjatoslav was the result of this intrusion, but the citizens of Kiev showed their sympathies for the dynasty of Monomach when accepting Mstislav's son Izjaslav II (1146–1154) and rejecting Vsevolod's brother Igor'. Izjaslav II's succession was, however, contested by his uncle George (Jurij), Prince of Rostov-Suzdal', the new principality in the northeast, and after a protracted struggle George, called Dolgoruki — the Longhanded — emerged victorious (1154–1157). The final result of the dynastic struggles was tragic for Kiev. George's son Andrew, called Bogoljubskij, took possession of Kiev (1169) in order to secure his right to succession against Mstislav, son of Izjaslav II. The city was pillaged and destroyed by fire, and Andrew (1157–1174) did not think it worth while to remain there. He installed his relatives in Kiev, returned to his northeastern principality and took up residence in Vladimir, a city which had superseded Rostov and Suzdal'. The decline of Kiev was accelerated during the reign of Andrew's brother Vsevolod III (1176–1212), who not only continued to reside in Vladimir but took the title of Grand-Prince of Vladimir instead of Kiev.

Contemporaneously with these dynastic struggles the Kievan

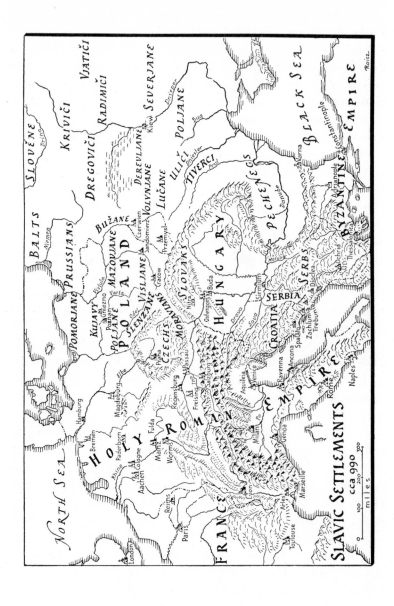

State was being completely transformed. The center of national wealth and political power was steadily moving from Kiev towards the northeast and the southwest. The principalities of Smolensk, Černigov, Polock, Perejaslavl', which were set up on the territories of the primitive tribes — the Radimiči, Drevljane, Severjane and Vjatiči — gradually increased in importance as their population grew, and Rjazan and Murom on the Oka were soon surpassed by the most northeasterly principality of Rostov-Suzdal', between the rivers Volga, Oka and Moskva.

The territories of the southwest were also becoming more important as factors in the national development. The primitive tribes there were amalgamated under the common name of Volynjane, and the territory they occupied was called the principality of Volhynia. The westernmost Russian outpost was the fortified place of Galič (Halicz), founded by Prime Vladimir about 1140, from which the whole region derived its name — Galicia. The temporary union of Galicia with Volhynia at the beginning of the thirteenth century seemed to open new possibilities for further Russian development, although in the event they were to be frustrated.

At the same time in the north, Novgorod was developing into a great colonial power. It was sending colonists and pioneers as far as the White Sea, the basin of Pečora and the upper Volga.

What was the reason for this transformation? The dynastic struggles of the Rurik dynasty for the possession of Kiev do not explain such a massive exodus of the population towards the northeast and the southwest. Similar struggles were occurring also in the new principalities. The main reason may have been the invasions of the Cumans which were particularly devastating. The *Russian Primary Chronicle* registered fifty invasions between the years 1061 and 1210, besides many local raids. For this reason, and anxious to find more security, the population moved from the Kievan principality to the new lands in the northeast and the southwest where colonization had begun.

Thus ended one glorious phase in Russian history: that of the Kievan State. The new period which followed was one of independent principalities held together by a common tradition and a common faith. This stage of evolution was interrupted by another Asiatic invasion, that of the Mongols, and darkness fell over the Russian lands for two long centuries. When new hope dawned in Russian hearts, all eyes turned not towards the south where stood Kiev, the cradle of Russian glory, but to the north, where on the territory of the principality of Suzdal'-Vladimir, Moscow had arisen. And it was from this new center that the idea of the unity of the Russian lands, born in Kiev and blessed by the Church, began to be realized anew.

II

A survey of the main features of Kievan civilization and an examination of the inner evolution of Kievan Russia are necessary in order to analyze the reasons responsible for the rise and fall of Kiev. The problems which should be studied in this respect are many; and it is impossible to touch upon them all. Atttention must therefore be concentrated upon those which seem particularly relevant.

The main source of the wealth and importance of Kiev in Europe lay in its commerce with the East. It seemed that Europe had, at last, discovered a new access to the treasures of Byzantium and the Middle East, an access which was not subject to Arab intervention. This does not mean that the Arabs did not pay any attention to what was to them an important problem; but probably the continuous struggle which they were waging with Byzantium and the Christian world in Italy and Spain prevented them from seeing the advantages of commercial intercourse with the West and from developing it more fully. In years of peace they did trade with Byzantium and some Western countries. It was, however, left to the Scandinavians to seek new ways by which commercial relations between Western Europe and the Middle East could be restored and freed from the interference of Arab pirates in the Mediterranean and Adriatic. This was achieved by the Scandinavian discovery of the Volga route to

the Caspian Sea and Bagdad and later by the even more important discovery of the *put' iz Varjag v Greki* — the route from
Scandinavia to the Greeks, following the Dnieper and the coast
of the Black Sea. Because of this, Kiev became one of the most
important commercial centers in Europe. From there the Scandinavian conquerors also secured the trade route leading to Central Europe, which seems to have been used earlier by the Goths.
This explains the interest which Vladimir and his successors took
in the so-called Red cities and Přemysl, uniting Kiev with
Cracow and the Vistula on one side and with Prague, the Danube
and Regensburg on the other. In fact, mention is made as early
as the tenth century of Russian merchants on the upper Danube
and in Prague.

These commercial relations would have become of immense
and lasting importance for Russia if the Kievan princes had been
able to obtain complete control of the mouths of the rivers forming the main commercial channels — the Dnieper, Dniester, Don
and Volga. Unfortunately, the continual invasions of nomadic
tribes coming from the interior of Asia prevented them from
doing this, and their failure proved the main handicap to Kievan
trade. The Khazars, however, understood the importance of commercial intercourse. After some time, even the Pechenegs were
brought to see reason, and they concluded special trading ar-
rangements with the Russians; but the Cumans and, after them,
the Mongols extinguished all hopes that normal commercial intercourse would be continued.

This was all the more serious because, in the meantime, the
West had on its own initiative opened a new Mediterranean route
towards the Middle East by establishing a number of Christian
states in Syria and Palestine after the First Crusade (1096–1099).
In spite of this, there was still the possibility of trade with Byzantium in the south and with Scandinavia, the Baltic countries,
Flanders and England in the north. The conquest of Constantinople by the Latins in 1204, however, put a definite end to a
prosperous relationship with what was left of Byzantium. In the
north, only Novgorod was left in a position to trade with north-

ern Europe, Germany and the interior of Russia — a circumstance which saved this city from the sad fate which overcame the rest of Russia.

Russian exports were largely limited to raw materials — furs, wax, honey, flax, hemp, tow, burlap, hops, tallow, fats and hides, not to mention, especially in the tenth century, slaves. There was also a certain amount of transit trade, the Russian merchants re-exporting to Central and Northern Europe goods which they had obtained from Byzantium such as precious stones, spices, rugs, silks and satins and weapons of Damascus steel.

At first, foreign money was used in commercial transactions. This is illustrated by numerous finds of Arab, Byzantine and Scandinavian coins in many different places, which are particularly numerous for the ninth and tenth centuries. Apart from these, especially in the markets of the interior, certain kinds of furs were used as currency. Later, there appeared a form of metal currency — *grivna* — the value of which, however, was not very stable. In the reign of Vladimir, silver and gold coins were minted bearing the Duke's emblem. This was the beginning of the Russian monetary system, although furs continued to be favored in barter.

2

It was natural that commercial relations should exercise an important influence on the economic, social and political evolution of Russia. There is, in fact, a great difference in this respect between Russia and that part of Central Europe which was transformed by the Germanic migrations. In the Carolingian period and afterwards, the national economy of Central Europe was centered in the manors of the aristocratic landowners. Cities began to spring up only in a much later period, the twelfth century, when artisans and merchants had found their place in the national economy. In Kievan Russia, the situation was different. Trade could develop only in cities, and the market place was the center where townsfolk and country people met. It soon be-

came associated with political life and administration. All public announcements were made in the public market, and judges
would open their enquiries into, say, a case of theft only after
the plaintiff had proclaimed the details of the incident in the
market place.

The most important citizens were, naturally, the merchants,
who frequently exerted a considerable influence on the economic and political life of the nation. They formed companies
and guilds for their own purposes. Their example was followed
by artisans who united in cooperative associations. The importance of the city in national life is illustrated by the existence of
the *veče*, the city assembly, an institution which was a characteristic of Kievan Russia. It developed from the old council
of family chiefs common to all Indo-European nations. As,
thanks to the merchants, national life became centralized in the
cities, these assemblies of family heads grew in importance. In
minor cities the assemblies limited their activities to dealing with
purely local matters, but the *veče* in the capital cities became a
weighty political institution. It was presided over by the mayor,
who called its members together whenever the necessity arose.
The *veče* would meet near the ducal palace, or in the square
before the cathedral church, or in the market place. Sometimes
it had a voice in deciding the succession to the throne. Sometimes it claimed the right to voice dissatisfaction with the ruling
prince, even going so far as to call for his abdication. Usually,
it supported the prince and his council in matters of legislation
and administration. The dukes of Kiev generally succeeded in
keeping the assembly under control; but in Novgorod the *veče*
achieved the zenith of its power.

Thus it came about that the city inhabitants became a significant element in the state, although they were far fewer than the
free peasantry, called *smerdi*.[1] These latter continued to live in
the *zadruga* (great families) and regarded the soil which they

---

[1] On the low social position of the *smerdi* see the study by Y. Blum "The
Smerdi in Kievan Russia," *The Amer. Slavic and East Europ. Review*
XII (1953), pp. 122–130.

tilled as being the common property of all members of the great families. On this basis the *verv'*, a local community similar to the Anglo-Saxon guild, developed and was superseded later by the peasant commune (*obščina, mir*). In addition to the free peasantry there were also peasants who worked on the estates of the boyars, and slaves.

The upper classes were formed from the natives — Slavs, *muži*, leaders of clans and tribes — or from aliens — Scandinavians. From the second half of the eleventh century, however, the distinction between them began to disappear, and both merged into one class of the privileged boyars. The melting pot for this transformation was the *družina* — the retinues of the princes, composed at first of Scandinavian warriors and servants. From the old members the duke chose his *posadniks*, or representatives in the provincial administration. From the members of the retinue the duke also chose the *tysjatsky*, the city governor, who was also the commander of the city militia. At the beginning, he must have been elected by the people and was considered to represent the people before the ruler. This practice was continued in Novgorod. The prince also chose the members of his private council, the *duma*, from among the older members of his *družina*. Besides them, the native boyars, bishops and representatives of the merchants were also regarded as the duke's councillors.

3

There is a problem which is still debated by specialists in early Russian history: the question of feudalism in the Kievan period. There is no room to discuss this in detail, but it is pertinent to recall what happened in this respect in Byzantium. Feudalism was not a Byzantine institution, and the emperors struggled hard to prevent the disappearance of the free peasantry and the concentration of landed property in the hands of a powerful aristocracy. But they were unable to arrest the course of evolution. The impoverishment of the free peasantry, due to high taxation and foreign invasions, played into the hands of the landed aris-

tocracy, who promised protection and help in return for the surrender of the free use of the peasants' land. A similar evolution
had occurred in Bulgaria, and the same symptoms can also be observed in Kievan Russia during the period of its decline and
before the onslaught of the Mongols. The *deti boyarskie* (sons
of the boyars) and the *zakladničestvo*, which we find in the later
Kievan period, were a Russian version of the Greek and Bulgarian *paroikoi* — free peasants who sought the help and protection of the rich and mighty.[1]

It is thus evident, even from this short review of the economic,
social and political conditions of Kievan Russia, that there was
a basic difference in this respect between the Kievan State and
the rest of Europe. The main reason for this difference was economic — the flourishing trade that went on between the North
and the East. This circumstance enhanced the importance of
cities in the national life and helped to replace the old tribal
organization by a regional grouping of the population around
cities as centers of administration. Nowhere else in Europe do
we find the coexistence of city states and monarchic institutions
such as developed in Kievan Russia. This was the basis of Kiev's
strength — and also of its weakness. This special social structure delayed the evolution of feudalism, which dominated the
scene in contemporary Europe; but the crisis in trade, brought
about by the invasions and by the activities of the Crusaders,
combined with the lack of monarchic strength, brought about
the collapse of Kiev.

4

The high level of Russian civilization in the Kievan period and
its character are indicated by what we have learned about the
economic evolution of the country and its relations with the rest
of Europe. The vast incomes which the princes gathered from
tribute paid by their subjects and from their personal participa-

---

[1] On the further evolution of Russian feudalism see G. Vernadsky's study
"Feudalism in Russia," *Speculum* XIV (1939), pp. 300–323.

tion in trade enabled them to indulge a remarkable activity in the field of architecture. The artistic inspiration naturally came from Byzantium but also from the West and from the Near East; but Russian artists soon learned the secrets which their masters revealed to them, and they improved upon them.

Another important feature of Kievan civilization is that it was not closed to Western influences. These can be traced in its literary achievements, its juridical evolution and its religious life, and the stepping stone for these influences was eleventh-century Bohemia.

First of all, Byzantium's legacy to Russia in art was particularly generous, and the first dukes of Kiev spent lavishly to take advantage of it. In 989, Vladimir built a church of the Assumption in Kiev which was destroyed by the Mongols in 1240. The church of the Holy Wisdom (St. Sophia), begun in Kiev by Jaroslav the Wise and built during the years 1037–1100, is a jewel of Byzantine art, erected and embellished by Greek artists; and to obtain a correct impression of Greek art and architecture of the eleventh century, it is necessary to study the church in Kiev. Later the church of the Holy Wisdom in Novgorod (1045–1054) — as well as the Nereditsa church (1198) — followed the pattern of the Holy Wisdom of Kiev, and its bold lines converging on a crown of thirteen cupolas must have appealed strongly to the tastes of the Russians since they made it one of the characteristic features of all their subsequent ecclesiastical architecture. Unfortunately little remains of Byzantine architecture and art of the same period on the soil of the Empire itself.

Kiev had its second school of arts, founded by Byzantine masters, who introduced the new architectural style of which the church of Our Lady's Assumption in the Monastery of the Caves in Kiev was the first typical example. It was constructed in 1089, but was almost completely destroyed in the second World War. Two other churches, those of the monasteries of St. Cyril (1140) and of St. Michael with the Golden Cupola (1108), followed the pattern of the church of the Assumption, and this style also found its way north of Kiev to Černigov.

Besides architecture, the decorative arts also received inspiration from Byzantium. The mosaics and frescoes of St. Sophia of Kiev were discovered in 1843 and have since attracted much attention from historians of art. They are of singular beauty, some of them exceptionally striking for their vigorous design and expressive reality. Native artists soon began to imitate their Byzantine masters. Amongst them, Olympius, a monk of the Monastery of the Caves, was especially gifted, and the mosaics of St. Michael with the Golden Cupola are attributed to him. He lacks the dexterity and refinement of technique of his Greek masters; but shows remarkable originality in the conception of his figures which, less rigid than those of St. Sophia, are much more life-like and varied. His work is one of the finest examples of medieval Russian religious art.

From the twelfth century there are also the frescoes of Novgorod and Vladimir, which are in part the production of native artists.

The practice of painting icons also owes its origin to Byzantine inspiration. In this respect, the famous icon, Our Lady of Vladimir, deserves special mention. Painted in the eleventh or very early twelfth century and of Byzantine origin, it has inspired millions of Russians and was from the first admired and imitated because of its touching and unaffected beauty. The painting of icons developed into a special Russian form of religious art, in which native originality found a remarkable expression.

5

In the sphere of literature, Kievan Russia was most fortunate in that, from the very beginning of its Christian life, it was in possession of all the treasures of the Old Slavonic literature bequeathed to Moravia by SS. Cyril and Methodius. These were salvaged by their disciples, when the Moravian Empire collapsed, and brought by them to Bulgaria. The Bulgarians considerably enriched this heritage before they transmitted it to the Russians. Thus the catastrophe which befell Bulgaria in the tenth century, when it became a Byzantine province, proved to be of inestimable benefit to Russia, for many Bulgarian refugees fled there carrying with them copies of Old Slavonic literary works.

Another agency, so far overlooked, which was instrumental in introducing Slavonic letters into Kievan Russia was Bohemia. Historians were not clear about the extent of the Přemyslide State and the spread of the Slavonic liturgy in the Czech lands; but it is now known that Slavonic literature flourished in Bohemia throughout the tenth and eleventh centuries. As to the extent of the Přemyslide State, it is also known that, after the loss of Cracow and what remained of White Croatia, the Přemyslides held Moravia and Slovakia until the beginning of the eleventh century, when these two countries were occupied by Boleslas the Great of Poland. Then, in the tenth century, Poland, Kievan Russia and Bohemia met in the Carpathian Mountains. This made access from Bohemia into Kievan Russia very easy and explains, for example, how the manuscript of *Vita Methodii* found its way into Russia. Indeed, the preservation of this literary treasure is due to that happy circumstance.

A short notice on Vladimir the Great in Thietmar's *Chronicle* seems to indicate that Czech missionaries were active in Kiev during Vladimir's reign, if not before. After recalling (Book VII, Chap. 72 in R. Holtzmann's edition) the adventures of the Polish Bishop Reinbern in Kiev — he was imprisoned by Vladimir because of his intrigues with Vladimir's son Svjatopolk, who had married a Polish princess — Thietmar admits that Vladimir atoned for his many sins by generous charities. Then he continues: "When he was weakened by age and after having reigned in the above-mentioned realm for long, he died. He was buried in the great city of Kiev, in the church of Christ's martyr and Pope, Clement, beside his wife mentioned above. Their sarcophagi are visible there, standing in the middle of the church."

Thietmar's information about Kiev seems reliable. He had no reason for inventing the existence of an imaginary church in Kiev. He evidently gathered his information on Boleslas's Rus-

sian expeditions from German — most probably Saxon — mercenaries who were in the Polish army.[1] Thietmar speaks of the
presence of Germans in Boleslas's army during his first expedition
in 1013 (Book VI, Chap. 91, ed. R. Holtzmann) and provides
particularly precise information on Germans in Kiev in Boleslas's
army in 1018 (Book VIII, Chaps. 31, 32, ed. R. Holtzmann).
They numbered 300 and were probably commanded by Henry
(Henricus) the Proud, who lost his life during the encounter with
the Russians. It can readily be imagined that the Germans who
volunteered to help Boleslas reinstate his son-in-law Svjatopolk
in Kiev and who were so much impressed by all that they saw
there were eager to visit the grave of Svjatopolk's famous father.

It should be stressed, moreover, that the passage on Vladimir's burial in the church of St. Clement was added to the
manuscript of the *Chronicle* by Thietmar himself and written by
his own hand. As R. Holtzmann pointed out in the introduction
to his critical edition of Thietmar's *Chronicle*, the original manuscript of the *Chronicle*, now in the *Landesbibliothek* in Dresden,
was written by eight scribes who put down in writing what the
Bishop dictated. Thietmar, however, made many corrections
with his own hand and added short passages to supplement information which he had omitted when dictating to his scribes.
He seems then to have been convinced of the genuineness of the
above information since he took pains to add it to his scribe's
copy with his own hand.

At the same time, it is a known fact that St. Clement was the
patron saint of the Slavonic liturgy, and the existence of a
church of St. Clement in Kiev would thus indicate that priests
of the Slavonic liturgy — from Bulgaria or from Bohemia — were
present in Kiev in Vladimir's time.

Thietmar's information, however, is contradicted by the *Russian Primary Chronicle*, which say that Vladimir was buried in
the church of Our Lady, which he had founded. The same
source, however, helps to explain this apparent contradiction.

[1] Cf. P. Schmitthenner, *Das freie Söldnertum im abendländischen Imperium* (München, 1934), p. 20.

The *Chronicle* describes how Vladimir, after surrendering the city of Kherson to the Byzantines, transported the relics of St. Clement from there to Kiev. It can thus be surmised that Vladimir deposited the relics in the church of Our Lady, where a special chapel was dedicated to St. Clement.[1]

The fact that Vladimir wanted to be buried in the chapel of St. Clement shows that he harbored a special veneration for the Saint, whose relics had been discovered, as it was thought at that time, by SS. Cyril and Methodius, the founders of the Slavonic liturgy, during their stay in Kherson. If so, they evidently left part of the relics in that city.

It is thus possible that the cult of St. Clement helped Bulgarian and perhaps also Czech missionaries, who regarded him as the patron saint of the Slavonic liturgy introduced by SS. Cyril and Methodius, to penetrate to Kiev in Vladimir the Great's time. If this is so, they naturally brought with them their treasures of Slavonic literature.

The Russians built their own literature upon these Bulgarian and Czech materials, adapting to their own needs the many translations from the Greek which were brought to them from Bulgaria. To a young nation on the threshold of its intellectual life, this rich store of letters was indeed a godsend and a blessing which was denied to the young Western nations.

6

It should also be stated that the Russians made very good use of the gift. In this respect Jaroslav the Wise did for the Russians what Symeon the Great did for the Bulgarians. The *Russian Primary Chronicle* pays deep homage to Jaroslav's merits for the advancement of learning in Kiev: "He applied himself to books,

---

[1] Cf. N. Zakrevskij, *Opisanie Kieva* (Moscow, 1868), vol. I, p. 281. Already I. M. Karamzin, in his History of Russia (*Istorija Gosudarstva Rossijskago* [St. Petersburg, 1844], 5th ed., vol. I, footnote 488 to ch. II, col. 136) gave detailed information on the treatment of the sarcophagi and of the relics of St. Vladimir during the Tataric invasion and in the seventeenth century.

and read them continually day and night. He assembled many scribes and translated from Greek into Slavic. He wrote and collected many books through which true believers are instructed and enjoy religious education. . . . His father Vladimir plowed and harrowed the soil when he enlightened Rus through baptism, while this prince sowed the hearts of the faithful with the written word, and we in turn reap the harvest by receiving the teaching of books. . ."

In another passage the *Chronicle* says that Jaroslav had deposited the books written on his orders in the church of the Holy Wisdom. It is permissible to suppose that this library formed the basis of a kind of academy founded by Jaroslav in Kiev. Another Russian chronicle relates that, about 1030, Jaroslav founded a school in Novgorod for both clergy and laymen, and in the *Life of St. Theodosius* the existence of a school in Kursk is attested (about 1023). Casual remarks in other similar writings authorize the conclusion that these schools were not the only educational institutions and that ladies were not excluded from learning.

Because the knowledge of reading and writing was widespread, the production of books increased. Specialists think that at least forty new translations of Greek works were made in the Kievan State before the Tatar invasion. Among them were: commentaries on the Epistles of St. Paul and on the Canticle of Canticles, the lives of some popular Greek saints (Andrew the Fool in Christ, Stephen of Surož, Theodore of Studion, the Miracles of St. Nicholas, Cosmas and Damian and St. Demetrius), the sermons of St. Theodore of Studion and the statutes of his monastery, the *Letter* of Peter of Antioch, Nicetas's commentary on the sermons of St. Gregory of Nazianzus, and an account of the construction of the church of the Holy Wisdom in Constantinople.

It was in Kievan Russia that Old Slavonic literature reached its highest level and inspired many original writings of great value. In particular, mention should be made of the discourse by the metropolitan Ilarion (Hilarion) "On the Law and Grace." The author gives a rhetorical description of the Old Testament

— the Law — and of the New Testament — the Grace — which is not without originality. Then he stresses the universal role of Christianity, "the religion of grace which has spread over the whole earth" and has in the end also reached new nations among whom "is the people of Rus." And then also for the Rus "the lake of the Law dried out while the fount of the Gospel welled up" . . . and after covering the whole earth, "overflowed upon us."

With these words Ilarion expresses his joy over the entry of the Russian nation into the Law of Grace, swelled with a patriotic pride that Rus, which is known and celebrated to all the ends of the earth, had become a member of the universal Christian commonwealth. Therefore, as all countries honor the teachers who had acquainted them with the Orthodox faith — Rome, St. Peter, Asia and Ephesus, St. John, India, St. Thomas, Egypt, St. Mark — so should the Russians praise their great khagan, Vladimir, their teacher and instructor. Then follows a panegyric on St. Vladimir, who is pictured, together with his son Jaroslav the Wise, in the Byzantine fashion as the ideal Christian ruler. The work ends with a long "Prayer for Russia" full of deep sentiment.

The work is written, according to Ilarion, not for the simple people, but for those "who had feasted to their fill on the sweetness of books." Its style is highly rhetorical, full of symbolical parallels, of metaphors, antitheses and other oratorical figures. The treatise shows the strikingly high level of civilization reached by the new Christian nation during the earliest period of its Christian life. It gives ample evidence of a rapid assimilation of Greco-Byzantine culture and of the Cyrillo-Methodian inheritance by the Russians of Kiev.

Another original work, showing that the literary *élite* of the Kievan period had reached quite a high cultural level, is the famous *Russian Primary Chronicle*, formerly called Nestor's Chronicle after one of its supposed compilers,[1] which was given

---

[1] For more details see S. H. Cross's introduction to his English translation of the Laurentian version in *Harvard Studies and Notes in Philology and*

its final shape at the beginning of the twelfth century. This *Chronicle* — called in Russian *Povest' vremennych let* — the "Tale of Bygone Years," is preserved in two versions: the Laurentian (written in 1377) and the Hypatian (written about 1420). In the Laurentian version it is followed by a North Russian chronicle which goes down to the year 1305 and in the Hypatian by a South Russian chronicle recording events in Kiev, Galicia and Volhynia down to the year 1292.

The authors of the *Chronicle* used numerous Greek, Russian and other sources. Among the Greek sources, the most important are the *Chronicle* of George Hamartolus and those of John Malalas and George Syncellus. The Greek *Life of Basil the Young* and the *Revelations of Methodius of Patras* were also known to the compilers. The account of the origin of Slavic literature is taken from a Moravian source.[1] Included in the narrative of the *Chronicle* are many Russian and Varangian tales, both oral and written, monastic legends,[2] biographies,

---

Literature XII (1930), pp. 77–135; new edition by O. P. Sherbowitz-Wetzor (Cambridge, Mass., 1953), pp. 3–50. Cf. also N. K. Gudzy, *History of Early Russian Literature* (New York, 1949, translated by S. W. Jones), pp. 117–146.

[1] It may have been a manuscript, since lost, in defense of St. Methodius's right of jurisdiction over his metropolis of Sirmium, which extended over Pannonia, Great Moravia and a part of Illyricum. The *Russian Primary Chronicle* (6396–6406: 888–898) stresses that Methodius was the successor of Andronicus, one of the seventy disciples of Christ, whom St. Paul appointed bishop of "Illyricum, whither Paul first repaired and where the Slavs originally lived." St. Paul was thus promoted to be the Apostle of the Slavic race, and from this race — says the chronicler — "we Russians too, are sprung." Moreover, in the introduction the author stresses the Slavic character of Noricum. R. Jakobson rightly points out that these affirmations could have been found by the chronicler in a Moravian apology of Slavonic letters and of Methodius's metropolitan rights. It should be noted that these details are not mentioned in the *Vita Methodii* which the Russian chronicler might also have known. For details see Jakobson's study (Olaf Jansen) "Český podíl," in the Czech publication *Co daly naše země* (Prague, 1940), p. 16 and his "Sources for Early History of the Slavic Church" in *Harvard Slavic Studies* II (1954), pp. 61 ff.

[2] See, for example, the recent study by D. Čyževskij, "Studien zur russischen Hagiographie. Die Erzählung wom hl. Isaakij," *Wiener Slavist. Jahr-*

martial stories and popular sayings. Some of these were independent writings and their preservation is due to the *Chronicle*.

The *Chronicle* is a remarkable literary achievement. Its style,
although lacking in unity because of the miscellaneity of its
sources, is fluent, vigorous, fresh, often laconic and delightful
to the reader. It is no exaggeration to classify the *Chronicle* as
one of the best produced in Europe during the Middle Ages by
virtue of its literary qualities and historical documentation.

The *Chronicle* does not start with the creation of the world as
do Byzantine chronicles, but with the division of the earth
among Noah's sons and goes straight to the history of Japheth
and the confusion of the tongues, insisting that "the Slavic race
is derived from the line of Japheth." It further stresses the unity
of all Slavic nations, a rare instance of national consciousness at
so early a period.

Unlike the Serbs and the Bulgarians, the Russians made full
use of the annalistic training they obtained from their Byzantine
masters. The *Russian Primary Chronicle* became the basis of
numerous other local annalistic compilations which continued its
tradition. During the twelfth and early thirteenth centuries the
following cities and principalities had their annalists: Perejaslavl'
in the South, Černigov, Volhynia, Kiev, Novgorod, Rostov, Suzdalian Perejaslavl', and Vladimir even boasted three chronicles.[1]
Numerous other works in later periods also drew on these compilations.

To this historical literature should be added the Slavonic
translation of Josephus's *History of the Judaic War*.[2] It is another
document testifying to the taste of the Kievan Russians for historical literature.

---

buch II (1952), pp. 22–49 on the story of four monks from the Monastery
of the Caves, told by the chronicler *ad annum* 1074.

[1] A good survey of Russian chronicles is given by D. S. Lichačev in his
study *Russkie letopisy, ich kulturno-istorič. značenie* (Russian chronicles and
their importance for Russian History and Civilization), published by U.S.S.R.
Academy (Moscow, 1947).

[2] See the edition and translation by V. M. Istrin, A. Vaillant and P.
Pascal, *La Prise de Jerusalem de Joseph le Juif* (Paris, 1934–38).

At the beginning of the twelfth century, the Kievan Prince Vladimir Monomach, who died in 1125, left to his children and subjects his *Poučenie*, a book of "Instruction" which was also called his "Testament." It is again a remarkable literary document which gives impressive evidence of a high cultural level at the princely court of Kiev. The author, a layman and ruler, is very familiar with the Holy Writ and the service books. He had also read the different "Instructions" which were so popular in Byzantium and some of which, for example, those of Xenophon and Marius, were included in Svjatoslav's *Sbornik* of 1076.[1] In a terse and effective style Monomach sketches his experiences of life, and the advice he gives to his children discloses the high moral qualities of this extraordinary prince. There are few Western princes who could have produced such a work in the vernacular.[2]

Equally original is the account which the Prince's contemporary, Abbot Daniel, wrote of the pilgrimage to the Holy Land and of conditions in Jerusalem during the reign of the Latin King Baldwin,[3] whom the Russian monk accompanied on his campaign against Damascus. There are in this book many pages of unusual charm and beauty, which make it an outstanding example of early Russian literature.

In respect of original work, St. Theodosius, Abbot of the Caves Monastery, who died in 1074, may be compared with the Metro-

[1] Cf. the short study by T. Čyževska, "Zu Vladimir Monomach und Kekaumenos," *Wiener Slavistisches Jahrbuch* II (1952), pp. 157–160, in which the author shows some parallel passages between Monomach's admonitions and those of the Greek Kekaumenos.

[2] I. M. Ivakin, *Kniaz Vladimir Monomach i ego Poučenie* (Prince Vladimir Monomach and his Instruction), Moscow, 1901. New edition by A. S. Orlov (*Vladimir Monomach*, Moscow, 1946) with Russian translation. See also S. H. Cross, "The Testament of Vladimir Monomach," *Harvard Studies and Notes in Philology and Literature* XII (1930).

[3] A. de Noroff, *Pélérinage en Terre Sainte de l'Igoumène Russe Daniel au commencement du XIIe siècle* (St. Petersburg, 1864, French translation and Russian text). The English translation was made from the French version by C. W. Wilson — *The Pilgrimage of the Russian Abbot Daniel in the Holy Land*, 1106–1107 (London, 1888, Library of the Palestine Pilgrims Text Society, vol. IV).

politan Ilarion. His sermons to the monks are simple and reveal that the Saint was well acquainted with the sermons of St. John Chrysostom, of Theodore of Studion and of Basil the Great. In some homilies Theodosius complained bitterly about the lack of discipline among the monks. His extreme humility and charity seem to have been partly responsible for that. He rejected all visible signs of his abbatial authority, refused to punish erring monks, and was too ready to receive the runaway brethren back into the community.

In spite of this, Theodosius has the great merit of having introduced order and discipline into the young Russian monastic life. His ideal was not the excessive asceticism of the Syrian and Egyptian hermits whose example had inspired his own teacher St. Anthony, but rather the community life, divided between prayer, ascetic practices, manual work and service to the world.[1] He obtained a copy of the Greek rule of the Monastery of Studion in Constantinople, had it translated into Old Slavonic, and introduced this Rule of St. Theodore of Studion, the great reformer of Greek monasticism, into Kiev.

Besides Theodosius's homilies, there exist a certain number of original sermons from the eleventh and twelfth centuries, written by anonymous authors, which would merit special study. Two other prelates, the Metropolitan Clement Smoljatič and Cyril, Bishop of Turov, deserve special mention. In one of Clement's letters which has been preserved, he defends himself against accusations of quoting Homer, Aristotle and Plato in his sermons. This shows that the Greek classics were known in Kiev at that early period, if not in originals, at least from anthologies. Cyril, who died in 1185, provides evidence in his sermons, letters and prayers that very soon after the nation's conversion its clergy mastered the works of the Greek Fathers and adapted them with skill and understanding. His contemporaries and followers did

[1] Cf. G. P. Fedotov, *The Russian Religious Mind* (Cambridge, Mass. 1946), pp. 110 ff. (Russian kenoticism). See also the introduction (by W. Fritze) to the translation of Theodosius's Life in E. Benz, *Russische Heiligenlegenden* (Zürich, 1953), pp. 76–81. Cf. also R. P. Casey, "Early Russian Monasticism," *Orient. Christ. Periodica* 19 (1953), pp. 372–423.

not hesitate to compare him with considerable justification with St. John Chrysostom. There were other writers in the Russia of this period who composed original works; but their productions have survived only in fragments. Two Bishops of Novgorod, Luke Židjata and Elias, are the best known.

There are numerous translations of Greek hagiographic writings: at least five so-called *Paterika* (collections of Lives of Saints); that of Palladius, from Sinai, the "Egyptian Paterik," that of Jerusalem, an alphabetical *Paterikon* and the Roman *Paterikon*, which were translated into Old Slavonic and read in Kiev. Several original works of this character came from Kiev, such as the *Life of St. Vladimir* by the monk Jacob, the *Lives of St. Boris and St. Gleb* (died 1015), one anonymous, ascribed to Jacob and the other by Nestor, a monk of the Monastery of the Caves, a *Life of St. Theodosius*, one of the founders of Russian monasticism (died 1074), also by Nestor of the Monastery of the Caves, and a *Life of St. Mstislav of Kiev* (1132).

One important contribution to early Russian literary activity was the *Pečerskij Paterik*, or collection of lives of saints, compiled in the famous Monastery of the Caves in Kiev. Besides some original items of information on this celebrated center of ascetic life, this work contains about thirty biographical sketches of local saints together with many legends. Some of this material had been written in the eleventh century, but most of it belongs to the thirteenth century when the whole collection was put together.

The *Paterik* is a very important source for the study of the spiritual life of Kievan Russia. Most of the local saints — Nicholas Svjatoša, one of the princes of Černigov, Prochorus the pigweed-eater, Spyridon the wafer-maker, Agapit the healer, Gregory the wonder-maker, Isaac the "holy fool in Christ," Moses the Hungarian, a war prisoner in Poland, Eustratius, a war prisoner in the Crimea where he was crucified by the Jews, Nicon the Dry, captive among the Cumans, Kukša, martyred by the pagan Vjatiči, Mark the cave-dweller, and others — were disciples or followers of the ascetic practices introduced into Kiev by Anthony and Theodosius, the founders of the Monastery and of Russian monasticism. In the lives and legends of the *Paterik*, Eastern ascetic traditions from Syria and Palestine can be traced which became familiar to the Russians through the intermediary of the Monastery of Studion in Constantinople and of Mount Athos.

The influence of Theodosius and his monastic ideas on Russian monasticism was more lasting than that of Anthony. His biography, one of the best works of this kind written in the Kievan period,[1] became a pattern for other Russian hagiographers and was a source of inspiration for many centuries to come to Russians who desired to embrace the religious life. It is not surprising that Theodosius was the first monk to be canonized by the Russian Church.

Juridical literature is also well represented by some original works such as the Greek and Russian "Ecclesiastical Rule" (*Tserkovnij Ustav* — about 1089), by the Metropolitan John II, and *Voprošanie* of Kirik (about 1130–1156), of which we possess only a few quotations. The first codification of Russian customary law, attributed to Jaroslav the Wise and called *Russkaja Pravda*, also belongs in its original form to the eleventh century.[2] Besides this original composition, there existed early in the Kievan period translations of handbooks of Byzantine law — especially the *Ecloga* and *Procheiron*. These reached Kiev from Bulgaria, together with the canonical *Collection of XIV Titles*, to which they were added. The "Agrarian Law" (*Nomos Georgicos*) was translated in the twelfth or thirteenth century. The *Collection of Canon Law* of John Scholasticus also

---

[1] It was translated into English by G. P. Fedotov (*A Treasury of Russian Spirituality*, London, 1950, pp. 14–49). Cf. the last edition of the *Paterik* by D. Abramovič (*Kievsko-Pečerskij Paterik*, Kiev, 1930). See the German translation of a great part of the *Paterik* in Benz's *Russ. Heiligenleg.*, op. cit., pp. 169–243 with a very instructive introduction by D. Čyževskij. *Ibid.*, pp. 76–156 a complete translation of Theodosius's Life.

[2] See the English translation of the *Pravda*, with bibliographical notices in G. Vernadsky's *Medieval Russian Law* (Columbia Univ. Press, New York, 1947), pp. 26 ff.

reached Kiev from Bulgaria soon after its Christianization. It contained some important *Novellae* of Justinian.

Such are the outstanding works of early Russian literature written, of course, in the Russian version of Old Slavonic, the only literary language of the Slavs at that time, with a strong and growing infiltration of vernacular elements. It should be noted that all these works were written in the vernacular, a remarkable achievement at that time, since we know that most of the Western nations did not start writing in vernacular prose until the thirteenth century at the earliest, and most of them only in the fourteenth.

In the field of belles-lettres, the Russians of the Kievan period showed the same taste as other nations of the time. Like the Bulgarians, they liked Old Testament stories mixed with tales from the Apocrypha and condensed in the so-called *Paleia*. Among the apocryphal writings which they obtained from the Bulgarians, "The Virgin Mary's Journey through the Inferno" and "The Story of Solomon and the Kitovras" were extremely popular. So also was "The Story of Barlaam and Josaphat," which was a variation of the life of Buddha adapted to the Christian mentality of the eighth century. Of course, the legendary *Life of Alexander the Great*, a product of the late Hellenistic age, appealed greatly to the Russians, as it did to all nations in the Middle Ages. This was translated in the eleventh or twelfth century, and also the great epic of the Byzantine frontiersmen in Asia Minor and of their fight against the Arabs — known as the *Digenis Akritas* — was translated in the twelfth or thirteenth century.

Besides the translations, original epic poems glorifying the deeds of national heroes must also have existed. These poems were transmitted orally before they were written down. The most original epic poem in manuscript, of which the Russians are justly proud, is *The Lay of Igor' 's Campaign*. It describes the disastrous expedition made in 1185 against the Cumans by Prince Igor' with some relatives and their retinues. The poet's words echo the sadness felt by all patriotic Russians when they learned about the defeat and witnessed new invasions of Russian land by the pagans. The poem reflects also in its vocabulary the lively intercourse the Russians of Kiev had with the Turkic nomads and describes better than the account of an annalist what the people had to suffer from the devastating nomadic invasion into the lands of Rus. The work seemed to many too beautiful and too perfect to have been composed at so early a period. Professor R. Jakobson,[1] however, definitely proved that it originated in the Kievan period soon after Igor''s unfortunate expedition against the Polovci.

Many epic poems which were transmitted orally and known in the Middle Ages, as for instance *byliny* or *stariny*, must have originated in the Kievan period to judge by their contents.[2] For some of them recall the deeds of Russian heroes fighting the nomads and the Jews, that is, the Khazars. The Kievan epic songs mostly glorified the heroes of Vladimir's *družina*. Ilja of Murom was their senior, and they reflect the rather democratic spirit which characterized the relationship between the duke and his retinue. Some poems originated in Polock and in Galicia about the twelfth century. Probably in the same period there appeared the early version of "Sadko the Rich Merchant," the famous poem, so typical of Novgorod with its commercial activity and its respect for wealth. In another Novgorodian epic — "Vaska Buslaev" — the restless and troublesome youth of the rich city is well portrayed.

[1] "Le Geste du Prince Igor" *Annuaire de l'Institut de Philologie et d'Histoire Orientales et Slaves* VIII (New York, 1948), in collaboration with H. Grégoire and M. Szeftel. An English translation of the Tale, made by S. H. Cross, will also be found there. A. Mazon (*Le Slovo d' Igor*, Paris, 1940) and H. Paszkiewicz (*The Origin of Russia*, London, 1954, pp. 336–353) are the latest opponents of the authenticity of the work. Cf. also R. Jakobson "The Puzzles of the Igor Tale on the 150th Anniversary of its First Edition," *Speculum* XXVII (1952), pp. 43–66, and K. H. Menges, "The Oriental Elements in the Vocabulary of the Oldest Russian Epos, The Igor's Tale," *Word* VII (1951), Supplement Monograph, No. 1.

[2] For details see R. Jakobson, E. J. Simmons, *Russian Epic Studies* (Philadelphia, American Folklore Society, 1949, vol. 42) pp. 14 ff.; R. Trautmann, *Volksdichtung der Grossrussen* (Heidelberg, 1935); N. K. Chadwick, *Russian Heroic poetry* (Cambridge, 1932).

III

So far original works and translations from the Greek have been analyzed; but Kievan Russia was also open to works coming from the West such as original Slavonic works and translations from the Latin. As was stated above, Vladimir opened a gate to Western Europe when he occupied the eastern part of modern Galicia. Recent discoveries have shown that Slavic literary activity continued in the Přemyslide Empire throughout the tenth and eleventh centuries; and it was from there that translations from the Latin and Slavonic original works found their way into Russia, not only to Kiev but also to Novgorod. The earliest was the original *Life of St. Wenceslas*, written in Bohemia in Old Slavonic soon after 929. The text has been preserved only in manuscripts copied in Russia. Another *Life of St. Wenceslas*, written in the tenth century in Latin by Gumbold of Mantua, was translated into Slavonic in Bohemia and at the same time considerably enlarged. The preservation of this work is due to the fact that it was taken to Kiev.[1] A Latin *Life of St. Vitus*, patron saint of Saxony and Bohemia, was also translated in Prague and is found in a Russian collection dating from the twelfth century, called the *Uspenskij Sbornik*. The Slavonic Life of Wenceslas's grandmother, St. Ludmila, now lost, was known in Kievan Russia and is preserved in its abridged form by the Russian Church in the Lessons of the Saint's feast.

Besides these works, the Czech origin of which is incontestable,

[1] It appears that the author of the *Life of St. Theodosius* (Feodosi) knew this *Legend of St. Wenceslas* and was inspired by this writing when composing Theodosius's biography. See for details the study by D. Čyževskyj "Anklänge an die Gumpoldslegende des Hl. Václav in der altrussischen Legende des Hl. Feodosij und das Problem der 'Originalität' der slavischen mittelalterlichen Werke" (*Wiener Slavisches Jahrbuch* I [1950], pp. 71–86). A detailed account of the numerous Western literary elements in Kievan literature and of their origins in Bohemia will be found in the following study: F. Dvornik, "Les Bénédictins et la christianisation de la Russie," *L'Eglise et les Eglises, 1054–1954* (Ed. de Chevetogne, 1954), pp. 323–349. Cf. also P. Devos, "Chronique d'hagiographie slave," *Analecta Bollandiana*, 72 (1954), pp. 426–438.

there exist a number of texts in Russian manuscripts dating from the fourteenth and fifteenth centuries which are certainly translations from the Latin into Slavonic. They were studied by A. I. Sobolevskij at the beginning of the present century, but the importance of these finds has, so far, been overlooked by most Slavic philologists. Some of these texts were almost certainly translated into Slavonic in Bohemia, whence they found their way into Kievan Russia. Among them are the *Life of St. Benedict of Nursia*, the *Martyrdom of Pope St. Stephen*, a short homily on the Baptism and Ascension of Jesus Christ, works on St. Cosmas and Damian and a sermon by St. Gregory the Great. Others, such as the sermons of SS. Peter and Paul on John the Baptist, and an Easter sermon, may be attributed to St. Methodius's favorite disciple, St. Clement, who fled to Bulgaria.[1]

2

But there is even more. Kievan Russia was open to more than literary influences from the West, and the Russian Church accepted the cult of Western saints. This explains how the cult of SS. Wenceslas and Ludmila, two Czechs, but of the Latin Church, came to be popular in Russia in the eleventh century. There are indications that the cult of St. Adalbert (Vojtěch), Bishop of Prague, the great friend of Otto III and Boleslas the Great of Poland, was known in Russia at the same period.

An interesting document in this connection is a prayer to the Blessed Trinity. It is of Western origin and could have found its way into Kievan Russia from nowhere but the Přemyslide Empire. It lists a number of Western saints and asks for their intercession: SS. Magnus, Canute, Olaf, Alban, Botulf, Martin, Victor, the Popes Linus, Anacletus, Clement and Leo, the saintly brothers Cyril and Methodius, Wenceslas and Adal-

[1] See R. Jakobson "Kernel of Comparative Slavic literature," *Harvard Slavic Studies* I (1953). The same author under the pseudonym "Olaf Jansen" gives a short and stimulating account of this literary intercourse in Czech Symposium (*Co daly naše země Eyropě a lidstvu* — What our lands gave to Europe and humanity — Prague, 1940, pp. 9–20).

bert. This prayer must have been composed at the end of the eleventh century and seems to have been popular in medieval Russia. It is found in different versions in Russian manuscripts dating from the fourteenth to the sixteenth century. The choice of saints is remarkable for its cosmopolitan character. SS. Magnus, Columban, Gall and Alban were held in great veneration in Germany; St. Canute is Danish; Olaf was a Norwegian ruler; Botolf, an Anglo-Saxon; St. Martin of Tours, a Gaul; St. Victor was popular in Switzerland, and the others are Slavic patron saints. The invocation of the Popes is also characteristic.

Another Old Slavonic prayer, for protection from the devil, has also a curious miscellany of saints, some of them taken from the prayer to the Blessed Trinity, together with SS. Lucy, Cecilia and Walpurga. There are other prayers in the collection which seem to be translated from a Latin original, especially those attributed to St. Gregory the Great and to St. Ambrose.

Perhaps the most characteristic evidence of the friendly religious intercourse that was carried on between Kievan Russia and the West is the inclusion of the feast of the translation of St. Nicholas's relics in the liturgy of the Russian Church. These relics were stolen in 1087 from Myra in Asia Minor by some Italian merchants, who brought them in triumph to their native city of Bari. The joy over the acquisition of the relics of so famous a miracle worker was so general in the Western Church that the Pope instituted a special feast commemorating the "translation of the relics of St. Nicholas." Of course, this feast does not exist in the Byzantine Church, which regarded that "translation" as an act of robbery; but it was introduced into Kievan Russia. An office of the translation was composed in Kiev in Old Slavonic soon after 1091, and thus the Russian Church joined eloquently with the Church of the West in celebrating the translation of the relics from the East.[1] It may be

---

[1] Here is a particularly telling passage from the Russian office: "The city of Bari rejoices and with it the whole universe exults in hymns and spiritual canticles . . . Like a star the relics have gone from the East to the West . . . And the city of Bari has received divine grace by thy presence.

that this translation considerably enhanced the popularity of St. Nicholas in the West, a popularity which is still echoed in the Anglo-Saxon world at Christmas, for Santa Claus is none other than the Greek miracle worker, St. Nicholas.

3

Another illustration of this friendly religious intercourse between the West and Russia is to be found in the *Life of St. Marianus*, abbot of a monastery in Regensburg, which was a Scottish foundation. We read there that a monk of the Abbey, named Mauricius, went to Kiev in order to ask "the king of the city" for a contribution towards the cost of completing the Abbey. Vladimir Monomach (died 1125) was the "king" referred to, and he gave the visiting monk a handsome donation in the form of a number of valuable furs. The Scottish monks of Regensburg must have been in frequent contact with Kiev, for probably towards the end of the twelfth century, they built a church and a monastery there to minister to the German colony and other foreign merchants who were trading with Russia. Later their foundation in Kiev was destroyed by the Mongol invaders.

Another document, written after 1132, describes how Western pilgrims returning from Russia were attacked by robbers and rescued by St. Godard. It seems clear from the context that the expedition was a religious pilgrimage to the shrines of Kiev. The party was not armed and was accompanied by a priest.

The main link in this intercourse with the West was the Abbey of Sázava near Prague, founded by St. Procopius (died 1053), a foundation which kept its Slavonic character until 1096. Among its treasures was a relic of SS. Boris and Gleb, who were canonized by the Russian Church in 1072 and there are some indications that even Olga, the first Kievan saint, was venerated in Bohemia.

All this intercourse took place at a time when the Eastern and

If now the country of Myra is silent, the whole world, enlightened by the holy worker of miracles, invokes him with songs and praise."

Western Churches were supposed to be in schism, brought about in 1054 by the excommunication of the Patriarch Cerullarius by the legates of the Pope. The Russian case shows that prevailing conceptions of the importance of this break in its effect upon the relations between East and West will have to be modified. The Russian Church, at least, did not attach too great an importance to this "schism," although it was governed by a Greek metropolitan and although anti-Latin polemical literature began to circulate in Russia from the end of the eleventh century.

Nor did the West seem aware of any religious rupture with Russia, as is proved by the frequent intermarriages between members of the Rurik dynasty and members of the principal European ruling families.

The consequences of the rift between Western and Eastern Christianity are to be observed in Russia's relations with the West only from the beginning of the twelfth century onwards. At that time the centralizing and Latinizing tendencies introduced by Gregory VII began to be more and more strongly felt in Bohemia and to penetrate into Poland. The result was the suppression of the Slavonic liturgy in Bohemia and a growing hostility towards the Slavonic rite in Croatia.[1] On the other

---

[1] In the *Life of Moses the Hungarian* (see the German translation in E. Benz's, *Russ. Heiligenleg.*, p. 199) there is an allusion to the persecution of monks being initiated by Boleslas the Great in Poland before his death in 1025. It is thought by some scholars that this persecution should be interpreted as a hostile action by the Polish King against monks of the Slavonic liturgy in Poland because it coincides with the first outburst of hostility against Slavonic monks in Bohemia. Such an interpretation is not impossible but highly hypothetical. Boleslas the Great was not hostile to the Slavonic liturgy. The first Polish historian, Anonymous Gallus, mentions, among the mourners at Boleslas's death, the clergy of the Slavonic liturgy. It is possible that the author of the Life confused this incident with what happened after Boleslas's death. The *Russian Primary Chronicle* mentions a revolt during which bishops and priests and boyars were killed in the year 1030. This may have occurred in connection with the intrigues of Bezprym who enlisted Russian support against his brother, Mieszko II, Boleslas's successor. In 1031 Bezprym became master of Poland. It may also be that Izjaslav's Polish wife, when admonishing her husband not to do any wrong to the monks of the Caves Monastery, had this incident in mind. According to the *Life of Theodosius* she is supposed to have said to her husband that,

hand, the animosity against Western Christians which arose from
the contact of the Greeks with the Crusaders inflamed anti-
Latin sentiments in Byzantium. At the same time, anti-Latin
propaganda was intensified by the Greek clergy in Kiev.

This growing antagonism is illustrated by the attitude of two
of the best Slavic historians of the period. On the one hand, the
Czech historian Cosmas, writing in Latin, ignored the work of
the two men who were mainly responsible for the Christianization of Moravia and Bohemia — SS. Cyril and Methodius — because of their connection with the schismatic East. On the other
hand, the anonymous monk of the Monastery of the Caves, when
preparing the definitive edition of the *Russian Primary Chronicle*, minimized the role of the Czechs in the growth of Kievan
Christian civilization, because they belonged to the Latin cultural world. When speaking of the founders of Slavonic letters
— SS. Cyril and Methodius — he avoids stressing the role of the
Popes in their activity. In this atmosphere, another Czech saint
— St. Adalbert — whose cult existed in Kiev in the eleventh century, appeared to the Russians in a distorted light, as a man who
was responsible for the suppression of the Slavonic liturgy. It is
no wonder then that the name of another Czech saint, a staunch
supporter of the Slavonic liturgy, St. Procopius, was not included
in the calendar of the Russian Church; for he was canonized by
Rome only in 1204. The change in the Polish mentality towards
the Russians is echoed in the invitation addressed by the Bishop
of Cracow to St. Bernard, when he was preaching the Second

---

when monks had been expelled in Poland, the country had "to suffer much
evil." Izjaslav's hostility against the Monastery cannot be interpreted as the
Prince's reaction against the monks who opposed his pro-Western policy.
In his *Life of St. Theodosius*, Nestor gives a plausible reason for the Prince's
animosity, namely the admission, by the Abbot Anthony, of one of his boyars
and one of his eunuchs to the monastic status without securing the Prince's
permission. Anthony's successor, St. Theodosius, is said to have been a
staunch supporter of Izjaslav in spite of the latter's pro-Western policy. It
seems that only in later tradition was this incident interpreted as representing
opposition by the monks to Izjaslav's attempts to obtain the Pope's help for
the recovery of his lost throne (see below, p. 276). Cf. R. Jakobson and J.
Simmons, *Russian Epic Studies* (Philadelphia, 1949), pp. 37, 38, 45 ff.

Crusade, not to forget the schismatic Russians in his efforts. Only then did the estrangement between Kiev and the Western Slavs become apparent, and the cultural intercourse between Kiev and the West came to a stop.

4

This change was discernible at first only among the educated classes. It took more time before this mistrust reached the ordinary people on both sides. It is no wonder, therefore, that Russia was regarded as a fabulously rich country and the home of valiant knights. From the allusions to Russian exports in the *chansons de geste*, a very clear picture may be obtained of what constituted trade with Russia. Furs, horses, precious cloths, gold and silver are mentioned — the last objects being evidently of Byzantine origin, but re-exported to the West by Russian traders. In one version of the romance of Beuve de Hamtoun, the old maritime Varangian route to Russia and the Black Sea from England, through the North Sea and the Baltic, is explicitly mentioned. The same poem relates that merchants from "great Russia" bought Beuve in Hungary as a slave and sold him in Armenia. This suggests that the wide connections of Russian merchants were notorious in Europe.

Another description of the old Varangian route, although it is not altogether clear, can be read in the ecclesiastical history of Hamburg written by Adam of Bremen. There he describes the route over the Baltic and Lake Ladoga to Novgorod, called by him Ostergard, and thence over Lovat and the Dnieper to Kiev and the Black Sea. Gervase of Tilbury also knew that the Russia of Kiev could be reached from Britain by way of the Baltic. The same Varangian route also figures on the first medieval maps — that of Henry of Mainz (1110) and the famous Hereford map of the world (1276–83). Finally, references to Russia are to be found in some English chronicles which echo the catastrophe which befell the Kievan State during the Mongol invasions — for example, in the continuation of Gervase of Canterbury's *Gesta*

Regum, in the *Annals* of Burton, in Matthew of Paris's *Chronica Maiora*. This catastrophe also made a great impression upon Chaucer, for he alludes to it in his *Canterbury Tales*, but after that, Russia disappeared from the accounts of Western chroniclers.

5

The frequent contacts between Kievan Russia and the countries of the West and the friendly relations which developed between them seem to puzzle many who think that, as an Orthodox land, Russia should have restricted her dealings to Byzantium alone. Some go so far as to contend that the princes of Kiev were vassals of the emperor, but this conception is quite false. Russia was never Byzantium's vassal. It is true that the metropolitan in Kiev was often a Greek prelate. Even when a Russian was elected, he had to be consecrated by the patriarch of Constantinople and confirmed in his office by the emperor. Such a situation was possible in Russia because the Russians had taken from Byzantium, besides the Christian faith, also the Byzantine and Christian version of the Hellenistic notion of the divinized king — the Law Incarnate or animate, the Basileus, successor of Constantine the Great, the only representative of God on earth, who wielded supreme power over all Christians. This alone explains the kind of subordination to Constantinople in which Russia was held during the first four centuries of her existence.

The supreme authority of the Orthodox Basileus was perfectly compatible with the political independence of the Grand Prince of Kiev and other Russian princes. The supreme legislative power of the Basileus over the whole of Christendom was expressed in Russia by the fact that the basic principles of Russian legislation — especially in religious matters — were Byzantine.[1]

---

[1] On the reception of Byzantine laws by the Slavs see the study by T. Saturník, *Příspěvky k šíření byzantského práva u Slovanů* (Contributions to the spread of Byzantine jurisprudence among the Slavs, Prague, 1922). In another study the author came to the conclusion that even the Pope Nicholas had sent Boris of Bulgaria a copy of the main parts of the Codex of

This helped both Byzantines and Russians to reconcile the idea of a supreme legislator in Constantinople with an independent growth of Russian law, in which sufficient allowance was made for the gradual absorption of Western principles after the first codification of the *Russkaja Pravda*, or "Russian Law," started by Jaroslav the Wise.

The Byzantine conception of the emperor as the representative of God on earth and the head of all Christians became the principle of all Russian religious and political life, and the Hellenistic-Byzantine notion of monarchy, as popularized by the Russian clergy under Greek tuition, lies at the very root of Russian political thought. We can trace the first stages of its growth in the *Izbornik* of Svjatoslav (1076) and in the Russian chronicles.

Geographical reasons explain why this conception was so readily adopted by the Russians and why it was able to take such deep root in Kiev. Russia was not an immediate neighbor of Byzantium, and therefore the Kievan princes were less tempted than the Bulgarian khagans to become masters of Constantinople and to replace the Basileus in his leadership of Christendom. On the other hand, the distance which separated both states minimized the danger of direct imperial intervention in the internal affairs of Russia.

Nevertheless, the fact that it was often a Greek who stood at the head of the Russian Church and was the country's cultural leader eventually proved to be somewhat beneficial to Russia, and the Kievan princes must have been well aware of it. It proved helpful when the state first came to be divided among the members of the Rurik dynasty. Because many metropolitans, and many bishops also, were foreigners, they were but faintly interested in local politics, but preferred to concentrate upon maintain-

---

Justinian and not the Lombard Law, as has been generally thought. ("Které zákony světské poslal papež Mikuláš I Bulharům r. 866?" — What kind of civil laws did the Pope Nicholas I send to the Bulgarians in 866?) in *Slovanské studie* (Prague, 1948), pp. 120–129. The problem deserves a special monograph.

ing peace and preserving unity rather than to take sides. The fact that he had to be confirmed in his office by Constantinople secured even to a metropolitan of Russian nationality more freedom of action. So it came about that the idea of the unity of the Russian nation and of Russian lands was saved and preserved by the Greek Church.

6

From the description of the relations of Kievan Russia with Byzantium and with the West, it becomes clear that the new Slav empire was in quite a good position to become an intermediary for Byzantine culture to penetrate Central and Western Europe. There were signs that Kievan Russia received from Byzantium not only theological learning but also the literary and philosophical treasures of the classical and Hellenistic periods, and it has been seen that Clement Smoljatič, Metropolitan of Kiev from 1147 to 1155, was accused of quoting Homer, Plato and Aristotle in his sermons more often than the Fathers of the Church. In Kievan Russia there certainly was a small *élite* of natives who were able to read classical works in Greek. The Greek metropolitans and the bishops who were sent to Russia were accompanied by secretaries, so that in every Russian diocese there may have been a small circle acquainted with Greek literature and philosophy. Besides, it is known that Russians developed the habit of visiting Byzantine centers of learning, Mount Athos being a favorite place of pilgrimage, and from such places Byzantine monastic traditions were transplanted into Russia. Russian artists sent for training to Byzantium brought back, in addition to the technical knowledge which they had acquired, a knowledge of Greek and of Greek manuscripts. There is also some evidence that Kiev made a start in carrying Greek culture to Central Europe, and it is surprising to see that Poland was the first country to benefit by this. A letter written in 1027 by Matilda, daughter of Hermann, Duke of Swabia, to Mieszko II of Poland, has been mentioned in which she praises the King's knowledge of Greek:

"Who ever mastered so many languages to God's glory? Though able to worship God worthily in your own tongue and in Latin, you did not consider this enough and chose to add Greek." This Polish prince could have learned Greek only from Greeks or Slavs living in Kievan Russia. In the *Life of St. Moses the Hungarian,* we learn, on the other hand, that monks from Mount Athos visited Poland.

These were promising indications of hopes which, unfortunately, never materialized, for there are no Slavic translations of complete classical works. A Russian who did not know Greek could acquaint himself with only a few fragments of Greek philosophical lore by reading the Slavic translation of *Dialectics* and similar collections, and also "Philosophical Chapters," written by John of Damascus, are based upon Aristotle. He could read some excerpts from Democritus, Plato, Aristotle, Philo, Epictetus and others in the collection of aphorisms translated into Slavonic in the twelfth century under the name *Pčela,* from *Melissa —* "Bee" (XIth century). The translation of two old Byzantine works on natural science, the *Christian Topography* by Cosmas Indicopleustes and the *Physiologus,* a popular handbook of natural history may also be mentioned.

This was, however, not enough. Russia needed more time to acquire from Byzantium all the heritage of classical and Hellenistic lore; but this was denied her. Before she could obtain what she needed, or even digest what she had already acquired, the decadence of Kiev, due to internal troubles, the decline of commerce and the Mongol invasion, had begun and steadily worsened. It was indeed Russia's greatest misfortune that she never had time to acquire and digest the full spiritual inheritance of Byzantium.

7

The division of Kievan Russia into principalities governed by members of the Rurik dynasty did not stop all cultural evolution, nor did it cut Russia off from contact with Western Europe. The cultural evolution developed in general in the direction which it

had been given by Kiev, and contact with the West was even intensified in the principalities of Galicia-Volhynia and Novgorod.
The principality of Suzdal', on the other hand, looked towards the
East, in the direction of the Volga river and the world of Islam.
Besides Kiev, these were the main new centers of Russian political life, the most prominent among the numerous principalities
whose number grew steadily as fathers divided their appanages
among their children.

The lands forming the principality of Galicia and Volhynia
grew in importance only in the twelfth century when the population from the Kievan principality began to migrate towards the
West where there was more security from the invasions of the
nomads. In 1199, they were united in the hands of a single member of the Rurik dynasty, Roman Mstislavič. Polish and Hungarian influences were particularly strong here and made themselves felt not only in the political field but also in the social
structure of the principality. Western feudal institutions soon
replaced the native democratic system of *veče*, and the powerful
aristocracy claimed its part in government in imitation of its
counterparts in other Western countries.

The principality of Novgorod, however, developed further the
native institution of the *veče* and became a kind of republic.
From the end of the twelfth century it elected its prince, who
ruled with the help of administrators appointed by the *veče*.
Only one of its princes became a military leader and a great national figure — Alexander Nevskij, who in 1240 defeated the
Swedes on the Neva river when they were menacing Novgorod.
The principality extended its territory considerably towards the
northeast and took control of the upper region of the trade route
down the Volga to the Near East. It became an important intermediary in commercial relations with the West, the bulk of the
commerce being in the hands of the German Hansa, and for several centuries the city remained susceptible to cultural influences
coming from the West.

8

The evolution of the principality of Suzdal' followed quite different lines. It was largely inhabited by Finns, most of whom had been assimilated by Russian colonists from Novgorod and the South. The Novgorodians introduced their democratic institutions into the cities which they founded; but the princes of Suzdal' kept them on a tight rein and did not permit the *veče* to attain any real importance. Andrew Bogoljubskij (1157–1174) was particularly adept in developing this policy. The principle of hereditary succession within the family was also introduced, and the basis laid for a strong and autocratic regime. In the period from the twelfth to the fifteenth century, a new ethnical type slowly developed here, and the differences in language, culture and outlook from that of the rest of Russia became more and more marked. The mixture of Slavic and Finnish stock and the climatic conditions of the principality gave this new ethnical type some characteristic features which still distinguish the Great Russians: endurance and patience tempered with a kind of fatalistic outlook. Nevertheless, the ethnical differentiation of the Eastern Slavs into Ukrainians, Byelorussians (White Russians) and Great Russians was not yet perceptible at this stage, although dialectical differentiation was already perceivable.

In the cultural sphere, Galicia and Volhynia were, of course, the lands which came most under Western influence. This influence made itself felt most in architecture, art and social conditions. From here Western influences also penetrated into Černigov, where they produced a combination of Romanesque and Byzantine features which in due course reached the principality of Vladimir-Suzdal'. Here, the new school flourished from 1157 to 1212 under the Grand Prince Andrew and his brother, Vsevolod III, the ancestor of the Grand Princes and Tsars of Moscow. The frescoes of the cathedral of Vladimir and those of the beautiful church of St. Demetrius were discovered only in recent years.

This territory was the eastern limit of Russian expansion during the Kievan period, and at a later stage in its evolution it became the meeting place of Western elements coming from Galicia through Černigov and from Novgorod and Eastern elements coming from Georgia, Armenia, Asia Minor and Persia. This blending of different cultural elements is mirrored most clearly in Suzdalian art. For example, the bas reliefs in the church of St. George in Iur'ev Polskij provide most interesting features of this combination, the Byzantine element predominating. Many of them have a definitely Oriental character; while others betray the strong influence of Western Romanesque. They best illustrate the role which the principality of Suzdal' played in the thirteenth century — for the church was built in 1230–1237 — as a meeting place of Byzantine, Oriental and Western influences.

In this principality can also be seen the first results of Russian expansion towards the East, which later assumed such amazing proportions. New cities arose — Tver', Jaroslavl', Moscow and Nižni' Novgorod. Moreover, a brisk trade with the Bulgars on the Volga and the countries beyond brought much wealth and prosperity. The Volga and the Caspian Sea reassumed their importance as trade arteries and links with the civilized Arab world, and the white stone of the new churches mentioned above was quarried in the Urals. With the West lying open, through the gateways provided by Černigov, Galicia and Novgorod, and the East beyond the Volga through Suzdal' and Vladimir, Russia seemed destined to carry her hybrid culture, enriched as it was by the influences of Byzantium and the West, far into the interior of Asia.

9

The prospects seemed hopeful for the future of Russia. A prince of Suzdal', Jaroslav (from 1222), also controlled Novgorod and was cooperating with his brother George (Iuri) II, Grand Prince of Vladimir-Suzdal' (from 1217). But these high hopes were not to be realized. They were dashed by the Mongol invasion. Already the first encounter with a reconnoitering force of Mongols in 1223, on the river Kalka near the Black Sea, proved disastrous

for the Russians and their last-minute allies, the Cumans. The
main invasion, led by the Mongolian Khagan Batu, the grandson
of Genghis-Khan, took place in 1237. First the Bulgars on the
Volga were routed. Then followed the attack on the principality
of Suzdal'. Rjazan', Suzdal' and Vladimir were destroyed, and in
the following winter all the Russian principalities were subdued
one after the other. In 1240 Kiev was burned down and Galicia
devastated. In vain Daniel of Galicia looked to the West for
help, even making the Pope the offer of union with the Western
Church, but all he received was a royal title conferred upon him
by Pope Innocent IV in 1253. It was a title which was used
afterwards by all the rulers of Galicia down to Francis Joseph
and Charles, Emperors of Austria. A new Tatar invasion in 1283
put an end to all Daniel's hopes, and the country drifted more and
more into the orbit of Polish interests. It fell completely under
Polish domination in the years 1340 to 1349 and shared Poland's
destiny until the year 1772.

Novgorod was the only principality to survive the onslaught.
Its flourishing trade with the West brought it into lively contact
with the German cities of the Hanseatic League. It grew rich
and retained sufficient independence to call itself Lord Novgorod
the Great. Here Western influences were more tangible than in
any other Russian city, without prejudice, however, to its Byzantine character. In arts and architecture Novgorod, with its de-
pendency of Pskov, followed at first the tradition of Kiev; but its
new school of architecture in the thirteenth and fourteenth centuries produced architects who showed great originality in their
transformations of the cupola model (e.g. the churches of St.
Nicholas at Lipna, St. Theodore Strateilates, the Holy Savior in
Kovaljovo and the church of Volotovo).

These churches exhibit fresh Byzantine influences which they
owe to the Greek artists of the period of the Paleologi, whose
contribution enabled Novgorod to take the lead in Russian art
throughout the fourteenth century; and as the tradition of the
artists of Novgorod was passed on to Moscow in the fifteenth century, it suffered no interruption. There also the Russian art of

icon painting was carried on without a break, achieving its peak
in the fourteenth and fifteenth centuries.

Novgorod thus succeeded in saving and even in improving
upon some cultural, social and political traditions which it had
inherited from Kiev. But this was not enough. The rest of Russia
remained largely cut off from all Western influences for more than
two centuries. This was the first Iron Curtain separating the main
part of Russia from the rest of Europe. To Russia's further misfortune, it was also difficult to preserve close relations with Byzantium, for the Mongols' Empire of the Golden Horde controlled
access to the Black Sea. Thus Russia could not add to what she
had inherited from Byzantium, which was indeed but a small
part of all that she might have acquired. The Emperor of Byzantium still acted as the head of the Orthodox Church in Russia and
his final decisions in religious matters were law there. The
Mongols did not interfere with the Church; on the contrary,
they respected the established religious institutions and exempted
the clergy from paying tribute and confirmed all their rights and
privileges. This, however, did not facilitate contact with the
tottering Byzantine Empire, whose influence steadily declined in
Russia.

The Tatars did not even dispossess the princes of their principalities. Instead of sending governors to the subjected lands,
they governed them through the intermediary of the native rulers.
The latter had to obtain their *jarlyk* — the confirmation by the
khans of their dignity. In order to get the *jarlyk*, they had to appear at Sarai, the residence of the khans, bearing generous gifts
for the khans and their entourages. The Mongol rulers expected,
however, an absolute loyalty from the Russian princes. Every
time they suspected disloyalty, they called them to Sarai and inflicted heavy punishment upon them, often torturing them and
sometimes putting them to death. In order to ensure a regular
payment of the tribute, called *vykhod*, the khans organized on
four occasions a census of the population. The memory of their
devastating invasions kept the terrified people in a state of submission for two hundred years.

In the meantime, Western Europe was making enormous progress in civilization. The West found its own route to Byzantium and the East, discovered their cultural treasures and began to assimilate them, with the result that, when Russia emerged from the darkness in the fifteenth century, she could hardly recognize the rest of Europe, transformed as it was by a new renaissance. Moreover, Russia herself appeared as a stranger to the West, and it is from this time that the distrust can be dated which she has often shown towards her neighbors. It was only in the tenth, eleventh and part of the twelfth centuries that Russia felt herself to be a full partner with others in the evolution of Europe.

The Slavs at the Crossroads

Federation in Otto III's Roman Empire or the Formation of a Great Slav State?

Otto III's new conception of the Roman Empire — St. Adalbert of Prague — Otto III, Boleslas the Great, Hungary and Dalmatia — The importance of Otto's plan for a European community — Henry II jettisons Otto's plan — The attempt of Boleslas the Great of Poland to form a great Slav state; debasement of the imperial idea — The Czech failure to secure Slav leadership.

There is yet another reason why Kievan Russia was denied the opportunity of playing the role of an intermediary between Byzantium and Western Europe: the failure of the attempts made by the Poles and the Czechs to form a great Slav state in Central Europe. Such a political formation would have been a great help to Russia, the more so as, at the time when these attempts were made, Bohemia and Poland were still to some extent in possession of the Greco-Slavic cultural inheritance bequeathed by SS. Cyril and Methodius.

As has been shown, the Slavs of Central Europe were being drawn more and more into the orbit of the new German Kingdom. When the German King became the Roman Emperor, it was to be expected that his interest in the Slavic East, then only partially Christianized, would become even more pronounced than in the past. Otto I's daring plans were, however, dashed by the revolt of the Slavs and the death of his son, Otto II, in Calabria (983). Otto II was one of the first of a long line of German kings, dukes and knights who paid with their lives for the realization of the medieval German dream — a universal empire, including Rome

and Italy and the rest of Christian Europe, and having as one of
its objects the diffusion of Latin culture, in German garb, to the
lands through eastern Europe and across the fertile plains inhabited by the Slavs. Otto II's marriage to the Byzantine princess, the courageous and intelligent Theophano, was regarded by
the Byzantines as a mild form of surrender to the Byzantine Emperor and an action which changed the so-called Western
Emperor from a rival into an ally. In this way, the Byzantines
thought, the unity of the Roman Empire, of which they regarded
themselves as the only lawful heirs, would be saved. Although
Otto I, who had asked for a Byzantine bride for his son, did not
view the marriage in quite the same light, it still looked as if a
new era had begun in the relations between East and West,
thanks to Theophano and to her son, the young Otto III, who was
half-Saxon and half-Greek. His education was largely in his
mother's hands, and from her he learned not only Greek but also
much classical lore.

This grounding in the classics was further developed by Gerbert
of Aurillac, the greatest contemporary Western scholar, who had
obtained his early education in Catalonia. He was an enthusiastic admirer of all the institutions of the old Roman Republic and
Empire. Combining his knowledge of classical lore with Christian traditions, Gerbert dreamed of a new Charlemagne – or
rather, a new Constantine the Great – who would revive the
Roman Empire, founding it, however, on Christian principles.
Perfect collaboration between the Emperor and the Church in
all matters should be the lodestar of the reborn Empire.

Gerbert filled the mind of his sensitive pupil with these lofty
ideas. He conceived of an Empire extending not only over the
West, but including also all the Slav lands. He expressed his
views in an enthusiastic outburst in one of his letters: *Nostrum,
nostrum est Romanum imperium. Dabit vires ferax frugum
Italia, ferax militum Gallia et Germania, nec Scithia desunt nobis
fortissima regna* – which may be interpreted as follows: "The
Roman Empire is ours, ours. Its strength comes from Italy bearing abundant fruits, from Gaul and Germany supplying it with

military might; but to our Empire belong also the most valiant
kingdoms of the Slavs."

Thanks to the intelligent way in which she managed affairs as
regent (983–991), Theophano succeeded, with the help of her
son's grandmother and the Archbishop of Mainz, in salvaging as
much as possible after the disastrous Slavic upheaval, and she
was able to hand over to her son a realm which was both consolidated and well administered. This enabled Otto III to make
an immediate start towards realizing his own and his teacher's
dream of a reborn Roman Empire. Therefore, in 998, the young
King crushed the powerful, aristocratic Roman family of the
Crescentii, who had monopolized the Papacy for themselves, and
he placed upon the papal throne his own teacher, Gerbert, known
from thence forward as Sylvester II (999–1003). Gerbert de-
liberately chose the name Sylvester as being reminiscent of Sylvester I, who — according to a legend which was already popular
in the West — had been the inspirer and influential partner of
Constantine the Great. Otto III was the new Constantine, and
from then onwards the government of the Christian world was to
be in the hands of the Emperor and the Pope, acting in mutual
accord.

The imperial court in Rome was reorganized, and many of the
old Roman and Byzantine titles were reintroduced into the imperial ceremonial. But there remained the problem of the Slavic
world. It was evident to the Pope and the young Emperor that
the practice of conversion and subjugation introduced by Otto
I had not succeeded. A new method had to be devised which
would not only produce better results but would also be more in
keeping with the new Roman imperial idea.

2

In this Otto was lucky enough to find another trusted friend
and sound adviser in the person of St. Adalbert, Bishop of
Prague. St. Adalbert (Vojtěch) visited Rome after a breach in
his relations with Duke Boleslas II of Bohemia and lived in the

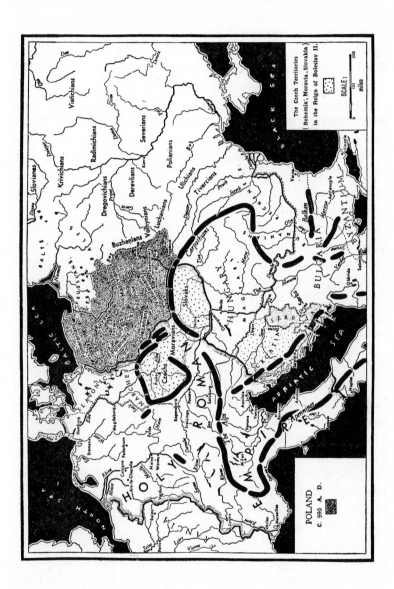

Abbey of SS. Alexius and Boniface. It was there that Otto III found him. Adalbert was a distant cousin of his, and, being somewhat inclined to mysticism, probably through his Greek mother, Otto saw Adalbert frequently and discoursed with him on religious matters. It was in Rome also that Adalbert received the news of the catastrophe which had befallen his family. But when the Archbishop of Mainz insisted that Adalbert should try once more to return to his diocese and the Pope endorsed the Archbishop's demands, Adalbert promised to do so. He asked the Pope's permission, however, to preach the Gospel to the pagans, should the Czechs refuse to accept him. Adalbert met the Emperor again in Mainz, where he was awaiting the return of the messenger with the expected refusal from Boleslas II.

Adalbert had considerable experience of missionary work. When he succeeded in uniting the whole of the Přemyslide Empire under his authority after the suppression of the bishopric of Moravia, he started missionary activities among the Magyars. Today the Magyars venerate Adalbert as one of their patron saints, and it may be that it was he who administered the sacrament of confirmation to their first Christian King, Stephen I.

During their meetings, Otto III learned from Adalbert that the best method of converting the Polabian and Baltic Slavs was peaceful evangelization and not forceful subjugation. Adalbert himself intended to put this true Christian missionary method into practice, and when he learned that Boleslas II definitely refused to accept him again as Bishop of Prague, he set off for Poland with the idea of going from there to preach the Gospel to the Veletians. But at the request of Boleslas the Great, he went instead to the Prussians, at whose hands he met a martyr's death in 997. His body was buried with great pomp by Boleslas the Great in Gniezno (Gnesen).

The news of Adalbert's martyrdom spread like wildfire over the whole of Europe. Otto III rejoiced at the news, because he had, from now on, a trusted friend in heaven, but all who knew Adalbert wanted to follow his example and preach the Gospel to the pagans on the Elbe and the Baltic. Indeed, several mis-

sionary centers were formed for this very purpose, where Italian,
German, Czech and Polish monks began to prepare themselves
for work in this field. In addition to the Abbey of SS. Alexius and
Boniface in Rome, Ravenna and Gniezno provided two such
centers. Otto III and Boleslas the Great gave every support to
the movement, and it looked as though a new era was beginning
for the Polabian and Baltic Slavs, an era of peaceful collaboration
with their Christian neighbors. The new Emperor had found a
true definition of his imperial duties towards non-Christian
nations.

3

But there were also Christian nations which had to be included
in the reborn Roman Empire. Such, for example, was Poland,
which had become under Mieszko I an important neighbor, independent, but willing to cooperate with the German King and
Roman Emperor. Hungary under its Duke Stephen I was also
entering the Christian community. The old aspirations of the
Carolingians to the Slavic lands in the South between the rivers
Drava and Danube and the Adriatic were not forgotten. And in
the distant East there was also Russia. The reborn Roman and
Christian Empire was destined to embrace all these new countries, but in order to interest them in the new idea of a Christian
commonwealth, built on the old Roman classical and imperial
traditions, new ways had to be found of respecting the independent position of the young states yet, at the same time, of
uniting them under the leadership of one emperor.

This new way was envisaged in Rome by the young Emperor
and his teacher Sylvester II, through a perfect collaboration between the *Sacerdotium* — or priesthood — and *Imperium* — or
political power. The first prince who was to be won to this idea
was Boleslas the Great of Poland. Here again, the memory of the
glorious martyr, St. Adalbert, played a great part, for Boleslas's
representative in Rome, who conducted the negotiations with
the Emperor and the Pope, was Adalbert's half-brother Gaudentius. As a result of their talks, Boleslas of Poland eagerly accepted

the new scheme. In order to stress before all Europe the importance of the fact that Poland was the first country to join the Roman Empire in its revived form as a federation of Christian princes under two leaders — the Emperor and the Pope — Otto III went in person to Gniezno. He assumed the title of "Servant of Jesus Christ" in order to make known to all Christians that he was carrying out a decision taken by the two heads of Christendom for the promotion of Christianity in the East. Boleslas the Great received the Emperor with great pomp, and a memorable ceremony took place at the grave of St. Adalbert which is still recorded in the annals of Polish history as the "Act of Gniezno." Duke Boleslas the Great was promoted to the rank of a Roman Particius and friend of the Emperor, and to him, as his representative in Poland, Otto surrendered all the rights over the Church there which he himself exercised in the Empire. The foundation of the archbishopric of Gniezno was solemnly made public and Gaudentius installed as its first titulary, the new metropolis comprising three bishoprics — that of Cracow, Kolberg (*Kołobrzeg*) on the Baltic, and Vratislava (Breslau). This organization may have been later completed by Boleslas, who seems to have founded a metropolitan see in Sandomierz for the eastern part of his realm.[1]

The second country to fall into line was Hungary. A special embassy sent by the Emperor and the Pope presented Stephen I with a royal crown, and from the two heads of Christendom the new King received the right to organize the hierarchy in his land. The first Archbishop of the Hungarians to be appointed was a friend and companion of St. Adalbert, Radla-Asteriscus.

From a letter sent by the Pope to Peter Orseolo, the Doge of Venice, who assumed the title of *Dux Dalmatiae* after his victories over the Croats, it can be concluded that both the Emperor and the Pope had planned to include this land in the new Roman Empire. The Emperor recognized the new title, and the Vene-

---

[1] H. Paszkiewicz, *The Origin of Russia*, pp. 380 ff., thinks that this metropolitan see was of Slavonic rite. This theory, however, has not yet been fully substantiated.

tian chronicler Dandolo exalts the friendly relations which existed between the Emperor and the Doge.

There were some signs that Otto III also intended to approach the Duke of Kiev and invite him to join the new Roman Commonwealth. At least, the *Russian Primary Chronicle* refers to an embassy sent by the Emperor to Kiev in the year 1001.

4

Historians still disagree about Otto's motives and plans, and many German scholars have deplored his weakness in handling the lesser nations; but they forget one thing. Now that the close collaboration between the Emperor and Pope Sylvester II, his mentor and the fount of his inspiration, is established as a fact, it is fairly certain that what they were engaged on was an interesting attempt to realize the medieval dream of a world dominion under the supreme temporal authority of the Emperor in association with the supreme spiritual authority of the Pope. It was also the only scheme emanating from a German source which could have been acceptable to both Germany and the other nations of Central Europe.

But Otto's plan can be viewed also from another angle. Under his rule, the Germans had their great chance to make a valuable contribution towards the cultural growth of Europe and towards bridging the ever growing gulf between East and West. Thanks to Theophano, the Byzantine Princess and German Queen, the contacts between Byzantium and Western Europe were renewed. Henceforward, it would have been possible for Byzantine cultural influences to penetrate to the very heart of Central Europe by way of southern Italy, where Byzantine power was firmly established, and the western Roman Empire, which Otto III's father and grandfather had tried to link to Byzantium's Italian possessions. The ties between the Byzantine imperial house and the German Saxon dynasty were about to be strengthened even more when Otto III asked for the hand of a Byzantine bride. A new era seemed to be dawning for Europe as Byzantium's cultural inheritance came within its grasp. For at that time the differences between East and West were not such as to preclude this friendly exchange. Had it endured, East and West would have been perhaps no more than geographical distinctions, and their cultural differences would have dwindled into insignificance. Working together, the German and Byzantine Emperors would have eliminated the Arab menace — from Sicily, at least — and they would have gained control over the trade between Byzantium and the Christian countries of the western Mediterranean.

5

Such were the possibilities which lay open for Europe at the beginning of the eleventh century; but they were dashed to the ground by the premature death of the young Emperor. The end of Otto III was sudden and unexpected. It happened at the moment when the Romans had revolted against him and he was about to crush them with the help of his cousin, Henry, Duke of Bavaria. The latter, who succeeded him as Henry II (1002–1024), was too narrowly German and he lacked Otto's wider and more far-reaching ideals.

First of all, he had no feeling for the classical memories of ancient Rome which were so dear to Otto. Instead of speaking of the rebirth of the Roman Empire, he concentrated on a renovation of the Frankish Empire (*Renovatio Regni Francorum*). He let himself be crowned in Pavia as King of Italy, thus setting a precedent completely at variance with the old imperial tradition, which had never known a king of Italy, but only a Roman emperor.

Boleslas the Great continued to regard himself as Germany's ally and a member of the Empire, exactly as Otto III had visualised it, in spite of some disappointments at the outset of Henry's reign. Soon, the Polish Duke was given the opportunity of intervening in Bohemia in favor of the last of the Slavniks, who had taken refuge at his court after the massacre of his family. When Boleslas II of Bohemia, who was responsible for this bloody deed, died, troubles broke out among his heirs; and Boleslas the Great, upon being approached by certain Czechs with a request that he should arbitrate, appointed the candidate who had taken refuge with him. This, however, proved a failure, as his protégé turned out to be quite incapable of ruling, and the Czechs complained that he was seldom sober. Boleslas the Great therefore removed him and proclaimed himself Duke of Bohemia. He occupied Moravia with Slovakia, the greater part of Bohemia, and soon, accompanied by the Slavnik Soběslav, he stood before the Castle of Prague.

The Emperor did not approve of what had happened, but he was prepared to recognize this conquest, if Boleslas was willing to declare Bohemia a fief of Germany. This the Pole refused to do, and so Henry proclaimed himself the avenger of the two surviving Přemyslides, who had taken refuge at his court. Boleslas had some reason not to trust the Emperor, yet his flat refusal was a tactical mistake. Henry II soon appeared in Bohemia with his protégés, and during the evacuation of Prague the last of the Slavniks was killed in the melee, and Boleslas the Great was forced to retire from the country.

6

This began a long war between Poland and the German King and Emperor. Boleslas jettisoned the whole imperial idea for which he had shown so much enthusiasm under Otto III and bent all his energies to create an independent Slavic empire including Poland, the Czech lands and a great part of the country inhabited by the Polabian and Baltic Slavs.

But when this great idea began to take shape, the Germans saw the danger signal; for Henry II did not favor the creation in Central Europe of a Polish-Czech empire, which would claim the allegiance of the Slavic tribes between the Elbe and the Oder and possibly of the Hungarians as well. He sensed that an obstacle was being erected in the way of Germany's drive towards the East. He was right, for the linguistic differences between the

Czechs and the Poles were at this time very slight, and if the two
nations had been able to live together for a generation or two,
they would have coalesced into a single political formation,
united by a common language. The possibilities in the cultural
field were equally significant. Bohemia was still bi-liturgical, and
Slavonic letters flourished in Prague. Traces of Slavonic liturgy
were to be found in Poland at that time and, in spite of the
rivalry between Poland and Kievan Russia over part of Galicia,
there was a prospect of new contacts with Byzantium through
Russia.

But again, all these possibilities were jeopardized by the Germans. Though Boleslas the Great kept Moravia and Slovakia and
mauled the German armies in many bloody battles, he could not
recover Bohemia. This key position, left in the hands of the
Germans, gave them entry into Central Europe, and this Henry
II saw clearly. He regarded Bohemia as a German fief, and the
Přemyslide dukes were subjected, from now on, to the greatest
humiliation, for Henry and his successors disposed of the Bohemian throne as they pleased.

During the German-Polish wars, the imperial idea as conceived
by Otto I and the noble Otto III and his partner, Sylvester II,
suffered a most serious setback. Henry's forces were not sufficient to check Boleslas the Great, and he therefore negotiated an
alliance with the Veletians, promising in return to tolerate their
paganism. So for the first time in history, a Christian king and a
Roman emperor fought a Christian prince with the aid of pagans.
This caused great bewilderment among the eleventh century
Christians, and the sentiments of Christian idealists were expressed in a very forceful way by a German, St. Bruno, a disciple
and admirer of St. Adalbert, and one of the missionaries who
had prepared to convert the pagan Slavs and Prussians. Although
of Germanic race, Bruno sympathized with his Slavic protector,
Boleslas the Great, and in a very eloquent letter tried to bring
the Emperor Henry II back to the imperial conception of Otto
III: "Is it right to persecute a Christian nation — he asks — and
to admit a pagan nation to friendship? How can Christ have

dealings with Belial? How can we compare light with darkness? Would it not be far better for you to earn the loyalty of a man with whose aid and counsel you could levy tribute from a pagan nation and turn it into a saintly and godly people? . . . . Is it not better to fight the pagans for the benefit of Christendom than to wrong Christians for worldly honors? . . . Would it not be more honorable and salutary to yourself to promote the growth of the Church, to work for the baptism of the heathen, thereby deserving in the eyes of God the title of apostle and to leave in peace a Christian prince who is offering you his help?" Nothing can illustrate better than these words the debasement of the imperial ideal under Henry II.

But there was even more to follow. Henry had to solicit the help of another Christian ruler — King Stephen I of Hungary — against Boleslas the Great. In vain did St. Bruno try to prevent this further humiliation of the imperial ideal. His efforts did not succeed, and Slovakia was conquered by the Magyars in two phases, the whole country being annexed by them after the death of Boleslas in 1025, and from that time down to the year 1918 Slovakia remained a part of Hungary.

Yet another incident which occurred during the reign of Boleslas influenced the relationship between Poland and Russia through the centuries which followed down to the present day. Boleslas intervened twice in Kiev in support of his son-in-law Svjatopolk. The first intervention occurred when Reinbern, Bishop of Kolberg, who accompanied Boleslas's daughter to Kiev on the occasion of her marriage, was thrown into prison together with the bride, because he intrigued against Vladimir. Then after Vladimir's death, he intervened again to assure his son-in-law's succession to the throne of Kiev. The description of Kiev by Thietmar of Merseburg is due to some German mercenaries who accompanied Boleslas on this expedition. Boleslas was successful in putting his son-in-law back on the throne; but the latter proved unworthy of the effort. The Pole left him to his fate, and he was defeated and driven out of the country by his brother Jaroslav the Wise. Nevertheless, as a reward for his intervention,

Boleslas kept the Red cities including Přemysl, i.e. modern eastern Galicia, this being only another incident in the rivalry between Russia and Poland for the possession of that country. The territory, however, returned to Russia during the reign of Boleslas's successor, Mieszko II. It became again a bone of contention under Boleslas the Bold, but reverted to Poland from the period of the Tatar invasions down to the time of the partitions of Poland, and became Russian again only in 1939 and 1945.

Boleslas the Great was also the first King of Poland. Under Otto III he contented himself with the title of a Roman Patricius, but it is probable that Otto intended to give him a royal title later. There was, of course, no hope of his obtaining a royal crown from Otto's successor; but there is some evidence that Boleslas approached the Pope on this matter. Finally, about 1025, he assumed the royal title on his own initiative and was crowned by the Archbishop of Gniezno. This was intended to be a final demonstration that he had severed all connections with the idea of the Roman Empire as conceived by Henry II.

It is a pity that Boleslas the Great did not succeed in founding a Polish-Czech empire in Central Europe, but his failure was mainly due to the rivalry and jealousies of the two Slav dynasties — the Polish Piasts and the Czech Přemyslides. Intent upon promoting their own political interests, the Přemyslides preferred a German alliance, but the Piasts, on the other hand, were at fault in their failure to appreciate Czech psychology. It is a pity that this great chance was missed; for at that time the Poles who had a succession of three able rulers — Mieszko I, Boleslas the Great and Mieszko II (1025–1034) — were the only nation in Central Europe which could have stemmed the German push towards the East and set up a state capable of dealing with them on an equal footing. It is true that Mieszko II ultimately failed, because the throne was usurped by his half-brother Bezprym (Vesprim) who was supported by the Russians and the Germans, and because the Czech Duke Oldřich refused to help him, but all the information available suggests that he was a very able ruler who would have been a match for all the difficulties he had to face.

7

The disorganization of Polish affairs which followed Mieszko II's death was exploited by the new Czech duke, Břetislav I, called the Restorer (1034–1055), a man of a daring and romantic nature. In popular books of Czech history, he is still depicted kidnapping his bride Judith from a convent school and using his sword to cut the chain with which the guards barred his way. Previously — about the year 1029 — Břetislav had conquered Moravia, but his attempts to win back Slovakia by helping the emperor Conrad II (1024–1039) against the Hungarians failed. Now he found compensation at the expense of Poland. His troops rapidly overran Silesia and Cracow in the autumn of 1038. Poznań was captured, and then Gniezno, the Polish capital, fell into his hands. A religious frenzy laid hold of the Czechs when the Duke's army approached the place where St. Adalbert lay buried, and the Bishop of Prague profited by the occasion to wring from the Czechs a solemn promise to avoid the sins that had driven Adalbert from Bohemia. According to the Bishop, the martyred saint had laid down a condition that his body should not be transferred to Bohemian soil until this promise was given. As this was forthcoming, the Czech army returned in triumph to Prague with the precious relics, to which was added also the body of Adalbert's brother, Gaudentius Radim, the first Archbishop of Gnesen, and the bodies of the first five Polish martyrs from Adalbert's school.

It seemed that the Czech Duke was about to realize the idea of Boleslas the Great. Prague was to become the capital of a great Slavic empire and the religious center of all the Western Slavic nations. But Břetislav overestimated his power. Just as in somewhat similar circumstances, when the Poles occupied Prague, the last members of the Czech dynasty called upon Germany for help, so Casimir I of Poland (1032–1052) took refuge at the court of the Emperor Henry III (1039–1056). The Germans could not tolerate the formation of a great Slavic empire under a Czech dynasty any more than under a Polish one. Henry

III invaded Bohemia, and after defeating the Czech army, forced
the Duke to approach his throne barefoot and thus purchase his
pardon. The Emperor permitted Břetislav to retain only Silesia
and Moravia and reduced him to the status of a German vassal.
In 1052, however, the Poles reconquered Silesia. The Emperor
decided that this country should belong to Poland and that the
Poles should pay the Czechs an annual tribute of 500 pounds of
silver and 30 pounds of gold in return. From that time on, Silesia
has remained a bone of contention between the two nations.

The embassy which Břetislav sent to Rome with the request
that Prague should be promoted to an archbishopric also failed
in its mission. The Romans were shocked by the forceful transfer
of saintly relics which had taken place and horrified by the manner in which the Czechs had plundered Polish churches. By good
fortune, Břetislav had provided his messengers with a substantial
share of the looted Polish gold and silver, and it was only this
which saved him from excommunication.

Břetislav's attempt to form a Czecho-Polish empire ended in
failure. It was an object which only a Polish dynasty could have
achieved, because Poland was stronger than Bohemia and was
also independent of Germany. The result of Břetislav's failure
was that Germany scored a second great victory in the battle for
Central Europe. The German king and Roman emperor was now
not only the recognized master of Bohemia, but of Poland also.

Casimir I did all he could to restore order in his land and is
rightly called "the Restorer" by the Poles; but he had to abandon
the royal title. Another result of Břetislav's fruitless effort was an
increase in the rivalry between the Poles and the Czechs for possession of Silesia. To this rivalry can be traced all the unhappy
feuds between them in the period after the first World War which
drove them into the bondage of their powerful neighbors.

10

The Slavs, The Empire, and The Papacy

The Contest between Empire and Papacy — The Popes seek allies among the Slav princes — Boleslas II of Poland, the Pope's agent in Hungary and Russia — Zvonimir of Croatia pays with his life for supporting the papal policy — The Papacy and the Serbs — The Czech Duke, a staunch supporter of the Emperor — Reversal in Poland in favor of the Emperor — The Czech Duke's vain hope of obtaining a foothold in Lusatia and Austria (Ostmark).

With the abortive attempt at the formation of a great Slavic state in Central Europe, an important, though little known, period in Slavic history and in the development of Slavic civilization comes to an end. Up to this time, the Western and Southern Slavs had been able to preserve some of the cultural inheritance which they had obtained from Byzantium through the intermediary of Byzantine missionaries led by SS. Cyril and Methodius. Then when the Magyar invasions cut off the Western Slavs from the source of this culture, other possibilities opened up in the newly converted Kievan Russia. It has been seen how intimate the contacts were between the Slavic clergy of Bohemia and that of Kiev, and there were fresh chances of a close relationship between Byzantium and the West during the reign of Otto III.

But the change of policy effected by Henry II and the ensuing victory which the Germans had won dashed all those hopes to the ground. Henceforward, the Czechs, the Poles, the Slovenes and, to a large extent, the Croats also had to turn towards the West, and only from there could they receive the cultural inspiration they needed. In theory they could obtain this inspiration from any Western nation, and in particular from Italy and France where culture had started to expand and rise to even higher levels; but in practice political considerations ensured that almost all cultural influences reached the Slavs through the intermediary of Germany, whose kings claimed the heritage of the Roman emperors.

The Papacy, an important factor in the spread of Western medieval civilization, was bound both by tradition and the policy inaugurated by Charlemagne to accept, or at least to respect, the principal claims of the new Roman emperors.

It was thus inevitable that the Slavs should become entangled in the struggle between these two powers — the Empire and the Papacy, the *Imperium* and the *Sacerdotium* — which, from the eleventh century onwards, directed the destiny of the Western Christian world. This struggle — called by historians the Investiture Contest — had arisen as a result of the introduction of a Germanic principle into Church practice. This principle was the ownership of places of worship, not by the Church or its representatives, but by the founders, who also reserved to themselves the right to appoint the ministers charged with the practice of worship. This system became the backbone of the whole political structure of the new German Reich, and in the tenth and eleventh centuries the bishops and abbots appointed by the emperors became the main buttress of the imperial power. The whole system of the *Reichskirche* was further elaborated under Henry II and Conrad II (1024–1039), while Henry III (1039–1056) introduced it into Lombardy. There was a danger that the German practice would also be introduced into Rome, for, with the object of raising the prestige of the Papacy, which had again become a pawn of the Roman aristocracy, Henry III appointed two German bishops as popes.

Violent opposition on the part of a reformist movement originating in Lorraine arose against the German practice, which if applied universally in detail would have split the Church into national religious bodies governed by the laity. The reformists wanted to reintroduce the former practice, according to which the bishops appointed the clergy and also took charge of the direction of religious affairs.[1] The movement penetrated Rome

[1] This reformist movement used to be wrongly identified with the reform of monasticism which originated in the famous French Abbey of Cluny. In

under the last Pope to be appointed by the Emperor, Leo IX
(1049–1054), who was Henry III's uncle and brought some of
the reformists with him from Lorraine to fill important posts in
the papal Curia. When one of the most active reformists, Hilde-
brand, became Pope Gregory VII (1073–1085), the differences
between the new German and the old Roman practices came to
a head. Gregory VII went much further than many of the reformists and in his famous *Dictatus Papae* set down the principles
of a new theory, which henceforth dominated the history of the
medieval Papacy — the superiority of the ecclesiastical over the
secular power.

Henry IV (1056–1106) was determined to defend his rights
as they were defined by the German practice. Thus in 1075
the great Investiture struggle started. It was settled in 1122 after
many vicissitudes and the appointment of anti-emperors and
anti-popes, long after the death of Henry IV and Gregory VII.
The so-called Concordat of Worms, which was then concluded,
was a compromise between the two practices. The emperor and
the nobles were left free to confer upon bishops and other prelates,
who had been elected and ordained, the investiture of their
dignity and endowment by presenting them with a scepter and
a ring.

2

The new, Western Slavic, states had naturally also accepted the
German practice; but during the struggle between the Emperor
and the Pope, they were given the chance to play an important
role, as their support was coveted by both sides.

It should be recalled that something similar happened in the
ninth century when Nicholas I launched his claim to world dominion. This Pontiff, and his successors, Hadrian II and John
VIII, also paid special attention to the emergence of the new
Slavic states in Central and Southeastern Europe, and they

---

fact the monks of Cluny were mainly concerned with monastic reforms and
had little in common with the reformists of Lorraine.

strove to tighten the bonds of devotion and protection which brought Boris of Bulgaria, Svatopluk of Moravia and Domagoj of Croatia under the tutelage of St. Peter. The ninth-century Papacy was merely aiming at the recognition of its spiritual supremacy over the Christian Churches and at stopping the threat of a dangerous expansion of the East Frankish (German) Church.

It was thus to be expected that when the Papacy of the eleventh century threw out its challenge, not to the German Church, but to the emperor, the Empire and its imperial ideology, Gregory VII and his successors would take special notice of the new states in Central and Eastern Europe, whether they were inside or outside the boundaries of the Empire, looking upon them as a providential means of checkmating Germany's expansion and of bringing the emperor to heel.

Indeed, the Papacy had already been looking towards these states for some time before the reign of Gregory VII, and the example of eleventh-century Poland indicated that the states would welcome the opportunity to side with the spiritual power against Germany. Such an attitude on the part of these states seemed to be dictated by the instincts of self-preservation, self-defense and independence.

The Popes seemed particularly to appreciate the importance of Bohemia in an eventual struggle with the emperors and they tried to bring its dukes into the orbit of their policy. This is the explanation for the special privilege granted by Rome to the Duke Spytihněv (1055–1061) and his successor Vratislav II (1061–1092) of wearing a miter and clerical tunic, a privilege which was restricted to bishops and abbots in the second half of the twelfth century. From that time on, only the emperors were allowed to wear these marks of distinction during the coronation ceremony. It is justifiable to see in this move the first step towards the claim, made later by the Papacy on the strength of the new ideology, that they could confer the royal dignity and title upon the world's secular rulers. The Czechs appreciated the privilege and gladly paid one hundred marks a year for it.

3

When Gregory VII had fully developed the new theory of the superiority of the spiritual over the temporal power, he found his most enthusiastic supporter not in the Czech Duke but in Boleslas II the Bold (1058–1079), the Duke of Poland. Thanks to the efforts of his father, Casimir the Restorer, Poland was again a mighty state when Boleslas II ascended the throne. He was determined to go further than his father and to reaffirm the independence of his country. He refused to pay the tribute for Silesia to Bohemia, and when the Emperor Henry IV summoned him to appear at his court, he ignored the summons and attacked Henry's protégé, the Czech Duke Vratislav.

Boleslas II was quick to perceive that the new papal ideology was less dangerous to him than the imperial ideology, and he threw in his lot with Gregory VII, supporting him with all his strength and influence. He was the main agent in organizing a kind of anti-imperial coalition in Central Europe. He started in Hungary, where he sided with the anti-imperial party and helped the Hungarians to repel the pro-German King Solomon. When this event took place, Gregory VII declared that Hungary was a fief of the Papacy. This was the first case of the practical application of the new theory.

Boleslas II also took action on behalf of the new idea in Russia. When Izjaslav, Prince of Kiev, was dethroned by Svjatoslav in 1068, he looked to the Pole for help. Boleslas II restored him to the throne of Kiev in 1069, but when Izjaslav was expelled from Kiev for the second time in 1073, he got a very cold reception in Poland. Boleslas II not only refused him his help, but concluded an alliance with Svjatoslav, the new ruler in Kiev. Izjaslav then approached the Emperor Henry IV but the latter also preferred to be on good terms with Svjatoslav. The *Russian Primary Chronicle* speaks of German ambassadors in Kiev in 1074 to whom Svjatoslav "in his pride" showed his riches — "innumerable quantity of his gold, silver and silks."

Izjaslav then addressed himself to Henry's adversary, Pope

Gregory VII. A letter sent in 1075 by Gregory VII to Izjaslav is extant in which the Pope mentions a request submitted to him by Izjaslav's son for the recovery of his father's dukedom from the hands of St. Peter. After acknowledging Izjaslav's homage, the Pope conferred the dukedom upon him, and at the same time he asked Boleslas II to change his unfriendly attitude towards Izjaslav.

Boleslas II was at first unwilling to do anything in Izjaslav's favor, and his new ally Svjatoslav sent him in 1076 a detachment of the Russian army to fight the Czech Duke. The Pope's attitude apparently wrought a change in Boleslas II; for he also shared the Pope's apprehension concerning the *rapprochement* between Henry IV and Svjatoslav. The *Russian Primary Chronicle* says that after the unexpected death of Svjatoslav (1076), his brother Vsevolod "succeeded to his throne". Then "Izjaslav advanced with Polish support and Vsevolod went forth against him". The brothers came to an agreement, however, and Izjaslav returned to Kiev.

The Pope's initiative, although successful, thanks to the military support of Boleslas II, brought no lasting results for the Papacy. Once Izjaslav came to a friendly agreement with his brother, he needed no foreign support, and the promises given to the Pope were soon forgotten. Izjaslav fell in battle in 1078 when helping his brother Vsevolod to regain Černigov from the hands of their nephews and was succeeded in Kiev not by his son, who had been his ambassador in Rome, but by his brother Vsevolod, who had no obligations towards the Pope. Boleslas II rewarded himself for his help by keeping the Red cities with Přemysl which he had already occupied in 1068. Although the Russian adventure did not succeed as the Pope had hoped, it is interesting to note that the new papal ideology struck an echo as far away as Kiev.

Poland was also the first country to which the new papal claims were fully applied. In 1076 Boleslas received the royal dignity and title at the hands of the Pope and was crowned by the Archbishop of Gniezno (Gnesen) in the Pope's name. This was an unmistakable challenge to the old theory that the imperial dignity was the one and only source of all political power in Christendom.

4

The new political theory on the supremacy of the spiritual power also penetrated to the Croats. It proved to be very useful to King Zvonimir, who in 1076 founded a new Croat dynasty. As he had no legal right to the succession, he needed the moral support of the Pope to buttress the dynasty and to bring the Dalmatian cities into closer union with Croatia. The text of the oath of allegiance to the Holy See is still extant, in which the King acknowledges that he had received the royal crown, scepter and sword from the Pope, to whom he promises obedience and fidelity.[1]

There was something deliberate and logical about all these moves which betrayed a carefully laid plan. It is noteworthy that Zvonimir was the brother-in-law of Kings Geiza (1074–1077) and St. Ladislas I (1077–1095) of Hungary, who were both openly anti-imperial and were supported by Boleslas II of Poland. This circumstance, together with Zvonimir's pro-papal policy, became in the end fatal to the national dynasty of the Croats. In 1089, Zvonimir convoked a national diet at Nin and tried to persuade his nobles to launch a crusade against the Pechenegs in order to help the Byzantine Empire. The King took this action at the request of the Pope Urban II (1088–1099), to whom the Emperor Alexis I Commenos (1081–1118) had

---

[1] As a token of his fealty, Zvonimir declared his willingness to pay a tribute of 200 Byzantine gold coins to the Pope. Gregory's action, taken quite independently of the emperor and intended to invest the Papacy with exclusive authority in all affairs relating to human society, contrasted strongly with the policy of Sylvester II. That Pope, the collaborator of Otto III, also took a lively interest in the same corner of Europe — Dalmatia, Hungary and Poland. But he always acted in concert with the Emperor, leaving all worldly affairs to Otto III and reserving to himself a substantial share in all decisions, whether religious or political, which concerned the welfare of Christendom.

appealed, promising in return to work for the reunion of the Churches, but the Croats did not relish the idea. Dissatisfaction with the King's foreign policy reached a climax; rioting broke out and Zvonimir was assassinated.

The only survivor of the old dynasty of Trpimir, Stephen II, who was then elected King, died soon afterwards, and there was no representative of the national dynasty left to follow him on the throne. Zvonimir's widow won the support of the majority of the nobles for the candidature of her brother, Ladislas of Hungary. As Zvonimir's next-of-kin, Ladislas accepted the invitation and he crossed the Drava in 1091 to take possession of Pannonian Croatia and Bosnia. In spite of opposition from some of the nobles, from the Pope, the Venetians, and from the Byzantines who had for some time been occupying Dalmatia with the help of petty national kings, Ladislas's brother, Koloman (1095–1114), the greatest ruler of the Arpad dynasty, succeeded (1097–1102) in securing the Croatian throne for the kings of Hungary.

The Act of 1102, by which Koloman promised on oath to respect the rights of Croatia and Dalmatia and to submit all important decisions concerning them to the national assembly, proved momentous for Croat history. Although the Croats had lost their national kings, at least they kept their kingdom. From that time onwards, the king of Hungary was recognized also as the king of Croatia and was represented in Croatia by a ban. The Croats were thus brought into ever closer contact with Central and Western Europe and became more and more estranged from their racial brothers, the Serbs. Here lie the roots of the differences between Croats and Serbs which have been so apparent in modern times.

The Croat case illustrates the great extent to which comparatively unimportant events can influence the future of a nation. Zvonimir's pro-papal policy was the innocent cause of profound changes in the history of the Croats.

5

New possibilities opened for the reformed Papacy in Serbia. It will be recalled that the Slavs of Dioclea were Christianized mostly by missionaries coming from the Byzantine metropolis of Dyrrhachium (Durazzo), which claimed jurisdiction over the whole coastal region. But claims were also put forward by the metropolitan of Spalato to whom the bishopric of Cattaro, within easy distance of Dioclea, was subject. The new bishopric of Stagno was founded on the initiative of Spalato while Ragusa was also rapidly gaining in importance. All these cities — Ragusa, Cattaro, Stagno, Antibari, Ulcinium, Scadra — were Latin although under Byzantine political supremacy, and Latin culture still flourished inside their walls in the eleventh century. It was natural that these cultural centers should exert influence over their Slavic neighbors and that the Slavic chieftains should be anxious to possess them. All this was an important asset for the Papacy and allowed Rome to play a prominent role in the evolution of medieval Serbia.

The first favorable occasion presented itself when the political situation among the Slavs of these regions had changed. During the wars with the Bulgarians, these Slavs looked to Byzantium for help; but when Bulgaria became a Byzantine province, a new era opened in the relations between the Serbian Slavs and the Byzantines. The Slavs of modern Serbia, finding Byzantine domination more and more oppressive, started a campaign for their own political independence.

The first center of political independence was formed not in the interior, in Serbia proper, but in the south, near the Adriatic, and comprised the land of Dioclea, Tribunje and Zachlumje. Vojislav is the first of its rulers to enter into the annals of history (about 1040). Vojislav was lucky enough in 1042 to succeed by a clever stratagem in destroying a Byzantine army which had been sent to punish him for his sympathetic attitude towards the unsuccessful Bulgarian revolt in 1040–1041. After that he was left alone, though it is probable that he had been able to acquire for his new realm two of the old Latin cities, Cattaro and Antibari.

Political independence from Byzantium also resulted in a change in the ecclesiastical orientation of the new state. The ecclesiastical supremacy of Dyrrhachium (Durazzo) ceased, and the new ruler was anxious to affirm his independence of Byzantium also in the ecclesiastical sphere. So it came about that the rising prestige of Rome was felt even in this distant country, on the confines of two civilizations.

The consequences of this new situation became fully apparent under Vojislav's son and successor, Michael. He was able to come to an understanding with the Byzantines (about 1052), who had to acknowledge the changed situation. Among the bishops established on the territory of the new political unit was the Bishop of Antibari, who gave evidence of great zeal and won the sympathies of the new ruler. Claiming to be the heir of the former metropolis of Dioclea, Bishop Peter addressed a request to the Pope Alexander II asking for the promotion of his see to the metropolitan status. The Pope granted the request (in 1067), confirming the jurisdiction of Antibari over the bishoprics of Dioclea, Cattaro, Palech (probably Dulcigno), Suacia (Svać), Scodra, Drivasto, Pulati, Serbia, Bosnia, and Trebinje. The Pope added the privilege that the archbishop should have a cross carried before him upon all solemn occasions, throughout the whole territory of his metropolis.

The catalogue of the bishoprics enumerated in the letter is very interesting for it shows the progress of evangelization among the Southern Slavs. To the bishoprics already founded from Dyrrhachium, two new Slavic foundations were added, those of Bosnia and Trebinje, but it is interesting to note that the bishopric of Serbia, which was definitely of the Byzantine rite and which had hitherto been subject to Ochrida, was thus subordinated to a Latin archbishop. The Pope must have been fully conscious of the special conditions prevailing in this territory; he stressed in his letter that Antibari should be the metropolis of all Latin, Greek and Slavic monasteries and institutions, because, he said, "they all belong to one Church."

It was a great success for the Papacy and its prestige among the Serbian Slavs was growing. Michael assumed the title of King, and is called by his contemporaries *Slavorum Rex*, but, impressed by the prestige of the reformed Papacy, he desired to have this dignity confirmed by Pope Gregory VII. This seems to be indicated in a letter written by Gregory on January 2, 1078, in which he replies to Michael's request that the Pope should send him a banner. There is a remarkable parallel in a similar petition presented by the Croat ruler Zvonimir. It is interesting to see how far the echo of the new order inaugurated by Gregory VII had penetrated and how eager the new Slavic rulers were to find in the new spiritual power protection against the political pretensions of the emperors of both East and West.

It appears also from Gregory's letter that Ragusa, which had been elevated to an archbishopric by Benedict VIII in 1022, had contested Antibari's claims to jurisdiction over the whole new state and that King Michael was supporting Antibari. The case was put to Rome again by Michael's son and successor, Constantine Bodin, in 1088. It did not appear to have troubled him at all that he had addressed himself to the wrong Pope — Clement III, who was Emperor Henry IV's creature set up in opposition to Urban II. Clement III saw the importance of the request and even showed himself eager to confirm the metropolitan status of Antibari, subordinating to its archbishop the nine bishoprics and "all monasteries, whether of the Dalmatians, Greeks or Slavs". The bishopric of Serbia (Rascia) had been under the independent Archbishop of Ochrida ever since 1020, and some ecclesiastical institutions now made subject to a Latin archbishop were dependent on Byzantium. So the initiative of the two rulers presents an interesting attempt — in disregard of the official schism existing between Rome and Byzantium since 1054 — at the creation of a new ecclesiastical body in which Latin, Greek and Slavic elements would be blended together under Roman supremacy through the intermediary of the archbishop of Antibari.

Constantine Bodin was an interesting figure. His anti-Byzantine sentiments were revealed by the fact that as a young prince he joined the Bulgars with his father's consent in their insurrection against Byzantium in 1073. He suffered defeat with the Bulgars, who had greeted him as their tsar, and spent a considerable time in Byzantine captivity; but later Venetian sailors hired by his father helped him to escape from Antioch, where he was incarcerated. He became co-regent with his father, whom he succeeded, and, although he had to recognize Byzantine supremacy, he made contact with the Normans, who were then occupying Apulia. While Byzantium under Alexius I was battling against new invaders, the Pechenegs, who brought the Empire to the brink of destruction, Bodin was quietly extending his sway over the provinces of Rascia and Bosnia and some other places belonging to the Byzantine theme or province of Dyrrhachium, as far as the river Drin (See map on p. 144).

But all was in vain. The success of the Dioclean kings and of the Popes was to be of short duration. Once Alexius I had settled his score with the Normans and the Pechenegs, he turned his attention to Bodin, defeated his army and made him captive. This was the end of Bodin's independent political career, although his dynasty continued to govern in Dioclea. The leadership of the Slavic tribes shifted towards the northeast to the province called Rascia or Rasa, which had been conquered by Bodin and placed under the care of his own Župan Vlkan. This ruler set about extending his dominions, but Alexius I reduced him to subjection in 1094, and once more the Serbs became Byzantine subjects.

At that moment Hungary emerged as a new actor upon the Balkan scene. There was a time in early Hungarian history when the newly converted nation was about to enter, at least partly, into the sphere of the Byzantine Church and civilization. Byzantine missionaries had been quite successful in the southern part of the country, but, owing to the activities of St. Adalbert, Bishop of Prague, to his companion Radla-Astericus, the first Hungarian Archbishop, and to German missionaries, Hungary was definitely won for the Latin Church and civilization. This situation, again imperilled after the conquest of Bulgaria, when Hungary became a neighbor of Byzantium, was to be more solidly defined in the second half of the eleventh century thanks to the intervention of the reformed Papacy in Hungarian affairs. Rome could thus hope to find in Hungary a protagonist of Latin interests on the confines of the Latin and Byzantine civilizations.

In actual fact, after securing Croatia against Byzantine attempts to regain Dalmatia, Hungary was able to play a very important part, even among the Serbian Slavs. This was made clear in 1120 when Bosnia, once annexed by Constantine Bodin and afterwards placed under Byzantine sovereignty, followed the example of Croatia — to which it had belonged before Bodin's annexation — and freely joined Hungary. Its national princes carried on as bans, governing in the name of the King of Hungary, who styled himself *Rex Ramae*, after a river in Bosnia, and in 1137, King Bela II (1131–1141) conferred the title of Duke of Bosnia upon his son Ladislas.

Hungary soon secured a foothold in Rascia when the daughter of the Župan Uroš I married the Hungarian King Bela II. This was confirmed when Uroš II lent a sympathetic ear to the pressing invitations from the Hungarians and the Normans who had invaded Greece. The Emperor Manuel Comnenus (1143–1180) drove the invaders out, crushed all the rebels in the two expeditions of 1149 and 1150, took the capital of Rascia and sent the Župan packing. In the words of the imperial poet Theodore Prodromus, the Emperor swooped — "like a golden-winged eagle upon the forests that sheltered Uroš, who fled with the swiftness of a deer and scurried to his hole like a rabbit."

Hungarian help was useless; for the Emperor, himself a doughty knight, defeated the Hungarian commander in single combat and took him prisoner. The Grand Župan Uroš II was forced to throw himself at the Emperor's feet and promise obedience, and Manuel held even the successors of Uroš firmly in his grip. The Grand Župan Stephen Nemanja (*ca.* 1167–1196) was obliged to abandon an attack which he undertook in company with the Venetians against Byzantine possessions in Dalmatia and Croatia. He was brought to Constantinople, where his martial bearing created a notable sensation and proved to be a most popular attraction in Manuel's triumphant procession through the city.

As long as Manuel Comnenus lived, the Serbs had no chance of achieving self-government. This great warrior and diplomat made a final daring bid from Constantinople to revive the Roman Empire. He not only recovered territories in the Balkans which Byzantium had lost, but also in 1164 he won back Dalmatia, with the exception of Zara and part of Croatia, and he turned Spalato into the temporary seat of a Byzantine *Dux Dalmatiae et Croatiae.* He intervened in Hungary, where he reduced King Bela III (1172–1196) practically to vassalage, and he was at one time also in touch with Vladislav II, King of Bohemia. He was the last Byzantine Emperor to adorn his name by adding to it, in the true Roman fashion, the pompous title of Ruler of Dalmatia, Bosnia, Croatia, Serbia, Bulgaria and Hungary.

Thus the ambitions of the popes to establish their supremacy over the Slavs of Serbia and of the coastal region were frustrated, for the time being at least. New possibilities were to be offered to Rome only after Manuel's death when Hungary was able to regain possession of Dalmatia and Croatia and when Stephen Nemanja, after occupying the former Dioclean kingdom, had become the real founder of medieval Serbia.

6

In support of the new political order he had inaugurated, Pope Gregory VII was pursuing a policy of encirclement against the emperor Henry IV. He enjoyed the support of the Polish King, but success depended on his ability to win over the Czech Duke, which he tried hard to do on several occasions. He first confirmed the coveted privilege of wearing the miter and clerical tunic which had been granted to the Duke's predecessor and he thanked the Duke most warmly for the regular payment of the hundred marks. It happened that Vratislav II was very proud of this particular privilege, because he had a good deal of trouble with his brother Jaromir, Bishop of Prague, whom he liked to annoy by parading in his vestments and miter during ecclesiastical ceremonies. The Pope tried to be agreeable to the Duke in his disputes with his brother, the Bishop; but it was not easy, for Jaromir completely ignored the new diocese which Vratislav had created in Olomouc (Moravia) in 1063 and took arms to win back for the diocese of Prague those of its possessions in Moravia which had been alienated in favor of the new foundation.

All the Pope's efforts to win over Vratislav were in vain; for the Czech Duke had made up his mind and he gave whole-hearted support to Henry IV. When the Saxons revolted against Henry and ruined his projected expedition against Poland, with the result that the Polish Duke started intriguing with the rebels, Vratislav II came to Henry's aid with powerful forces and displayed exceptional bravery at the battle of Unstrut. Lambert of Hersfeld's chronicle echoes the Saxons' bitter feelings against the Czechs, who after defeating them did not even have the decency to desist from the collection of booty after nightfall. The Czech chronicler Cosmas (II, Chap. 35) also stresses that the Czechs distinguished themselves by their bravery in this campaign, and as for Vratislav II, he remained faithful to Henry IV even after Canossa.

Henry IV went to the length of making Jaromir, Bishop of Prague, his Chancellor, to the great joy of the Duke, who thereby got rid of his episcopal brother, at least for the time being. At the battle of Flarchheim Vratislav's Czechs fought so tenaciously that they saved, if not the defeated imperial army's laurels, at least its honor. They even captured the golden spear carried by Rudolph, the papal candidate for the imperial throne, and for long afterwards this was the trophy which was proudly borne before the Czech duke on all special occasions. When Henry IV besieged Rome in 1083, the Czechs in his army were the first to enter the Eternal City — but not as pious pilgrims.

Up to now, Gregory had failed completely to draw the Czech Duke to his side, and even the Bishop of Prague went over to Henry IV. But worse was in store. After his great victory over the Pope, Henry IV held a Reichstag at Mainz in April, 1085;

with great pomp and ceremony, in the presence of all the princes of the Empire, he conferred the royal title on the Duke of Bohemia and with his own hands placed the crown upon his head as a fitting reward to his most faithful vassal for all the services he had rendered.

But the ceremony was more than that; it was a public challenge flung at the new ideology preached by Gregory VII and the reformists. Henry IV, the chief protagonist of the old order that rested upon a century-old tradition, was determined to proclaim that the Papacy was not the sole source of all spiritual and temporal power, but that temporal power issued from the *Imperium,* which God had predestined to govern the world. The right to confer a royal title upon prince or duke belonged, he argued, not to the pope, but to the emperor.

This becomes even more evident in view of the fact that, according to Cosmas (II, Chap. 37), the title conferred upon Vratislav II, was "King of Bohemia and Poland." The significance of this is still mooted among specialists; but the true explanation can be found only if the conflict between the Empire and the reformed Papacy on the problem of creating the right world order be taken into consideration. Henry IV chose this way of protesting against the Polish Duke's acceptance of this royal title from the Pope, with its consequent implicit denial of the right of the Emperor to interfere in the affairs of Poland. For a misdemeanor so detrimental to the imperial dignity, the Poles were not only deprived of their royal crown, but they lost it to the Duke of Bohemia, who took precedence over the Polish Duke as a reward for his loyalty to the Emperor.

Another benefit accruing to the new King of Bohemia lay in the fact that his claim against Poland over the Silesian tribute received imperial sanction, and Bohemia became the authorized trustee for the Empire's interests in the East.

As a reward for the services rendered by the Chancellor Jaromir — better known to the Germans by his other name of Gebhard — the Emperor suppressed, at the same Reichstag, the bishopric of Olomouc and replaced the whole Přemyslide territory under the sole jurisdiction of Prague. It was on this occasion also that the famous charter was issued in Mainz which was destined to become a most controversial and hotly contested document, as it is the only piece of evidence giving precise details about the foundation and extent of the bishopric of Prague and the policy of Otto I.

7

Henry IV could risk taking these steps without fearing any reaction from Polish quarters, as, in 1085, when he honored Vratislav with the Polish title, the situation in Poland had changed completely. Boleslas II had been displaced on the throne by his brother Władisław (Ladislas) Herman (1079–1102). One of the main reasons that led to Boleslas's downfall was his quarrel with Stanislas, Bishop of Cracow. The grounds for this are not precisely known, as Stanislas's martyrdom was later romanticized out of all recognition. The only tangible statement about him is given by the first Polish chronicler, Anonymus Gallus (I, Chaps. 27, 28), who reports that the Bishop was quartered — a punishment inflicted upon traitors — for his treasonable attitude towards the King; but he adds that while he has no wish to exculpate the treacherous Bishop, yet Boleslas II had no right, as an anointed ruler, to inflict such a punishment upon another of the Lord's anointed.

This statement seems to imply that Boleslas believed, rightly or wrongly, that the Bishop had been implicated in a conspiracy against him. Subsequent events were to prove abundantly that a conspiracy did take place with the object of overthrowing Boleslas in favor of his brother Władisław (Ladislas) Herman.[1]

[1] The plot was apparently hatched by some Polish aristocrats, probably headed by Sieciech, whose influence became paramount under the new ruler. Of course it enjoyed the full support of Henry IV, whose Chancellor Jaromir-Gebhard had spent some time in Poland in his youth and had many influential friends there. The Czech Duke Vratislav would also have welcomed a change upon the Polish throne. It is not impossible, therefore, that the Bishop of Cracow either made common cause with the conspirators or, at least, expressed himself too freely in favor of the King's brother.

Although it is impossible to say to what extent the accusations against the Bishop were well founded, his execution did Boleslas no good. The conspirators seized Cracow (1079) and the King had to seek refuge in Hungary, where he died in the following year under mysterious circumstances. A similar fate overtook his son, who was invited by his uncle in 1086 to return to Poland.

The story of the quarrel between the Bishop and the King was embellished by succeeding generations and surrounded by a dazzling halo of a religious and moral complexion, which made Stanislas of Cracow grow to the legendary stature of a martyr for Church reform and the gallant protagonist of the Gregorian ideology against an impious king. At the time when this legend reached its zenith, Stanislas was canonized (1253) and became the first Polish saint and the national hero. His relics were considered all the more valuable, as the Poles had previously lost the treasures which the Czechs had stolen from Gniezno — above all the body of St. Adalbert. By this time, Cracow had long outstripped Gniezno in the political sphere, and the canonization of its Bishop naturally raised it to further prominence in the religious and cultural life of Poland. The pious Bishop no doubt deserved supreme honors for his saintly life and terrible end; but it is a curious instance of the irony of fate that the King, who had been the warmest supporter of the Gregorian new order and the key collaborator of the Pope in his policy of the "encircle-ment" of the Emperor, should be relegated by the worshippers of his victim to a place among the most bitter opponents of the Gregorian reform! [1]

[1] It seems, however, that the original tradition concerning Boleslas must have survived to the fourteenth century. According to a popular legend Boleslas returned home from his exile and lived in secret as a monk doing penance for his sins. He was regarded as a saint. For more details on his cult see the study by J. Zathey quoted above (p. 172) on "Remnants of some lost MSS. in the Warsaw National Library," pp. 78–81. Cf. also P. David, "Casimir le moine et Boleslas le pénitent," *Études histor. et litt. sur la Pologne mediévale,* V (Paris, 1932), pp. 28–38. H. Paszkiewicz (*The Origin of Russia,* pp. 394–404) advanced the theory that "the conflict between the King and Bishop arose from the rivalry and antagonism between two rites in Poland, the Latin and the Slavonic one." Boleslas is supposed to have

It was not the only mystery in the history of Boleslas II's end, for it is not known exactly what parts were played in this drama by Henry IV and his faithful ally, Vratislav II of Bohemia. The scarcity of historical sources does not permit any further assertion than that both of them not only welcomed, but supported the change, and the policy of the new Polish ruler amply bears this out. Władisław Herman gave up his royal title and contented himself with that of a duke. The Duke of Bohemia gave him his daughter in marriage; Herman completely abandoned his predecessor's line of action and became a warm supporter of the imperial order, even going so far as to rally to Henry's anti-Pope.

So the policy of "encirclement" from the East, devised by Gregory VII with such good prospects of success in order to check a refractory Emperor, broke down completely in the end. Obviously, without the participation of the ruler of Bohemia, nothing solid and lasting could be achieved in this part of Europe, and once again the central position of Bohemia, making it a link between the Empire, Poland and Hungary, proved to be an indispensable factor in any manoeuvring against Germany, or from Germany against her eastern and southeastern neighbors. Henry IV's discovery of a faithful vassal and ally in Vratislav II was another turning point in the development of Central and Southeastern Europe, and it raised a barrier against which all the schemes of the reformed Papacy were shattered.

It is therefore justifiable to say that the help which Vratislav II was able to lend to Henry IV has not been sufficiently valued by historians of this period. At the same time, Vratislav himself must have been a shrewd politician since despite his championship of an excommunicated Emperor, he managed to remain on the best of terms with Gregory VII, who never dared to subject him to anything worse than a fatherly admonition. There may be an additional reason for Vratislav's dislike of Gregory VII. There is in Gregory's register (Book VII, Letter II) a letter in which the Pope emphatically refuses to grant the Czechs the privilege of

---

favored the latter. Unfortunately, the evidence for such a supposition is very slight and doubtful.

having the liturgy said in the Slavonic language. The Pope invokes the authority of St. Peter in admonishing the Duke severely to desist from such "vain temerity." It is important to note that in spite of his sympathies with Henry IV, the Duke was an ardent Czech patriot and anxious to have the Slavonic liturgy once more confirmed by the Pope. This shows that the Slavonic liturgy was still used in Bohemia in 1079 after a short interruption. The Curia's unfavorable attitude explains at the same time why it disappeared from Bohemia soon afterwards.

In spite of this disappointment, Vratislav II did not throw in his lot with the Emperor's anti-Pope until after Gregory's death and even then, with an eye to business, he asked to be excused his yearly payment for the miter privilege, a request which the anti-Pope did not in the least relish.

8

It may be asked why the Czech Duke was so eager to join Henry and to identify the fate of his country with that of Henry's Germany. Some historians have painted the Czech Duke as impelled by a lofty conception of a vassal's duty to his supreme liege lord and have extolled him as one of the noblest characters of his day. There may have been a good deal of noblemindedness in his attitude; but he certainly had other motives as well. The policy of *sacro egoismo*, so often cherished by the Přemyslide dynasty in the past, seems to have had something to do with his behavior. The geographical position of their country naturally made the Bohemian rulers think twice before making any decision which was not likely to be countenanced by Germany. Vratislav II decided to make the best of his unfavorable position, to extend the dominion of his House within the Empire as much as he could, and to pay for this by rendering to the Emperor such services as he would be likely to appreciate most. Throughout the period of his close association with Henry IV, Vratislav seems to have coveted the Marks of Meissen and Lusatia — countries inhabited by the Sorbian tribes — and of the Austrian Mark. As Boleslas the Brave entertained similar aspirations, these ambitious plans were naturally a source of rivalry between Vratislav and Poland.

However, in spite of the Emperor's promises and a successful termination of his struggle against the anti-imperial margraves of those territories, Vratislav II did not succeed in the end. When the dangers threatening from Poland and from the rebellious margraves were over, he was ordered by the Emperor to return the territories to their original German overlords. He kept a few possessions in the Mark of Meissen and hoped that the Emperor would finally let him have the territory as a fief of the Empire; but in 1088, to his utter disgust, Meissen was presented to Henry of Ostmark. This considerably cooled the King's ardor for Henry IV's cause, and although he did not leave the Emperor's service, he abstained thenceforth from giving him military aid. Not even the reversal of the Mainz decision concerning the bishopric of Olomouc, Vratislav's pet foundation, succeeded in reviving his zeal for the Emperor's cause.

Thus, Vratislav's policy towards the Empire did not bring to Bohemia all the advantages that had been expected. It is true that the prestige of Bohemia within the Empire benefited considerably; but it is also true that by identifying his own interests so closely with those of the Empire, the ruler of Bohemia lost the opportunity of pursuing a foreign policy of his own, for his neighbors regarded him as nothing more than the local representative of the Empire and a champion of imperial interests. The same factors also ruined every effort made by Poland and Hungary to create an anti-imperial and anti-German coalition. If the opportunity to do this had arisen and been seized, the support of the reformed Papacy would have made this coalition a valuable factor in arresting or retarding the eastward penetration of German influence for a long time to come.

It is particularly interesting to study the Emperor's reluctance either to establish or to further Czech influence in the Slavic marches on the middle Elbe. Was it just blind chance or the instinctive feeling of a German that these territories should be saved for Germany by being kept secure from any Czech or

Polish influences? But Vratislav's ambition to gain possession of the Bavarian Ostmark — the future Austria — inaugurated a tradition in the Přemyslide policy which was to haunt many of his successors. In the end, under Přemysl II Ottokar, it resulted in the formation of a vast realm which was destined to be the foundation of Habsburgian power.

The Baltic and Polabian Slavs: The Wends

The Wends' hatred of Christianity and the causes of it — Political organization of the Wends — Abortive attempt at the formation of a Christian Slavic dukedom on the Baltic — The crusade against the Wends — Albrecht the Bear gets Brandenburg — Submission of the Obodrites and Rani — Economic changes in Germany, colonization of the East, foundation of cities and the new role of Magdeburg — Colonization of the Sorbs.

The evolution of Western Europe and of Germany in particular during the eleventh century was of vital importance for the future of another branch of the Slavic race — the Baltic and Polabian Slavs, otherwise known as the Wends. It has been seen what an important part in German, Polish and Czech history these Slavs played during the tenth and early eleventh centuries. The Poles and the Czechs made attempts to attach some of the Wendish tribes to their own states. The Poles succeeded at least in extending their supremacy over the Pomeranians; the Czechs strove hardest to win over the Lusatian Slavs. But all these efforts were thwarted by the German kings. The first wave of the famous German *Drang nach Osten* helped the Germans to obtain a firm, permanent hold in Lusatia and a temporary supremacy in Brandenburg and over the Vagrian Slavs in modern Holstein. Here a bloodthirsty insurrection against German rule had the effect of retarding the German penetration for a considerable time.

But when the Germans won their first great battle for the domination of Central Europe by crushing all the prospects of the foundation of a great Slavic empire, either by the Poles or by the Czechs, the fate of the Baltic and Polabian Slavs was sealed. It was clear that sooner or later the German *Drang nach Osten* would recommence and that it would bite deeply into the lands of the Wends on the Baltic and the right bank of the Elbe. The Slavic tribes of this part of Europe were faced by the two great powers of the medieval world: the Roman Empire, as renovated by the Germans, and the Papacy. And for this very reason, they were at a great disadvantage. The imperial crown indeed passed from the Saxon dynasty to that of the Salians (1024–1138) and then to that of the Hohenstaufen (1138–1268), and the main interests of the king-emperors were concentrated in the South — in Lombardy and the Papal State. But the Slavs had as their nearest neighbors Saxon dukes, counts and margraves whose greed for new possessions was in no way abated by the diversion of the emperor's interests towards the South.

It has been shown how the Germanic ecclesiastical system was applied to the lands of the Slavs from the moment of their subjugation during the reign of Otto I. This system of proprietary churches, combined with the "land hunger" of the Saxon aristocracy, was responsible for the development of new missionary methods which were hardly calculated to appeal to the Baltic and Polabian Slavs. They saw clearly that christianization meant submission not only to the holy Roman emperor as the head of Western Christendom, but also to Saxon nobles, and that it implied a loss of freedom and of political independence. The colonization of conquered territories by German settlers involved the danger that those territories and their peoples would lose their own nationality. These considerations made the Wends extremely hostile towards Christianity. They adhered to their own gods in opposition to the German God, who threatened to take from them their liberty, their land and their language.

Hence there arose in this part of Europe a bitter hostility towards Christianity which helps to explain the appalling extremes to which the Slavs were prepared to go in their hatred of German missionaries. The viciousness which was displayed was in no wise solely caused by the native fury of these untutored pagans, but was to a very large extent due to the new missionary methods adopted by the German Church, methods which had little in common with those employed by the primitive Christians. It is justifiable to say that if St. Boniface of Crediton, the patron saint of the Germans, had employed similar methods, the Germans would have reacted in the same way as the Slavs did.

This, of course, made it impossible for the Slavs of these regions to seek the protection of the other medieval power, the Papacy. This was all the more dangerous in the eleventh century, when the religious enthusiasm of the recently converted Western nations was approaching frenzy. It manifested itself in the crusading movement under the leadership of the reformed Papacy, which found its first outlet in the East, where it had as its goal the liberation of the Holy Land from the Mohammedans. But once the idea of the holy war was introduced into the thought of medieval Christians, they saw no reason why it should not be applied elsewhere, such as against pagans or heretics. That is indeed what happened. From these seeds grew those abortive manifestations of medieval Christian zeal — the Crusades, the conversion of pagans and heretics by force, and the Inquisition with all its implications.

2

When studying the history of the Baltic and Polabian Slavs, it is necessary to bear in mind that they were grouped in several political organizations. The most westerly Slavonic outpost was the state of the Obodrites, who also ruled several other tribes, including the Vagrians, the Polabians and the Varnians. The Obodrite State was a monarchy, and during the period of its greatest extent it comprised the eastern part of Holstein and most of Mecklenburg-Schwerin. It flourished during the eleventh and the first half of the twelfth century.

The State of the Veletians was a kind of republic of federated tribes, and it varied in size at different periods. Territorially, it stretched along the Baltic from the mouth of the Warnow river, near Rostock, to the mouth of the Oder, comprising further inland the region between the Elbe and the Oder and bordered by the

land of the Sorbian tribes, Silesia and central Poland. The worship
of Svarožič was the principal tie binding all the tribes together.
His temple in Radgošč, the capital of the Ratarians, the most
powerful tribe of the confederacy, was its political center. It was
the meeting place for the representatives of the various tribes
who formed the supreme legislative and administrative authority
of the State.

The Veletian State flourished in the tenth and the first half of
the eleventh century, and during this period the Veletians played
an important role in Polish and Czech history. It will be remembered that Henry II made an alliance with them against the
Polish King Boleslas the Great.

During the second half of the eleventh century, serious disputes
and conflicts arose among the tribes of the confederacy, resulting
in a disintegration of the State, which caused some tribes to join
the Obodrites, while others had to submit to the princes of
Pomerania.

After the decline of the cult of Svarožič, the pagan Polabian
and Baltic Slavs shifted their allegiance to the supreme god of
the Ranians, a deity known as Svientovit. The Ranians inhabited
the island of Rujana (Rana — Rügen). Their tiny State was a
monarchy ruled by a native dynasty, which rose to be an important maritime power at the end of the eleventh and during the
twelfth century. At this time, the capital, Arcona, was the holy
city of all pagan Baltic and Polabian Slavs, while the powerful
fleet of the Ranians enjoyed undisputed mastery in the Baltic
Sea. So mighty was their reputation that even Christian rulers
who wished to win their favor were obliged to send gifts to their
god.

From the middle of the tenth century onwards, the Pomeranians
found themselves within the orbit of Polish interests. The country
seems to have been divided from the earliest days of its recorded
history into two parts, Eastern and Western Pomerania. It was
ruled by two dynasties, one of which may have been founded by
a Piast prince to whom Mieszko I had entrusted the government
of the country. The reconquest of Pomerania and its Christian-

ization were finally achieved by Boleslas III of Poland.[1] But by that time, the Germans had also reached the frontiers of Pomerania, and thenceforth Poland and Germany vied for its possession, Germany finally emerging as the victor.

The State of the Sorbs, which was the heir of White Serbia, played a notable role, as has been seen, in the seventh and ninth centuries. But the Sorbs lost their independence in the tenth century, when their land was engulfed by the first wave of the *Drang nach Osten.* German counts then governed the whole territory, parts of which were also from time to time given by the German kings as fiefs to Czech and Polish dukes.

3

Detailed information concerning the history of these Slavic peoples from the tenth century onwards is lacking, except in the case of the Obodrites. For this posterity is indebted to Helmold, who was a German missionary among them in the twelfth century. What he has to say about them is supplemented by the Danish chronicler Saxo Grammaticus. According to these two sources, the Obodrite State had become an important maritime power on the Baltic. The Slavs must have learned their seamanship from the Norsemen and the Danes, with whom their relations were in turn friendly and hostile from the beginning of the ninth century.

About the middle of the eleventh century the Obodrites had a chance of becoming a really important power on the Baltic, after their defeat at the hands of a Danish-Saxon coalition. In 1043, their duke, Gottschalk,[2] who had taken refuge at the Danish court, returned to his country and took up the reins of govern-

---

[1] For more details on the reconquest and rechristianization of Pomerania by Boleslas III, see below, p. 313.

[2] Gottschalk was the grandson of Mistivoj who led the rebellion in 983 and destroyed Hamburg, whereas his father, whom Helmold calls Udo, "a bad Christian," was murdered by a Saxon deserter. At the time of his father's death, Gottschalk was at school at St. Michael's Monastery in Lüneburg. He left Saxon territory and in revenge for his father's murder wrought terrible havoc among the Saxons.

ment. He was a Christian, and the Danes rewarded him for the services he had rendered them during his stay at their court by giving him the hand of the Danish Princess Sigrid. Gottschalk did everything in his power to spread Christianity in his own land by peaceful means and he found a valuable associate in Adalbert, Archbishop of Bremen (1045–1072), one of the best and most progressive prelates whom northern Germany had ever known.[1] The diocese of Oldenburg (Stargard) was divided, and two more bishoprics were founded at Mecklenburg and Ratzeburg, while several new religious institutions were brought into being in these regions.

The activity of this far-seeing and valiant Duke conveys the impression that he was aiming at nothing less than the creation of a powerful Slavic dukedom on the Baltic, a Christian dukedom that might have grown into a sort of northern Bohemia, in feudal relationship with Germany, but autonomous and independent. Such a scheme, with the assistance of the irresistible Archbishop, had every chance of success. It would also have fitted in well with the interests of the Emperors Henry III and Henry IV, who were both suspicious of the Saxon dukes, the famous Billungs, and would have welcomed the rise of a feudal dukedom on the Baltic, loyal to the crown and as mistrustful as they towards the Saxon rulers; for neither Gottschalk nor the Archbishop made any attempt to hide their anti-Saxon sentiments.

But in 1066 the mighty Saxon Duke and other nobles jealous of his power brought the downfall of Adalbert. This was a great blow to Gottschalk and precipitated a formidable revolt of the Veletians, who incited the Obodrites to join them. Gottschalk was killed at Lenzen, where a priest was immolated on the altar. Similar scenes were enacted at Ratzeburg and Mecklenburg.

---

[1] Adalbert planned to transform his archdiocese into a northern patriarchate, which would include northern Germany, the dukedom of the Obodrites, Denmark, Sweden, Norway, Iceland and Greenland. The character sketch of this interesting personality written by his great admirer Adam of Bremen is one of the best studies of the kind composed in the Middle Ages. Adam also testifies to the friendship and good understanding that existed between the Archbishop and the Duke Gottschalk.

Bishop John was martyred with many others, and his head was offered up to the god of the Veletians. Helmold and Adam of Bremen give us vivid descriptions of the horrors of this war. Gottschalk's subjects were forced to renounce their new faith; Hamburg was razed and Saxony devastated. Such was the disappointing end of the scheme of Gottschalk and Adalbert which represented the one and only opportunity these Baltic Slavs ever had to find statehood within the Christian community of nations.

The leadership of the pagan Slavs was assumed by the chief of the insurgents, one Cruto, and seemingly endless hostilities broke out between the Saxons and his Slavs. Eventually, Gottschalk's son Henry was able, with the assistance of the Danes, the loyal Slavs and the Saxon Duke, to defeat the pagan coalition (about 1093) and to become head of the Obodrite State. As the Rani continued to raid his territory, he surprised them on their own island in the winter of 1113 or 1114 by crossing the frozen sea. Nevertheless, so firmly was paganism entrenched among the Obodrites that Henry did not dare to take any active steps for the propagation of Christianity.

After Henry's death and the murder of his sons, the Emperor Lothair III gave the Obodrites a Danish duke; but a revolt broke out on a national scale. The Danish ruler was swept away and two of the Slav leaders, Pribislav, Henry's nephew, and one called Niklot, divided the country between them.

Pribislav lost his independence in 1143, and the territory which he had ruled was incorporated in the county of Holstein-Sturmarm. At this time St. Vicelin, a German missionary, succeeded in converting him to Christianity. But when the Bishop of Stargard visited Lübeck, where Pribislav resided, in about 1156, and exhorted him and his people to be good Christians and not to make piratical expeditions against the Danes, Pribislav answered, according to Helmold (Chap. 84): "Your words, O venerable Bishop, are God's words and lead us to salvation. But how shall we enter upon that way when so much evil ensnares us? . . . . Your princes deal so harshly and severely with us that, because of oppression by taxes and burdensome services, we had as soon death as such life. Behold, this year . . . . we paid to the Duke a thousand marks, besides that to the Count (of Holstein) so many hundreds, and all this is as nothing, but every day they afflict us and oppress to the point of destruction. How can we then devote ourselves to the new faith, build churches and receive baptism, when we have daily flight before our eyes?" Because of all this, explained the prince, the only way in which they could get an honest living was to rove the seas and plunder the Danes and any other they came upon. Pribislav's words give a vivid picture of the missionary methods employed by the Saxons for which the Saxon Duke and the Count of Holstein were responsible. It is not surprising that the results were as they were.

4

The rest of the Slavs refused so stubbornly to have any dealings with the German God that the German clergy began to consider adopting really violent methods to convert them. This general feeling which was prevalent among them is reflected in a famous proclamation issued in the name of the Archbishop of Magdeburg. After describing the impiety of the Slavs, their persecution of Christians and their abominable paganism, it urges the Saxons and Germans to invade these neighboring lands and seize them. The present inhabitants are an abomination; but their country "is extremely rich in meat, honey, grain and birds, abounding in all the products of earth's fertility . . . Therefore — so the exhortation concludes — you can both save your souls there and, if you so desire, make acquisition of the best land to live on."

The Archbishop of Magdeburg, St. Norbert, was among the first to use force against the pagans. In 1129 he launched a military expedition against Havelberg, "the seat of iniquity"; but the raid had no durable results. In 1136 the city was recaptured by the pagans and the church which St. Norbert had built was torn down.[1]

[1] Curious to relate, when Bishop Otto of Bamberg visited Havelberg on his second missionary expedition to Pomerania, the Slavic Duke and his

These incidents were a bad omen. They show how the idea of a crusading expedition against the stubborn pagans was able to take root. However, it was St. Bernard of Clairvaux who permitted himself to be an inspiration of the crusading spirit. When he came to Germany to preach the Second Crusade, which seemed to be necessary after the fall of Edessa, the last remnant of the Christian states in the Near East, he found little enthusiasm in spite of his remarkable oratorical powers. Unfortunately, the first practical result of his preaching was the massacre of the Jews in Mainz. The Emperor Conrad III eventually succumbed to his exhortations; but the Saxons remained unmoved. They suggested that they had many infidels to deal with nearer home and that it would be much better to divert a detachment of crusaders to destroy paganism among the Slavs on the right bank of the Elbe.

Bernard must have been totally ignorant of the true conditions prevailing in the lands of the Slavs, but as is usual with born orators he was carried away by his own eloquence, his blind enthusiasm and the sublimity of his conception of the fight against anti-Christ. So when in March 1147 he was called to Frankfurt, where the King was holding his Reichstag and debating the new Crusade with his nobles, he approved the idea of taking the sword against the Slavs and addressed his notorious epistle (letter 457) to all the princes and bishops of the Reich, calling upon them to unite and fight the pagans — "until with the help of God either their religion or their nation be exterminated." (". . . *donec auxiliante Domino aut ritus ipse aut natio deleatur.*")

These were fatal words, which still embarrass admirers of this extraordinary personality and prove once again how easy it is even for great men to be bewitched by the lure of their own fiery imaginations, to blind themselves to reality and to forget completely the very principles which they themselves advocate.

It was not until after the Frankfurt decision, and until Bernard had lavished the same blessings and privileges on the crusade

---

people blamed the saintly Archbishop of Magdeburg for their hostility towards Christianity, saying: "If only we had another archbishop we would be willing to become Christians."

against the Slavs as upon that against the Moslems, that the Saxons really warmed up to their pious undertaking — and then it was not only the Saxons and the Germans, but the Czechs and the Poles as well. In Poland, the Second Crusade was preached by Cardinal Humbold, and the Bishop of Cracow asked Bernard not to overlook the schismatics, his neighbors the Russians, and to work for the moral regeneration of the whole of "Sclavinia." In Bohemia, Zdík, Bishop of Olomouc, who was in close touch with Bernard and was also working to promote the Second Crusade, had some personal knowledge of both the infidels in Palestine and the pagans of the North, for not only had he made a pilgrimage to the Holy Land but he had also undertaken a missionary tour in 1141 among the pagan Prussians, following in this the tradition of St. Adalbert. It may be that the failure of his first venture suggested to him that some more robust methods were required to convert these tough and stubborn unbelievers.

In Germany there were a few level-headed princes who realized the foolishness of such an enterprise. Among them Adolf of Schauenburg, Count of Holstein, understood the position better than anyone else, and for this reason he looked upon the preparations for the crusade against the Slavs with the gravest misgivings; yet feeling himself unable to divert the would-be crusaders from their purpose, he preferred to stand aloof and refuse to have anything to do with the venture. Unfortunately, he had few imitators and there were many others who hoped to find profit in a venture of this sort.

The leaders of the crusade were the men who had the closest interests in extending their domination over the country of the Polabian and Baltic Slavs — Henry the Lion, Duke of Saxony,[1]

---

[1] The ducal dynasty of the Billungs became extinct in 1106, and the Duchy of Saxony was given by the Emperor Henry V to Lothair of Supplinburg. When Lothair became King of Germany in 1137, he gave the Duchy to Henry the Proud, Duke of Bavaria and grandson of the last of the Billungs. King Conrad III, however, refused to allow Henry to hold two duchies and gave Saxony to Albrecht the Bear, who was also a grandson of the last Billung. Albrecht failed to maintain himself in Saxony and renounced the Duchy after Henry's death in favor of his rival's young son, Henry the Lion.

Albrecht the Bear of the Nordmark, Conrad Wettin of Meissen and Adalbero, Archbishop of Hamburg. The main effort was directed against the Baltic Slavs — the Obodrites and the Pomeranians. Niklot, the Duke of the Obodrites, tried to forestall the storm by a counterattack, but in the end he was hard-pressed in his fortress of Dubin, the Danes blockading him from the sea; however, the intervention of the fleet of the pagan Rani saved the situation. The Danish fleet was partly destroyed and the Danes retired from the scene. So the first of the crusaders' attempts to besiege Niklot remained inconclusive.

The military results achieved by the crusaders' second army, which was composed mostly of ecclesiastical contingents, were even poorer. They laid siege to Szczecin (Stettin), and the *Annals* of Vincentius of Prague give a lively description of the tragicomedy which Bishop Zdík of Olomouc, one of the zealous prelates in arms, witnessed, to his utter dismay, under the walls of that city. When the crusaders were investing it and planting crosses everywhere to mark their saintly intentions, they were amazed to see the supposedly pagan Slavs doing precisely the same and raising the sign of the cross upon their ramparts. A solemn embassy then approached the headquarters of the besiegers, headed, to the Bishop's utter amazement, by a prelate in full pontificals. Some of these episcopal braves must have felt decidedly crestfallen when they realized that the prelate whom they sought to convert was a genuine bishop and none other than Adalbert, Bishop of the Pomeranians and a German to boot.

The embassy asked the besieging prelates what their intentions were. It was pointed out that if they wanted to convert the Pomeranians to Christianity they had been forestalled by another bishop, Otto of Bamberg, who had come to Szczecin (Stettin) in more suitable attire, and that if they wanted to confirm the Pomeranians in their faith they must have forgotten that such things were not done at the point of the sword but by the word of God. This opened the besieging bishops' eyes to the real purpose of the crusade, Saxon greed for Slavic lands, and they made haste to conclude a peace with the Prince of the Pomeranians, Ratibor, the successor of Warcisłav, and with Bishop Adalbert. Their losses had thus been in vain and the annalist adds the laconic remark: "They found it somewhat difficult to bring to a satisfactory conclusion an undertaking which they had not rushed into for God's interests."

As the sieges of Dubin and Demmin dragged on, dissensions broke out among the princes conducting them. The Saxons began to realize that the devastation which they were inflicting upon the Slavic lands was only damaging their own prospects and ruining a country whose wealth they coveted. Already famine was decimating the population and turning the country into a desert. So when the Slavic princes Niklot and Pribislav declared their willingness to embrace Christianity, the crusade was called off.

Although the Slavs had not actually suffered defeat, the crusade had a crippling effect upon their strength. The subjection of the Obodrites to Saxony was final and their power of resistance against German infiltration remained broken. The moral effect of these expeditions was equally regrettable, for the Slavs became Christians under duress and received baptism for reasons of political expediency, while obdurately clinging to their paganism in secret.[1] Neighborly intercourse, which had been so full of promise in the years preceding the crusade, was suspended again. The Slavs were sullen and seized every opportunity to vent their feelings against both the Saxons and the Christian religion. In the circumstances, there was but slender hope that the Slavs would ever accept the Christian faith of their own free will — a poor result for an undertaking started with such enthusiasm and blessed so naïvely by St. Bernard. It is little wonder that the great Abbot of Clairvaux was so bitterly criticized by his contemporaries, since the two ventures he so warmly recommended — the crusade against the Turks and the expedition against the Wends — had ended in disappointing failures. He was, however, right in retorting that the main responsibility for

[1] Recently a short but exhaustive account of this crusade was given by N. Gracianskij in *Voprosy Istorii* (1946), nos. 2–3, pp. 91–105 ("Krestovyj pochod 1147g. protiv Slavjan i ego rezultaty").

the failure lay with those princes who fought principally for their own selfish ends. This was certainly true of the Slavic crusade, and the Polish incursion against the Prussians which followed it was only Boleslas the Curly's way of punishing them for the help they had given to his rival brother Władisław and for their frequent raids on Polish territory. Here again, religion served as a pretext.

But for all their participation in the crusade, the Poles were certainly among the losers. The peace which the crusaders had forced upon Ratibor of Pomerania only tightened the German grip on that country. Magdeburg found easier access to Pomerania, while a similar situation was created in the land of the Obodrites. Adolf of Schauenburg, whose hopes for a tolerable *modus vivendi* on the Saxon-Slavic borders had been shattered forever, did all he could to reorganize the devastated areas; but the principal gains fell to the Saxon Duke Henry the Lion, who collected tribute from the Obodrites without — according to Helmold — worrying about the propagation of Christianity among them, so long as he got his spoils. The Metropolitan of Hamburg-Bremen, Hartwig, was more conscientious, and in 1149 he revived the sees of Oldenburg and Mecklenburg, consecrated as their incumbents Vicelin and Emmehard and, in the words of Helmold (I, 69), "sent them into a land of want and hunger where Satan had fixed his residence followed by every foul spirit." This may not be a very cheerful description of the renascent dioceses, but it was exactly what Helmold thought of the state of Christianity in those lands. Soon afterwards, before 1154, even the diocese of Ratzeburg had been restored.

The work of the new bishops did not progress well among the Slavs. Vicelin, the Bishop of Oldenburg, was hampered not only by the deterioration in the Slavic mentality after the crusade but also by the differences which arose between the Duke, as represented by the Count of Schauenburg, and the Archbishop of Hamburg-Bremen over the right of investiture in the reconstituted dioceses. Then Vicelin died in 1154.

But slow as the progress of evangelization was among the Obodrites, the small amount achieved did bring them into conflict with some other tribes of the Veletian group under their control — the Kicini and the Circipani, who refused to become Christians and to pay their share of the tribute due to the Saxon Duke. In 1151, a joint expedition under Niklot, Adolf of Schauenburg, and the Duke defeated them. Their principal temple was destroyed and they had to pay tribute.

5

It was Albrecht the Bear who eventually obtained a firm foothold among the Veletians. He was befriended by the Slavic prince Pribislav, Duke of Branibor-Brandenburg, now a sincere and devout Christian. Pribislav, fearing that after his death the pagans would again get the upper hand in his country and having no direct heir, willed his territory, perhaps not entirely voluntarily, to Albrecht of the Nordmark. Albrecht took over the country in 1150 after the death of Pribislav and, after crushing a pagan reaction led by one of the late Prince's relations, Jaczo, he started a campaign of Christianization and colonization.

His final capture of Brandenburg, which became the cradle of Prussia, was a turning point in the history of Central and Eastern Europe and a fresh milestone on the way of the German drive towards the East. On this territory, near the town of Spandau, lay a village called Bralin [1] which was destined to become the glittering capital of the new Germany between the Elbe and the Oder: Berlin. Near Berlin, Potsdam was destined to rise to fame as the Prussian Versailles. The glory of Potsdam was therefore raised upon foundations laid by the conquest of Brandenburg. This affiliation was unconsciously symbolized by Frederick William I — the founder of Prussian military might — when, in the

[1] It was the Bear's son, Albrecht II, left the sole margrave after the death of his brother Otto II, who captured the Slavonic settlement called Barlin or Bralin, opposite Kolno (Kölln), and bridged the Spree. The future capital of the Prussian monarchy was thus as early as 1209 in the hands of the Ascanians of Brandenburg, the forerunners of the Hohenzollerns.

eighteenth century, he built a military orphanage near his royal palace of Potsdam with the stones which — as the legend says — the Wends had so painstakingly carted from the Bohemian mountains, by way of the rivers Elbe and Havel, to Branibor-Brandenburg, to erect the magnificent temple to their god Triglav on the hill which dominated the city. If the tradition is reliable, then it took the Prussian King's execrable taste to destroy this last witness of Wendish pagan civilization, which even Albrecht the Bear and his bishop had respected when they contented themselves with transforming the temple into a church of the Blessed Virgin.[1]

6

The conquest of Havelberg and of its territory definitely sealed the fate of the Veletians. That of the Obodrites was sealed by another hero of this second wave of the *Drang nach Osten*, the famous Duke of Saxony, Henry the Lion. For some time bloody fighting raged between the Obodrites and the Duke, the latter being generally the more successful. If he had only concentrated his efforts on the conquest of the Slavic lands and had not become entangled with the Emperor and numerous German nobles because of his ambitious plans, he would doubtless have subjugated the whole coast of the Baltic, including Pomerania. The complications encountered in Germany, however, forced him to accept a compromise. The country of Pribislav became definitely German, but in Mecklenburg, Pribislav, the son of Niklot, who was slain in battle, was reinstated as the Duke's vassal and became a Christian. So it happened that the dynasty of Mecklenburg, founded by Niklot, continued to rule over the country, even when both were Germanized, down to the year 1918.

[1] Cf. C. Schuchhardt, *Arkona, Rethra, Vineta*, 2nd ed. (Berlin, 1926), p. 63 and J. Strzygowski, *Die Altslavische Kunst* (Augsburg, 1929), pp. 146 ff. T. Palm expresses his doubts about the origin of the church. His arguments are not convincing, although the problem should be re-examined by experts (Thede Palm, *Wendische Kultsttätte* [Lund, 1937], pp. 94–97).

The conquest of the island of Rujana (Rana — Rügen) by Waldemar of Denmark in 1168 made an end of this small Slavic maritime power. Although at first this island was placed under Danish overlordship, it was Christianized and colonized by Germans. Germanization, indeed, made such startling progress that in the fourteenth century there was on the island only one couple who still spoke the native Slavic language.

7

The conquest of the lands of the Obodrites and Veletians was achieved at a time when Germany was about to experience a great economic transformation. The overpopulation of the old settlements in the western part of Germany, the most developed part of the country, created a need for extending the arable land. This was done by clearing forests and draining marshes; but owing to the primitive methods of contemporary agriculture, this extension was soon found to be inadequate. The peasantry was forced to seek new opportunities, which included emigration to newly conquered lands. The overpopulation was even more marked on the coastal plain of modern Holland and Belgium, where the Flemings were particularly eager to migrate. Some of them were settled by the Archbishop of Bremen-Hamburg near Bremen and it may be that St. Vicelin, the missionary to the Obodrites, saw during his stay in that city how successful this experiment in colonization had been. This may have induced him to suggest to Adolph of Schauenburg, Count of Holstein-Sturmarm, to call foreign settlers into his lands, devastated as they were after the wars. In this manner the colonization of this part of the Slavic territory may have started. There was, however, another more important reason why the rulers of the depopulated lands called in foreign immigrants. This was the firm refusal of the native Slavic population to become Christian. In spite of their defeat and their promises to accept the new faith, the Slavs continued to give the "German God" a wide berth, showing increasing reluctance to submit to a religion that was forced upon them at the point of the sword. In order to fill their churches, the bishops had to import foreign colonists.

The first attempts at colonization made by the Count of Holstein-Sturmarm, Henry the Lion of Saxony, and Albrecht the Bear are vividly described by Helmold. The activities of Albrecht in this field seem to have impressed the annalist most. He writes (I, 89): "He brought over large numbers of Hollanders, Zeelanders and Flemings and had them live in the strongholds and villages of the Slavs. As churches multiplied and the income from the tithes grew to enormous sums, the dioceses of Brandenburg as well as of Havelberg benefited greatly by the influx of colonists."

That is how the great migration of Flemish and other colonists towards the East started. The process was accelerated by the foundation of new cities. The rise of a new class of the populace — the burghers — is another feature of the economic transformation of Germany which started in the twelfth century. Henry IV saw the importance of this new class in the life of the nation and he became the royal patron of the burghers on the Rhine. His example was followed by some far-seeing members of the higher aristocracy, among them Henry the Lion and Albrecht the Bear, who had assumed the title of Margrave of Brandenburg. The new *Stadtrecht* penetrated from Bavaria and Saxony as far as the Baltic and served as the model for the new code of urban law of Lübeck and the other foundations which derived from this city. Lübeck became in the following century the Queen of the Baltic, which became a German sea after the overthrow of Danish power at the battle of Bornhöved in 1227.

Beyond the Elbe, Magdeburg entered upon a new career. This city developed rapidly and by 1188 boasted the first written code of urban law, with its famous *Schöffenkolleg* or College of Aldermen. By 1241 the code was completed with a provision for a town council, the high water mark of urban legislation. Thus, the Law of Magdeburg (*Magdeburger Recht*) made its triumphant debut in what had been the Slavic East, to be later adopted by the new towns of the Marches of Meissen and of Brandenburg, and eventually to penetrate into Silesia, Prussia, Poland, Bohemia and Hungary. The Magdeburg *Schöffenstuhl* (Bench of Jurors) functioned as a High Court, to which any town which had adopted the *Magdeburger Recht* could appeal in all its thorny juridical problems. Thus the idea of Otto I came to be realized in a way of which the Emperor had never dreamed. This was the more remarkable because the *Landrecht* (Manorial Law) which had found its readiest acceptance east of the Elbe and which contributed greatly to the juridical education of the Slavs was the famous *Sachsenspiegel*, also a product of Eastphalia, the eastern part of Saxony, where Magdeburg was situated.

A notable share in this German penetration of the Slavic lands fell to the new Orders: the Premonstratensians, founded by St. Norbert in 1119, and the Cistercians, founded by St. Bernard in 1113. The latter were particularly prominent. They soon developed a new kind of economic administration which was destined to revolutionize the old system, already in decay. The foundation of Cistercian abbeys contributed to the progress of colonization in the Baltic region, in Pomerania, in Brandenburg and in Lusatia.

8

In Lusatia, the Slavic population was reduced to serfdom, working for its masters, cultivating its lands and paying tribute for what had previously been its own property. For many years, the Slavs lived in complete isolation from their masters, under their own chiefs, the *župans*, who exercised the lower functions of the judiciary and policed such villages and districts as were not yet considered to be under the private ownership of the master class. It was on these general lines that the lands of the Sorbs developed until the beginning of the twelfth century, when the great colonizing drive started. The reasons for this colonization were the same as those which had been operative in the lands of the Obodrites and the Veletians: depopulation following the wars and the lamentable failure of the German clergy in its endeavors to convert the native Wends. Churches existed only in German fortified places, and German priests served only German garrisons. The Sorbs flatly and stubbornly refused to adopt the religion of their conquerors. "This made it necessary for any further progress (of Christianity) to alter the composition of the population." [1] The change was effected in the Sorbish country, as it had been in other regions beyond the Elbe, through colonization, since there seemed to be no other way of Christianizing the lands between the Saale, the Elbe and the Bober.

The Germanization of the country, however, made slow progress. Lusatia has a very checkered political history, having been coveted by many German princes and Czech kings. The fact that the sovereignty was frequently transferred from one duke to another partly explains why a remnant of the Sorbish nation — about 150,000 — still exists to this day.

This, briefly, is the history of the creation of the new Germany on the Baltic and between the Elbe and the Oder. It was a great achievement; but the German Reich and nation had to pay for it with the loss of the Flemish lands, of Alsace, Lorraine and Burgundy. While the attention of the nation was riveted on the East, and imperial interests in the West were neglected, nations which had long been members of the German kingdom developed their own states — Holland, Belgium and Luxemburg — or were absorbed by France. And today, possession of a great part of the new "Colonial Germany" (beyond the Elbe) is being contested once more by Slavs.

[1] A. Hauck, *Kirchengeschichte Deutschlands* (Leipzig, 1913, 4th ed.) IV, p. 578.

The Downfall of Poland and Bohemia:
Westernization of Their Culture

Boleslas III, Poland's last hope — The consequences of the division of Poland into duchies — German progress in Pomerania and German colonists in Poland — The Teutonic Order and Poland; the margraves of Brandenburg — Disintegration of Bohemia into imperial principalities — Přemysl Ottokar I restores Bohemian prestige — Social and political development in Bohemia — Bohemia's cultural progress — Poland's social differentiation and political evolution — Polish civilization, literature and art.

The effects of the economic transformation of Germany during the twelfth century on the fate of the Slavic lands between the Elbe and the Oder and on the Baltic do not complete the picture. This process did not stop at the Oder. Overpopulation and economic changes were its motive forces, and the duke of Saxony and the margraves knew well how to exploit its momentum for their own purposes. Very soon, German colonists were to cross the Neisse, the Oder and the Bohemian Forest in order to establish new peasant settlements and thriving towns among two other Slavic peoples — the Poles and the Czechs.

This development was brought about by different factors. First of all, Poland and Bohemia at that time had not reached a point in the growth of their populations where their inhabitants were forced to seek new arable lands. On the other hand, their princes soon perceived the economic advantages accruing to them by the influx of colonists and the establishment of towns and they were eager to welcome foreign peasants and artisans. The political ascendancy of Germany, of course, was an important factor in this evolution, the more so because both Poland and Bohemia were experiencing political decadence, which al-

BRITISH MUSEUM
READING ROOM LIBRARY

most resulted — particularly in Poland's case — in the disintegration of the state. It was this which also greatly helped the Germans to obtain their stranglehold over the Slav lands on the Elbe
and eventually to establish themselves firmly in Pomerania.

At the beginning of the twelfth century there were some signs
that the decline of Poland might be arrested. The country was
led by a courageous ruler in the person of Boleslas III, called
Wrymouth (1102–1138), who had all the qualities of Boleslas
the Great. When the Emperor Henry V (1106–1125) asked him
to follow the example of his predecessor, Władysław (Ladislas)
Herman (1079–1102), and to recognize the Emperor's overlordship, Boleslas professed his readiness to support the imperial
program, but only to the extent to which it operated in the
western states. He declared himself willing to help the Emperor
in his task of protecting the Church and propagating the faith;
but warned him to keep out of internal Polish affairs. The Emperor then played off Bohemia and Boleslas's brother Zbigniew
against Poland and invaded that country. Boleslas and his troops
met the threat valiantly and the Emperor's plans miscarried. The
first Polish chronicler, called Anonymus Gallus, comments upon
this campaign in a pungent vein and his account ends on a note
of grim humor: "The Emperor decided to withdraw and carried
away no tribute but his own dead."

The reign of this gallant Polish prince augured well also for
the Slavs on the Baltic. Just before the German princes had
started their victorious drive against the Obodrites and the Veletians, Boleslas III succeeded in reuniting Pomerania and Poland.
However, he left Western Pomerania under its native princes
as his vassals and this proved to be a most dangerous concession.
He then made a new effort to christianize the Pomeranians. With
the help of St. Otto, Bishop of Bamberg, he succeeded in converting Pomerania to Christianity, insisting hopefully on the
proviso that the newly converted land was not to be included in
the German *Reichskirche*, but was to come under the jurisdiction
of the Polish Church. Had Boleslas III seen his plans through,
there might have been a prospect of saving at least a portion of

CARNEGIE INSTITUTE
OF TECHNOLOGY LIBRARY

Baltic and Polabian Slavdom; but Germanic influence was already too strong and in order to save Pomerania for Poland, Boleslas had to agree to a compromise — the creation of the independent missionary diocese of Wollin [1] and the inclusion of Pomerania and the Slavic island of Rügen as German fiefs in the Empire (1135). This was the first step towards the German absorption of Pomerania. It inevitably recalls a similar occasion when Mieszko I, about to gather the Pomeranians under his authority, had to consent to an analogous compromise with the Emperor's representative, Count Gero. Ever since the first days of its unification, Germany had harbored the secret design of securing a hold on the Baltic Sea as the best way of guaranteeing safe expansion.

2

Setting his face against any further imperial interference in Poland's domestic affairs for the purpose of reducing it to the level of Bohemia, Boleslas III divided his realm among his four sons, stipulating that the senior member of the Piast dynasty should always occupy the rank of premier duke and ruler of Poland with Cracow as his capital. With the best of intentions, this great Pole thus opened the door to the period of the division of Poland into duchies, the most bewildering period in the country's history, and one whose intricacies are still a nightmare to every student of Poland's past. The country remained divided into several hereditary dukedoms — Great Poland with Gniezno (Gnesen), Little Poland with Cracow, Mazovia, Sandomierz and Silesia — which were again often subdivided into smaller territories given to the members of the reigning families.

Great harm was done to the ideal of Polish unity, as every duchy had its own interests to look after to the detriment of the country as a whole. Moreover, soon after Boleslas III's death the dignity of the premier duke became an object of conflict among the members of the dynasty. Thus the emperors had all the opportunity they needed for making mischief. In 1146 Conrad

[1] It was transferred to Kamin in 1188.

III failed to take a firm hold over Poland when he intervened in favor of his brother-in-law Władysław (Ladislas), the eldest son of Boleslas III, who was expelled from Cracow and from his duchy of Silesia by his brother Boleslas IV. Frederick Barbarossa, however, almost reduced Poland to the level of Bohemia, and in 1157 Boleslas IV, the Curly Haired (1146–1173), the premier duke of Poland, had the humiliation of being forced to promise regular attendance at the Emperor's court, participation in the Italian campaign and the payment of a large sum of money in return for the honor of becoming one of the imperial dignitaries as a sword bearer and of joining his Czech colleague who was proud to officiate at imperial banquets as a cupbearer (*Mundschenk*).

The order of succession to the "seniorate" established by Boleslas III was again neglected after the death of Boleslas IV. His legitimate successor, Mieszko III, called "The Old" (1173–1177), although an able ruler, became unpopular because of his strong monarchical tendencies and lost Cracow to Casimir II the Just (1177–1194), the youngest and probably posthumous son of Boleslas III. Thanks to the support of the aristocracy and the higher clergy Casimir was able to keep Cracow in spite of several attempts made by his older brother to recover the lost possession. A new principle — that of hereditary succession to the "seniorate" — was introduced by Casimir II. Thanks again to the support of the aristocracy, after Casimir's death his son Leszek, called "the White" (1194–1227), became premier duke and kept the Duchy of Cracow as his heritage. In spite of the efforts of Casimir the Just — who united Little Poland with Mazovia and Kujavja — and of his successors to form a solid political group around Cracow, the division of Polish territory among the different branches of the Piast dynasty went on, to the great disadvantage of the Polish nation. All this weakened Poland's resistance to the penetration of German influences into the country.

But the turn of Fortune's wheel saved Poland from being incorporated in the Empire. The Italian question was absorbing the

Emperor's attention, and although the forces of the Empire were not sufficient for sustained and simultaneous pressure in south and east, the great Hohenstaufens were dreaming of another renovation of the Roman Empire. It soon became evident that their dreams were inspired less by the ideals of Charlemagne and Otto I — not to mention Otto III — than by the ambition to rival the Caesars and their centralized Roman monarchy. Henry VI and Frederick II did not look so much to the northeast where Christianity needed their help, as to the southeast where abundant riches and a great historical inheritance excited their greed. They failed, however, to reckon with the Papacy, whose prestige throughout Western Europe had grown considerably. The Papacy was not prepared to tolerate prevarication which fell so far short even of Henry IV's ideals. Once again, in the need of the Popes to find political and ideological allies against a dangerous rival, Poland found its opportunity. The Pope used his good offices frequently during the twelfth century to mediate between the Polish dukes and to keep a valuable eastern ally on good terms; and as a warning to the Germans to keep their hands off Poland, Innocent III (1207) and Innocent IV (1253) both declared that that country was directly dependent upon the Roman See. The ecclesiastical organization of all the Polish duchies under the jurisdiction of the Archbishop of Gniezno and Peter's Pence, a special tax which Poland had paid to the Apostolic See since the days of Casimir I, served to remind every Pole, irrespective of which duchy he belonged to, of his country's common purpose, interests and unity. It was because of this that when the Duke of Silesia, Henry IV (Probus), had succeeded in imposing his rule on Little Poland with Cracow, he applied as a matter of course to the pope for the royal crown. His sudden death in 1290 put an end to his plans.

3

But the division of Poland had results which were to harm not only that country but the Slavic peoples of Central Europe as well. The worst feature of Boleslas III's scheme was that instead of attaching Pomerania to the neighboring Duchy of Greater Poland, he allotted it to the senior duke, and as the senior duke's territory was not always contiguous to Pomerania, he was unable to assist that country at times when his help was most needed, nor was he disposed to take the same interest in it as he took in his own duchy and the immediately adjacent lands. To Poland's lasting detriment Western Pomerania — although it retained its Slavic character and was ruled by princes of a Piast branch — drifted into the sphere of German influence and was made a principality of the Empire in 1181. Poland's attempt to link Eastern Pomerania to itself was equally unsuccessful. Swiętopełk, the best ruler that country ever had, refused to take orders from Poland, and the Senior Duke Leszek the White, who appealed to the sword, perished by it in 1227. Eastern Pomerania's independence was but another step towards the loss by Poland of the whole of Pomerania.

Poland's dismemberment into duchies ruled by different branches of the Piast dynasty and bound together only by the declining authority of the senior duke soon lulled the Poles into disregarding the danger which threatened from Germany — that same danger which had been so valiantly warded off by Boleslas the Great, Mieszko II, Boleslas II and Boleslas III. The more distant duchies, especially Mazovia and Kujavja, safely ensconced behind a protecting screen of other Polish duchies and Slavic territories, whose rulers were bent on their eastern expansion, were absolutely blind to the danger.

The emperors' inability to give their full attention to the eastward drive somehow facilitated this process of disintegration. A concentrated and consciously directed attempt at expansion might well have roused the Poles to the menace and forced them to unite in the face of common danger, for anti-imperial embers were still smoldering throughout the land. But as the German margraves acted on their own responsibility as independent princes, the Poles thought little of the threat and allowed matters to drift.

To make things worse, the Piasts who governed Silesia invoked the aid of the Germans to enforce their authority over the Duchy against the pretensions of other Piasts, with the result that after the German-educated sons of Władysław (Ladislas), the eldest son of Boleslas III, had come to power in 1173, German influence and sympathies had free access to the territory. Frederick Barbarossa knew what he was doing when he forced Boleslas IV to establish them definitely in that Duchy. Silesia was a borderland of Germany and the margraviates of Meissen and Lusatia established in old White Serbia were in German hands, a circumstance which made things very easy for the Germans. Presently, the dukes started imitating the margraves of the Slavic territories by encouraging German colonists to settle. The famous song *Nach dem Osten wollen wir reisen* (We Will Wander Towards the East), which the twelfth-century German colonists adopted as a sort of national anthem, began to echo on the Polish plains.

The Silesian dukes, of course, profited greatly from the colonial movement. Their wealth and prestige grew immensely. The new situation is best illustrated by reference to the achievements of Henry I the Bearded, Duke of Breslau, who secured Cracow in 1229. Within a few years, half of Great Poland was in his possession. Although he was under strong German cultural influence, this Duke aimed at nothing less than a revival of the Polish kingdom, his son, Henry II the Pious, being the one whom he expected to fulfil his plans. Allied with the Papacy against the Emperor Frederick II and supported at home by the clergy, Henry II was well on the way to realizing his father's dream when an unforeseen catastrophe intervened. The Mongols, after destroying Kiev, invaded Poland. The Duke with his small army of Polish and German knights tried to halt the invaders and perished with the flower of his force at the battle of Lignica (1241) and only the fact that the Mongols turned aside to ravish Hungary saved the rest of Poland and Germany.

4

It must be understood that all these happenings in Silesia meant little to the Poles of the more remote duchies. The classical illustration of their ignorance of what was brewing was the arrival of the Teutonic Order on the borders of Prussia (1228) at the invitation of Conrad, Duke of Mazovia. The Hungarians had shown greater discernment. When Bela I called the Knights to his assistance against the Cumans, the successors of the Pechenegs who were invading the Balkan peninsula, he soon discovered that they were making attempts to create a German enclave in Transylvania and Wallachia and expelled them unceremoniously from the country. But heedless of the experience of Hungary, Conrad invited the Teutonic Knights to settle in Chelmno, the easternmost Polish province, to pacify and convert the Baltic Prussians. It would be difficult to find, even at that period, a more flagrant instance of cunning, bad faith, trickery and truculence than was exhibited in the relations of the Order with Conrad of Mazovia and the Prussians. From the outset, the Knights were determined to establish a German State in the East. Their plan had the approval of Frederick II, who declared in advance that any land they might acquire would be a part of the Empire. This was quite contrary to the intentions of the Duke, who had been led to understand that both the Knights and their conquests would be feudally dependent upon his Duchy.

In the forty years between 1230 and 1270, the Knights, with the assistance of a number of "crusaders", subdued the whole territory which is modern East Prussia; but here too Christianization amounted to colonization. The country was packed with German immigrants, for the remnants of the native population refused obstinately to have anything to do with a faith which was forced on them by the sword. These were the beginnings of the greatness and glory of Prussia. Though the purpose for which the Knights had been called was achieved, they did not rest content with their gains, but cast envious eyes towards the mouth of the Vistula, where Danzig lay. This time, they overreached themselves and Swiętopełk of Eastern Pomerania gave them a lesson which they badly needed.

Another danger threatened Poland from the west. The margraves of Brandenburg, who were also covetous of Eastern Pomerania, had the cunning to capture the strategic outpost of Lubusz, on the confluence of the Warta and the Oder, with the intention of using it as a springboard for further moves forward. After the death of Swiętopełk, they crossed the Warta and helped themselves to a slice of the country they coveted. Fortunately, Mestwin II of Eastern Pomerania saw the trap which was being prepared, and in 1294 he made a present of his territory to Přemysl (Przemysław) II, the Duke of Greater Poland. The situation was eased for the Poles, and in order to show his firm purpose, Přemysl II had himself crowned King of Poland. This was too much for the margraves to swallow. Never fastidious in their methods, they instigated his assassination in 1296 and thus secured the removal of a dangerous rival. With no formidable opponent left in Poland the way lay open for the margraves for further penetration into the Slavic East.

5

Bohemia also went through a period of political decadence in the twelfth century. Here again the main reasons for it were the growth of German power under Frederick Barbarossa, and the jealousies which were generated among the members of the reigning family by an unsatisfactory law of succession. According to the order established in 1054 by Břetislav I, the oldest member of the reigning house was to be the sovereign of the State and had to exercise undivided rule over Bohemia. The younger princes were to receive lands in Moravia. Shortly after its introduction, this order was changed by Břetislav II (1092–1110) in favor of his brother Bořivoj, and protracted civil wars ensued. Thus the emperors were presented with a series of opportunities for interfering in the affairs of Bohemia. Lothair went so far as to declare that no prince had the right to ascend the throne of

Bohemia before receiving the country as a fief from the German king. Soběslav (1125–1140) successfully opposed this claim; but by granting the Czech dukes the dignity of being hereditary cupbearers, Conrad III tied them still more closely to Germany. In their pride at having a certain influence upon the elections of German kings, the Czech dukes were induced to take a more lively interest in German affairs and to imitate their German colleagues.

The consequences of this development were soon evident. The Duke Vladislav II (1140–1173), who established his right to rule the country with German help, became a faithful follower of Conrad III, whom he had accompanied on his Crusade. For the help which he gave to Frederick Barbarossa on his Italian campaign, Vladislav II received Upper Lusatia as a fief, together with the title of King.[1]

Although this title was meant to be hereditary, new wars for the succession broke out in 1173 after Vladislav's abdication and retirement to the monastery of Strahov, and it fell into disuse. Frederick Barbarossa took such cunning advantage of the jealousies of the princes and their quarrels that the Přemyslides themselves were scarcely aware of the disintegration of their realm into three imperial principalities, the Duchy of Bohemia, the Margraviate of Moravia and the Bishopric of Prague — with a fourth in the making, the Bishopric of Olomouc. Only the timely deaths of Barbarossa (1152–1190) and of his successor Henry VI (1190–1197) saved the Czechs from the fate which was imperceptibly overtaking the Slavs between the Elbe and the Oder.

6

It was in the year of Henry VI's death that the Czechs had the good fortune to acquire a most able ruler in the person of Přemysl Ottokar I (1197–1230), a man who showed himself to be remark-

[1] The relations between Vladislav II and the Byzantine Emperor Manuel I Comnenus are examined in a short study by F. Dvornik in *Sborník Bidlův* (Prague, 1928, pp. 58–70: "Manuel I Komnenos a Vladislav II, král český," in Czech with a résumé in French).

ably skilful in exploiting the struggle for the imperial succession in such a way as to serve his own country's ends. He secured the confirmation of his own royal hereditary title by the two rivals for the title of imperial dignity — Philip, Duke of Swabia, and Otto of Brunswick, son of Henry the Lion. The latter was supported by Pope Innocent III (1198–1216), who also recognized the Czech ruler's royal title. Přemysl Ottokar's clever manoeuvres were finally crowned in 1212, when the Hohenstaufen Emperor Frederick II (1211–1250) confirmed his royal privileges in a special letter bearing the seal which Frederick used as King of Sicily. This document, called the Golden Sicilian Bull, regulated the relations between Bohemia and the Empire, setting them on a new and firm basis. The internal independence of the Bohemian kingdom was assured and its boundaries decreed inviolable. The Bohemian king's obligation to provide 300 men for the emperor's Italian coronation expedition could be redeemed by a nominal payment of 300 marks, and the king's attendance at the Reichstag was expected only when it was held in one of three cities near the Czech border — Nuremberg, Babenberg or Merseburg. Bohemia was saved.

7

From the eleventh century onwards, the fate of the Czechs, the Slovaks and the Poles was definitely and intimately linked with the fate of Western Europe and it was from that quarter that all the patterns originated which inspired and influenced their social, religious, literary and cultural progress. In this respect, the Czechs had the advantage not only of geographical situation — which, however, had caused them to be dependent upon the Holy Roman Empire — but also of the Old Slavonic literary tradition, which was far from forgotten and which helped them greatly to develop their own language and literary activity. For these reasons the progress of medieval civilization on the Western pattern was more remarkable in Bohemia than in Poland. From the thirteenth century onwards, and especially in the literary field, the Czechs were able to provide some precious inspiration to the Poles.

In their political and social evolution the Czechs were handicapped during the eleventh and twelfth centuries by the old Slav principle that the country was a kind of appanage of the reigning house, all of whose members ought to have a share in its government. This principle led to the division of the country into small principalities and it has been shown how the rivalry of the Přemyslide princes was about to cause the disintegration of the Dukedom and to place all the separate dukes in a position of dependence upon the emperor. Fortunately, this fate was averted at the last moment. The circumstance that the members of the Přemyslide dynasty were not numerous and that the branches of the family in the different appanages slowly died out (between 1200 and 1204) saved Bohemia from sharing the fate of Poland and of Kievan Russia. The place of Bohemia in the Empire was finally defined and the autonomous status of the Kingdom confirmed by the Sicilian Golden Bull. The hereditary character of the Czech succession was made clear, although the principle of primogeniture, not without some control, was introduced only at a later date.[1]

The power of the duke was primitively regarded as absolute and he was not obliged to share it with anybody. He nominated the officers of his court and the governors of the provinces, which were probably formed on the basis of the unification of the Czech tribes in the ninth and tenth centuries. The duke alone controlled their administration and all his officers were selected from among his own retinue. The provinces were administered from castles which were the residences of the governors appointed by the duke. The provincial governor commanded the castle garrison and also any body of troops raised by levy in the province in the event of war. At court, various offices were introduced later on the Western pattern.

The origins of the Czech aristocracy were also influenced by Western — especially German — usage. Under primitive condi-

[1] It was made definite in 1341. It was necessary even then, however, that the heir's rights should be confirmed by the nation and acknowledged by the emperor.

tions, the people were divided into freemen and bondmen. Some individuals among the freemen became conspicuous in virtue of their wealth or because they were in the immediate service of the prince and thus above the level of the common people. The Czech name for aristocracy — *šlechta* — indicates the German influence on the rise of this class, just as the Polish word *szlachta* does, both words having been formed from the Old High German *slahta* (modern German *Geschlecht*), meaning "race." Moreover, time brought a distinction between the high aristocracy and the low aristocracy, the latter being that class of freemen who were able to do their military service on horseback. After the German custom, the princes and the high aristocracy started making use of bondmen to perform various duties at their courts and households.

The influence of the high aristocracy in the administration of the State developed on the same lines as it had followed in Germany and the rest of Western Europe. The high aristocracy and, to some extent, the high clergy, were the first to organize themselves into a distinct class claiming some of the prince's sovereign rights. This transformation was achieved in the period from the middle of the twelfth century to the beginning of the fourteenth century. From the second half of the twelfth century onwards, for example, the high aristocracy had sufficient influence to intervene, sometimes effectively, in questions concerning the succession to the throne.

This situation prepared the further evolution of Bohemia's constitution. From the beginning of the thirteenth century on, the Czech State can be described as dualistic, because political power was vested not only in the prince, but also in the privileged classes, referred to as the Nation. A striking illustration of this development is given by the fact that, from that time onwards, the class described as the higher aristocracy used its own seal, which was impressed upon state documents alongside the royal seal.

The lower aristocracy did not enjoy such a privileged position. As a class it was established rather late, that is, only in the fourteenth century, when the cities had formed their organization and begun their successful claim for political rights as a special burgher class.

8

In purely cultural matters, Bohemia made great progress from the twelfth century onwards and for this the clergy were mainly responsible. The first wave of Western influence upon the religious affairs of Bohemia showed itself in a growing hostility to the use of the Slavonic language in the liturgy. But although Latin prevailed, other Church reforms introduced by Gregory VII — celibacy of the priesthood and a stern clerical discipline — were accepted only after a very hard struggle during the second half of the twelfth century. The Bishop of Olomouc, the learned and zealous Zdík, was the main promoter of these reforms.

The Westernization of Czech Christianity was further promoted through the intermediary of new Benedictine foundations — Opatovice (c. 1086), Postoloprty (end of XIth cent.), Kladruby (c. 1115), and Rajhrad, Hradiště, Třebíč in Moravia — and of the new Premonstratensian and Cistercian orders. The main Premonstratensian foundations were those of Strahov (1142) and of Doksany (for nuns), and those of the Cistercians were Sedlec, near Kutná Hora (1142), and Velehrad (1205). Some Benedictine foundations were also given to the new orders. These orders brought into the country new agricultural methods and their foundations became important centers of education and links with the rest of the cultural West — France and Germany. In 1159 the Knights of St. John of Jerusalem were settled in Prague.

The chapters of canons also became important centers of cultural life. Besides the chapter at the cathedral church, the one of Vyšehrad in Prague was founded in the eleventh century. About the same time chapters were founded in Olomouc, in Stará Boleslav (in memory of St. Wenceslas, who was martyred there), and in Litoměřice. The chapters of Mělník, near Prague, and of Sadská came into being at the beginning of the twelfth century.

Also during this so-called Romanesque period remarkable progress was made in the arts in Bohemia, though Czech production limited itself to copying patterns and motifs from the West and trying to adapt them to Czech taste. It has been seen how Czech religious architecture had developed from the early Christian and Byzantine provincial styles endowed with certain Romanesque features into a characteristic style of church design — rotundas with one apse. This spread to Hungary, Poland and Germany, and many new churches of this type were built in Bohemia in this period. The church of St. George in Prague, rebuilt in 1142, is the most remarkable monument of Romanesque art in Bohemia.

In sculpture and painting, Bohemia followed mainly German patterns. The Abbot of Sázava, Božetěch, is said to have been an original sculptor. Unfortunately only fragments are left of most of the sculptured decorations of churches. The most original work of the twelfth century is the tympanum at St. James near Kutná Hora. It is surpassed only by the tympanum of the church of St. George in Prague. Also, considerable progress was made by Czech artists in minor arts such as illumination of manuscripts and miniature painting. Four productions of this kind from the eleventh century deserve a special mention: the codices of Vyšehrad, of St. Guy (Vít) in Prague, of Cracow, and of Gniezno, the last two of Czech origin. From the twelfth century some Psalters — for example, those of Mělník, of Vyšehrad, and of Ostrov — testify to the high standard the minor arts had achieved in Bohemia.

Czech literary development from the eleventh century onwards was also strongly influenced by Western traditions coming not only from Germany but also from France. The first Czech chronicle was written in Latin by Cosmas, Dean of the Chapter of Prague (about 1045–1125), who had studied at Liège in Belgium. Cosmas was a great Czech patriot, although hostile to the Slavonic liturgy, and a married man to boot. His *Chronicle* was continued by many, including a canon of Vyšehrad, covering the years from 1126 to 1142, a monk of Sázava those from 1126 to 1162, Canon Vincentius those from 1140 to 1167, and Abbot Jarloch the years 1167 to 1198. All these chronicles are important sources for the history of this period. Canon Vincentius was a devoted adviser of King Vladislav II and well acquainted with life at the court of Frederick Barbarossa, and Abbot Jarloch gave a detailed description of the deeds performed by the Czechs during the siege of Milan by the imperial army.

All these chroniclers, Cosmas in particular, show vast knowledge of classical lore and of contemporary literary production in Western Europe and this is an indication that the education of the Czech intellectual *élite* was on the same level as in Western countries.

Writing in Czech progressed slowly. From the eleventh and twelfth centuries there are only some Czech and Old Slavonic glosses in gospels and in compositions written in Latin, namely the homilies used in the Abbey of Opatovice, the Latin manuscript of Jeremiah's Prophecies in Olomouc, and the *Mater Verborum*, a kind of contemporary encyclopedia. There may possibly have existed some hymns and songs in Czech. The composition of the first strophe of the oldest version of St. Wenceslas' hymn and of the prayer "Hail Mary" in Czech verse may be attributed to this period.

When compared with the literary production of Moravia during the ninth century and that of Bohemia during the tenth and eleventh centuries, the literary harvest of the twelfth century was rather scanty. One of the reasons for this is the suppression of Old Slavonic in the liturgy and in literature. The Czechs abandoned the literary language which was common to all Slavs, and the creation of a Czech literary language required some time.

The prominent promoter of this new course was the first Czech chronicler Cosmas. He ignored in his work the cultural achievements of the Slavonic period in Czech history, although he seems to have known its literary productions and to have made use of

328   EARLY SLAVIC CIVILIZATION

information contained therein. In spite of that, the *Annals* of the Benedictine Abbey of Hradiště in Moravia, written about 1150, still echo the old tradition, and the second writer to continue the *Chronicle* of Cosmas, an anonymous monk of Sázava, comes back to it. He copied the oldest Latin legend of St. Ludmila and used an Old Slavonic legend of St. Procopius, founder of Sázava, in his biography of the Saint. This tendency grew and found expression in 1204 when Přemysl Ottokar I obtained from the Pope, together with the confirmation of his royal title, the official canonization of St. Procopius, with whose name the Old Slavonic tradition in Czech lands was so intimately connected. The Slavonic liturgy and literature could not, however, be reinstated.

By the wholesale liturgical replacement of Slavonic by Latin, the Church lost a very effective means of educating its faithful through a liturgy which could be generally followed because it was performed in a language easily understood by everybody. This circumstance was also partly responsible for the survival of many pagan usages among the simple people. On the other hand, of course, with the loss of the Old Slavonic liturgy, Bohemia was definitely drawn into the orbit of Western Latin civilization.

9

The social and political evolution of medieval Poland presents some features of similarity with developments in Bohemia; but in other respects it differs considerably from anything which was achieved in this period by other Central European nations. As in Bohemia, the power of the duke was absolute, once the unification of the tribes had been effected by the Piast dynasty. The great Piasts, from Mieszko I to Boleslas III the Wrymouth, created a monarchic system which gave evidence of great strength and vigor, blended with intelligence.

In the social sphere, primitive Poland knew neither aristocracy nor feudalism. All members of the clans were free, with the exception of prisoners-of-war and slaves. Class distinction, however, showed itself at an early date. It was natural that the elders of the clans (*starosta*) should begin to regard themselves as being superior to the rest of the people. All freemen were potential soldiers; but the princes maintained their own retinues and Mieszko is said to have had 3,000 in his standing army. The members of these retinues or cadres were not only warriors and commanders of freemen in the field, but also governors of the duke's fortified castles, which were the centers of political administration in the country.

In this way, there began slowly to emerge a class of privileged men, distinguished by their wealth, which was derived from the booty of war or from gifts from their liege-lord, or by the prominent position which the ruler called upon them to occupy. The number of the privileged grew considerably during the period of the disintegration of Poland into separate duchies, as each duke had his own court and his own retinue; for the necessity of defending the frontier and waging war called for a plentiful supply of knightly warriors who were better trained than the ordinary freemen. The dukes used to reward them for their services by gifts of land and they soon began to regard themselves as different from the people. This is how the class of the lower nobility originated. The peasants were attached to the noble families or to ecclesiastical institutions. A fairly sharp division into classes — magnates, knights and the people, still freemen in principle — began to become more clearly marked.

Besides the magnates, who were the intimates of the princes and his main advisers, the high clergy soon won an important position in the state. They were the educated class. It was they who looked after the duke's correspondence with other rulers and who composed his legal documents and juridical pronouncements. The clergy were also the first to secure important privileges and guarantees against encroachments by the state. This was achieved at the Assembly of Lęczyca (1180), convoked by Casimir the Just, who was anxious to secure from the higher aristocracy and the higher clergy sanction for the revolutionary change of his father's statute. In consideration for the privileges which he then granted, Casimir carried his point that the Duchy of Cracow and the "seniorate" should henceforth be hereditary in his dynasty.

These privileges were later extended, thanks to the efforts of Henry Kiętlicz, Archbishop of Gniezno (1199–1219), the foremost protagonist in Poland of canonical reform in the spirit of Gregory VII. It was due to the beneficial influence which the Church exercised in Poland as the main defender of the national unity amid dynastic partition that its high dignitaries were able to maintain their position as a privileged class.

Although the change in Boleslas III's statute made at Lęczyca was sanctioned also by the Pope and by the Emperor, it was rejected by the other branches of the Piast dynasty. The dynastic struggles which issued from this situation gave the higher aristocracy the welcome opportunity of acquiring more influence in the state. The first occasion presented itself after Casimir's death, during the struggles between his son Leszek the White and Leszek's uncle Mieszko the Old.

10

In purely cultural respects, Poland also made great progress from the eleventh century onwards. Again the clergy were in the van of this progress, although the education of native priests to succeed foreign missionaries was slow. Progress in Christian practice was also rather laborious after the first outburst of enthusiasm during the reign of Boleslas the Great, which was, of course, dominated by the memory of two great saints: St. Adalbert and St. Bruno of Querfurt. Benedictines, and later Premonstratensians, Cistercians and Franciscans, became important links between Poland and the cultured West. As has already been mentioned, the Church reforms of Gregory VII were accepted in Poland much later than they were in Bohemia — definitively only in the first half of the thirteenth century.

In the eleventh and twelfth centuries Poland swarmed with foreign priests, coming not only from Germany but also from France, Belgium and Italy. This is illustrated by the fact that the first Polish historian was an anonymous ecclesiastic, called Gallus because he is believed to have been a Frenchman or a Walloon. He lived in Poland between 1110 and 1135 and in his *Chronicle*, written in Latin, he preserved many Polish legends. He was fond of quoting the classics, particularly Sallust — an indication that he had read widely.[1] His work was continued by two bishops of Cracow — Matthew Choleva and Vincent Kadłubek, the work of the latter being particularly popular. He was educated in Paris and died in 1223 as a Cistercian, these two details being an illustration of the general situation among the better educated clergy in Poland at that period. His work, tracing Polish history from the legendary period up to 1200, is important for the study of the reign of Casimir the Just, in whose favor he is much biased.

Besides the chronicles, the Latin legends of St. Adalbert were very popular in Poland. Bruno of Querfurt, a friend of Boleslas the Great, wrote a biography of Adalbert of which there are two editions. An account of Adalbert's passion was written by a German priest who had lived in Poland, and a third legend was written by a native priest in Poland. More hagiographical works were composed in Poland in the thirteenth and fourteenth centuries. In the thirteenth century the first definitive edition was set down of the Polish hymn in honor of Our Lady in *Bogurodzica*. This is of much older origin and the first part may be attributed to St. Adalbert.

The new foundations of the Benedictines and the abbeys of the new Cistercian and Premonstratensian orders became the centers of cultural progress in Poland. The Benedictines achieved great merit for the rechristianization of the country under Casimir the Restorer. A later tradition attributes to him the foundation of the Abbey at Tyniec near Cracow and of that at Leubus in Silesia. Boleslas II founded the abbey at Mogilno near Gniezno and that at Lubin near Poznań.[2]

[1] Cf. the most recent monograph by M. Plezia, *Kronika Galla*, published by the Polish Academy (S. II, vol. XLVI), Cracow, 1947.

[2] On the activity of the Benedictines in Poland see the monograph by P. David, *Les Bénédictins de l'Ordre de Cluny dans la Pologne médiévale* (Paris, 1939).

Boleslas II also re-established the episcopal foundations erected in 1000, adding to them Płock in Mazovia. St. Norbert, the Archbishop of Magdeburg, made a last attempt in 1133 at subordinating all Polish bishoprics to the jurisdiction of his metropolis. His request was granted by Innocent II, but as the bishops of Poland paid no attention to the decision, the papal bull remained a dead letter and it was annulled in 1136.

Under Boleslas III Benedictines were established at Łysa Góra and in Breslau. Cistercians from France and Germany erected abbeys in the twelfth century in the following places: Jędrzejów (1140), Łekno and Ląd (about 1150), Leubus (1150), Sulejów (1176), Wąchock (1179), Oliva in Pomerania (about 1178), Koprzywnica (1185). The Premonstratensians appeared in Poland before 1140, founding abbeys at Kalisz, Brzesk and Witów. But their activity was not so widespread nor so popular as that of the Cistercians. The Knights of St. John of Jerusalem were established in Zagość (c. 1165) and in Poznań (Posen) in 1184, and the Templars at Opatów.

Chapters of canons, set up in all episcopal cities, were also important cultural centers. Their libraries were enriched by the acquisition of many manuscripts of French, Belgian and German origin, especially under Casimir the Restorer and Władysław Herman.

With Casimir the Restorer begins also the development of Polish medieval architecture and art. Cracow, the first center of Polish Christianity during the Great Moravian period of its history, could boast a new cruciform stone church, that of SS. Felix and Adauctus, built in the style which was in vogue in Cologne whence Casimir had brought Benedictine missionaries. The same prince constructed the oldest Polish basilica, that of St. Leonard, in Cracow on the Wawel, his place of residence. Only a few ruins remain of what was an imposing Romanesque edifice, with three naves, apses and two towers. Only a small part is preserved of the Romanesque church of St. John the Evangelist, built in Mogilno under Boleslas II. Unfortunately the first Romanesque cathedral of Gniezno, finished in 1097, has disappeared almost completely. It had two naves with apses and two towers. This style, probably imported from Hildesheim and Merseburg, became the pattern of Polish cathedrals constructed during the twelfth century in Poznań and Cracow.

Płock was another important centre of arts in the twelfth century. Its Romanesque cathedral, finished in 1144, combined church architecture with fortification. The church of Łęczyca near Płock, from the same period, is partly preserved. Different types of Romanesque architecture are presented by the cathedral of Breslau (Wrocław) and the churches of Czerwińsk, of St. John in Prandocin, of St. Andrew in Cracow and of St. Nicholas in Wysocicze. Numerous small Romanesque churches were built in the eleventh and twelfth centuries, some of them on the pattern of small rotundas with apses, a style imported into Poland from Bohemia.

When the reform movement of Cluny had reached Poland, the style of Cluny was also adopted by the reformed Polish abbeys. The first church of this kind was that of SS. Peter and Paul in Kruszwica. Many churches are said to have been built in the twelfth century by Peter Włast, Count of Breslau, a great benefactor of the Benedictines and of regular canons whom he brought to Poland from France. French Romanesque patterns were also imitated by the architects who built the churches founded by him. The best example of this kind was the church of St. Vincent near Breslau, finished in 1148. At the end of the twelfth century and during the first half of the thirteenth Polish architecture shows some new tendencies. The churches of Our Lady in Strzelno and in Inowrocław were built partly in stone and partly in brick but the church of St. John in Poznań (1187) was built completely in brick. The Cistercians naturally brought their own artistic traditions to Poland and their abbeys and churches were all built in the traditional Cistercian style, imposing in its simplicity.

In decorative arts Poland produced some good work during this period. The churches were decorated with a preference for relief sculptures of fantastic beasts and plants. Only fragments of this kind of decoration are preserved. The tympanum of the church in Łęczyca — Madonna with angels — deserves special mention. The best specimens of decorative art were produced by the artists who decorated the church of St. Vincent near Breslau. Good sculptured portraits of the founder, Peter Włast, and of some of his contemporaries are preserved. In general, some tympanums from the churches founded by Peter and still preserved demonstrate that Polish sculpture reached its highest quality in Silesia.

A masterpiece of Polish Romanesque decorative art is the bronze door of the cathedral of Gniezno by an unknown artist. Its plastic decorations were executed in the years 1129 to 1137 and represent scenes from the life of St. Adalbert.

A Polish counterpart of the Czech Božetěch was the master Leopard. Some think that he might be the artist who produced the bronze door of Gniezno. The plastic decorations on the doors of the cathedral at Płock also deserve to be mentioned. They were probably executed, however, not by German but by French craftsmen.

In the minor arts, the Poles did not produce anything very remarkable in this period. The libraries of the dukes, chapters and abbeys could, however, boast many beautifully illuminated manuscripts, imported from Germany, France and Bohemia. Only in the thirteenth century were some examples of Polish minor arts produced under the inspiration of the traditions brought by the Cistercians, for example, the Book of Eight Prophets, the Psalter of Trzebnic, both now in Warsaw, and the Gradual of the Sisters of St. Claire, now in Cracow.

It is interesting to note that although Poland was a neighbor of Russia and thus open to Eastern, especially Byzantine, influences, the Poles were not as much affected by these as might have been expected. Some traces of Russian influence can, however, be noted. Byzantine jewelry seems to have found admirers in Poland, but in other respects the Poles looked for inspiration only to the Latin West. At the end of the twelfth century, Poland, like Bohemia, was definitely included in the sphere of Western Latin civilization.

It should, however, be stressed that both countries, and especially Poland, tried to be in direct contact with French civilization. In this respect the relations of Poland with Liège and with some other Belgian centers are particularly interesting. There are some indications that Polish merchants were in lively contact with the Flemish cities in the eleventh, twelfth and thirteenth centuries.[1] This gives ground for the view that many incentives in the cultural development of Poland in this period came directly from Flanders and the French-speaking centers. The role of Cologne and the Rhineland — mentioned above — in Polish history at this period should not be forgotten either.

It is important to note how the Poles tried to keep in direct touch with French and Belgian cultural centers, and to avoid the mediation of eastern Germany, which was less developed at that time than Belgium and France.

CONCLUSION

Such then, briefly stated, was the political, cultural and social development of the Slavs, from the dawn of their history to the middle of the thirteenth century. As we have seen, at the end of the twelfth and at the beginning of the thirteenth centuries, almost all the Slavic states experienced profound crises that threatened their very existence. A better future seemed, however, to beckon to the Slavs from the thirteenth century on. In most of the Slavic political formations we witness an unexpected rise to new heights in the political and cultural development of Europe.

Bohemia was the first to rise to a new importance in Central Europe. Profiting from the decline of medieval Germany and from the strife for the imperial crown, the last kings of the Přemyslide dynasty extended their influence within the Empire. Přemysl Ottokar II (1253–1278) won the inheritance of the Babenbergers

[1] For details and bibliographical indications, see the short monograph by J. Sobieski, *Jean de Pologne à Louvain (1253)* (Bruxelles, 1950), pp. 9–32. Cf. also the short study by C. Osieczkowska, "Connections between Medieval Art of Poland, Bohemia, Belgium, and France," published in the *Bulletin of the Polish Institute of Arts and Sciences in America* II (October, 1943), no. I, pp. 163–167.

in the Alpine region and became founder of modern Austria. Through the Austrian lands he came into direct contact with Italy, a circumstance which had its importance in the cultural development of Bohemia. Emboldened by this success, he extended his hand to grasp the imperial crown, but lost his life in battle with his rival Rudolf of Habsburg, and his achievements in Austria became the basis of the rise of the Habsburg dynasty.

His son, Wenceslas II, the wealthiest king of Europe, because of the rich silver mines discovered in Bohemia, tried his chances in the East, and succeeded in uniting Poland with Bohemia. Hungary offered its crown to him. A new political formation was rising in Central Europe, a mighty formation, with Prague as its center. The premature death of Wenceslas II and the assassination (1306) of his son Wenceslas III, the last Přemyslide, extinguished all these high hopes.

It was reserved to Charles IV of the dynasty of Luxemburg to realize the dreams of the Přemyslides. As Roman Emperor and King of Bohemia, Charles IV made Prague the capital of the Empire, an independent metropolis, and the seat of the first university founded in Central and Eastern Europe (1348). Bohemia rose to an unusual height in political and cultural life. This "golden age," however, did not last. A national, religious and social crisis followed in the wake of this rise and plunged the country into the chaos of the Hussite wars. The Czechs heroically defended their own "Reformation," inaugurated by John Hus, against the armies of the crusaders, and won undying military fame, but the achievements of the "golden age" were lost to a great extent in the crisis. In vain did their moderate reformers claim official recognition by the Pope of those concessions yielded to them at the Council of Basel (1433). Although the Czechs made considerable progress in the cultural field, they continued to be harrassed by religious strife and crisis.

A new hope rose for them under the Polish dynasty of the Jagiellonians when Poland, Bohemia and Hungary were united. But the dynasty of Habsburg took over the inheritance of the Jagiellonians; and the Czechs, favoring the new Reformation

and opposing the Habsburg King Ferdinand II, lost their independence in a single battle in 1620. The Kingdom of Bohemia
was gradually incorporated as a province into the Habsburg
Monarchy.

The Southern Slavs also rose to a new importance in the thirteenth century. Profiting by the decline of Byzantine political
power which set in after the death of Manuel I Comnenos
(1180), the Bulgarians revolted (1185). Their leaders, John and
Peter Assen and especially Kalojan (1197–1207), laid the foundations of the second Bulgarian Empire. The Serbs, under their
great Župan Nemanja, also shook off the political yoke of Byzantium, and the new Serbian State extended its sway from Serbia
proper over the former Dioclean kingdom and over some Latin
cities on the Adriatic. The conquest of Constantinople by the
Latins, in 1204, offered new opportunities to Bulgarian and
Serbian rulers. Their support was solicited by the Greeks, the
Papacy and the new Latin Empire. The Bulgarian Tsar John
Assen II (1218–1244) almost succeeded in realizing Symeon the
Great's dream — the conquest of Constantinople. Both countries
made considerable progress in their political, economic and
cultural evolution and played an important role in contemporary
southeastern Europe.

When Bulgarian prestige, which was at its highest in the thirteenth century, diminished, Serbia came forward and for some
time took the leadership in the Balkans. The greatest Serbian
Tsar Stephen Dušan (1331–1355) even succeeded in bringing
about a kind of federal union with Bulgaria. Realizing the danger
from the Turks, who had succeeded in getting a firm hold on
Greek soil, he proclaimed himself champion of Christian interests
and made preparations for the conquest of Constantinople. Sudden death prevented him from realizing his aim and from uniting
the Christian forces against the Turkish menace. The Turkish
wave first swallowed Bulgaria and overran the lands conquered
by Dušan. It moved forward, gradually engulfed the whole of
Serbia and Bosnia, inundated the plains of Croatia and broke
into Hungary, to be stopped only under the walls of Vienna. Then

the wars of liberation started, fought mostly by Slovak, Czech, German and Croat regiments under Austrian generals, a struggle which resulted first in the liberation of Hungary and Croatia and which ended only in the twentieth century for the Balkan nations.

A new life started also in Eastern Europe. Poland, torn by continuous internal strife and disturbed by the growing German influence, finally found its unity under a national king. In the reign of Casimir III the Great (1333–1370) the Poles advanced rapidly to new fame. Casimir stopped the menacing progress of the Teutonic Order, consolidated Polish lands and, supported by Hungary, his ally, assured Poland a place of honor in Central and Eastern Europe.

On the foundations built by Casimir, the Jagiellonian dynasty continued to erect a new empire. The dynastic union with Lithuania — comprising many Russian principalities, with Kiev, liberated by the Lithuanians from the Tatars — was soon completed by the dynastic union with Bohemia and Hungary. Even the proud Teutonic Order had to acknowledge Polish supremacy, which extended from the Baltic Sea to the Black Sea. It was at this time that Poland experienced its literary and cultural renaissance, the achievements of which are remarkable.

The union with Lithuania was, however, one of the main reasons for a new crisis which was predestined in the end to prove fatal to Poland. Russia was, in the meantime, from the end of the thirteenth century, also finding a new center round which its national and cultural life started to revolve — Moscow. The princes of this small principality revealed a rare ability in acquiring new territories, which they administered very wisely. Securing from the Tatar khagans the title of Grand Prince and the privilege of levying for the khagans the tribute due to the Tatars by all Russian principalities, they outgrew all their rivals in Russia. After securing the support of the Russian Church, when the Metropolitan of Kiev settled in Moscow, the rulers of Moscow became leaders of the national struggle for freedom. The Grand Prince Dmitri (1359–1389), who secured the first Russian victory over the Tatars on the River Don, became the legendary symbol of this struggle which ended in 1480, under Ivan III, with the definite liberation of all Russia from the Tatars.

Soon, however, the consequences of the isolation of Russia from the rest of Europe for over two hundred years became apparent. The Russia of Moscow was very much different from Kievan Russia. The grand princes of Moscow developed a strong monarchic régime, centralizing all the power in the hands of a single ruler. Soon they started to claim dominion over all Russia, even over the principalities which had joined the Polish-Lithuanian commonwealth. Rejecting the new cultural treasures offered them by the Poles, the Russians entrenched themselves in their own Orthodox traditions and refused to accept anything from the nation which ruled over lands claimed by Moscovite princes as their *otčiny* — rightful inheritance from their forefathers.

This mentality prompted the Russians to sever relations also with the Greeks after the latter had accepted, for a short period, the Union with the Latins proclaimed by the Council of Florence (1439). Basil II declared himself the only lawful protector of Orthodoxy, represented by the Russian Church, and soon Russian ecclesiastic theoreticians started to declare Moscow the third Rome, rightful successor of Rome and Constantinople. Unimpressed by the claims to Byzantine inheritances, the Moscovite princes pressed only their right to lands formerly ruled by their masters, the Tatar khagans, and to "Russian" land under Poland-Lithuania, although two new Slavic nations were coming into being in those lands — the Ukrainians and the Byelorussians.

The first Tsar Ivan IV, the Terrible (1533–1584), started the Russian drive toward the Baltic Sea, on one side, and beyond the Volga and the Urals into the wide Siberian plains. An immense empire was rising, proud in its isolation from the rest of Christianity, looking for leadership only to its tsar and patriarch, the head of its Church.

The two Slavic nations clashed in a bloody and prolonged conflict when, after the extinction of the Rurik dynasty, the Poles made an attempt to put a Polish prince on the Moscovite throne. National and religious bias grew in Russia during this period of troubles. The new dynasty of the Romanovs (from 1613 on) continued the policy of the Ruriks and eagerly joined Prussia in plans for dividing Poland, weakened by the decline of royal power and the growth of the influence on State affairs of the uncontrollable assemblies of the aristocrats. Instead of the slow penetration of Western cultural, technical and economic achievements, which Russia needed and which could have reached it peacefully through Poland, came the avalanche-like inrush, for which the Russians were not ready, when Peter the Great suddenly opened the gates that had hitherto permitted only a trickle of Western ideas to enter Moscovite Russia. This violent inrush is responsible for many a crisis that swept over Russia.

All this development opens new and varied vistas on the history of the Slavs and on their political and cultural relations with the rest of the world. The achievements realized during this medieval and postmedieval era provided the chief inspiration for the Slavic nations when they were engulfed in the empires of Germany, Austria-Hungary, Turkey, and Moscovite Russia. It is the conserved memory of their storied past that has always inspired the Slavs in their ever-recurring struggles for freedom, and it will never fail to have significance for them.

Only the scholar who is familiar with this rich and eventful history will be able to comprehend the Slavic mentality and understand the present and future history of the Slavic people. It is for this reason that this period of the rise and crisis of medieval Slavdom deserves a more thorough study.

ABBREVIATIONS USED IN THE BIBLIOGRAPHY

Bonn C.S.H.B.   *Corpus Scriptorum Historiae Byzantinae*, also called the Byzantine Corpus of Bonn.

F.R.B.   *Fontes Rerum Bohemicarum*, ed. J. Emler, Prague, 1871.

M.G.H.   *Monumenta Germaniae Historica.*

–   Auct. Ant.: *Auctores Antiquissimi.*

–   Dipl.: *Diplomata.*

–   Ep.: *Epistolae.*

–   S.: *Scriptores.*

–   S. Rer. Langob.: *Scriptores Rerum Langobardicarum.*

–   S.N.S.: *Scriptores Nova Series.*

–   S. in us. schol.: *Scriptores in usum scholarum.*

Muratori, S.R.I.   *Scriptores Rerum Italicarum*, ed. Muratori.

M.P.H.   *Monumenta Poloniae Historica*, ed. E. Bielowski, Lwóv, Kraków, 1864–93.

S.R.H.   *Scriptores Rerum Hungaricarum*, Budapest, 1938–40.

Teubner   *Bibliotheca Teubneriana*, Leipzig.

P.G.   Migne, *Patrologia Graeca*, 140 vols., Paris, 1844–65.

P.L.   Migne, *Patrologia Latina*, 221 vols., Paris, 1844–64.

BIBLIOGRAPHY

1. General

The early history of the Slavs is usually treated very briefly in books dealing with the general history of the different Slavic nations. Therefore, only the best known works in English, French and German are quoted in this bibliography. More abundant bibliographical indications will be found in the following works: —

Kerner, R. J., *Slavic Europe. A Selected Bibliography in the Western European Languages* (Cambridge, Mass., 1918).
Strakhovsky, L. I., *A Handbook of Slavic Studies* (Cambridge, Mass., 1949).

General books on early Slavic history and civilization are few, but the following give a short introduction to the subject: —

Bogusławski, E., *Einführung in die Geschichte der Slaven* (Jena, 1904).
Brückner, A., *Der Eintritt der Slaven in die Weltgeschichte* (Berlin, 1909).
Cross, S. H., *Slavic Culture through the Ages* (Cambridge, Mass., 1948).
Halecki, O., *Borderlands of Western Civilization* (New York, 1952), pp. 1–78.
Léger, L., *Les anciennes civilisations slaves* (Paris, 1921).
Mousset, A., *The World of the Slavs* (New York, 1951).
Niederle, L., *La race slave, statistique, démographie, anthropologie* (Paris, 1911), trans. from Czech by L. Léger.
——— *Manuel de l'antiquité slave* (2 vols., Paris, 1923, 1926).
Trautmann, R., *Die slavischen Völker und Sprachen, eine Einführung in die Slavistik* (Göttingen, 1947).

2. Handbooks on the General History of Slavic Nations and of Byzantium

Antonoff, V., *Bulgarien vom Beginn seines staatlichen Bestehens bis auf unsere Zeit, 679–1917* (Berlin, 1917).
Braun, M., *Die Slawen auf dem Balkan* (Leipzig, 1941).
Cambridge History of Poland from the Origins to Sobieski (1696) (Cambridge, 1950).

David, P., *Les Sources de l'histoire de Pologne à l'époque des Piasts* (Paris, 1924).

Doroshenko, D., *History of the Ukraine* (Edmonton, 1939).

Diehl, Ch., Marçais, G., *Le Monde Oriental de 395 à 1081* (Paris, 1936), (Histoire générale, ed. G. Glotz, Hist. du Moyen Age, vol. III).

Dyboski, R., *Poland in World Civilization* (New York, 1950).

Forbes, N., et al., *The Balkans: A History of Bulgaria, Serbia, Greece, Rumania and Turkey* (Oxford, 1915).

Gapanovitch, J. J., *Historiographie russe (hors de la Russie)* (Paris, 1946).

Halecki, O., *A History of Poland* (New York, 1943).

Hrushevsky, M., *A History of the Ukraine* (New York, 1941).

Iorga, N., *Histoire des Etats balkaniques jusqu'à 1924* (Paris, 1925).

Kovalevsky, P., *Manuel d'histoire Russe* (Paris, 1948).

Krofta, K., *A Short History of Czechoslovakia* (New York, 1934).

Lednicki, W., *Life and Culture of Poland* (New York, 1944).

Lipšic, E. E., *Byzanz und die Slaven* (Weimar, 1951).

Luetzow, C. F., *Bohemia* (New York, 1934).

Mazour, A. G., *Russia, Past and Present* (New York, 1951), pp. 1–74.

Ostrogorsky, G., *Geschichte des byzantinischen Staates*, 2nd ed. (München, 1952).

Pares, B., *A History of Russia*, 2nd ed. (New York, 1937).

Platonov, S. F., *History of Russia* (New York, 1925).

Prokeš, J., *Histoire tchéchoslovaque* (Paris, 1927).

Ristelhuber, R., *Histoire des peuples balkaniques* (Paris, 1950).

Rose, W. J., *Poland – Old and New* (London, 1948).

Schevill, F., Gewehr, W. M., *A History of the Balkan Peninsula* (New York, 1933).

Seton-Watson, R. W., *A History of the Czechs and Slovaks* (London, 1943).

Slatarski (Zlatarski), V. N., and Haneff, N., *Geschichte der Bulgaren* 2 vols. (Leipzig, 1917–1918).

Songeon, G., *Histoire de la Bulgarie des origines à nos jours, 485–1913* (Paris, 1913).

Stadtmüller, G., *Geschichte Südosteuropas* (München, 1950).

Temperley, H., *History of Serbia* (London, 1917).

Thomson, S. H., *Czechoslovakia in European History* (Princeton, 1953).

Tompkins, S. R., *Russia through the Ages; from the Scythians to the Soviets* (New York, 1940).

Vasiliev, A. A., *History of the Byzantine Empire 324–1453*, 2nd ed. (Wisconsin Univ. Press, Madison, 1952).

Vernadsky, G., *A History of Russia*, 2nd ed. (New Haven, 1930).

—— *Political and Diplomatic History of Russia* (London, 1937).

Vojnović, L., *Histoire de Dalmatie*, 2 vols. (Paris, 1934).

CHAPTERS I AND II

THE ORIGINS AND MIGRATIONS OF THE SLAVS
PRIMITIVE SLAVIC CIVILIZATION

SOURCES

Greek and Byzantine

Agathias, *Historiarum libri V*, ed. Bonn *C.S.H.B.*

Constantinus Porphyrogenitus, *De administrando imperio*, ed. Bonn *C.S.H.B.*, ed. G. Moravczik, R. J. H. Jenkins (with English translation) (Budapest, 1949).

—— *De Ceremoniis*, ed. Bonn *C.S.H.B.*; ed. A. Vogt., *Collection Budé* (Paris, 1935–1940).

—— *De Thematibus*, ed. Bonn *C.S.H.B.*; ed. Pertusi, A. (*Studi e Testi*, 160, Rome, 1952).

S. *Demetrii Miracula*, *P.G.*, 116.

Genesius, *Regum libri IV*, ed. Bonn *C.S.H.B.*

Georgius Pisides, *Bellum Avaricum*, ibid.

Kekammenos Kerameus, *Strategicon*, ed. B. Vasilevskij and V. Gernsted (St. Petersburg, 1895).

Leonis Tactica, *P.G.*, 107.

Leo Diaconus, *Historiae*, ed. Bonn *C.S.H.B.*

Le Grammaticus, *Chronographia*, ibid.

Malalas, Joannes, *Chronographia*, ibid.

Maurikios, *Strategicon*, ed. J. Scheffer (Upsala, 1664).

Menander Protector, *Fragmenta . . . de legationibus*, ed. C. Müller, *Fragmenta histor. Graecor.* (Paris, 1885) IV.

Nicephorus, *Historia syntomos*, ed. Bonn *C.S.H.B.*, ed. *Teubner* (1880).

Priscus Panites, *Historiae Byzant. fragmenta*, ed. C. Müller, *Fragmenta histor. Graecor.* (Paris, 1868) IV.

Procopius Caesariensis, *De Bello Gothico*, ed. Bonn *C.S.H.B.*, ed. *Teubner* (1905). With English translation in the *Loeb Classical Library*.

Ptolemaeus Claudius, *Geographiae libri octo*, ed. and English translation by E. L. Stevenson (New York, 1932).

Theophanes, *Chronographia*, ed. Bonn *C.S.H.B.*, ed. de Boor (Leipzig, 1885).

Theophanes Continuatus, ed. Bonn *C.S.H.B.*

Theophylactes Simocates, *Histor. libri VIII*, ed. Bonn *C.S.H.B.*, ed. *Teubner* (1887).

Latin Sources

Chronicum patriarch. Gradensium, *M.G.H. S. Rer. Langob.*

Documenta historiae croaticae periodum antiquam illustrartia, ed. F. Rački, *Monumenta spect. hist. Slav. meridion.*, publ. by the Academy of Zagreb (1877) vol. VII.

Fontes historiae religionis Slavicae, ed. K. H. Meyer, in the collection *Historiae religionum*, ed. C. Clement (Berlin, 1931) vol. IV.

Fredegarius Scholasticus, *Chronicon.*, *M.G.H. S. Rer. Merov.*, II.

Jordanes, *Getica*, *M.G.H. Auct. Ant. V.*

Origo Gentis Langobardorum, *M.G.H. S. Rer. Langob.*

Paulus Diaconus, *Historia gentis Langobardorum*, *M.G.H. S. Rer. Langob.*

Plinius Secundus Caius, *Historia Naturalis*, ed. in the *Loeb Class. Library* with English translation (1938).

Ravennatis Anonymi Cosmographia, ed. M. Pinder and C. Parthey (Berlin, 1860).

Strabo, *Rerum Geographicarum libri XVII*, ed. *Teubner*.

Tacitus, *Cornelius*, ed. Allen (Boston, 1913).

—— *De origine et situ Germanorum*, ed. Y. G. C. Anderson (Oxford, 1938).

Thomas Archidiaconus, *Historia Salonitana*, ed. F. Rački, *Monumenta spect. hist. Slav. meridion.*, XXVI published by the Academy of Zagreb (1894).

Syriac, Arab and others

Alfred the Great, *A Description of Europe* . . . , ed. J. Bosworth (London, 1855).

Bar Hebreus (Abulfaragius, Georgius), *Chronicon Syriacum*, ed. P. I. Brunns and G. G. Kirsch (Leipzig, 1789). English translation by E. A. Wallis Budge, *The Chronography of Gregory Abul Faraj* (London, 1932).

Edrisi, *Geographie d'Edrisi*, ed. P. A. Jaubert, publ. by the Société de Géographie, vols. V, VI (Paris, 1824 etc.).

Harvararsaga, ed. S. Bugge, *Det Norske Oldscriftselskabe Samlinger*, VIII (Christiania, 1865).

John of Ephesus, *Ecclesiastical History*, ed. Assemani Bibliotheca orient. (Roma, 1719). German translation by Schönfelder, *Die Kirchengeschichte des Joh. v. Eph.* (Munich, 1862).

John of Nikion, *The Chronicle*, ed. Zotenberg (Paris, 1883), English translation by H. Charles (London, 1916).

Massudi, *Prairies d'or*, transl. C. Barbe de Meynard and Pavet de Courteille, 9 vols. (Paris, 1861–1877).

Zacharias Rhetor, *Die sogenannte Kirchengeschichte*, German translation by K. Aehrens and G. Krüger, *Teubner* (1899).

BIBLIOGRAPHY

Brady, C., *Legend of Ermanaric* (Univ. of California Press, 1943).

Brückner, A., *Mitologia Slava* (Bologna, 1923).

Cvijić, *La peninsule balkanique* (Paris, 1918).

Childe, Gordon, *The Aryans* (London, 1926).

—— *The Danube in Prehistory* (Oxford, 1929).

Cross, Samuel H., *Slavic civilization through the Ages* (Harvard Univ. Press, 1948).

—— "Gothic Loan Words in the Slavic Vocabulary," *Harvard Studies and Notes*, XVI, no. 193.

—— "Primitive civilisation of the Eastern Slavs," *The Amer. Slavic and East Europ. Review*, V (1946), pp. 51–81.

Czekanowski, J., "The Racial Structure of Silesia," *Baltic and Scandinavian Countries*, III (Torun, Gdynia, 1937).

Dvornik, F., *Les Slaves, Byzance et Rome* (Paris, 1926), pp. 1–31.

—— *The Making of Central and Eastern Europe* (London, 1949), pp. 268–314 (Origins of Serbs, Croats and Russians).

Geidel, H., "Alfred der Grosse als Geograph," *Münchener Geograph. Studien*, XV (1904).

Gregoire, H., "L'Origine et le nom des Croates et des Serbes," *Byzantion*, XVII (1944–45).

Haller, J., *Der Eintritt der Germanen in die Geschichte* (Berlin, 1944).

Howorth, H. H., "The Spread of the Slavs," *Journal of Anthrop. Inst. of Great Britain and Ireland*, VII, VIII (London, 1878–79).

Jakobson, R., "Slavic Mythology," *Funk and Wagnall's Standard Dictionary of Folklore Mythology and Legend* (New York, 1950), pp. 1025–1028. (Up-to-date bibliography.)

—— Slavic Languages (New York, 1949).

Jakobson, Pírková, Svatava, "Slavic Folklore," *ibid.*, pp. 1019–1025.

Jazdzewski, K., *Atlas to the Prehistory of the Slavs*, 2 vols. (Lodz, 1948). (Bibliography, vol. I, pp. 19–25.)

Kostrzewski, J., *Les Origines de la civilisation Polonaise. Préhistoire — protohistoire* (Paris, 1949).

Lot, F., *Les Invasions barbares*, 2 vols. (Paris, 1937).

—— *Les Invasions Germaniques* (Paris, 1934).

Máchal, H., "Slavic mythology," *Mythology of all races*, VIII (Boston, 1918), pp. 227–314.

—— "Essai comparatif sur la mythologie Slave," *Revue des Etudes Slaves*, XXIII (1947), pp. 48–65.

Mansikka, V. J., *Die Religion der Ostslaven*, vol. I. Quellen (Helsinki, 1922).

Minns, E. H., *Scythians and Greeks* (Cambridge Univ. Press, 1913).

Niederle, L., *Manuel de l'antiquité Slave* (Paris, 1923, 1926) (A French résumé of his great work in Czech, *Slovanské starožitnosti* — Slavic Antiquities, published in Prague in several volumes from 1902 to 1924).

Palm, Th., *Wendische Kultstätten* (Lund, 1937).

Pirchegger, H., *Geschichte der Steiermark* (Gotha, 1920).

Roesler, E. R., "Über den Zeitpunkt der slawischen Ansiedlungen an der unteren Donau," *Sitzungsber. d. K. Akad. d. Wissensch., phil-hist. Kl., Vienna*, LXXIII (1873), pp. 77–126 (still useful).

Rostovtsev, M., *Iranians and Greeks in South Russia* (Oxford, 1922).

Šafařík, P. J., *Slavische Altertümer*, 2 vols., German translation by Mosig v. Aehrenfeld (Leipzig, 1843–1844).

Schránil, I., *Die Vorgeschichte Böhmens und Mährens* (Berlin, 1928).

Unbegaun, B. O., "Les religions des anciens Slaves," in *Mana, les Religions de l'Europe ancienne*, III (Paris, 1948), pp. 387–445 (bibliography).

Vasmer, M., *Untersuchungen über die ältesten Wohnsitze der Slaven* (Leipzig, 1923).

—— "Die Urheimat der Slaven," *Der Ostdeutsche Volksboden*, W. Volz, ed. (1939), pp. 56–66.

—— "Die ältesten Bevölkerungsverhältnisse Russlands im Lichte der Sprachforschung," *Vorträge und Schriften*, Heft. 5 (Preuss. Akad. der Wissensch., 1947).

Wienecke, E., *Untersuchungen zur Religion der Westslaven* (Leipzig, 1940).

CHAPTER III

THE FRANKS, BYZANTIUM AND THE FIRST SLAVIC STATES

SOURCES

Byzantine

Cedrenus Georgius, *Compendium Historiae*, Bonn *C.S.H.B.*
Chronicon Paschale, Bonn *C.S.H.B.*
Constantine Porphyrogennitus, *De admin. Imperio*, Bonn *C.S.H.B.*
——— *De caeremoniis*, Bonn *C.S.H.B.*
Georgius (Hamartolus) Monachus, *Chronicon*, Bonn *C.S.H.B.*, ed.
     de Boor, Leipzig, 1904 (Teubner).
Georgius Monachus Continuatus, *Chronicon*, Bonn *C.S.H.B.*
Leo Diacomus, *Historia*, Bonn *C.S.H.B.*
Leonis Tactica, *P.G.*, vol. 107.
Nicephorus Patriarcha, *Opuscula Historica*, Bonn *C.S.H.B.*, ed. de
     Boor, Leipzig 1870 (Teubner).
Procopius, *Opera*, Bonn *C.S.H.B.*, *History of the Wars*, translated by
     H. B. Delving, *Loeb Classical Library* (New York, 1914–40).
Theophanes, *Chronographia*, Bonn *C.S.H.B.*, ed. de Boor, Leipzig,
     1883 (Teubner).
Zonaras, Joannes, *Epitome Historiarum*, Bonn *C.S.H.B.*

Latin

Annales Bertiniani, *M.G.H.S.*, I.
Annales Fuldenses, *M.G.H.S.*, III.
Annales Laurissenses, *ibid.*, I.
Annales Quedlingburgenses, *ibid.*, III.
Annalista Saxo, *Annales*, *ibid.*, III.
Dandolo, *Chronicon Venetum*, in *Muratori*, XII.
Diocleae Presbyter, *De Regno Slavorum*, in Lucius, *De Regno Dal-*
     matiae (Amsterdam, 1666).
Einhardus, *Annales*, *M.G.H.S.*, I.
——— *Vita Caroli Imper.*, *ibid.*, II.
Fredegarius Scholasticus, *Chronica*, *M.G.H.S. Rerum Merovingicarum*,
     II.
Gesta Dagoberti, *M.G.H.S. Rerum Merovingicarum*, II.

BIBLIOGRAPHY

Antonoff, V., *Bulgarien vom Beginn seines staatlichen Bestehens bis*
     auf unsere Tage, 679–1917. (Berlin, 1917).

Brutzkus, J., "The Khazar Origin of Ancient Kiev," *The Slavonic and East European Review*, XXII, no. 58 (May 1944, American Series).

Dümmler, E., *Über die älteste Geschichte der Slawen in Dalmatien, 549–928* (Vienna, 1856).

Dvornik, F., *Les Slaves, Byzance et Rome au IXe siècle* (Paris, 1926) chap. I, II.

—— *Les Légendes de Constantin et de Méthode* (Prague, 1933).

—— *National Churches and the Church Universal* (London, 1944).

—— *The Making of Central and Eastern Europe* (London, 1949), chap. I.

Gérard, Ch., *Les Bulgares de la Volga et les Slaves du Danube; le problème des races et les barbares* (Paris, 1939).

Hauck, A., *Kirchengeschichte Deutschlands*, 4th ed. (Leipzig, 1900–1906), vols. I and III.

Runciman, S., *A History of the First Bulgarian Empire* (London, 1930), pp. 1–70.

Slatarski, V. N., *Geschichte der Bulgaren*, I (see General Bibliog.).

Stutz, U. "The Proprietary Church as an Element of Medieval German Ecclesiastical Law," in *Barraclough's Studies in Medieval History*, II (Oxford, 1938), pp. 35–70.

CHAPTER IV

THE MORAVIAN EMPIRE AND ITS GREEK APOSTLES SS. CONSTANTINE-CYRIL AND METHODIUS

SOURCES

Anastasius Bibliothecarius, *Epistolae sive praefationes*, P.L., 129, ed. E. Perels, G. Laehr, *M.G.H. Ep.*, VII, pp. 395 ff.

Libellus de conversione Bagoariorum et Carantanorum (from 870, 871) and *Epistola episcoporum Bavariensum ad Johannem P. IX scripta a. 900*, ed. in *M.G.H.S.*, XI, pp. 1–15, P.L., vol. 131, col. 34–38.

Hadrianus II papa, *Epistolae*, P.L., 122, *M.G.H. Ep.*, VI.

Joannes VIII papa, *Epistolae*, P.L., 126, cols. 651–969, ed. E. Caspar, *M.G.H. Ep.*, VII.

Lavrov, P.A., *Materialy po istorii voznik. drevn. slav. pism.* (Leningrad, 1930), edition of old Slavonic sources concerning SS. Constantine-Cyril and Methodius.

Nicetas Paphlago, *Vita S. Ignatii Patriarchae*, P.G., 105, cols. 488 ff.

Nicola I papa, *Epistolae et decreta*, P.L., 119; *M.G.H. Ep.*, VI (ed. Perels).

Photius patriarcha, *Epistolae, P.G.,* 102.

Regesta Imperii, vol. I, *Die Regesten des Kaiserreiches unter den Karolingern,* ed. S. F. Böhmer and Mühlbacher (Innsbruck, 1899–1908).

Theophylactus Ochridensis, *Vita S. Clementis Episcopi Bulgarorum, P.G.,* 126.

"Vita Constantini," French translation by F. Dvornik in *Les Légendes de Constantin et de Méthode* (Prague, 1933), pp. 349–380.

"Vita Methodii," *ibid.,* pp. 381–393. *Ibid.,* pp. 339–348 bibliographical indications on editions of the two biographies and other Slavonic sources.

Vita S. Naumi (Nahumi), see Bibliog. Kusseff, M.

BIBLIOGRAPHY

Alexander, P. J., "The Papacy, the Bavarian Clergy and the Slavonic Apostles," *The Slavonic Year Book* (American Series, 1, 1941).

Amann, E., "Jean VIII," *Diction. de Théologie Catholique* (1924), VIII, cols. 602–613.

——— "Photius," *ibid.* (1935), XII, cols. 1536–1604.

——— "L'Epoque Carolingienne," *Histoire de l'Eglise,* ed. A. Fliche and V. Martin (Paris, 1937), VI.

Bury, J. B., *A History of the Eastern Roman Empire* (London, 1912).

Dümmler, E., *Geschichte des Ostfränkischen Reiches,* 3 vols. (Leipzig, 1887–1888).

Dvornik, F., *Les Slaves Byzance et Rome au IXe siècle* (Paris, 1926).

——— *Les Légendes de Constantin et de Méthode* (Prague, 1933).

——— *The Photian Schism. History and Legend* (Cambridge Univ. Press, 1948).

——— "The Photian Schism in Western and Eastern Tradition," *The Review of Politics,* X (Notre Dame Univ. Press, 1948).

——— "Western and Eastern Traditions of Central Europe," *ibid.,* VII (1947).

Jagić, V., *Entstehungsgeschichte der Kirchenslavische Sprache,* 2nd ed. (Berlin, 1913).

——— "Conversion of the Slavs," *Cambridge Medieval History* (London, 1927), IV, pp. 215 seq.

Kusseff, M., "St. Clement of Ochrida," *The Slavonic and East European Review,* XXVII (London, 1948–49), pp. 193–215.

——— "St. Nahum," *ibid.,* XXIX (1950–51), pp. 139–152 (English translation of the Slavonic Short Life of St. Nahum).

Lapôtre, A., *L'Église et le Saint Siège à l'époque Carolingienne* (Paris, 1895).

Marquardt, J., *Osteuropäische und Ostasistische Streifzüge* (Leipzig, 1903).

Perels, E., *Papst Nikolaus I and Anastasius Bibliothecarius* (Berlin, 1920).

Schubert, H. von, *Die sogenannten Slavenapostel Constantin und Methodius* (Heidelberg, 1916).

Snopek, F., *Die Slavenapostel*, in *Opera Academiae Velehradensis*, vol. V (Kremsier, 1918).

Strauss, M., *Beziehungen Karls des Grossen zum byzantinischen Reich* (Breslau, 1877).

Trautmann, R., "Leben und Werk der Slavenapostel Konstantin und Method," *Zeitschrift für deutsche Geisteswissenschaft*, II (1939), pp. 147 seq. (with bibliography).

CHAPTER V

AFTER THE DESTRUCTION OF THE MORAVIAN EMPIRE GERMANY AND THE RISE OF BOHEMIA AND POLAND

SOURCES

Annales Altahenses Maiores, M.G.H.S., XIX.

—— *Bertiniani, ibid.*, I.

—— *Cracoviensis Capituli, ibid.*, XIX.

—— *Cracovienses Vetusti, ibid.*, XIX.

—— *Einhardi, ibid.*, I.

—— *Fuldenses, ibid.*, I.

—— *Hildesheimenses, ibid.*, III.

—— *Juvavenses Maiores, ibid.*, XXX.

—— *Quedlinburgenses, ibid.*, III.

—— *Ratisbonenses, ibid.*, XVII.

—— *Sazavae*, F.R.B., II.

Anonymi Gesta Hungarorum, F.R.H., I.

Anonymus Gallus, *Chronicae Polonorum*, M.P.H., I.

Bruno of Querfurt, *Passio S. Adalberti*, F.R.B., I.

Canaparius, *Vita et Passio S. Adalberti*, F.R.B., I.

Christianus, *Vita S. Venceslai*, F.R.B., I, ed. J. Pekař, *Die Wenzels und Ludmila Legenden und die Echtheit Christians* (Prague, 1906).

Cosmas Pragensis, *Chronicae Bohemorum libri. III*, M.G.H. S.N.S., II.

Ibrahim ibn Jacub, *Arabische Reiseberichte*, ed. G. Jacob (Berlin, 1927).

Passio S. Adalberti, F.R. B., I.

Slavonic Legends on S. Wenceslas, *F.R.B.*, I; ed. Vajs, J., Vašica, J. in *Sborník staroslov. památek* (Prague, 1929).

BIBLIOGRAPHY

Brackmann, A., "Der Römische Erneuerungsgedanke und seine Bedeutung für die Reichspolitik der Deutschen Kaiser," *Sitzungsber. d. Preuss. Akad. Hist. Phil. Kl.* (1932).

——— "Die Anfänge des Polnischen Staates," *ibid.* (1934).

——— "Reichspolitik und Ostpolitik im frühen Mittelalter", *ibid.*, (1935).

Bretholz, Z., *Geschichte Böhmens und Mährens bis zum Aussterben der Przemysliden* (Leipzig, 1912).

Doenniges, S. W., *Jahrbücher des deutschen Reichs unter Otto I* (Berlin, 1839).

Dvornik, F., *S. Wenceslas, Duke of Bohemia* (Prague, 1929).

——— "The First Wave of the Drang nach Osten," *Cambridge Historical Journal*, VII (1943).

——— *The Making of Central and Eastern Europe* (London, 1949), pp. 11–135, detailed bibliography.

Grégoire, H., "L'habitat primitif des Magyars," *Byzantion*, XIII (1938), pp. 262–278.

Homan, B., *Geschichte des Ungarischen Mittelalters* (Berlin, 1940), I, pp. 1–170.

——— "King Stephen the Saint," *Archivium Europae Centro-Orientalis*, IV (Budapest, 1938).

Kętrzyński, S., "The Introduction of Christianity and the Early Kings of Poland," *The Cambridge History of Poland*, I (Cambridge, 1950), pp. 16–42.

Kirchberg, I., *Kaiseridee und Mission unter den Sachsenkaisern und den ersten Saliern von Otto I bis Heinrich III, Hist. Studien*, Heft 259 (Berlin, 1934).

Lintzel, "Zur Geschichte Ottos des Grossen," *Mitteilungen d. Oesterr. Instit. f. Geschichte*, 48 (Wien, 1934).

Loserth, J., "Der Sturz des Hauses Slavnik," *Abhandl. f. Oesterr. Geschichte*, Bd. 65 (1895).

Lot, F., *Les derniers Carolingiens, Bibl. de l'Ecole des Hautes Etudes*, 87 (Paris, 1891).

Lüdtke, F., *Heinrich I, der Deutsche* (Leipzig, 1934).

Lüttich, R., *Ungarnzüge in Europa im 10 Jahrhundert, Hist. Studien*, Heft 84 (Berlin, 1910).

Macartney, C. A., *The Magyars in the ninth century* (Cambridge, 1930).

— — *Studies in the Earliest Hungarian Sources, Etudes sur l'Europe Centre-Orientale*, XVIII, XXI (Budapest, 1938, 1940).

— — *The Medieval Hungarian Historians* (Cambridge, 1953).

Naegle, A., *Kirchengeschichte Böhmens*, 2 vols. (Wien, 1915, 1918). (Dealing with the oldest period only from the German point of view.)

— — *Der heilige Wenzel* (Warnsdorf, 1928).

Palacký, F., *Geschichte von Böhmen*, 3rd ed., 5 vols. in 10 (Prague, 1864–96).

Pekař, J., *Die Wenzels und Ludmila – Legenden und die Echtheit Christians* (Prague, 1906).

Roepell, R., and J. Caro, *Geschichte Polens*, 5 vols. (Hamburg-Gotha, 1840–88). (From the origins to 1506.)

Stasiewski, B., *Untersuchungen über die Quellen für die älteste Geschichte und Kirchengeschichte Polens* (Breslau, 1933).

Thoss, A., *Heinrich I, der Gründer des ersten Deutschen Volksreiches* (Goslar, 1936).

Vaczy, P. von, *Die erste Epoche des Ungarischen Königtums* (Pecz, Fünfkirchen, 1935).

Voigt, H. G., *Adalbert von Prag* (Berlin, 1898).

Waitz, G., *Jahrbücher des Deutschen Reichs unter König Heinrich I.* (Berlin, 1863).

Winterswyl, L. A., *Otto der Grosse und das erste Reich der Deutschen* (Berlin, 1937).

Wojciechowski, Z., *Mieszko and the Rise of the Polish State* (Toruń-Gdynia-London, 1936).

Zeissberg, H., "Miesco I – der erste christliche Beherrscher Polens," *Sitzungsber. d. k. Akad. Phil. Hist. Kl.* (Wien, 1867).

CHAPTER VI

THE SOUTHERN SLAVS, FRANKS, BYZANTIUM AND ROME

SOURCES

Acta Concilii VIII (869–870), Mansi, *Conciliorum amplissima Collectio*, 31 vols. (Florence, Venice, 1759 seq.), XVI.

Acta Concilii unionis (879–880), *ibid.*, XVII.

Annales Bertiniani, M.G.H.S., I.

— — *Fuldenses, ibid.*, I.

354   EARLY SLAVIC CIVILIZATION

—— *Hildesheimenses, ibid.,* III.
—— *Laurissenses, ibid.,* I.
—— *Quedlinburgenses, ibid.,* III.
—— *Weissenburgenses, ibid.,* III.
Constantinus Porphyrogennitus, *De Admin. Imperio. De Thematibus,* ed. see Ch. I, II.
—— *Vita Basilii,* ed. Bonn *C.S.H.B.* (in *Theophanes Cont.*).
Dandolo, *Chronicum Venetum,* ed. Muratori, *S.R.I.,* XII.
Diocleae Presbyter, *De Regno Slavorum,* in Lucius, *De Regno Dalmatiae* (Amsterdam, 1666).
Georgius Cedrenus, *Compendium Histor.,* ed. Bonn *C.S.H.B.*
Georgius Monachus Continuatus, *Chronicon,* ed. Bonn *C.S.H.B.*
Innocentius III Papa, *Epistolae, P.L.,* 214–215.
Joannes VIII Papa, *Epistolae, M.G.H. Ep.,* VII.
Joannes Diaconus, *Chronicon Venetum, M.G.H.S.,* VII.
Liber Pontificalis, ed. L. Duchesne, 2 vols. (Paris, 1886, 1892) II, the lives of Nicolas I, Hadrian II, John VIII, Stephen VI.
Liudprandus Cremonensis, *De Legatione Constant.; Antapodosis, M.G.H.S.,* III, Engl. translation by F. A. Wright, The Works of Liudprand of Cremona (London, 1930).
Nicolaus I, Papa, *Epistolae, M.G.H. Ep.,* VI.
Nicolaus Mysticus Patriarcha, *Epistolae, P.G.,* 111.
Romanus I Lecapenus Imperator, *Epistolae,* ed. Sakkelion, in *Deltion,* vol. I (Athens, 1884).
Scylitzes, Joannes, *Historia,* copied in Cedrenus Georgius, *Historiarum Compendium,* ed. Bonn *C.S.H.B.*
Stephanus VI, Papa, *Epistolae, M.G.H. Ep.,* VII.
Theophanes Continuatus, ed. Bonn *C.S.H.B.*

BIBLIOGRAPHY

Dvornik, F., *Les Slaves, Byzance et Rome* (Paris, 1926), pp. 71–105, 216–322.
Farlati, D., *Illyricum Sacrum* (Venice, 1751), oldest Church History of Illyricum.
Feher, B., *Bulgarisch-Ungarische Beziehungen in dem V–XI Jahrhunderten* (Budapest, 1921).
Gelzer, H., *Das Patriarchat von Achrida* (Leipzig, 1902).
Ilić, J. A., *Die Bogomilen in ihrer geschichtlichen Entwicklung* (Sr. Karlovci, 1923).
Jireček, C., *Geschichte der Bulgaren* (Prague, 1877).
—— *Geschichte der Serben* (Gotha, 1911).
—— "Die Romanen in den Städten Dalmatiens während des Mittel-

alters," *Sitzungsber. K. Akad. Phil.-hist. Kl.* (Wien, 1902), vols. 48–49.

Lucius, J., *De regno Dalmatiae et Croatiae* (Amsterdam, 1666).

Miller, W., *The First Bulgarian Empire*, in the *Cambridge Medieval History*, IV.

Mutafčiev, P., *Bulgares et Roumains dans l'histoire des pays Danubiens* (Sofia, 1932). Critical reviews of ultra Rumanian views exposed in Iorga's work, *Formes Byzantines et realités Balkaniques* (Bucarest, Paris, 1922). Cf. N. Banescu, *L'ancien Etat bulgare et les pays roumains* (Bucarest, 1947).

Obolensky, D., *The Bogomils* (Cambridge, 1948).

Rambaud, A., *L'Empire Grec au Xe siècle* (Paris, 1870).

Runciman, S., *The Emperor Romanus Lecapenus* (Cambridge, 1929).

—— *A History of the First Bulgarian Empire* (London, 1930).

Schlumberger, G., *L'Epopée Byzantine à la Fin du Xe siècle* (Paris, 1896–1905).

—— *Un Empereur Byzantine au Xe siècle* (Paris, 1890).

Šišić, F., *Geschichte der Kroaten* (Zagreb, 1917).

Spinka, M., *A History of Christianity in the Balkans* (Chicago, 1933).

Chapter VII

OLD SLAVONIC CULTURE AND LITERATURE AND THEIR BYZANTINE BACKGROUND

Dvornik, F., *Les Slaves, Byzance et Rome* (Paris, 1926), pp. 282–322 (literary activity of Methodius' disciples in Bulgaria).

—— *Les Légendes de Constantin et de Méthode* (Prague, 1933), pp. 212–226 (Byzantine influences in Moravia), 339–349 (documents concerning SS. Cyril and Methodius).

Filov, B., *Early Bulgarian Art* (Berne, 1919).

—— *Geschichte der Altbulgarischen Kunst* (Berlin, Leipzig, 1932), 1–46 (First Bulgarian Empire).

Gaster, M., *Ilchester Lectures on Greeko-Slavonic Literature* (London, 1887).

Georghieff, S., *Les Bogomils et Presbyter Kosma* (Lausanne, 1902).

Grabar, A., *Recherches sur les influences orientales dans l'art balkanique* (Paris, 1928).

—— "Peinture religieuse en Bulgarie," *Orient et Byzance*, I (Paris, 1928), pp. 54–116.

Jagić, V., *Entstehungsgeschichte der Kirchenslavischen Sprache*, 2nd ed. (Berlin, 1913).

Jakobson, R., "Kernel of Comparative Slavic Literature," *Harvard Slavic Studies* I (1953).

—— "Some Russian Echoes of the Czech Hagiography," *Annuaire de l'inst. de Philol. et d'Hist. Orient. et Slaves*, VII (1939–44), pp. 155–180.

Jireček, C., *La civilisation Serbe au Moyen Age* (Paris, 1920).

Krek, *Einleitung in die slavische Literaturgeschichte*, 2nd ed. (Prague, 1887).

Lingenthal, Zachariae von, *Beiträge zur Geschichte der Bulgarischen Kirche, Mémoires de l'Acad. des Sciences*, série VII (St. Petersbourg, 1864).

Lützow, Count Francis, *A History of Bohemian Literature*, 2nd ed. (London, 1902), chap. I.

Miatev, K., *Die Keramik von Preslav, Monumenta Artis Bulgariae*, IV (Sofia, 1936).

Millet, G., *Ancien Art Serbe* (Paris, 1919).

—— "L'Art Byzantin chez les Slaves. Les Balkans. Recueil dédié a Th. Uspenskij," *Orient et Byzance*, IV (Paris, 1930).

Murko, M., *Geschichte der älteren südslawischen Literaturen* (Leipzig, 1908).

Novaković, S., *La Zadrouga; les communautés familiales chez les Serbes* (Paris, 1905).

Obolensky, D., *The Bogomils* (Cambridge, 1948) detailed bibliography.

Pekař, J., *Die Wenzels und Ludmila Legenden und die Echtheit Christians* (Prague, 1906).

Poulík, J., *Jižní Morava* (South Moravia in the old Slavonic period) Brno, 1948–1950 (with a résumé in English. Publication of important archaeological material).

—— *Staroslovanská Morava* (Moravia in Old Slavonic Period), Prague, 1948 (with a summary in English).

Probitch, A., *L'architecture religieuse bulgare* (Sofia, 1924).

Puech, H. C., Vaillant, A., *Le traité contre les Bogomiles de Cosmas le prêtre* (Paris, 1945).

Pupin, M. J., *South Slav Monuments*, I, Serbian Orthodox Church (London, 1918).

Pypin, A., Spasovič, V., *Histoire des litteratures slaves*, traduit du Russe par E. Denis (Paris, 1881), pp. 77–124 (Bulgarian lit.), 213 seq. (old Serbian lit.), 399 seq. (Slavonic lit.).

Šafařík, P., *Geschichte der südslavischen Literatur* (Prague, 1864–65), I. Old Slavonic and glagolitic literature.

Schmid, H. F., *Die Nomokanonübersetzung des Methodius* (Leipzig, 1922).

Sharenkov, V. N., *A Study of Manchaeism in Bulgaria with Special Reference to the Bogomiles* (New York, 1927).

Stanoyevich, M. S., *Early Jugoslav Literature* (New York, 1922), pp. 1–28.

Spinka, M., *A History of Christianity in the Balkans* (Chicago, 1933).

Weingart, M., "Die Anfänge der tschechischen Kultur und die erste kirchenslawische St. Wenzels-Legende," *Prager Rundschau*, vol. V (1935).

Chapter VIII

THE RUSSIA OF KIEV

Sources

Adamus Bremensis, *Gesta Hamburgensis Ecclesiae Pontificum, M.G.-H.S. in us. schol.* (1917).

Anna Comnena, *Alexias*, ed. Bonn *C.S.H.B.* Engl. transl., Dawes, E.A.S. (London, 1928).

Anonymus Gallus, *Chronica Polonorum, M.P.H.* (1864), vol. I, pp. 301–481.

Attaliates, Michael, *Historia*, ed. Bonn *C.S.H.B.*

Cedrenus (Scylitzes), *Historiar. Compendium*, ed. Bonn *C.S.H.B.*

The Chronicle of Novgorod (1016–1471), transl. by R. Michell, N. Forbes (London, 1914).

Cinnamus (Kinnamos), Ioannes, *Epitomae Historiarum*, ed. Bonn *C.S.H.B.*

Constantine Porphyrogenitus, *De Admin. Imperio*, ed. Bonn *C.S.H.B.* (See Bibliogr. ch. I, II).

—— *De Ceremoniis, ibid.*

Cosmas Pragensis, *Chronica Bohemorum*, ed. *F.H.B.*, I, ed. *M.G.H.S. in us. schol.* (1923).

Fritzler, K., *Zwei Abhandlungen über altruss. Recht. Die sogenannte Kirchenordnung Jaroslavs ein Denkmal russ. german. Rechts* (Berlin, 1928).

Goetz, L. K., *Das russische Recht*, 4 vols. (Stuttgart, 1910–1915) vol. I, pp. 6–65. (German translation of the Ruskaja Pravda.)

—— *Deutsch-russische Handelsverträge* (Hamburg, 1916), pp. 14–72, 231–304.

Ibn Foszlan — in Frähn, C. M., *Ibn Foszlans und anderer Araber Berichte über die Russen älterer Zeit* (St. Petersburg, 1823).

Leo Diaconus, *Historiae Libri decem*, ed. Bonn *C.S.H.B.*
Manasses Constantine, *Chronicon*, ed. Bonn *C.S.H.B.*
Photius Patriarcha, *Epistolae P.G.*, 102.
—— *In Rossorum incursionem Homiliae I–II*, ed. Nauck, A., *Lexicon Vindobonense* (St. Petersburg, 1867), pp. 201–232.
Russian Primary Chronicle, Engl. transl. by Cross, S. H., *Harvard Studies in Philology and Literature*, XII (1930), (bibliography on the chronicle and its edition). New ed. by O. P. Sherbowitz-Wetzor, *Mediev. Acad. Publ.*, no. 60 (Cambridge, Mass., 1953).
Saxo Grammaticus, *Gesta Danorum*, ed. Holder, A. (Strassburg, 1886); ed. Olrik, J., Raeder, H., 2 vols. (Copenhagen, 1931).
Symeon, Magister and Logothetus (Pseudo-Symeon), *Chronicon*, ed. Bonn *C.S.H.B.*
Thietmar of Merseburg, *Chronicon*, *M.G.H.S.*, III; *S.S.N.S.*, IV (1935).
Vernadsky, G., *Medieval Russian Laws* (New York, 1947), (Engl. translation of the *Ruskaja Pravda* and of the Charters of Dvina, Pskov and Novgorod, with bibliography).

BIBLIOGRAPHY

Ainalov, D. V., *Geschichte der russ. Monumentalkunst*, 2 vols. (Berlin, Leipzig, 1932–33), I.
Alpaton, N., Brunov, N., *Geschichte der altruss. Kunst* (Augsburg, 1932).
Anisimov, A. J., *Our Lady of Vladimir* (Prague, 1928).
Arne, T. J., *La Suède et l'Orient* (Upsala, 1914).
Baumgarten, N. de, "Généalogies et mariages occidentaux des Rurikides russes du Xe and XIIIes." *Orientalia Christiana*, XXXV, XCIV (Rome, 1927, 1934).
—— "Olaf Tryggwason, Roi de Norvège," *ibid.*, no. 73 (1931).
—— "Aux Origines de la Russie," *Orient. Christ. Anal.*, no. 119 (1939).
—— "S. Vladimir et la Conversion de la Russie," *Orient. Christ.*, XXVII (1932).
Benz, E., *Russiche Heiligenlegenden* (Zürich, 1953).
Buxton, D. C., *Russian Medieval Architecture* (Cambridge, 1934).
Casey, R. P., "Early Russian Monasticism," *Orient. Christ. Period.*, XIX (1953), pp. 373–423.
Chadwick, N. K., *The Beginnings of Russian History* (Cambridge, 1946).
—— *Russian Heroic Poetry* (Cambridge, 1932).
Conant, K. J., "Novgorod, Constantinople, and Kiev in Old Russian Church Architecture," *The Slavonic and East Europ. Review*, XXII (Amer. Series IIIa) (1944), pp. 75–92.

—— Cross, S. H., *Medieval Russian Churches* (Cambridge, Mass., 1949).

Cross, S. H., "Jaroslav the Wise in Norse Tradition," *Speculum*, IV (1929).

—— "The Scandinavian Infiltration into Early Russia," *ibid.*, XXI (1946).

—— "Medieval Russian Contacts with the West," *ibid.*, X (1935).

—— "The Earliest Medieval Churches in Kiev," *ibid.*, XI (1936).

Dvornik, F., "The Kiev State and its Relations with Western Europe," *Transactions of the R. Hist. Society*, XXIX (London, 1947).

—— *The Making of Central and Eastern Europe* (London, 1949), pp. 59–70, 167–184, 236–268, 298–305.

—— "Les Bénédictines et la christianisation de la Russie," in *L'Eglise et les églises*, éditions de Chevetogne (1954), pp. 223–349.

Eck, A., *Le Moyen Age Russe* (Paris, 1933).

Eckhardt, Hans von, *Russisches Christentum* (München, 1947).

Fedotov, G. P., *The Russian Religious Mind: Kievan Christianity* (Harvard University Press, 1946).

Grégoire, H., Jakobson, R., Szeffel, M., "La Geste du Prince Igor," *Annuaire de l'Inst. de Philol. et d'Hist. Orient. et Slaves*, VIII (New York, 1948).

Grekov, B., *The Culture of Kiev Rûs* (Moscow, 1947).

—— and Jakoubovski, *La Horde d'Or* (Paris, 1939).

Goetz, L. K., *Das Kiever Höhlenkloster als Kulturzentrum des vormongol. Russlands* (Passau, 1904).

Gudzy, N. K., *History of Early Russian Literature*, transl. by S. W. Jones (New York, 1949), (rich bibliography in Slavic).

Hrushevsky, M., *A History of the Ukraine*, transl. by O. J. Frederikson (New Haven, 1941).

—— *Geschichte des Ukrainischen Volkes* (Leipzig, 1906).

Kliuchevsky, V. O., *A History of Russia*, transl. by C. J. Hogarth, 2 vols. (New York, 1911–12), I.

Koch, H., "Byzanz, Ochrid und Kiev 987–1037," *Kyrios*, III (Berlin, 1938).

Kondakov, N. P., *The Russian Icon*, transl. by E. H. Minns (Oxford, 1925).

Krappe, A. H., "La chute du paganisme à Kiev," *Revue des études Slaves*, XVII (Paris, 1937).

Laehr, G., "Die Anfänge des russ. Reiches," *Historische Studien*, H. 189 (Berlin, 1930).

Leib, B., *Rome, Kiev et Byzance à la fin du XIe siècle* (Paris, 1924).

Medlin, Kenneth W., *Moscow and East Rome* (Geneva, 1952), pp. 58–61.

Miliukov, P. N., Seignobos, Eisenmann, L., *Histoire de Russie* (Paris, 1932), I.

Mavor, J., *An Economic History of Russia*, 2nd ed. (London and Toronto, 1925), I.

Mousset, A., *Histoire de Russie* (Paris, 1945).

Mirsky, Prince D. S., *A History of Russian Literature* (New York, 1927).

Muratov, P. P., *Les icones Russes* (Paris, 1947).

Nemitz, F., *Die Kunst Russlands* (Berlin, 1940).

Noroff, de A., *Pélérinage en Terre Sainte de l'Igoumène Russe Daniel au commencement du XIe siècle* (St. Petersbourg, 1864).

Paszkiewicz, H., *The Origin of Russia* (London, 1954).

Philipp, Werner, *Ansätze zum geschichtlichen und politschen Denken im Kiewer Russland* (Breslau, 1940).

Platonov, S. F., *History of Russia*, transl. by Aronsberg (New York, 1925).

——— *Histoire de la Russie des origines à 1918* (Paris, 1929).

Pokrovsky, M. N., *History of Russia*, transl. by Clarkson, J. D., Griffiths, M. R. M. (New York, 1931), (written from the Marxist point of view).

Rambaud, A., *History of Russia*, 3 vols. (Boston, 1886), I.

Réau, L., *L'Art russe des origines à Pierre le Grand* (Paris, 1922).

Rice, D. Talbot, *The Beginnings of Russian Icon Painting* (Oxford, London, 1938).

——— *Russian Icons* (London, New York, 1947), (The King Penguin Books).

Russian Fairy Tales, transl. by N. Guterman, folkloristic commentary by R. Jakobson (New York, 1945).

Rouet de Journel, M. J., *Monachisme et monastères Russes* (Paris, 1952), pp. 1–39.

Stählin, K., *Geschichte Russlands* (Berlin, Leipzig, 1923), I.

——— *La Russie des origins à la naissance de Pierre le Grand* (Paris, 1946).

Stender-Peterson, A., "Die Varägersage als Quelle der altruss. Chronik," *Acta Jutlandica*, VI (Kobenhavn, 1934).

Sumner, B. H., *A Short History of Russia* (New York, 1943).

Thompson, V., *The Relations between Ancient Russia and Scandinavia and the Origin of the Russian State* (Oxford, London, 1877).

Vasiliev, A. A., *The Russian Attack on Constantinople in 860* (Cambridge, Mass., 1946).

Vernadsky, G., *Political and Diplomatic History of Russia* (Boston, 1936).

—— *Ancient Russia* (New Haven, 1943).

—— *Kievan Russia* (New Haven, 1948).

Voyce, A., *Russian Architecture* (New York, 1948), pp. 1–41.

Wilson, C. W., *Pilgrimage of the Russian Abbot Daniel in the Holy Land, 1106–1107* (London, 1888), The Library of the Palestine Pilgrim's Text Soc., IV.

Zernov, N., "Vladimir and the Origin of the Russian Church," *The Slavonic and East Europ. Review*, XXVIII (1949–50), pp. 123–138, 425–438.

CHAPTER IX

THE SLAVS AT THE CROSSROADS

SOURCES

Adalbert, St. Bishop of Prague, *Brunonis Passio S. Adalberti*, F.R.B., I.

—— Canaparius, J., *Vita et Passio S. Adalberti, ibid.*

—— *Passio S. Adalberti* (attributed wrongly to Sylvester II) *ibid.*

Annales Cracovienses Breves, M.G.H.S., XIX.

—— *Capituli, ibid.*

—— *Vetusti, ibid.*

—— *Kamenzenses, ibid.*

—— *Mechovienses, ibid.*

—— *Polonorum, ibid.*

—— *Quedlinburgenses, ibid.*, III.

—— *Sazavae*, F.R.B., II.

Anonymi Gesta Hungarorum, F.R.H., I.

Anonymus Gallus, *Chronicae Polonorum*, M.P.H., I.

Böhmer, J. F., *Regesta Imperii* (Innsbruck, 1893), II.

Brunonis, *Vita Quinque Fratrum*, M.G.H.S., XV, 2.

—— *Epistola*, M.P.H., I.

—— *Passio S. Adalberti*, F.R.B., I.

Chronicon Pictum Vindobonense, S.R.H., I.

Chronicum Hungarico Polonicum, S.R.H., II.

Cosmas Pragensis, *Chronicae Bohemorum libri III*, M.G.H.S.N.S., II.

Dalimil, *Czech Chronicle*, F.R.B., III.

Diplomata Ottonis III, M.G.H. Dipl., II.

Endlicher, S., *Rerum Hungaricarum Monumenta Arpadiana* (St. Gallen, 1849).

Epitaphium Chrabri Boleslai, M.P.H., I. Cf. P. David, *L'Epitaphe de Boleslas Chrobry, Etudes hist. et lit. sur la Pologne médiév.*, II (Paris, 1928).

Gerbert (Pope Sylvester II), *Lettres de Gerbert*, publ. by J. Havet,
*Collection des textes pour servir à l'étude et à l'enseignement de
l'histoire* (Paris, 1889).
Henry II. Abaldi Episc. Traiectensis, *Vita Henrici II Imperatoris*,
M.G.H.S., IV.
—— *Adalberti Diaconi Vita S. Henrici Imperatoris, ibid.*
John XII, *Decreta Joannis XII Papae, P.L.*, 133.
Legenda S. Stephani Regis, Legenda Maior et Minor, S.R.H., II.
—— a Hartvico episc. conscripta, *ibid.*
Matilda of Suabia, *Letter to Mieszko II, M.P.H.*, I.
Pulkava, *Chronica Bohemorum*, ed. G. Dobner, *Monumenta Historica
Bohemiae* (Prague, 1764–85), III.
Reginonis Chronicon, M.G.H.S., I, *M.G.H.S. in us. schol.*
Russian Primary Chronicle, Engl. transl. by Cross, S. H., *Harvard
Studies in Philol. and Liter.*, XII (1930).
Thietmar, episc. Merseburgensis, *Chronicon, M.G.H.S.N.S.*, IX (1935).
Translatio S. Godehardi, M.G.H.S., XII.
Vita Godehardi episcopi, auctore Wolpherio, *M.G.H.S.*, XI.
—— *Gunteri Eremitae, M.G.H.S.*, VI.
Vita S. Romualdi, auctore Petro Damiano, *P. L.*, 144; cf. *M.G.H.S.*, IV.
pp. 846–854.
—— *S. Wolfkangi episcopi*, auctore Othlone, *M.G.H.S.*, IV.
Wiponis, *Gesta Chuonradi II, M.G.H.S.*, XI.

BIBLIOGRAPHY

Baethgen, F., "Zur Geschichte der ältesten Deutsch-Polnischen Beziehungen," *Altpreussische Forschungen* (1936).
Brackmann, A., *Deutschland und Polen* (München, Berlin, 1933, cf.
also the Polish Answer to Brackmann's interpretation in the Polish
Historical Review *Kwartalnik Historiczny*, 1934).
—— "Die Anfänge des Polnischen Staates," *Sitzungsber. d. Preuss.
Akad. Hist. phil. Kl.* (1934).
—— "Kaiser Otto III und die staatliche Umgestaltungen Polens und
Ungarns," *Abhandl. d. Preuss. Akad.* (1939).
—— *Magdeburg als Hauptstadt der deutschen Ostens* (Leipzig, 1937).
Bresslau, H., *Jahrbücher des deutschen Reiches unter Konrad II*, 2
vols. (Leipzig, 1879, 1884).
Cartellieri, A., "Otto III Kaiser der Römer," *Judeich-Festschrift* (Weimar, 1929).
—— *Die Weltstellung des deutschen Reiches 911–1047* (München,
Berlin, 1932).

David, P., "La Pologne et l'évangélisation de la Poméranie," *Etudes hist. et lit. sur la Pologne médiév.*, 7 (Paris, 1928).

Dvornik, F., *The Making of Central and Eastern Europe*, London, 1949, pp. 136–236.

Eichengrün, F., *Gerbert (Silvester II) als Persönlichkeit* (Leipzig, Berlin, 1928).

Franke, W., "Romuald von Camaldoli und seine Reformtätigkeit zur Zeit Ottos III," *Hist. Studien*, 107 (Berlin, 1913).

Füllner, W., *Der Stand der deutsch-slawischen Auseinandersetzung zur Zeit Thietmars von Merseburg* (Jena, 1937).

Giesebrecht, W. von, *Geschichte der deutschen Kaiserzeit*, 5th ed. (Leipzig, 1881–85), I, II.

Haller, J., *Das altdeutsche Kaisertum* (Stuttgart, 1934).

Hampe, K., "Kaiser Otto III und Rom," *Histor. Zeitschrift*, 140 (1929).

——— *Deutsche Kaisergeschichte in der Zeit der Salier und Staufer*, 6th ed. (Leipzig, 1929).

——— *Das Hochmittelalter. Geschichte des Abenlandes von 900–1250* (Berlin, 1932).

Hauck, A., *Kirchengeschichte Deutschlands*, III (Leipzig, 1896).

Hirsch, S., Waitz, G., Usinger, R., Pabst, H., Bresslau, H., *Jahrbücher des deutschen Reiches unter Heinrich II* (Berlin, 1862–75).

Hóman, B., *Geschichte des ungarischen Mittelalters* (Berlin, 1940), I, pp. 173–243.

——— "King Stephen the Saint," *Archivium Europae Centro-Orientalis*, IV (1938).

Jedlicki, M. Z., "La création du premier archévêché polonais," *Revue Hist. du Droit Francais et Etranger* (1933).

——— "Die Anfänge des polnischen Staates," *Histor. Zeitschrift*, 152 (1935).

Kehr, P., "Das Erzbistum Magdeburg und die erste Organisation der Christl. Kirche in Polen," *Abhandl. d. Preuss. Akad. d. Wissensch.* (Berlin, 1920).

——— *Die Urkunden Ottos III* (Innsbruck, 1890).

Kirchberg, J., "Kaiseridee und Mission unter den Sachsenkaisern und den ersten Saliern von Otto I. bis Heinrich III, *Histor. Studien*, 259 (Berlin, 1934).

Mikoletzky, H. L., *Kaiser Heinrich II und die Kirche* (Wien, 1946).

Roepell, R., *Geschichte Polens* (Hamburg, 1840).

Salle de Rochemaure, Duc de la, *Gerbert (Silvestre II)* (Paris, Rome, 1921).

Schramm, P. E., *Kaiser, Rom und Renovatio, Studien der Bibl. Warburg*, XVII (Berlin, 1929).

——— "Kaiser, Basileus und Papst in der Zeit der Ottonen," *Histor. Zeitschrift*, 129 (1929).

Schünemann, K., *Die Deutschen in Ungarn bis zum 12 Jahrhundert*, *Ungarische Bibliothek*, VIII (Berlin, Leipzig, 1923).

Sulimirski, T., *Poland and Germany* (London, 1942).

Ter Braak, M., *Kaiser Otto III* (Amsterdam, 1928).

Uhlinz, K., *Geschichte des Erzbistums Magdeburg unter den Kaisern aus dem sächsischen Hause* (Magdeburg, 1887).

Voigt, H. G., *Adalbert von Prag* (Berlin, 1898).

——— *Bruno von Querfurt, Mönch, Eremit, Erzbischof der Heiden und Märtyrer* (Stuttgart, 1907).

CHAPTER X

THE SLAVS, THE EMPIRE AND THE PAPACY

SOURCES

Anna Comnena, *Alexias*, ed. Bonn *C.S.H.B.*, Engl. transl. Dawes, E.A.S. (London, 1928).

Annales (See Polish Annals, Bibliogr. Ch. IX).

Anonymi Gesta Hungarorum, *F.R.H.*, I.

Anonymus Gallus, *Chronicae Polon.*, *M.P.H.*, I.

Bernoldi Chronicon, *M.G.H.S.*, V.

Bertholdi Annales, *ibid.*

Brunonis, *Liber de bello Saxonico*, *ibid.*

Chronicon pictum Vindobonense, *S.R.H.*, I.

Chronicum Hungaro-Polonicum, *S.R.H.*, II.

Cinnamus (Kinnamos), Ioannes, *Epitomae Histor.*, ed. Bonn *C.S.H.B.*

Cosmas Pragensis, *Chron. Bohem.*, *M.G.H.S.N.S.*, II.

Dalimil, *Czech Chronicle*, *F.R.B.*, III.

Dandolo, *Chronicon Venetum*, ed. in Muratori, *Script. Rer. Italie*, XII.

Diocleae Presbyter, *De Regno Slavorum*, ed. in Lucius, *De Regno Dalmatiae* (Amsterdam, 1666).

Friedrich, G., *Codex Diplomaticus et Epistolaris Regni Bohemiae* (Prague, 1905–1917), I.

Gregorius VII, *Registrum Gregorii VII*, ed. E. Caspar, *Das Register Gregors VII*, in *Epistolae selectae ex Monumentis Germaniae historicis*, 2 (Berlin, 1920, 1923).

Lamberti Annales, *M.G.H.S.*, V.

Michael Attaliates, *Historia*, ed. Bonn *C.S.H.B.*

Nicetas Acominatos Choniates, *Historia*, ed. Bonn *C.S.H.B.*

Psellus Michael, *Chronographia*, ed. Sathas, C., *The History of Psellus* (London, 1899), French transl. Renauld, E., *Michel Psellus, Chronographie*, 2 vols. (Paris, 1926–28). Engl. transl. by E.R.A. Sewter, *The Chronographia of M. Psellus* (London, 1953).

Theodorus Prodromus, *Opera*, *P.G.*, 133.

Thomas, archipresbyter Spalatensis, *Historia Salonitana*, ed. Lucius, J., *De Regno Croatiae et Dalmatiae*; Rački, *Monumenta spectantia ad histor. Slavor. meridional*, VII (Zagreb, 1877).

Vincentius Pragensis, *Annales*, *F.R.B.*, II; *M.G.H.S.*, XVII.

Vita Henrici IV imperatoris, *M.G.H.S.*, XII.

Zonaras, *Epitome historiae*, ed. Bonn *C.S.H.B.*

BIBLIOGRAPHY

Chalandon, F., *Essai sur le règne d'Alexis Ier Comnène* (Paris, 1900), pp. 137–154.

—— *Jean II Comnène et Manuel Ier Comnène* (Paris, 1912), pp. 383–415, 469–492.

David, P., *Boleslas le Preux dans les légendes épiques polonaises et scandinaves* (Paris, 1932).

—— *Casimir le Moine et Boleslas le Pénitent* (Paris, 1932).

Deer, J., *Die Anfänge der ungarisch-kroat Staatsgemeinschaft, Etudes sur l'Europe Centro-Orient.*, IV (Budapest, 1936).

Duchesne, L., "Le Provincial Romain au XIIe siècle," *Mélanges d'archéologie et d'histoire*, 24 (Paris, 1904). (Important for the study of ecclesiastical organisation of Dioclea.)

Fabre, P., *La Pologne et le Saint Siège du Xe au XIIIe siècle* (Paris, 1896).

Holtzmann, R., "Die Urkunde Heinrichs IV für Prag vom Jahre 1086," *Archiv. für Urkundenforschung*, VI (Berlin, 1918).

Hóman, B., *Geschichte des Ungarischen Mittelalters* (Berlin, 1940), I, pp. 243–403.

Jedlicki, M. Z., "Les Rapports entre la Pologne et l'Empire Germanique," *La Pologne au VIIe Congrès internat. des sciences historiques* (Varsovie, 1933), III.

Jireček, C., *Geschichte der Serben* (Gotha, 1911), vol. I.

Lucius, *De regno Dalmatiae et Croatiae* (Amsterdam, 1666).

Šišić, F., *Geschichte der Kroaten* (Zagreb, 1917), pp. 281–384.

Temperly, H. W. V., *History of Serbia* (London, 1919), pp. 18–41.

Thompson, J. W., *Feudal Germany* (Chicago, 1926).

CHAPTER XI

THE BALTIC AND POLABIAN SLAVS (THE WENDS)

SOURCES

Adam of Bremen, *Gesta Hammaburgensis ecclesiae pontificum, M.G.H. in us. schol.* (third ed.).

Annales Hildesheimenses, M.G.H.S., III.

Annalista Saxo, *Chronicon, M.G.H.S.,* VI.

Arnoldus, *Chronica Slavorum, M.G.H.S. in us. schol.*

Bernardus, S., *Epistolae, P. L.,* 182.

Chronicon Magdeburgense, M.G.H.S., XIV.

Helmold, *Chronica Slavorum, M.G.H. in us. schol.,* Engl. transl. by F. J. Tschan, *The Chronicle of the Slavs by Helmond,* in *Records of Civilization,* No. XXI (New York, Columbia University Press, 1935).

Otto Frisingensis, *Chronica sive Hist. de duabus civitat.* (liber VII) *M.G.H. in us. schol.,* Engl. transl. by ch. ch. Mierow, ed. by A. P. Evans, Cl. Knapp in *Records of Civilization* (Columbia University Press, 1928).

Ottonis et Rahevini, *Gesta Frederici I. Imper., M.G.H. in us. schol.* (1912).

Pulkava, *Chronica Bohemorum,* ed. Dobner, G., *Monumenta Histor. Bohemiae,* III (Prague, 1764–85).

Saxo Grammaticus, *Gesta Danorum,* ed. Holder, A. (Strassburg, 1886), ed. J. Olrik, H. Raeder, 2 vols. (Copenhagen, 1931).

Thietmar of Merseburg, *Chronicon, M.G.H.S.,* III, *N.S.,* IX.

Vita Norberti archiep. Magdeburgensis, M.G.H.S., XII.

Vitae Ottonis episcopi Bambergensis, auctore Herbordo, Ebbone, monachi Prieflingensis, *M.G.H.S.,* XII.

Widukind, *Chronica Saxonum, M.G.H.S. in us. schol.,* German translation by Hirsch, P., *Widukinds sächsische Geschichten* (Leipzig, 1931, *Die Geschichtschreiber der deutschen Vorzeit,* Bd. 33).

BIBLIOGRAPHY

Andree, R., *Wendische Wanderstudien: (zur Kunde der Lausitz und der Sorbenwenden),* (Stuttgart, 1874).

Aubin, H., *Von Raum und Grenzen des deutschen Volkes* (Breslau, 1938).

Barthold, F. W., *Geschichte von Rügen und Pommern* (Hamburg, 1840).

Beyer, "König Krato und sein Geschlecht," *Mecklenburgische Jahrbücher,* XIII (1848), pp. 1–55.

Brackmann, A., *Magdeburg als Hauptstadt des deutschen Osten im frühen Mittelalter* (Leipzig, 1937).

Brückner, A., *Die slavischen Ansiedelungen in der Altmark und im Magdeburgischen* (Leipzig, 1870).

Böhmer, A., *Vicelin; ein Beitrag zur Kritik Helmolds und der älteren Urkunden von Neumünster und Seeberg* (Wiemar, 1887).

Bronisch, F., *Die slawischen Ortsnamen in Holstein und im Fürstentum Lübeck* (Sonderburg, 1901).

David, D., *La Pologne et l'évangelisation de la Poméranie aux XIe et XIIe siècles* (Paris, 1928).

Dvornik, F., "The First Wave of the Drang nach Osten," *Cambridge Historical Journal*, VII (1944).

Eggert, O., "Die Wendenzüge Waldemars I und Knut VI von Dänemark nach Pommern und Mecklenburg," *Baltische Studien*, Neue Folge, 29 (1927), pp. 1–152.

Ernt, A., "Kritische Bemerkungen zur Siedlungskunde des deutschen Ostens, vornehmlich Brandenburgs," *Forschungen zur Brandenb. und Preuss. Geschichte*, 23 (1910).

Fock, *Rügensch-pommersche Geschichten aus 7 Jahrhunderten*, 6 vols. (Berlin, 1861–72).

Giesebrecht, L., *Wendische Geschichten aus den Jahren 780–1182*, 3 vols. (Berlin, 1843).

Giesebrecht, W. von, *Geschichte der deutschen Kaiserzeit*, 5th ed., 6 vols. (Leipzig, 1881–89).

Gley, W., *Die Besiedelung der Mittelmark von der slawischen Einwanderung bis 1624* (Stuttgart, 1926).

Haag, G., "Die Völker um die Ostsee von 800 bis 1000," *Baltische Studien*, 28 (1877).

Hampe, K., *Der Zug nach dem Osten. Die kolonisatorische Grosstat des deutschen Volkes im Mittelalter* (Leipzig, 1921).

Hauk, A., *Kirchengeschichte Deutschlands* (Leipzig, 1911, seq.), III, IV.

Jaster, A., *Die Geschichte der askanischen Kolonisation in Brandenburg* (Breslau, 1934).

Jatzwenk, J., *Sorbische (Wendische) Bibliographie*, 2nd ed. (1952).

Juritsch, G., *Geschichte des Bischofs Otto I von Bamberg* (Gotha, 1889).

Kötzschke, R., *Quellen zur Geschichte der ostdeutschen Kolonisation im 12 bis 14 Jht.* (Leipzig, 1912).

Krensch, E., *Kirchengeschichte des Wendenlands* (Paderborn, 1927).

Lehmann, R., *Aus der Vergangenheit der Niederlausitz* (Cottbus, 1925).

—— *Geschichte des Wendentums in der Niederlausitz* (Langensalza, 1930).

Ludat, H., *Legenden um Jaxa von Köpen. Deutsche und slawische Fürsten im Kampf um Brandenburg in der Mitte des 12 Jhts.* (Deutschland und der Osten), (Leipzig, 1936).

Lorentz, F., *Geschichte der Pomoranischen (Kaschubischen) Sprache* (Berlin – Leipzig, 1925).

—— Fischer, A., Lehr-Spławinski, T., *The Cassubian Civilisation* (London, 1935), (gives bibliography in Polish).

Luedtke, F., *Kaiser Lothar der Sachse. Deutschlands Wendung zum Osten* (Berlin, 1937).

Mansikka, V. J., *Religion der Ostslaven* (Helsinki, 1922).

Meitzen, A., *Die Ausbreitung der Deutschen in Deutschland und ihre Besiedelung der Slawengebiete* (Jena, 1879).

Metzenthin, E., "Zur Besiedelung der Mittelmark," *Forschungen zur Brandenb. und Preuss. Gesch.*, 48 (1935).

Müller, E., *Beiträge zur Siedlungskunde Neu-Vorpommerns und der Insel Rügen* (Greifswald, 1911).

Ohnesorge, W., "Ausbreitung und Ende der Slawen zwischen Nieder-Elbe und Oder. Ein Beitrag zur Geschichte der Wendenkriege, zur Charakteristik Helmolds, sowie zur historischen Topographie und Namenkunde Nordalbingiens," *Zeitschr. for Lübeck. Gesch. und Alt.*, XIII (Lübeck, 1911).

Platen, C. G. von, "Ursprung und Nachkommenschaft des rügenschen Königshauses," *Baltische Studien*, XXXI (1929).

Poole, A. L., *Henry the Lion* (Oxford, 1912).

Rische, A., *Geschichte Mecklenburgs vom Tode Heinrich Borwins I bis zum Anfang des 16 Jh.* (Berlin, 1901).

Roepell, R., *Über die Verbreitung des Magdeburger Stadtrechts* (Breslau, 1857).

Rost, P., *Die Sprachreste der Drevano – Polaben im Hannoverschen* (Leipzig, 1907).

Rudloff, A., *Geschichte Mecklenburgs vom Tode Niclots bis zur Schlacht bei Bornhöved. Zeit der Christianierung und Germanisierung* (Berlin, 1901).

Schuchhardt, C. von, *Arkona, Rethra, Vineta* (Berlin, 1926).

Schulze, E. O., *Die Kolonisierung und Germanisierung der Gebiete zwischen Saale und Elbe* (Leipzig, 1896).

Schultz, T., *Gesammtgeschichte der Ober und Niederlausitz*, 2 vols. (Halle, 1847, 1882).

Sommerfeld, W. von, *Geschichte der Germanisierung des Herzogtums Pommern oder Slavien bis zum Ablauf des 13 Jh.* (Leipzig, 1896).

Sulimirski, T., *Poland and Germany, Past and Future* (London, 1942).

Tangl, "Der Aufruf der Bischöfe der Magdeburger Kirchenprovinz zur Hilfe gegen die Slaven aus dem Anfang des 12 Jhts.," *Neues Archiv*, XXX (1905).

Tetzner, F. O., *Die Slawen in Deutschland* (Brunswick, 1902).

Thompson, J. W., *Feudal Germany* (Chicago, 1928).

Trautmann, R., *Die Wendischen Ortsnamen Ostholsteins, Lübecks, Lauenburgs und Mecklenburgs* (Neumünster, 1939).

Tschan, F. J., *The Chronicle of the Slavs by Helmold, Priest of Bosan* (New York, 1935), (detailed bibliography in German).

Pauls, Volquart, Scheel, O., *Geschichte Schleswig-Holsteins* (Neumünster in Holst. 1934, seq.).

——— *Mecklenburgische Geschichte*, 2 vols. (Wismar, 1913).

Wagner, R., *Schwerin, Die Wendenzeit* (Berlin, 1899).

Wattenbach, W., "Die Germanisierung der östl. Grenzmarken des deutschen Reiches," *Histor. Zeitschrift*, IX (1863), pp. 386–417.

Wendt, G., *Die Germanisierung der Länder östlich der Elbe, 780–1181* (Liegnitz, 1884–89), (two parts in 1 vol.).

Wehrmann, M., "Die Lehr und Predigtätigheit des Bischofs Otto von Bamberg in Pommern," *Baltische Studien* (1924), XXVI, pp. 157–189.

Widajewitz, J., *The Western Slavs on the Baltic* (Torun, London, 1936), (The Baltic Pocket Library).

Wiesener, W., *Die Geschichte der Christlichen Kirche in Pommern zur Wendenzeit* (Berlin, 1889).

Wilman, R., *Jahrbücher des deutschen Reiches unter der Herrschaft Ottos III* (Berlin, 1840).

Witte, H., "Wendische Bevölkerungsreste in Mecklenburg," *Forschungen zur deutschen Landes- und Volkskunde*, XVI (1907), pp. 1–124.

Zeissberg, H., "Otto III und Boleslaw I von Polen," *Zeitschrift für die österreich. Gymnasien*, 18 (1867).

——— "Die öffentliche Meinung im XI Jh. über Deutschlands Politik gegen Polen," *ibid.*, 19 (1868).

——— "Die Kriege Kaiser Heinrichs II mit Herzog Boleslaw I von Polen," *Sitzungsber. d. K. Akad. Wiss., phil. hist. Kl.*, 57 (Wien, 1868).

CHAPTER XII

THE DOWNFALL OF POLAND AND BOHEMHIA.
WESTERNIZATION OF THEIR CULTURE

SOURCES

Annales Opatovicenses, F.R.B., II.

Anonymus Gallus, *Chronica Polonorum and his continuators, the bishops Matthew Choleva and Vincent Kadlubek, M.P.H.,* I, II. Cf. also *M.G.H.S.,* XXIX (Ex Rerum Polonicarum Scriptoribus S. XII et XIII, extracts published by M. Perlbach).

Codex diplomaticus Poloniae, 4 vols. (Varsoviae, 1847–1887).

Codex diplomaticus Maioris Poloniae, 5 vols. (Posnaniae, 1877–1908).

Codex diplomaticus et epistolaris Moraviae, ed. A. Boczek, 10 vols. (Brünn, Olmütz, 1835–78).

Codex juris Bohemici, ed. H. Jireček, 5 vols. (Prague, 1868–98).

Cosmas, *Chronica Bohemorum,* and his continuators, a canon of Vyšehrad (from 1126 to 1142), a monk of Sázava (from 1126 to 1162), the canon Vincentius (from 1140 to 1167), the Abbot Jarloch (from 1167 to 1198), *F.R.B.,* I, II.

Friedrich, G., *Codex diplomaticus et epistolaris regni Bohemiae,* 2 vols. (Prague, 1907–12).

Otto of Freising, *Gesta Friderici Imperatoris, M.G.H. in us. schol.*

BIBLIOGRAPHY

Bachmann, A., *Geschichte Böhmens,* 2 vols. (Gotha, 1899, 1905).

—— *Geschichte Böhmens und Mährens,* 4 vols. (Reichenberg, 1921–25).

Breitenbach, O., *Das Land Lebeus unter den Piasten* (Fürstenwalde, 1890).

Bretholz, B., *Geschichte Böhmens und Mährens bis zum Aussterben der Przemysliden, 1306* (Leipzig, 1912).

The Cambridge History of Poland (Cambridge, 1950):

Boswell, A. Bruce, "The Twelfth Century: from Growth to Division, 1079–1202," pp. 43–60.

—— Territorial Division and the Mongol Invasions, 1202–1300," pp. 85–108.

David, P., "The Church in Poland, from its Origin to 1250," pp. 60–85.

Dyboski, R., *Outlines of Polish History* (London, 1931).

David, P., "Recherches sur l'histoire de la Poméranie polonaise," *Revue des questions historiques,* XX, XXI (1932, 1933).

Fabre, P., *La Pologne et le Saint Siège du Xe au XIIes* (Paris, 1896).

Greuber, B., *Die Kunst des Mittelalters in Böhmen*, 4 vols. (Wien, 1871–79).

Grunhagen, C., *Geschichte Schlesiens*, 2 vols. (Gotha, 1884–86).

Hausdorf, G. P. A., *Die Piasten Schlesiens* (Breslau, 1933).

Maschke, E., *Polen und die Berufung des Deutschen Ordens nach Preussen* (Danzig, 1934).

Neuwirth, J., *Geschichte der bildenden Kunst in Böhmen* (Prague, 1893).

Niessen, P. von, "Die staatsrechtlichen Verhältnisse Pommerns in den Jahren 1180 bis 1214," *Baltische Studien*, XVIII (1914).

Prokop, A., *Die Markgrafschaft Mähren in kunstgeschichtlicher Beziehung* (Brünn, 1904), I.

Salis, F., "'Forschungen zur älteren Geschichte des Bistums Kumin," *Baltische Studien*, XXVI (1924).

Schafer, D., "Lothars III Heerzug nach Böhmen," *Historische Aufsätze für K. Zeumer* (1910).

Schlesische Bibliographie, published by the Historische Kommission für Schlesien (Breslau, 1927, ff.).

Simonsfeld, H., *Jahrbücher des deutschen Reiches unter Friedrich I* (Leipzig, 1908).

Wiesener, W., "Die Gründung des Bistums von Pommern und die Verlegung des Bischofesitzes von Wollin nach Kamin," *Zeitschrift für Kirchengeschichte*, X, pp. 1–53.

Winter, E., *Tausend Jahre Geisteskampf im Sudetenland* (Leipzig, 1938), pp. 12–41.

INDEX

Aaron, Bulgarian ruler, 141.
Abaev, V. I., 12.
Abbasid dynasty, 191.
Aboba, 158, 161.
Abramić, M., 155.
Abramavič, D., 236.
Achilles, Church of Saint, 159.
Adalbero, Archbishop of Hamburg, 303.
Adalbert, Archbishop of Bremen, 298 ff.
Adalbert — Vojtěch, Saint, Bishop of Prague, 114, 240, 244, 258 ff., 266, 269, 282, 288, 330, 331.
Adam of Bremmen, 46, 245, 298, 299.
Adam-Klissi, 17.
Adauctus, Saint, 332.
Adolf of Schauenburg, Count of Holstein, 302, 305, 308.
Adriatic Sea, 36, 40, 41, 42, 60, 69, 70, 85, 122, 136 ff., 218, 261.
Aegean Sea, 42.
Aetius, Roman general, 30.
Afghanistan, 26.
Agapit, Saint, the healer, 235.
Agathias, Byzantine writer, 24.
Agathon, Pope, 77.
Agathon, Moravian archbishop, 97, 163, 164.
"Agrarian Law," see *Nomos Georgicos*.
Agrippa, 15.
Ahura Mazda, Iranian deity, 50.
Alamanni, Germanic tribe, 68.
Alania, 28.
Alans, Sarmatian tribe, 25, 26, 155.
Alban, Saint, 240, 241.
Albania, 141.
Albania, Caucasian, 65.
Albigensians, 139.
Albrecht the Bear, Duke of Saxony, 302, 306 ff.
Albrecht of the Nordmark, 306.
Alcuin, Charlemagne's minister, 76.
Alessio, 165.

Alexander, Byzantine Emperor, 128 ff.
Alexander II, Pope, 280.
Alexander the Great, Life (Romance) of, 185, 237.
Alexander Nevskij, 250.
Alexius I Comnenus, Byzantine Emperor, 277, 282.
Alexius and Boniface, Abbey of Saints, 260, 261. See also Boniface, Saint.
Alfred, Anglo-Saxon King, 27, 85, 105.
Alisso, 15.
Alps, 41, 42, 44, 60, 69, 85.
Alsace, 311.
Ambrose, Saint, 241.
Ammianus Marcellinus, 29.
Amsa, Vedic deity, 50.
Anacletus, Pope, 240.
Anahita, Iranian goddess, 50.
Anastasius of Sinai, 178.
Andrew, Church of Saint, 333.
Andrew Bogoljubskij, Russian prince, 215, 251.
Andrew the Fool in Christ, Saint, 229.
"Andrich" (Oldřich), Czech Duke, 208, 268.
Angelarius, Methodius' disciple, 177.
Angles, Germanic tribe, 68.
Anglo-Saxons, 85.
Anne, Byzantine princess, wife of Prince Vladimir, 207.
Anno, Bishop of Freising, 92.
Anonymus Gallus, Polish chronicler, 173, 243, 287, 313, 331 ff.
Antês, 23, 24, 25, 27, 28, 29, 36, 38, 54, 58, 59, 65.
Anthâib, 28.
Anthony, Saint, 234, 236.
Anti, see Antês.
Antibari, 165, 279, 280, 281.
Antioch, 282.
Aphrodite, Greek goddess, 50.
Apollinaris of Ravenna, Saint, 171.

Date Due

S

EP 16 '57

NOV 5 70

NOV 18 70

Demco 293-5

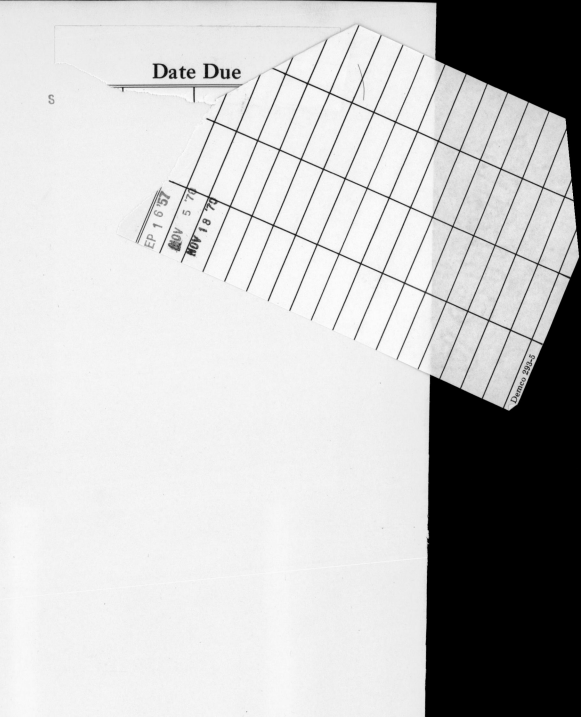